European Security and Defence Policy: the first ten years (1999-2009)

Esra Bulut, Caty Clément, George Dura, Sabine Fischer, Benedikt Franke, Richard Gowan, Giovanni Grevi, Eva Gross, Damien Helly, Isabelle Ioannides, Daniel Keohane, Daniel Korski, Xymena Kurowska, Dov Lynch, Claudia Major, Michael Merlingen, Luis Peral, Kirsten E. Schulze, Thierry Vircoulon

Preface by Álvaro de Vasconcelos

Edited by Giovanni Grevi, Damien Helly and Daniel Keohane

Institute for Security Studies

European Union

43 avenue du Président Wilson

75775 Paris cedex 16

tel.: +33 (0)1 56 89 19 30

fax: +33 (0)1 56 89 19 31

e-mail: info@iss.europa.eu

www.iss.europa.eu

Director: Álvaro de Vasconcelos

ISBN 978-92-9198-157-1

QN-80-09-910-EN-C

Acknowledgements

The editors wish sincerely to thank a number of people for their support during this project. Firstly, we wish to thank the contributors to this book, without their cooperation it would not have been possible. We also wish to thank the numerous EU officials, national diplomats and operations personnel who gave up their valuable time for interviews or to give comments on drafts, and who would prefer to remain anonymous. Many thanks also to Álvaro de Vasconcelos, the Director of the EUISS, for his support, and to various EUISS colleagues – these include Gearóid Cronin for his language editing, Hanno Ranck for graphic design, and Marie Antonini-Alvarez for research help. Finally, for their extensive help with research, we wish to thank Charlotte Blommestijn, Project Assistant, and the following interns at the EUISS: Monika Brzoska, Katrin Buchmann, Igor Garcia-Tapia, Kasper Gimsing, Pol Morillas, Florina-Laura Neculai and Marta Zajaczkowska. Any factual errors are, of course, our responsibility.

Paris, October 2009

Contents

Preface

ESDP: A reality check

2009 was the 'year of ESDP' at the EUISS with the release of two publications marking the first ten years of the European Security and Defence Policy. The EUISS set out to produce two books: one – this volume – consists of a retrospective examination of the last ten years, including a detailed account and analysis of each individual ESDP mission, while the other, *What ambitions for European defence in 2020?*, seeks to define what should be the ambition for European defence in the coming decade.

European Security and Defence Policy: the first ten years (1999-2009), which has involved the in-house research team almost in its entirety and drawn in further contributions, has brought to light, with the methodological persistence and thoroughness of the archaeologist, working layer by layer, stone by stone, all past and current ESDP missions' achievements and shortcomings. It examines in depth virtually all issues relevant to ESDP, its institutions and their workings, the available resources and their use, as well as the way it relates to other international organisations, mainly the UN, NATO, the OSCE and the African Union. With this multi-authored volume, the EUISS is now able to offer a manual of ESDP, that will hopefully serve as a reference book for the use of all those interested in the development of European security and defence policy, in both its civil and military aspects.

What is striking is not so much that the main policy conclusions drawn from both exercises should practically be the same. What is rather more striking is that by looking closely at twenty-three EU missions one by one, from the first mission in Bosnia to the naval operation off the coast of Somalia, a larger picture emerges of the future contours and development of ESDP. ESDP is already maturing, and indeed in different ESDP missions elements of its future shape can already be inferred. Building on the last ten years' best practice, as the present study suggests, will allow for substantially enhanced effectiveness in the ten years to come, and make it easier to reverse the three major deficits both EUISS volumes identify in parallel: the political deficit or the Common Foreign and Security Policy (CFSP) gap, insufficient coherence and inadequate capabilities.

Examining the EU monitoring mission in Georgia, Sabine Fischer demonstrates that an enormous gain of efficiency is achieved by integrating a mission into a well-defined strategy under 'strong leadership' unanimously backed by Member States. EU action to prevent a dangerous escalation of war on its doorstep was decisive also because it was swift, and part of the reason for this timeliness relates to unity of purpose. The need to bridge the political deficit is a main recommendation for the next ten years. The EU mission in Georgia proves that it is quite possible to overcome the political gap that has weakened the impact of other EU missions. Looking at the current mission in Kosovo, Giovanni Grevi concludes that more thinking needs to be devoted 'to the connection between foreign policy and ESDP', and expresses the hope the Lisbon Treaty will indeed help bridge the gap.

Advantages in terms of coherence that can be gained by unifying EU external action emerge just as clearly from the detailed analysis of the various missions in the Balkans, where many European Commission projects are also being implemented alongside ESDP operations. As Eva Gross states, highlighting the EU's excellent record as a crisis management actor in the former Yugoslav Republic of Macedonia (FYROM), the 'linear application and devolution from a military to a civilian ESDP mission followed by Community programmes' was crucial to the success of the EU's intervention there. This is true even though, as has often been observed, strong inter-pillar coordination has in many cases been lacking, including in the Balkans. The double-hatted EU representation to the African Union in Addis Ababa is a foretaste of things to come. Damien Helly points out that it 'is seen as a very successful experience so far', and one that must certainly be carefully studied in the process of establishing the European External Action Service. But the need for coherence does not merely refer to the ability to give a common thrust to EU diplomacy, but perhaps more decisively to the necessity to ensure that national policies are part of it as well. Examples of the failures of coordination between EU Members States both among themselves and within the Union are catalogued far too frequently in these pages, Afghanistan being a case in point. The Union needs to overcome the coherence deficit without weakening EU legitimacy for the sake of effectiveness.

The benefits of pooling are equally obvious when it comes to the universally recognised capability gap, and bridging this is certainly a major challenge for the future. The sheer size of some operations, like the civilian EULEX mission in Kosovo, and the 'successful' *Althea* military mission in Bosnia, show that sufficient usable military resources and capacities exist within the Member States to generate enough forces to meet the commonly established operational goals. However, as the Chad mission has notably made plain, operational capabilities are lacking in a certain number of areas and, from a purely European point of view, there is vast waste in terms of spending and much duplication in other areas owing to the multiplicity of national procurement programmes. This is clearly demonstrated by Daniel Keohane who argues that military resources can be maximised if Member States simply 'coordinate more of their demand and spend their defence budgets more efficiently.' In fact bringing capabilities up to speed where they are lacking will require not more but better spending.

The future of ESDP – or rather, of the Common Security and Defence Policy (CSDP), as it is renamed in the Lisbon Treaty – is not solely predicated on the capacity of the Europeans to work together, but almost as crucially on their ability to work with others. Americans are already taking part in the civilian mission in Kosovo, and the Russians joined in the military mission in Chad. Operation *Atalanta* offers perhaps the best illustration however of what the future holds. European navies patrol the sea lanes off the coast of Somalia together with the navies of 20 countries including all major powers, notably China and India. Global interdependence creates the conditions for the actual development of effective multilateral cooperation in the UN framework, which is furthermore a source of unquestionable legitimacy. Richard Gowan notes that 'linking ESDP to the UN has let the EU present its defence identity as part of a global collective security strategy.' This will, very probably, be even more the case in the future since the UN is the preferred, and indeed almost exclusive, framework for emerging powers to contribute to international peace.

Looking at the span of ten years that have passed since the inception of ESDP to the current state-of-play after the second Irish referendum on the Lisbon Treaty, it is tempting to restate, on the strength of the present analysis, what Nicole Gnesotto wrote in a previous EUISS volume covering the first five years: 'the Union can boast really spectacular results' with the launching and further development of ESDP.[1]

---

1. Nicole Gnesotto (ed.) *EU Security and Defence Policy: the first five years (1999-2004)*, EU Institute for Security Studies, Paris, 2004.

For European defence to fulfil the Europeans' ambitions and make a distinctive and decisive contribution to international peace in the years ahead, the EU needs to implement many of the recommendations put forward by the authors in order to deal with the shortcomings revealed in the reality check they have performed on 'ESDP@10'. As the great Spanish poet Antonio Machado wrote, *'se hace camino al andar'* – 'walking is how you learn to walk'.

Álvaro de Vasconcelos

Director of the EUISS
Paris, October 2009

Introduction

Giovanni Grevi, Damien Helly and Daniel Keohane

In December 1998 the French and British governments signed an agreement at St. Malo, which paved the political path for EU governments to launch the European Security and Defence policy (ESDP) at the Cologne European Council summit in June 1999. The St. Malo Declaration stated that the European Union 'must have the capacity for autonomous action, backed up by credible military forces, the means to decide to use them, and a readiness to do so, in order to respond to international crises'. Has ESDP met those expectations? This EUISS book analyses the first ten years of ESDP from 1999 to 2009. It shows that ESDP has had some impressive results over the last decade, and draws conclusions from this experience for meeting future challenges.

The book is divided into two parts. Part One contains three chapters covering ESDP institutions, resources and partnerships. The first chapter on ESDP institutions analyses how ESDP decision-making has developed, for both civil and military crisis management. The second chapter, on ESDP resources, looks at the civil and military resources available for ESDP operations, as well as the capability development plans that EU governments have put in place. The final chapter in Part One of this book, considers the important relationships between ESDP and the United Nations (UN), the North Atlantic Treaty Organisation (NATO), the Organisation for Security and Cooperation in Europe (OSCE) and the African Union (AU). Each partnership has been different, both politically and operationally, but each has contributed to the development of ESDP.

Arguably, the most significant aspect of the first ten years of ESDP has been the large number of operations that EU governments have carried out in this framework, some 23 missions since the first was launched in 2003. Part Two of this book contains 21 chapters analysing every ESDP operation to date (two chapters analyse two operations). Since 2003, EU governments have conducted a wide range of ESDP operations in Europe, Africa, the Middle East and Asia.

Aside from geography, they have also greatly varied in task, from traditional military peacekeeping in Bosnia and Herzegovina to helping reform the Georgian judicial system to training the Afghan and Iraqi police forces.

The editors chose this two-part structure, and these specific aspects of ESDP for two reasons. First, it is important to explain in detail, and as comprehensively as possible, how ESDP functions, how it is resourced, and how it cooperates with other international organisations (which has been a significant factor for most ESDP operations). Each of these aspects has evolved during the last decade, and such developments provide the backbone of the EU's ability to take action. Second, taken as a whole the 23 operations have not yet received as much attention in academic literature as other aspects of ESDP, albeit some individual operations have been widely analysed. An analysis of each mission is compiled in the second part of this book to help develop the study and analysis of both individual operations and the general operational *acquis* for ESDP missions.

Given this distinctive and innovative approach, this book does not thoroughly address other important dimensions of the debate on ESDP. It does not analyse the specific strategic positions and approaches of individual EU Member States towards ESDP in detail, although differences between Member States are referred to, when relevant, in each chapter. Much has already been written over the last decade on different national positions towards ESDP, and various divisions at various times between 'Europeanists' and 'Atlanticists', 'peacekeepers' and 'war fighters', and the inherent tension between ESDP as a policy and ESDP as a political project.[1] However, the aim of this book is to provide a comprehensive policy, rather than political, analysis.

Nor does the book specifically analyse the evolution of the EU's strategic outlook, which has changed dramatically since 1999. After the war in Kosovo in 1999, the geographic focus of the then 15 EU governments, understandably, was on the Balkans, and on the use of military resources. Today, as shown by the variety of ESDP operations, the 27 EU governments have greatly expanded both their geographical perspective and their mix of policy options. EU governments agreed on a European Security Strategy (ESS) in 2003, which has provided the strategic framework for EU foreign and security policy – of which ESDP forms an integral part. EU governments

---

1. For example see Jolyon Howorth, *Security and Defence Policy in the European Union* (Basingstoke, Hampshire: Palgrave Macmillan, 2007); Charles Grant, *Is Europe doomed to fail as a power?* (London: Centre for European Reform, July 2009).

assessed the implementation of the ESS in 2008, and their conclusions highlighted the value of the holistic approach of the EU to international security, and its ability to deploy diplomats and development workers, judges and police, and – when necessary – soldiers.[2]

One of the difficulties of analysing ESDP is that some data is not gathered centrally or is not publicly available. Although there is a vast amount of official papers and academic literature available to anyone who wishes to study ESDP, not all aspects are well documented or analysed, especially for some operations. As a result, all the authors in this book have conducted a range of interviews with EU officials, national diplomats and/or operations personnel. The contributors to this book were selected for their expertise and proven track record of independent analysis; and all of them are independent academics, analysts or think tankers – with the exception of Dov Lynch from the OSCE, who previously was a Senior Research Fellow at the EUISS and writes here in a personal capacity. The editors sent precise guidelines to all contributors on the structure of their chapters, and with regard to operations on the need to assess both the achievements and shortcomings of each mission.

In Part Two of this book, each of the 21 chapters on ESDP operations contains a data box at the beginning. The purpose of the boxes is to summarise what the operation was supposed to do, its size, budget and which countries contributed to it. Readers should note, however, that operations change over time and their personnel rotates. Changes in mission mandates also have various kinds of implications (composition of the personnel, capabilities required, budgets etc.). All this means that it is almost impossible to fix the evolution of an ESDP operation in time, so the boxes are meant as indicative guides.

In particular, readers should note that grasping the details of the financing of ESDP operations is sometimes more of an art than a science. This is especially true for military operations, since the data available on common costs for military operations only indicates roughly ten percent of the overall costs of an operation. As a result, the operational budgetary figures used in this book to assess total costs of some missions are mainly estimates. For the figures on mission strength, operations staffs rotate and mandates can change, requiring increases or decreases in personnel. Therefore, mission strength numbers reported in the boxes are either dated or

2. For more on the European Security Strategy see Álvaro de Vasconcelos (ed.), 'The European Security Strategy 2003-2008: Building on common interests', *Report* no. 5, European Union Institute for Security Studies, February 2009; Sven Biscop and Jan Joel Andersson (eds.), *The EU and the European Security Strategy: Forging a Global Europe* (New York: Routledge, 2008).

are peak strength figures (and sometimes both). Lastly, to provide an overview of Member States' contributions to ESDP operations, the editors have collected data in the annexes at the end of this book covering, respectively, military and civilian operations. The same caveat as above applies here, as the data can only reflect national contributions to ESDP operations at a given moment in time.

In sum, this book should serve as an initial reference work on the first ten years of ESDP, which has greatly evolved and developed since its birth at the EU Cologne summit in June 1999. The book tries to provide a comprehensive and detailed outline of different aspects of ESDP, to contribute to an informed debate about the future development of that policy. As Javier Solana, the EU's High Representative for the Common Foreign and Security Policy, told an EUISS conference: 'Development of ESDP's crisis management capacity is crucial to contributing effectively to international peace and security. It is the missing link. EU foreign policy used to be about declarations. Now the EU puts people in large, visible numbers on the ground and takes risks for peace.' [3]

---

3. Remarks by Javier Solana, 'ESDP@10: what lessons for the future?', Brussels, 28 July 2009.

Part One

1. ESDP institutions

Giovanni Grevi

Introduction

The European Security and Defence Policy (ESDP) is an integral part of the EU Common Foreign and Security Policy (CFSP), which 'shall include all questions related to the security of the Union' (Article 17.1 TEU). The institutional frameworks of CFSP and ESDP broadly overlap, although the specific operational character of ESDP has triggered the creation of a distinctive sub-set of institutions primarily charged with the planning and conduct of crisis management operations.

The institutions and procedures underpinning ESDP have undergone a process of almost permanent expansion and reform over the last ten years. Ultimately, this process responds to the basic requirement expressed by the Saint Malo Declaration that the Union must have the capacity for autonomous action backed up by credible military forces and 'the means to decide to use them and a readiness to do so.' This entails that 'the Union must be given appropriate structures and a capacity for analysis of situations, sources of intelligence and a capability for relevant strategic planning.'[1] While at the time of Saint Malo the focus was on military crisis management, the argument has since applied to both the military and the civilian dimensions of ESDP. In other words, the Union must be given the 'capacity to decide' in this policy domain.

To be sure, as stressed below, EU Member States *take* the final decisions in this policy area, based on the unanimity rule. However, these decisions are achieved following a complex process of decision-making that normally entails extensive, institutions-based intergovernmental interaction. When looking at

---

1. British-French summit at Saint-Malo, 3-4 December 1998, Joint Declaration on European Defence. In Maartje Rutten (ed.), 'From Saint Malo to Nice. European Defence: core documents', *Chaillot Paper* no. 47, EU Institute for Security Studies, Paris, May 2001, pp. 8-9.

CFSP/ESDP institutions and their development, therefore, the accent is put on how political decisions are *shaped* in the interplay between the European and national levels of governance.

In this perspective, the capacity to decide can be defined as the ability to formulate, adopt and implement decisions. In terms of ESDP, this capacity entails five key functions, namely the ability to agree common political and strategic priorities, to develop the conceptual framework for EU crisis management, to collect adequate information and generate joint analysis, to harness and expand the military, civilian and financial resources available to the Union, and to carry out crisis management operations.

The institutional framework of ESDP is meant to ensure that these functions are effectively fulfilled, while pursuing the convergence of national positions and improving the coherence of EU action. As such, institutional engineering tackles the basic paradox at the core of this policy domain. The main strengths of ESDP, namely the engagement of Member States and the wide policy toolbox of the Union, can also prove the sources of serious constraints and shortcomings. In a policy domain governed by unanimity and with limited scope for flexibility at Treaty-level, the capacity to achieve a decision is crucially predicated on the convergence of national positions towards a common one. The effectiveness of the resulting decisions depends, on the other hand, on the mobilisation of all relevant actors and all necessary instruments in a coherent fashion at every stage of the decision-making process. Achieving convergence and enhancing coherence take time and require a permanent balancing act between national interests and institutional perspectives. However, both political convergence and policy coherence remain inescapable conditions for generating effective action at EU level. There lies the challenge at the core of ESDP decision-making.

This chapter is divided into four main sections. First, some preliminary considerations are outlined to frame the analysis of ESDP institutional reform and practice, highlighting the principal factors affecting the pace and direction of reform. This section paves the way for a more detailed exploration of the institutional architecture of ESDP, where the features and prerogatives of the main institutional actors are described, while outlining their progressive evolution. The third section addresses the ESDP decision-making process, with a focus on the planning of military and civilian crisis management operations. This is a good vantage point to illustrate the complicated interaction between Brussels-based structures in delivering the operational output of ESDP. The fourth and final section of this chapter turns to the reforms envisaged by the Lisbon Treaty, pending ratification. The innovations of the Lisbon Treaty carry considerable implications for CFSP and ESDP, notably with a view to enhancing the coherence of the EU foreign and security policy and to enable the further convergence of Member States' positions.

Framing institutional reform

Since the launch of ESDP, Member States have been pooling human resources and expertise in Brussels to establish a critical institutional mass to foster and steer cooperation while preserving the ultimate authority to take decisions. In short, while the power to veto initiatives remains at the national level, the ability to take action is shifting to the European level. In this context, it is important to stress the basic complementarity between the Council Secretariat headed by the Secretary General/High Representative for CFSP (SG/HR for CFSP) on the one hand and the Brussels-based inter-governmental committees dealing with CFSP and ESDP on the other. The former is charged with two basic functions. First, supporting the Presidency in running the meetings of the General Affairs and External Relations Council (GAERC) and of the policy-making committees dealing with CFSP/ESDP. Second, providing policy input on horizontal issues (concepts, capabilities, training etc.) and on envisaged action (policy options, military and civilian expertise). National representatives meet in Brussels-based committees to shape decisions at the technical and political level. Their proceedings enable the consensual definition of EU positions and the adoption of final legal acts by the Foreign Ministers in the GAERC. The multi-level interaction between these two sets of bodies – the Secretariat and the committees – is particularly intensive when it comes to deciding on an EU crisis management intervention and to the planning, conduct and support of ESDP missions.

The evolution of ESDP structures and procedures can only be understood against the broader background of developments at three other levels, namely the wider process of institutional reform launched in 2002 with the Convention on the Future of Europe, the European strategic debate and the operational experience gained by ESDP missions as of 2003. In particular, the discussion on the international profile of the Union and on corresponding institutional reforms in the run-up to the Constitutional treaty in 2004 and the adoption of the European Security Strategy in 2003 set the stage for the evolution of ESDP institutions reviewed in this chapter.

In this context, two broad phases can be pointed out. First, the pioneering stage following the Saint Malo Declaration, when the ESDP institutional framework was rapidly set up from scratch in 2000/2001 and progressively expanded, so as to enable the Union to undertake the first crisis management operations in 2003. Second, based on early operational experience and on parallel conceptual developments and political debates, the phase of progressive (albeit incomplete) deepening and consolidation that started in 2004/2005 and led to the adoption and implementation of the Hampton Court agenda between 2006 and 2008. The analysis of the institutional dimension of ESDP focuses here on the developments that have occurred since 2004.

Three main 'waves' of reform can be identified for the purposes of this analysis while acknowledging that, in practice, different strands of conceptual and institutional innovation do not simply follow each other but overlap and interplay. The focus on establishing a comprehensive approach to crisis management over the years 2003/2005 has been followed by a stronger emphasis on the need to strengthen ESDP crisis management structures and capabilities as such in 2006-2008. Since mid-2008, a third trend can be detected, with the accent somewhat shifting back to the need to better situate ESDP in a broader political context, and chain of command, by linking it more closely to CFSP as well as to the instruments and resources of the Commission.

The different perspectives and interests of EU Member States, and notably of those endowed with the largest resources and the strongest, or most distinctive, security cultures, are a very important factor driving institutional reform in the field of ESDP. In synthesis, the linking thread consists here of the permanent and creative, although not always constructive, dialectic between three broad visions of ESDP. France has consistently pushed for enhancing the military dimension, and therefore the military expertise, decision-making structures and capabilities, of ESDP, so as to make of the Union a credible and autonomous actor in this domain. The UK, while sharing France's emphasis on enhancing the military capabilities of EU Member States, has been keen on preserving the central role of the Atlantic Alliance as the main forum for European defence and has been wary of duplicating at EU level institutional structures, such as permanent Headquarters, already available to NATO and to individual countries. Some Nordic countries and Germany, have on the other hand insisted on fostering the civilian dimension and resources of ESDP, building on the comprehensive approach of the EU to crisis management, from conflict prevention to post-conflict stabilisation. The institutional features of ESDP largely embody the evolving compromise between these three perspectives, with the input and mediation of Brussels-based institutions themselves.

The lessons and implications of the growing operational experience of ESDP are a second important variable affecting the direction and priorities of the reform process. Following the hard test of the first missions deployed in 2003/2005, from the Western Balkans to Georgia and Africa, various shortcomings were identified that depended not only on inadequate inter-pillar coordination and on the limited resources available to ESDP but also on the weakness of existing ESDP crisis-management structures in terms of intelligence, planning, command and control, political guidance and mission support. Hence the sustained, although surely not definitive, effort between 2006 and 2009 to reinforce the ESDP structures tasked with these key enabling dimensions of effective crisis management.

Lastly, the emphasis on a comprehensive approach and inter-pillar coordination has arguably increased and waned in parallel to perspectives for Treaty reform. The latter seemed forthcoming up to June 2005 and seems within reach following many setbacks, after the positive result in the second referendum on the Lisbon Treaty in Ireland in October 2009. As illustrated below, the Lisbon Treaty includes far-reaching reforms essentially directed to overcome the dysfunctional separation between different pillars in the area of external relations. In between these two phases, the informal Hampton Court summit in 2005 paved the way for a rationalisation of crisis management structures within the Council Secretariat, a few months after the French and Dutch No votes in the referenda on the Constitutional Treaty.

The institutional architecture

The Member States and the Council Secretariat lie at the core of CFSP and ESDP policy-making. National political leaders meet in the European Council at the level of Heads of State and Government and in the GAERC configuration at the level of Foreign Ministers. Diplomatic and military representatives meet in a variety of committees preparing and informing the proceedings of the Political and Security Committee (PSC). The Council Secretariat, headed by the SG/HR for CFSP (since 1999, Javier Solana), has been expanding in size and remit to provide policy advice and coordination for ESDP as well as military and civilian expertise for crisis management.

The Commission is 'fully associated' with the work carried out in the field of CFSP (Article 27 TEU) and plays an important role in the context of ESDP in essentially two ways. First, it administers the CFSP budget and, second, it works with the Council at different stages of the decision-making process so as to promote coherence between ESDP initiatives and Community instruments and assistance. The interaction between the Council and the Commission has been growing in scope and relevance, albeit not always in effectiveness, as ESDP has been moving from theory to operational practice. The European Parliament enjoys rather limited prerogatives of consultation and information in the field of ESDP. However, as the EP is one branch of the budgetary authority of the Union (the other being the Council), its democratic scrutiny of ESDP has been growing in parallel to its involvement in the debate on the size, expansion and management of the CFSP budget.[2]

The European Council, the GAERC and the Presidency of the Council

The European Council is the highest political authority of the EU and, as such, is responsible for defining the principles and general guidelines of CFSP, including for matters with defence implications. In particular, the European Council decides on the common strategies addressing areas of particular interest for EU Member States (Article 13 TEU). ESDP matters, as such, rarely climb the decision-making ladder up to the level of the Heads of State and Government sitting in the European Council (together with the President of the Commission) but the deliberations and decisions of this body are of crucial importance for the development of ESDP. Strategic foreign policy decisions naturally impact on the security and defence policy of the Union as they define the framework and priorities for its development.

The summit meetings in Cologne and Helsinki in 1999, Feira and Nice in 2000, Goteborg and Laeken in 2001 and Brussels in December 2003, among others, have provided essential input to establish ESDP and to define the strategic outlook and profile of the Union.[3] The adoption of the European Security Strategy (ESS) in December 2003 was a landmark development in this context. Between 2002 and 2004, the European Council has also approved important documents on EU/NATO relations, envisaging new procedures to streamline the cooperation between the two organisations.[4] In 2007/2008, successive European summits launched and concluded the review of the implementation of the ESS, which entailed a particular focus on

---

2. See Chapter 2 on the resources of ESDP in this book.

3. European Council, Cologne, 3-4 June 1999; European Council, Helsinki, 10-11 December 1999; European Council, Santa Maria da Feira, 19-20 June 2000; and European Council, Nice, 7-9 December 2000. See Rutten, op. cit. in note 1, pp; 41-45, 82-91, 120-39, and 168-221. European Council, Goteborg, 15-16 June 2001 and European Council, Laeken, 14-15 December 2001. See Maartje Rutten (ed.), 'From Nice to Laeken. European Defence: core documents', *Chaillot Paper* no. 51, EU Institute for Security Studies, Paris, April 2002, pp. 30-63 and 110-42. European Council, Brussels, 12 December 2003, in Antonio Missiroli (ed.), 'From Copenhagen to Brussels: European Defence: core documents', *Chaillot Paper* no. 67, EU Institute for Security Studies, Paris, December 2003, pp. 292-338. References to the specific decisions adopted in successive summits are made, as relevant, in what follows.

4. See Chapter 3 on ESDP partnerships, pp. 127-38.

the development of ESDP capabilities.[5] The adoption at summit level of framework documents such as, for example, the Joint Africa-EU Strategy and action plan in December 2007, also contributes to define the broader political context of ESDP and to devise a regional approach to security and defence. In addition, at the end of each Presidency term, the European Council receives the detailed Presidency report on ESDP – an important document taking stock of progress achieved and priorities ahead.

The GAERC is the central forum of political negotiations and decision-making in the domain of CFSP and ESDP. The proceedings of the European Council are prepared by the Foreign Ministers in the GAERC, meeting in its External Relations configuration following the distinction between General Affairs and foreign policy matters introduced at the Seville European Council of June 2002. Based on the guidelines outlined by the European Council and/or on its own deliberations, the GAERC defines and implements the CFSP/ESDP by adopting joint actions, common positions and Council decisions (Articles 13 and 14 TEU). Joint actions and common positions are legal instruments committing Member States to act in conformity with them when conducting their foreign and security policy although national decisions in this field fall outside the jurisdiction of the European Court of Justice and can therefore be challenged on political but not on legal grounds. When it comes to ESDP *stricto sensu*, the GAERC is the top decision-taking authority, in particular with regard to the planning and the launch, through a joint action, of crisis management operations. The GAERC also monitors and provides impetus to the evolution of the capability development plans under the military and civilian Headline Goal processes. *Ad hoc* annual meetings take place in November to review achievements and detect shortfalls.

Together with the Commission, the Council is responsible for ensuring the overall consistency of the external activities of the Union, encompassing its external relations, security, economic and development policies (Article 3 TEU). In the context of the CFSP, the Council is tasked with ensuring the unity, consistency and effectiveness of the EU's action (Article 13.3 TEU).

Unanimous decision-making is the rule for CFSP and ESDP, although the constructive abstention of Member States representing up to one third of the weighted votes in the Council is foreseen to allow the adoption of a decision committing the Union

---

5. European Council, Brussels, 11-12 December 2008, Report on the implementation of the European Security Strategy 'Providing security in a changing world', in Catherine Glière (ed.), 'European security and defence: Core documents 2008', *Chaillot Paper* no. 117, EU Institute for Security Studies, Paris, July 2009, pp. 453-86.

while excluding the countries abstaining from the obligation to apply it (Article 23.1 TEU). The Treaty envisages minor exceptions to the unanimity rule and provides for majority voting to adopt acts implementing previous decisions as well as to appoint EUSRs. However, consensual decision-making is predominant. In the particular case of ESDP, when a decision is taken to launch an operation, an original form of permissive consent often applies in practice when Member States agree on undertaking a mission in the context of ESDP but decide not to contribute to it.[6]

In a typically inter-governmental area such as CFSP and ESDP, the rotating Presidency of the Council of the EU plays an important role in establishing the working agenda and, to some extent, setting the priorities of the Union. More specifically, the Presidency is tasked with representing the Union in CFSP matters and with the implementation of relevant decisions, which may also entail the negotiation of international agreements (Articles 18 and 24 TEU). In practice, since the appointment of the first SG/HR for CFSP in 1999, the so-called CFSP Troika in charge of relations with third countries includes the Foreign Minister of the country holding the Presidency, the SG/HR himself and the Commissioner in charge of External Relations. The Foreign Minister of the country holding the next Presidency in line may also take part in the work of the Troïka.

The Presidency is directly and closely involved in the proceedings of ESDP. The representatives of the country holding the Presidency chair the PSC and all the other CFSP/ESDP committees, with the exception of the EU Military Committee. Besides, the Presidency PSC Ambassador sits on the so-called Crisis Management Board envisaged under the post-Hampton Court process and participates in the CFSP and ESDP planning meetings, supported by the Council Secretariat (see below). The rotation of the Presidency affects the ESDP agenda in an uneven way, as only a handful of countries (not necessarily the largest ones only) have the will, expertise and resources to make a real impact on it.

Concerning ESDP, the main issue with the rotation of the Council Presidency lies less with the accumulation of incoherent flagship initiatives than with the lack of a sustained commitment to pursue long-term programmes, whether in terms of capacity- or institution-building. In an effort to provide more continuity to EU policy-making, the practice of establishing priorities and work programmes covering the terms of three successive presidencies has been adopted. Besides, the interaction

---

6. Cyprus has formally abstained from adopting the joint action on the EU rule-of-law mission in Kosovo (EULEX Kosovo). This has been reportedly the first and only case of recourse to constructive abstention as provided for in the Treaty in the context of ESDP.

between the Presidency, the other Member States and the Council Secretariat is central to improving the level of consistency and continuity.

The CFSP/ESDP institutional framework at a glance

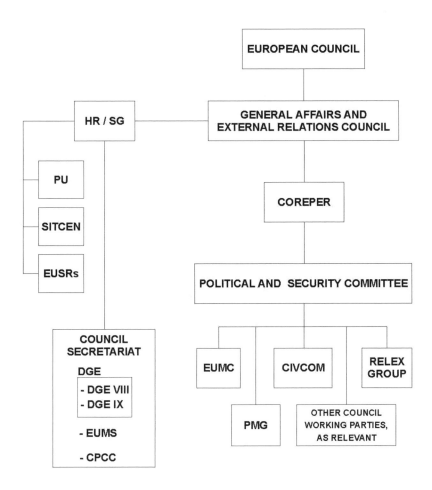

This chart is meant to map the main institutions and bodies involved in CFSP/ESDP decision-making. The important roles of the European Commission and of the European Parliament in this policy area are explained in the text of this chapter, as is the interaction between all of these institutions.

The Political and Security Committee

The establishment of the 'family' of Brussels-based ESDP committees has been one of the two major institutional innovations marking the launch of ESDP, the other being the appointment of Javier Solana as the first SG/HR for CFSP in June 1999. As stressed above, these two developments should be regarded as closely connected. The SG/HR and his staff in the Council Secretariat require permanent, senior national interlocutors to 'feel the pulse' of the capitals, provide policy input and adequately support CFSP and ESDP proceedings. National representatives benefit from the expertise and institutional memory of the Council Secretariat, and from the regular delivery of 'EU-made' information and policy options fuelling, among other factors, the inter-governmental debate.

Of course, the work of ESDP committees should be regarded in conjunction with that of other committees, providing specific geographical or thematic expertise in the context of CFSP and external relations.[7] In fact, limited exchanges and coordination between all these committees, due to time and workload pressures as well as to different 'cultures' and priorities, complicates efforts to achieve overall coherence and a truly comprehensive approach to crises. However, this chapter maintains a more limited focus on ESDP as such. The PSC is central to the family of ESDP committees which includes the EU Military Committee (EUMC), the Political Military Group (PMG), the Committee for Civilian Crisis Management (CIVCOM), the group of Foreign Relations (RELEX) Counsellors and the Nicolaidis group.

First sketched out in various policy papers submitted by Germany and France following the Saint Malo Declaration and in the conclusions of the Cologne European Council in June 1999, the broad remit of the PSC was outlined in annex to the presidency report on ESDP to the Helsinki summit six months later. The committee was set up on an interim basis in February 2000[8] and established as a permanent body in January 2001, following the specification of its job description in the annex to the ESDP Presidency report to the Nice European Council in December 2000.[9] At the same time, the PSC found its way into Article 25 TEU via the Treaty of Nice. The new Committee effectively replaced the Political Committee, including Political Directors based in respective capitals and meeting twice per Presidency,

---

7. Council document 11602/09, List of Council preparatory bodies, 30 June 2009. This document lists a total of 36 working parties in the fields of external relations, security and defence and development.

8. Council Decision 2000/143/CFSP setting up the Interim Political and Security Committee, 14 February 2000. *Official Journal* L 49, 22 February 2000.

9. Council Decision 2001/78/CFSP setting up the Political and Security Committee, 22 January 2001. *Official Journal* L 27/1, 30 January 2001.

as the engine of CFSP and in particular ESDP. PSC meetings involve, in addition to national representatives, relevant Council officials (depending on the agenda of the meeting) and a representative from the Commission. This format is replicated, at different levels of seniority and for different areas of expertise, in other ESDP committees. While the PSC is normally chaired by the representative of the country holding the Presidency, provision is made for the SG/HR to chair the committee, following consultation with the Presidency, in particular in the event of a crisis. This clause has not been activated yet but anticipates the solution envisaged for the PSC chairmanship under the Lisbon Treaty.

At first, the PSC appeared somewhat squeezed between the powerful political directors in various EU capitals and the very senior Ambassadors to COREPER II, the highest placed inter-governmental committee of the EU charged with the overall preparation of the GAERC and of the European Council. However, the new committee has quickly defined its own niche and has been consistently expanding it, in parallel to the rise of ESDP, the growing political engagement of the EU in crisis areas and the launch of numerous crisis management operations.[10] The PSC was the only committee in town that could consistently sustain and oversee the fast development of ESDP. This became the platform of the power and identity of the PSC.

The Annex to the Nice Presidency conclusions describes the PSC as the 'lynchpin' of ESDP and CFSP, dealing with all aspects of these policies and playing a central role in the definition of the EU's response to a crisis. According to Article 25 TEU, the PSC should monitor the international situation and contribute to the definition of CFSP by delivering opinions to the Council, including on its own initiative. The above-mentioned Annex lists in some detail the attributions of the PSC, which is tasked with maintaining a 'privileged link' with the HR for CFSP, providing guidance to other committees on CFSP matters, monitoring the implementation of agreed policies, and driving the capability development process, among other issues.

The core of the PSC responsibilities lies, however, in the area of crisis management proper. In times of crisis, the PSC is charged with examining the situation, assessing the various policy options and making a proposal to the Council defining the political interests and objectives of the Union and indicating a recommended course of action. Once an ESDP operation has been decided upon and launched, Article 25

---

10. On the development of the PSC, see among others Simon Duke, 'The Lynchpin COPS. Assessing the workings and institutional relations of the Political and Security Committee', Working Paper 2005/W/05, European Institute of Public Administration, Maastricht, 2005.

TEU envisages that the PSC exerts the political control and strategic direction of the operation under the responsibility of the Council. The latter can also authorise the PSC, for the purpose and duration of the operation, to take relevant decisions. This is a rare instance of explicit, albeit potential and circumscribed, delegation of decision-taking authority by the Council to a committee of national officials. To sum up, in the sensitive field of crisis management, the PSC disposes of considerable powers of policy advice and recommendation in the run-up to formal decisions as well as political direction, monitoring and evaluation in the implementation phase.

As described in the following sections, the PSC exercises its functions in constant interplay with other ESDP committees and the Council Secretariat. The Nicolaidis Group, set up in 2003 to manage the growing workload of the PSC and named after its first chairman, is tasked with ensuring the preparation of the PSC proceedings on a quasi-daily basis.[11] In this context, national representatives can raise issues of particular concern to respective countries and anticipate other matters deserving thorough discussion by the PSC. The Coordination Unit of Directorate General E for External and Political-Military affairs (DG E) in the Council Secretariat supports the so-called CFSP and ESDP planning meetings (see below), where the agenda of the PSC is discussed and organised over the medium term.

The PSC has developed a distinctive working style and 'club atmosphere' that allows for substantial exchanges within the limits of the political instructions or guidelines that each delegation receives from national capitals.[12] PSC Ambassadors consistently express a growing sense of belonging to a distinctive circle of decision-makers and, by and large, share the ambition to make CFSP and ESDP work. Formal and informal codes of conduct have been emerging that inform the style of negotiation and debate, putting a premium on the ability to persuasively articulate national positions and to adjust them with a degree of flexibility in search of consensus, as opposed to simply stating national lines. Of course, the degree of flexibility that delegations can afford varies depending on the particular importance of the issues at stake for each Member State. Besides, some of the most divisive matters, such as the Iraq crisis in 2003, were kept firmly off the PSC agenda.

---

11. Council of the European Union, 'Creation of a preparatory group for the PSC', Doc. 8441/03, 14 April 2003.

12. See Jolyon Howorth, 'The Political and Security Committee: a case study in supranational inter-governmentalism', in Renaud Dehousse (ed.), *The Community Method in Perspective: New Approaches* (New York: Palgrave, 2009).

And yet, the function of the PSC as a 'transmission belt' between Brussels and national capitals constitutes the main platform of this committee's influence. PSC Ambassadors dispose of extensive information and expertise from multiple sources in Brussels, as well as from the EU Special Representatives, the Heads of ESDP civilian missions and the military commanders in the field. The practice of joint reports produced by the heads of national diplomatic missions in the field has also been expanding. Most importantly, PSC Ambassadors are in the best place to convey to colleagues in Member States where the scope for compromise lies and what the most effective (in the sense of both acceptable and workable) policy options may be. From this standpoint, the work of the PSC has been crucial in reaching agreement on the launch of more than twenty ESDP operations in six years. That said, given the time-consuming nature of crisis management decision-making, including the planning and the implementation of various operations at the same time, and the often technical character of the dossiers on its agenda, the PSC can only perform adequately if supported by the other members of the ESDP committees' family.

The EU Military Committee, the Political Military Group, the Committee for Civilian Crisis Management and the Foreign Relations (RELEX) Counsellors

The EU Military Committee (EUMC) is 'the highest military body established within the Council' and provides military advice to the PSC as well as military direction to the EU Military Staff (EUMS).[13] It was set up as an interim military body in March 2000 and as a permanent committee in January 2001. The EUMC is composed of the Chiefs of Defence – that is, the highest military authorities – of the Member States, but normally meets at the level of their military representatives: senior three star officers based in Brussels. For those Member States that are not also NATO members, with the exception of the representatives of France, Belgium and Luxembourg, the members of the EUMC are double-hatted as military representatives to the NATO military committee as well. The EUMC meets in the Chiefs of Defence configuration if and when required, normally twice a year.

In particular, the committee meets at this level to select its own Chairman, a four star flag officer who is appointed by the Council for a term of three years. The EUMC is therefore the only ESDP committee which is not chaired by a representative of the rotating Presidency. The chairman of the EUMC exercises four important roles, namely providing military advice to the HR, participating when relevant in PSC meetings and attending Council meetings when decisions with defence implications need to be tak-

---

13. Council Decision 2001/79/CFSP setting up the Military Committee of the European Union, 22 January 2001. *Official Journal* L 27/4, 30 January 2001.

en, issuing directives and guidance to the EUMS and acting as the primary point of contact with the Operation Commander of an ESDP military operation.

As described below in some detail, the EUMC plays an important role in the planning of ESDP military operations as the top level source of military advice at the interface between the EUMS, which produces military assessments, the other services of the Council Secretariat (DGE VIII), the SG/HR and the PSC, where the political-military profiles of an envisaged operation are discussed all along the planning process. On a more regular basis, the EUMC monitors the conduct of ongoing ESDP military operations and steers the work of the EUMS on all dimensions of military ESDP, including crisis management concepts, procedures and exercises and issues related to military capabilities.

The Political Military Group (PMG) stands somehow in between the EUMC and the CIVCOM, the two top advisory bodies for, respectively, military and civilian ESDP. The COREPER decision establishing the group in its final shape in April 2001 includes a very vague mandate, namely assisting the PSC by carrying out preparatory work on ESDP.[14] As a result, and unlike other ESDP committees, the PMG lacks a specific mission and profile, except dealing by and large with the political dimension of military issues. This is reflected in its composition, including national representatives from both ministries of foreign affairs and defence. It is therefore, to some extent, up to the Presidency of the EU Council to decide how best to use the group and that depends, among other factors, on the relative prominence of political-military and civil-military issues on the EU agenda.

Aside from its contribution to preparing PSC debates on political-military issues, the PMG has been developing a distinctive civilian-military expertise and has sought to apply it more specifically to the domain of Security Sector Reform (SSR). This is a policy area where the potential for civ-mil synergy is clear and the PMG has played an important role in 2008 in devising the concept of pools of SSR experts who could be mobilised in deployable teams and could enhance EU capabilities and expertise on SSR. Furthermore, in keeping with the fact the DGE VIII for political-military affairs is in charge of managing the SSR operation EUSEC RD Congo, the PMG is the committee responsible for overseeing the conduct of this mission, which is aimed at helping reform the Congolese army. The PMG has also been particularly involved in the planning stages of the EU SSR operation in Guinea Bissau, which includes both a military and a civilian component.

---

14. COREPER Decision amending COREPER decision of 5 July 2000 on the establishment of a Politico-Military Working Party. See Council Document 7992/01, 12 April 2001.

As envisaged at the Helsinki summit, the Council adopted the decision to establish the CIVCOM in May 2000 and mandated it with providing information, formulating recommendations and giving advice on the civilian aspects of crisis management to the (then) interim PSC.[15] The guidelines for the work of the new Committee very much focussed on the capability dimension of civilian crisis management. Promoting inter-pillar coherence in this domain and coordinating national and EU resources were other important aspects of the CIVCOM's original mandate.

The role of CIVCOM has of course very much evolved over time, with the launch of the first civilian crisis management missions in 2003 marking a turning point. Since then, the planning and monitoring of civilian missions has taken up the bulk of the committee's time. By and large, the CIVCOM is supposed to perform similar tasks as the EUMC on the civilian side, notably in providing workable options for civilian crisis management to the PSC. This makes of it a key body for ESDP policy-making but also puts it under serious strain.

The CIVCOM has been suffering from the relative fragility of civilian ESDP structures in the Council Secretariat compared to the military ones. Understaffing has always affected the work of DGE IX in charge of civilian crisis management and no *ad hoc* structure for the planning, guidance and support of civilian ESDP operations existed until the Civilian Planning and Conduct Capability (CPCC) was set up in 2007. Besides, unlike the representatives at the EUMC, the CIVCOM members do not dispose of a preparatory working group to address technical profiles and prune the agenda of their meetings.

Against this background, the CIVCOM had to confront both a quantitative and a qualitative challenge. On the one hand, 17 civilian missions have had to be planned, launched, conducted and (six of them) terminated over the last six years. On the other, civilian crisis management in the context of ESDP was a new policy field for the Union and for some of its Member States alike. It therefore generated new requirements in terms of expertise not only in the field but also in Brussels. Most CIVCOM members have been and by and large remain generalist diplomats with limited earlier experience of the planning and conduct of civilian crisis management missions. Learning by doing has therefore been a quite common feature of the professional experience in CIVCOM. As such, however, the role of the CIVCOM as the repository and the vehicle of a rich institutional memory is even more important for Member States. In supporting the emergence of a new policy field, the

---

15. Council Decision setting up a Committee for civilian aspects of crisis management, 22 May 2000. *Official Journal* L 127/1, 27 May 2000.

members of the CIVCOM have played a key role of liaison with national capitals as well, striving to raise awareness of the strong demand for EU civilian crisis management and of the consequent capability requirements.

Albeit from a different standpoint, providing viable options and technical expertise is the main role of the RELEX Counsellors working group as well. The role of RELEX Counsellors is discreet but essential, in so far as they oil the ESDP machinery with specific advice on the institutional, financial and legal profiles of ESDP decision-making. This working group was set up in 1994 following the establishment of a single institutional framework by the Treaty of Maastricht and the consequent expansion of COREPER's competence to CFSP matters.[16] The additional workload persuaded national representatives to create a new body – the CFSP Counsellors – tasked with examining horizontal issues with legal or financial implications and coordinating the agendas of COREPER and the Political Committee, then in charge of CFSP.

Following the launch of ESDP and the creation of the PSC, the group changed name to Foreign Relations (RELEX) Counsellors. RELEX Counsellors draft, in close cooperation with the other CFSP/ESDP structures, all the legal acts adopted in the context of CFSP and ESDP, including punitive measures. They also oversee the legal aspects of the evolving bureaucratic framework in this policy area, including for example the creation of new bodies such as the European Defence Agency or the European Security and Defence College. In so far as the budget is concerned, the RELEX Counsellors group performs a crucial role with the active participation of the Commission representative therein. They discuss the 'financial statement' – that is, the money made available – corresponding to all joint actions and other initiatives financed under the CFSP budget. In carrying out this task, they need to ensure that the budget is allocated in a balanced way across the different actions to be supported, and they negotiate the procedures allowing for the quick disbursement of funds for preparatory actions and procurement in the context of ESDP.[17]

The Secretary General/ High Representative for CFSP, the Policy Unit and Directorate General E for External Relations and Political-Military Affairs

The General Secretariat of the Council supports and informs the proceedings of Brussels-based committees and of the GAERC in ESDP decision-making. From this standpoint, various sets of actors can be pointed out within the General Secretariat,

---

16. COREPER Decision establishing the CFSP Counsellors Working Party, 26 July 1994. On 24 November 1999, the COREPER decided that the tasks of the RELEX Working Party should be transferred to the CFSP Counsellors Working Party, which would be renamed Foreign Relations Counsellors Working Party.

17. See Chapter 2 on ESDP resources, pp.93-6.

namely the SG/HR, the Policy Unit, the DG E for External Relations and Political-Military Affairs and the distinctive 'operational' bodies serving ESDP, namely the EUMS and the CPCC. The presentation here follows this breakdown, although it is clear that, in practice, these bodies work together in permanent cooperation to shape and implement ESDP.

Based on the Treaty of Nice, the job description of the SG/HR is rather modest. Articles 18 and 26 TEU confer to the new post (envisaged by the Treaty of Amsterdam in 1997 but actually created in 1999) the basic task of assisting the Presidency of the Council in CFSP matters. That entails contributing to the formulation, preparation and implementation of policy decisions and, on behalf of the Council and at the request of the Presidency, conducting political dialogue with third parties. Three tasks can therefore be extrapolated from Treaty provisions, namely (informal) policy proposal, policy implementation and external representation. The appointment of a senior politician – Javier Solana – to what some Member States regarded as the post of a top civil servant made a key difference and allowed for a dynamic, entrepreneurial interpretation and application of the letter of the Treaty.

The launch of ESDP, parallel to the appointment of the first SG/HR, offered the latter a suitable platform to establish the new post on the map in Brussels and beyond. The SG/HR has invested considerable political and personal capital in the development of the new policy area by keeping it on the radar screen of the Foreign Ministers and also of the European Council, by engaging himself directly in crisis diplomacy (often as a preliminary step to the mobilisation of ESDP instruments) and, finally, by shaping a consistent discourse about the distinctiveness, purpose and requirements of the new policy.

The participation of the SG/HR in the GAERC and in the European Council has provided scope for channelling ESDP dossiers at the highest political level. Through the services of the Council Secretariat, the SG/HR maintains a permanent working relationship with the PSC and has sometimes participated in the meetings of the committee when issues of particular political relevance were addressed. In addition, the SG/HR receives the advice of the Chairman of the EUMC on military matters while the Director General of the EUMS and the Civilian Operations Commander (CivOpCdr) are placed under his direct authority within the Council Secretariat.

When it comes to the operational dimension of ESDP, the SG/HR chairs *ad hoc* (albeit quite rare) top-level crisis management meetings bringing together senior officials from all relevant departments in the Council and is formally in the chain of command of ESDP civilian missions. On the military side, while not directly involved in the military direction of ESDP operations, the SG/HR is tasked with assisting the Presidency and the Council as relevant and ensuring, for example, the coherence of the EU's response and the coordination with other international actors. Finally, the EU Special Representatives, who perform an important diplomatic role in crisis areas providing local political guidance to the leadership of ESDP operations, act under the strategic oversight and political direction of the PSC and the operational direction of the SG/HR. In short, the position of the SG/HR is at the centre of the institutional hub of CFSP and ESDP. The hub, however, includes a variety of other bodies under his authority.

The expansion of the CFSP/ESDP institutional structures in the Council Secretariat has enabled the SG/HR to exercise, within the limits of available time, such multiple tasks, in addition to his political and diplomatic role in the context of CFSP. Conversely, these bodies have benefited from the political profile of the SG/HR in their dealings with national officials in Brussels and in capitals. The so-called Policy Unit (PU) has played an important role in triggering the evolution of the Council Secretariat towards a more proactive role in policy-making.[18] The (then-called) Policy Planning and Early Warning Unit, established in 1999, works under the direct authority and responsibility of the SG/HR and includes roughly one seconded diplomat from each Member State as well as a representative of the Commission and officials from other departments of the Council Secretariat.

Through the PU, the HR disposes both of a dedicated service to fuel decision-making upstream with policy option papers and of a plug into national capitals via the diplomats serving in the Unit. In practice, the commonly called Policy Unit (following the attribution of the early warning function to the Joint Situation Centre in January 2003) has been working closely with the private office of the HR. While not primarily in charge of ESDP, the PU has played an important role in the formulation and development of this policy area and remains involved in its proceedings. The Director of the PU, who regularly appears before the PSC, sits on the recently revamped Crisis Management Board (CMB), which reviews the overall coherence and effectiveness of the CFSP/ESDP approach to crisis areas and co-chairs with the PSC representative of the country holding the Presidency the so-called CFSP planning meetings, which organise the agenda of the PSC over the medium term.

---

18. The Declaration 6 attached to the Treaty of Amsterdam envisaged the creation of the Policy Planning and Early Warning Unit and charged it with four essential tasks, namely monitoring and analysing developments of relevance to CFSP, assessing EU foreign policy interests and identifying issues for future action, ensuring timely analysis and early warning and producing policy option papers as a contribution to policy formulation.

The Joint Situation Centre, also directly attached to the SG/HR, is charged with providing analysis and risk assessments to CFSP/ESDP bodies drawing from both open source intelligence and confidential information and assessments coming from EU Member States or other EU sources. In close cooperation with the Intelligence Division of the EUMS (see below), the SitCen plays a key role in informing the planning process with adequate analysis of the situation on the ground and performs an important early warning function.

The DG E of the Council Secretariat plays a fundamental role in the conception and development of ESDP. In particular, DG E services contribute to formulating policy priorities, supporting coordination, steering the evolution of military and civilian crisis management concepts and capabilities, running crisis management exercises and providing input at the political strategic level to EU crisis response. The Coordination Unit of DG E is tasked with supporting the proceedings of the PSC and the RELEX Counsellors working group by providing input on specific dossiers and a broader secretariat function.

The Director General of DG E chairs the Crisis Management Board and regularly attends PSC meetings as the most senior Council official. In this capacity, he is accompanied by the directors of political and operational crisis management structures, or of geographical departments, as relevant.

Directorate VIII (DGE VIII) for political-military affairs and Directorate IX (DGE IX) for civilian crisis management are the key bodies in charge of ESDP within DG E. Their specific contribution to the framing of the EU's response to crisis starts upstream, when the appropriateness of the EU's intervention in a given crisis situation is debated. Once the decision to consider intervention is taken and the planning process starts, as described below in some detail, DGE VIII and DGE IX take the lead at the political-strategic level, with a view to drafting the crisis management concept for either military or civilian operations. In this function, DGE VIII closely cooperates with the EUMC and the EUMS as important institutional interlocutors and sources of expertise on the planning of crisis management operations. Over time, and within the particularly narrow limits of the inter-governmental consensus on defence issues, DGE VIII has provided a significant impetus to the development of the military dimension of ESDP and has accumulated considerable institutional memory and expertise. In particular, DGE VIII is in charge of managing the sensitive dossier of ESDP-NATO relations, including the application of the Berlin Plus agreements and the negotiation of the technical arrangements necessary to streamline EU-NATO cooperation in theatre.

At its creation in 2001 DGE IX found itself in a different institutional position from DGE VIII. Political-military structures did not exist within the EU before the launch of ESDP but relevant expertise was abundant at national level and could be pooled in Brussels, provided that the political will to do so existed. Conversely, national administrations disposed of limited and fragmented know-how on civilian crisis management and, at first, this area did not feature high on the political agenda of most EU Member States. Likewise, while military operations undertaken in the context of ESDP could rely on the EUMS and on NATO's or national operational HQs to exercise planning, command and control, neither the structures not the concepts of civilian planning, command and control were defined at first. As a result, the remit of DGE IX expanded over time, with the bulk of the work shifting from developing concepts and listing theoretically available capabilities to actually planning and overseeing operations and scrambling for very rare national resources, in close cooperation with the CIVCOM.

DGE IX made considerable strides in all respects. For example, a Police Unit was created to improve the planning and oversight of the ESDP police missions undertaken in Bosnia Herzegovina and FYROM. DGE IX had to provide the equivalent of a strategic and an operational HQ for all civilian missions, while being responsible for complex mission support functions and working with the Commission to improve procedures for rapid financing and procurement.

As the number of ESDP civilian missions grew rapidly between 2003 and 2005, it became clear that the otherwise remarkable performance of DGE IX could not make up for the gap between the demand for EU intervention and the limited institutional capacity to plan, monitor and evaluate several civilian missions at once. At their informal meeting in Hampton Court in October 2005, EU leaders decided to address this growing capability-expectations gap.[19] In the context of the so-called post-Hampton Court process, plans were made to strengthen the crisis management structures of the Council Secretariat, with a particular focus on the civilian dimension.

In his letter to the Council Presidency of June 2006, the SG/HR outlined five sets of reforms directed at reinforcing the Secretariat's assessment, planning and implementation capacity. Concerning the latter dimension, the SG/HR envisaged

---

19. Following the recommendations for further work established at the summit in Hampton Court on 27 October 2005, the SG/HR addressed a set of proposals to the British Presidency of the EU in December 2005 with a view to improving the defence capabilities of EU member States, strengthening the EU crisis management structures, increasing CFSP funding and finding ways to finance ESDP civilian operations rapidly, and improving the EU coordination in the Balkans. In June 2006, the SG/HR sent a progress report on these four sets of issues to the Austrian Presidency of the EU.

the creation of the Civilian Operations Commander (CivOpCdr), responsible for the conduct of each civilian operation. The approval of this innovation by the Council paved the way towards the setting-up in August 2007 of the new Civilian Planning and Conduct Capability (CPCC), headed by the CivOpCdr and essentially responsible for the operational planning, command and control of civilian missions (see below). As a result, following a phase of stalemate due to much of its staff being transferred to the new CPCC, DGE IX retained responsibility for strategic planning (up to the finalisation of the crisis management concept), for developing concepts and conducting crisis management exercises, for gathering and analysing lessons learned from all civilian missions, as well as for a range of other horizontal issues.

The Hampton Court agenda envisaged other innovations for ESDP decision-making within the Council Secretariat, namely the creation of a Crisis Management Board and of new formats charged with drafting the crisis management concept (policy group) and with devising military, civilian or civilian-military strategic options (planning group). The common denominator of these proposals was not to create new structures but to ensure that all relevant bodies acted coherently within the Secretariat at different stages in the crisis management process. The policy group and the planning group have never been formally set up as such although relevant actors are expected to convene as appropriate during the planning phase.

The Crisis Management Board was supposed to meet when a new ESDP operation was contemplated, bringing together senior staff with geographic, military or civilian responsibility within the Council Secretariat under the chairmanship of the SG/HR himself. The purpose was to clarify respective tasks and responsibilities at the highest level and to review the performance of ESDP operations. Not least due to the charged agenda of the SG/HR, the CMB hardly ever met in this particular configuration but over two years on, in late 2008, it has been revamped under the lead of the Director General of DG E.[20] The 'new' CMB has been meeting every two weeks or so since the beginning of 2009 and brings together, besides the Director General of DG E, the PSC Ambassador of the country holding the Presidency, the Director of the PU and senior officials from political and operational crisis management departments (DGE VIII, DGE IX, the EUMS and the CPCC). The purpose is to ensure regular and consistent monitoring of ongoing crisis management operations, to enhance coherence between CFSP priorities and ESDP interventions, and to enable a better flow of information between different Council bodies.

---

20. It is foreseen, however, that another top-level crisis management body looking at the broader political dimension of a crisis situation can still be chaired by the SG/HR.

The EU Military Staff and the Civilian Planning and Conduct Capability

The EU Military Staff was set up in January 2001 with the basic mandate to provide military expertise and support ESDP.[21] Within the Council Secretariat, the EUMS is directly attached to the SG/HR and works under the military direction of the EUMC. Starting from a small cell of uniformed personnel, the EUMS has expanded to include almost 200 seconded military officers and its prerogatives have undergone significant evolution. The creation of the Civil-Military Cell in summer 2005 and the implementation of the Hampton Court and post-Wiesbaden agendas in 2008 represent important steps in this context. The EUMS was given two main sets of tasks, namely to perform early warning, situation assessment and strategic planning for ESDP military operations, and to contribute to the process of elaboration, assessment and review of the military capability goals. In this latter function, the EUMS has been supposed to work in close coordination with the EDA since the setting-up of this agency in 2004.[22]

In exercising these tasks, the EUMS acts under the direction of the EUMC and provides its expertise to that committee, while working in close cooperation with DGE VIII and the Joint Situation Centre in the Council Secretariat. Within the Council Secretariat, the former leads the definition of the political frame of EU military action, while the latter exchanges intelligence with the EUMS (see below).

Without anticipating the details of the planning process, the EUMS is essentially in charge of providing military expertise upstream, in the phase of strategic planning. Up to early 2007, the EU disposed of two options for the subsequent phase of operational planning and conduct of ESDP military operations, namely access to NATO's operational HQ capabilities under the Berlin Plus mechanism, or using national HQs to be augmented with multinational staff to run an ESDP operation. The controversial debate on equipping the Union with an operational HQ for autonomous EU crisis management operations led to the first stage of EUMS reform. Meeting in Brussels in April 2003, France, Germany, Belgium and Luxembourg proposed that interested states progressively establish an operational HQ available to the EU.[23] In short, this would have provided the Union with a third option in the form of a permanent, fully-fledged operational HQ. The UK and other Member

---

21. Council Decision 2001/80/CFSP on the establishment of the Military Staff of the European Union, 22 January 2001. *Official Journal* L 27, 30 January 2001.

22. See Chapter 2 on ESDP resources.

23. See the final statement issued at the meeting in Tervuren, 29 April 2003, in Missiroli (ed.), op. cit. in note 3. For an insightful analysis of the political dimension of the summit and of its follow up, see Philippe de Schoutheete, 'La cohérence par la défense. Une autre lecture de la PESD', *Chaillot Paper* no. 71, EU Institute for Security Studies, Paris, October 2004.

States swiftly opposed this proposal, perceived as duplicating NATO and national assets and weakening the transatlantic link. The ensuing debate resulted in a compromise between France, the UK and Germany in November 2003, endorsed by the European Council in December, whereby the links between the EUMS and NATO's HQ (SHAPE) would be upgraded by setting up liaison cells in both institutions.[24]

Besides, a Civil-Military Cell (Civ-Mil Cell) was set up within the EUMS with a view to enhancing its planning capacity and providing the nucleus of the new EU Operation Centre.[25] The latter would not amount to a standing operational HQ but could be activated *ad hoc*, with a view to mounting individual military or civil-military operations, by a decision of the Council. In this case, the Civ-Mil Cell would be responsible for generating such autonomous capacity. This complex compromise paved the way for the creation of the Civ-Mil Cell in May 2005 and for achieving, with considerable delay, the full capability to activate the Operations Centre in January 2007. As a result, the EU disposes of a third option for the planning and conduct of ESDP operations, although only by default, when Member States decide not to have recourse to NATO's assets and national HQs are not available.

The CivMil Cell included two branches, namely the civil-military strategic planning branch and the permanent staff providing the nucleus of the Operations Centre. The former was tasked with strategic contingency planning and with contributing to crisis response strategic planning for military, civilian and joint civil-military operations, bringing a distinctive civilian-military dimension. The Commission was represented in the Civ-Mil cell by two experts. The nucleus of the Operations Centre essentially performed a 'housekeeping' role, ensuring that the facilities of the Centre would be ready for activation within days, but also developed standard operating procedures for all HQs available to the EU (including national ones) and coordinated the flow of 'augmentees' to multinationalise national HQs when used for an ESDP operation.

The Civ-Mil Cell has been affected by broader obstacles to implementing civil-military coordination in the context of ESDP and has therefore struggled to inform the ESDP strategic planning process with a real civil-military dimension. The inclusion

---

24. See 'European defence: NATO/EU consultation, planning and operations' in Missiroli (ed.), op. cit. in note 3, pp. 322-323. This document was agreed by France, Germany and the UK on 29 November 2003, subsequently endorsed by the Italian Presidency of the EU and approved by the Brussels European Council in December 2003.

25. See Gerrard Quille, Giovanni Gasparini, Roberto Menotti, Nicoletta Pirozzi and Stephen Pullinger, 'Developing EU Civil Military Coordination: The Role of the new Civilian Military Cell', Joint Report by ISIS Europe and CeMISS, Brussels, June 2006. For the precise attributions of the new Civ-Mil Cell, up to the review of its remit in 2008 (see below), see Council Decision 2005/395/CFSP amending Decision 2001/80/CFSP on the establishment of the Military Staff of the European Union, 10 May 2005. *Official Journal* L 132/7, 26 May 2005.

of the Civ-Mil Cell in the EUMS raised reservations as to the suitability of the Cell to develop a civil-military interface drawing on *both* the military and the civilian experience and distinctive requirements. Among other activities, the Civ-Mil Cell has contributed to the reflection on Security Sector Reform (SSR), a concept central to the mandate of an increasing number of ESDP operations and that lends itself well to civil-military coordination. In practice, it has provided important added value in supporting DGE IX first, and subsequently the CPCC in the planning of civilian missions, from the Aceh Monitoring Mission in 2005 to the EU Monitoring Mission in Georgia in 2008. In this context, the Civ-Mil Cell has made military know-how, intelligence and logistical planning capabilities available to assist the planning and deployment of ESDP civilian missions.

The structures of the EUMS and of the Civ-Mil Cell underwent further reform in 2008, in application of the Hampton Court and post-Wiesbaden agendas. These reforms responded to the pressing requirement to strengthen the crisis management structures of the Council Secretariat, based on the lessons of operational experience and given the ambition to undertake more demanding missions. In the context of the post-Hampton Court process the SG/HR proposed to the Council in June 2006 the creation of a stronger situation and risk assessment capacity. This would bring together the resources of the Intelligence Division of the EUMS and those of the SitCen so as to pool information at the civil-military level and make better analysis available to other ESDP bodies. The new Single Intelligence Analysis Capacity (SIAC) was consequently set up.

The SG/HR also proposed enhancing the capacity to monitor military and civilian operations, notably when crises or critical contingencies emerge. The new Watch-keeping capability (WKC) follows ESDP operations 24/7 and ensures the ability to swiftly exchange and process operation-specific information, thereby establishing a better link between the operational HQ and the EUMS on the military side, and the Civilian Operations Commander and the Head of Mission on the civilian side. The WKC was declared fully operational in August 2008 and is placed within the Operations Division of the EUMS, while working under the functional authority of the Civilian Operations Commander in so far as civilian missions are concerned.

Aside from these useful but quite circumscribed innovations, the informal meeting of Defence Ministers in Wiesbaden in May 2007 stressed that the EUMS suffered from broader shortcomings. These concerned its ability to contribute to strategic planning and to envisage the force requirements of ESDP operations at an early enough stage for Member States to assess what contribution they could provide. The difficulties and delays encountered in the planning and force generation process of the EUFOR RD Congo operation provided important lessons in that respect. It was broadly acknowledged that the problem lay both in the small size of the EUMS planning structures and in the uneven professionalism of its personnel. A new debate opened up on the need to constitute a much stronger EU capability for the planning and conduct of autonomous military operations.

Following the mandate of Wiesbaden, and amidst enduring divergence between Member States on the scope and ultimate purpose of reform, the SG/HR submitted to the Council in November 2007 a relatively limited set of measures to strengthen the EUMS's ability to conduct strategic planning. These included both improving the recruitment process of EUMS staff, only a minority of which is selected through competition as opposed to national quotas or 'flag posts', and slightly expanding the EUMS with five more officers. Together with five others reassigned within the EUMS, the five new officers serve in the new Military Assessment and Planning Unit (MAP) of the CivMil Cell. The MAP is in charge of advance planning, both generic and contingency (see below), so as to provide decision-making bodies with military expertise on the potential scenarios for EU intervention before a crisis occurs.

As a consequence of these innovations, in 2008 the EUMS was reorganised as follows. The 'new' CivMil Cell includes two branches, namely its traditional civil-military strategic planning branch and the new MAP branch. The permanent nucleus of the Operations Centre has been moved to the Operations Division. The latter, charged with monitoring ongoing operations and providing political-military advice, includes therefore a crisis response branch, the new WKC and the nucleus of the Operations Centre. In short, the CivMil Cell includes the personnel in charge of advance and strategic planning, while the Operations Division cooperates at different levels with the relevant operational HQs to oversee the conduct of military operations.

On the whole, the series of piecemeal reforms illustrated above contributes to improving the capacity of the EUMS to fulfil its functions, but questions remain as to its ability to undertake the strategic planning of more demanding military operations. The planning staff remains relatively small and disposes of little reach-back capacity to access specific expertise when need be, for example in planning naval operations.

The EU Military Staff

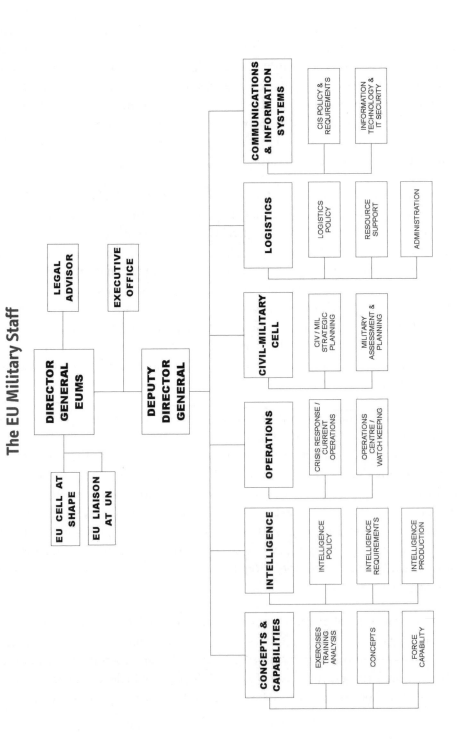

This graph is based on a chart published in Impetus, *the Bulletin of the EUMS, Issue 6, Autumn/Winter 2008.*

On the civilian side, the creation of the CPCC was meant to address existing short-comings in the ability to plan, conduct and support the fast-growing range of ESDP civilian missions. Established in August 2007, directly attached to the SG/HR and headed by the new post of Civilian Operations Commander, the new structure has a multidisciplinary team of about 70, half of them coming from DGE IX and other services of the Secretariat, and half having joined as seconded national experts. It includes three departments, respectively tasked with the planning, conduct and support of civilian operations. As such, the CPCC represents a genuine and quite unique institutional innovation, supposed to respond to the pressing demands for more professional planning, better operational direction, permanent monitoring of ongoing missions (including through the WKC) and adequate mission support. The civilian chain of command is adjusted accordingly, with the CivOpCdr replacing the EUSRs in the operational chain of command.[26] The CivOpCdr exercises the command and control of all civilian ESDP missions at the strategic level, issues instructions to the HoMs and provides them with advice and technical support. HoMs, on the other hand, exercise the command and control of respective missions in theatre.

Like the EUMS, the CPCC is a body tasked with informing decision-making with distinctive technical expertise. Unlike the EUMS, however, the CPCC is charged with operational planning, which follows the adoption of the crisis management concept, and with the conduct of all civilian missions, while strategic planning remains in principle a prerogative of DGE IX. In the military domain, the EUMS is primarily charged with contributing to strategic planning, whereas the operational planning and conduct are the responsibility of the designated operational HQ for each individual operation. In both cases, the distinction between strategic and operational planning is much less clear-cut than it looks on paper: the CPCC and the EUMS provide their expertise to inform the whole planning process.

The CPCC has performed an important role in the planning and launching of three civilian missions, namely EU SSR Guinea Bissau, EUMM Georgia and EULEX Kosovo. In many respects, however, the CPCC remains work in progress. In particular, the operational planning branch is too small, and required assistance from the CivMil Cell and other EUMS divisions on the logistical, communication and medical aspects of the planning and support of the EU mission in Georgia in September 2008. In addition to its principal operational tasks, the CPCC is charged with complementary responsibilities to those of DGE IX on a range of important

---

26. The EU Special Representatives remain in the 'political' chain of command of ESDP civilian missions and are responsible to provide HoMs with local political guidance, in consultation with the CivOpCdr.

horizontal matters such as input to the civilian capabilities development process, training issues, civilian crisis management exercises and the collection and analysis of lessons identified, among others. In principle, DGE IX is responsible for defining the policy goals and for driving policy developments on all these matters. In practice, the division of tasks between DGE IX and the CPCC is blurred and requires more fine-tuning to improve cooperation and coordination.

The European Commission

The Commission is fully associated with the work carried out in the field of CFSP (Article 27 TEU) and disposes, alongside Member States, of a right of initiative in this domain. Since ESDP is an integral part of CFSP, these provisions apply to this field as well. In practice, the broader politics surrounding the launch and development of CFSP have defined the scope for the actual implementation of Treaty provisions. When crafting CFSP, Member States have refrained from pooling sovereignty at the EU level and have reserved for themselves a pivotal role in decision-making, from initiating policies to taking final decisions by unanimity. The creation of the position of SG/HR for CFSP at the top of the Council Secretariat reflected the determination to seek ways to better cooperate in foreign policy matters while preserving a clear distinction between intergovernmental structures and procedures on the one hand and the Community method, which applies to other areas of external action, on the other. The launch of ESDP in 1999/2000, with a strong focus on its military dimension, confirmed this trend. Crisis management within the second pillar was to translate into rapid, potentially robust interventions benefiting from the political endorsement and the clout of all Member States.

Against this background, the Commission has never formally exercised its right of initiative in the context of CFSP and has focused on the Community dimension of external action, notably including external economic relations, development cooperation, trade and humanitarian assistance. In so doing, well before the creation of CFSP, the Commission has framed and implemented a wide range of policy tools establishing structural relations with third parties, whether individual countries, sets of states such as the Africa, Caribbean and Pacific (ACP) group of developing countries, or regional organisations. Over time, the political dimension of these relations has been growing, including a security component largely pertaining to crisis prevention activities, the consolidation of democratic governance and of the rule of law, and the support of human rights. In parallel, the issue of coherence between CFSP and Community programmes has acquired ever more prominence, as a basic requirement for the effectiveness of the EU as an international actor. With the launch of ESDP, the debate on coherence has gained a new key dimension, concerning the application of the wide toolbox of the EU to crisis areas.

The Commission provides an important contribution to the ESDP at many levels, although this is a policy domain where inter-institutional relations have often been strained by controversy on respective prerogatives and competences. On the ground, the interplay between ESDP activities and relevant Community instruments all along the crisis or conflict cycle is crucial to the success and long-term sustainability of EU action. In Brussels, the Commission contributes to the debate on the EU approach to crises and on envisaged ESDP operations through the participation of Commission officials in all relevant ESDP committees and through permanent, if not always smooth, cooperation with the Council Secretariat. In particular, the Commission is responsible for administering the CFSP budget, which covers the operational expenditure of civilian ESDP.[27]

From an organisational standpoint, over the last ten years, the Commission has been shaping up its internal structures to match the development of CFSP and of ESDP in particular. Following the appointment of the SG/HR in 1999, a new CFSP Directorate was set up within DG RELEX and has since steadily expanded into the sizeable Directorate A, about 70 officials strong, headed by the Commission representative to the PSC and responsible for coordinating the Commission's input to CFSP. The Directorate includes four units, whose respective remit somewhat mirrors the division of tasks between CFSP/ESDP structures. The unit of the European Correspondent, named after the correspondents responsible for the CFSP dossier in national foreign ministries, is tasked with the overall procedural coordination of the Commission's activities in the area of external relations and CFSP. Among other tasks, the unit assists on a permanent basis the Commission's representative to the PSC. In addition, it is responsible for managing the Commission's end of the COREU (*Correspondance européenne*) network of diplomatic exchanges with Member States and the Council Secretariat.

The unit for crisis response and peace-building performs a wide range of tasks to ensure the prompt formulation and delivery of crisis and disaster response by the Commission. In particular, the unit is in charge of the planning and adoption of crisis response measures via the Instrument for Stability that finances, among other actions, a wide range of complementary measures to ESDP operations.[28] The unit takes the lead within RELEX on key policy dossiers for crisis response and stabilisa-

27. This important task is addressed in the chapter dealing with ESDP resources and capabilities.
28. See Chapter 2 on ESDP resources, pp. 96-8.

tion such as SSR and manages the so-called crisis room – a tool to collect and distribute open source information and intelligence.

The CFSP operations unit includes the Commission representatives to CIVCOM and to the RELEX Counsellors Group. It manages the CFSP budget and deals, therefore, with the often pressing requirements of ESDP civilian operations in terms of finance and procurement. In this context, the unit is responsible for ensuring that ESDP civilian operations act within the rules of sound financial management of the Community. Finally, the security unit provides the Commission's interface with the political-military dimension and relevant ESDP bodies. Officials sitting in the security unit represent the Commission in the EUMC, the PMG and various other Council Working Groups. The unit is also in charge of counter-terrorism, non-proliferation of weapons of mass destruction, conventional disarmament and other transnational threats to health and infrastructures. In addition, the security unit prepares the long-term measures for capacity-building and crisis preparedness envisaged under the Instrument for Stability.

The range of the Commission's structures involved in crisis- or conflict-relevant activities, from prevention to peace-building, is of course broader than the services dedicated to CFSP/ESDP as such. While their comprehensive mapping goes beyond the scope of this contribution, these structures include the ECHO Directorate General responsible for the delivery of humanitarian relief, the Monitoring and Information Centre situated in DG Environment[29] as well as all the geographic services in DG RELEX and in DG Development (in so far as ACP countries are concerned) in charge of relations with third countries or regions. Within RELEX, Directorate B on multilateral relations and human rights is responsible for relations with the UN (including the DPKO) and the OSCE, among other issues. Moreover, the 130 delegations of the Commission on the ground play an important role both as a source of information and expertise and in managing and implementing external assistance.

The Treaty provides that the Council and the Commission are responsible for ensuring the consistency of the EU's external activities. In seeking to promote coherence and consistency, scope for interaction can be identified at many levels, although practice often falls short of potential. First, in terms of information and analysis, the delegations of the Commission on the ground and services in Brussels feed the situation assessments carried out by the Joint Situation Centre, although a truly

---

29. The Monitoring and Information Centre constitutes the operational platform of the EU Civil Protection Mechanism, which coordinates national and EU efforts in emergency response to natural disasters within and outside the Union.

shared and comprehensive evaluation of emerging or ongoing crises is often lacking.

Second, mutual information and consultation on respective initiatives and policies has been improving in quantity and quality, with the Commission representatives in CFSP/ESDP committees performing as the main but not exclusive transmission belts. However, reporting on respective activities does not necessarily amount to joint policy making.[30] More broadly, this also applies to the Commission's work on drafting country strategy papers (CSPs) or action plans for neighbouring countries, defining the priorities for Community external instruments and assistance. The lifetime of CSPs is seven years, broken down into two multi-annual indicative programmes. The time horizon of CSPs exposes a tension between the requirement for predictability of development assistance, the demand for mainstreaming conflict-sensitivity in Community programmes, and the flexibility and responsiveness that crisis management entails. Policy-makers in both the Commission and in the Council Secretariat feel that upstream inter-institutional consultation is limited when drafting strategic papers addressing third countries. On the other hand, in the context of crisis response, considerable progress can be detected with the implementation of the new Instrument for Stability, as illustrated separately.[31]

Third, in the planning phase of ESDP operations, the Commission is involved both in the proceedings of all ESDP committees and in the so-called Crisis Response Coordination Teams, set up to accompany the drafting of the crisis management concepts but, in practice, not always central to this process. Besides, Commission officials take part in fact-finding missions to establish the requirements of envisaged ESDP operations. In addition to their focus on specific financing and procurement issues, they can bring useful perspectives on potential Community measures flanking ESDP action and on the broader Community approach to stabilisation and institution-building in a given theatre.

From a functional standpoint, Security Sector Reform (SSR) has emerged as a key domain for inter-institutional cooperation in crisis theatres. Successful engagement requires a structural linkage between short- and long-term measures and a comprehensive approach often encompassing all the branches of the security sector – police, justice, prison system, army and the political bodies charged with oversee-

---

30. Catriona Gourlay, 'Civil-Civil Coordination in EU crisis management' in Agnieszka Nowak (ed.), 'Civilian crisis management: the EU way', *Chaillot Paper* no. 90, EU Institute for Security Studies, Paris, June 2006, pp. 105-122.

31. See Chapter 2 on ESDP resources, pp. 96-8.

ing them.[32] As stressed in the second part of this book, cooperation has not been forthcoming in the early years of ESDP. In Brussels, the Commission and the Council Secretariat have drafted two separate concept papers, each addressing SSR in the areas of respective competence.[33] In the field, attempts at coordination between ESDP missions and Community programmes, when undertaken, have in most cases produced little by way of synergy between EU actors and instruments. The case of RD Congo, where two ESDP SSR missions are deployed in parallel to Community programmes, is particularly telling in this respect.[34] The area of rule of law has proven particularly controversial, with the Commission concerned that this traditional domain of EC intervention could be encroached upon by ESDP missions, including police missions whose mandate extended to the interface between police and criminal justice.

More recently, awareness of the imperative of coordination in SSR has led to some progress in critical theatres such as Afghanistan and Kosovo. Officials from the Commission and the Council Secretariat have showed more willingness to discuss the division of labour at an early stage in the planning of respective measures and mechanisms for exchanging information in the field have been reinforced. Such *ad hoc* progress, however, cannot replace a systemically comprehensive approach to SSR, which would require a single EU concept paper, more joined up bureaucratic structures and tighter coordination mechanisms in the field.

Beyond the area of SSR, the complexity of the issues involved in the demarcation of respective competences was highlighted when the Commission decided to take the Council to the European Court of Justice in the so-called 'ECOWAS' case in February 2005.[35] In short, the Commission challenged the legality of a Council Decision providing support for ECOWAS in the area of small arms and light weapons (SALW), implementing a Joint Action on the EU contribution to combating the accumulation and spread of SALW, on grounds that such an initiative would be in breach of the Community's competence, under the Cotonou agreement. In other words, the question was to define respective competences at the interface of development policy and security policy. Eventually, the Court ruled in favour of the Commission and the contested decision was annulled. This court case provides a good example

---

32. See David Spence and Philipp Fluri (eds.), *The European Union and Security Sector Reform*, Geneva Centre for the Democratic Control of Armed Forces (London: John Harper Publishing, 2008).

33. Council of the European Union, 'EU Concept for ESDP support to Security Sector Reform (SSR)', 12566/4/05, 13 October 2005; Communication for the Commission to the Council and the European Parliament, 'A Concept for European Community Support for Security Sector Reform', COM(2006) 253 final, 24 May 2005.

34. See the chapters on EUPOL Kinshasa, EUPOL RD Congo and EUSEC RD Congo in this book.

35. Case C-91/05, Commission of the European Communities v Council of the European Union. Action for annulment under Article 230 EC. The judgement of the Court was delivered on 20 May 2008.

of poor inter-institutional relations and should encourage much closer dialogue upstream with a view to ensuring the full consistency of the EU's external activities, as mandated by the Treaty and required in the field.

The European Parliament

The role of the European Parliament (EP) in CFSP/ESDP is essentially twofold. On the one hand, it engages in the political debate on CFSP/ESDP priorities and implementation, thereby strengthening the democratic accountability of EU decision-making bodies. On the other hand, as one of the two branches of the EU budgetary authority together with the Council, the EP adopts and scrutinises the CFSP budget. Article 21 TEU stipulates that the Presidency consults the EP on the main aspects and basic choices of CFSP and ensures that its views are taken into consideration. Besides, the Presidency and the Commission are tasked to regularly inform the EP on the development of CFSP.[36]

Aside from plenary sessions, where CFSP and ESDP matters are often addressed and an annual debate on the implementation of CFSP is held, the Foreign Affairs Committee (AFET), the Sub-committee on Security and Defence (SEDE) and the Committee on Budget are the key bodies in charge of the parliamentary proceedings on foreign, security and defence policy. Clearly, in the inter-governmental domain of CFSP/ESDP, the EP's budgetary powers represent a strong leverage for the Parliament to gain access to decision-makers and to enhance its influence in the policy debate.[37] Relations between the Council and the EP were strained in the 2005/2006 period, on account of little transparency and insufficient consultation, with the AFET and budgetary committees blocking the approval of the CFSP budget. The situation has improved since, following the adoption of the new Inter-Institutional Agreement (IIA) in 2006, as the gap between the demand and the supply of information to the Parliament has been steadily narrowing.[38]

At a political level, the dialogue between the EP, the Presidency and other CFSP/ESDP actors has been growing in scope over the years. Since January 2007, the SG/HR has appointed a Personal Representative for Parliamentary Affairs who acts as an interface between the institutions and manages exchanges at all levels. Besides,

---

36. Daniel Thym, 'Beyond Parliament's Reach? The Role of the European Parliament in the CFSP', *European Foreign Affairs Review*, vol. 11, no. 1, 2005, pp. 109-27.

37. As illustrated below, inter-institutional conciliation meetings take place at least five times a year to monitor the CFSP budget and expenditure, discuss the evolution of ESDP operations and address upcoming financial needs. See Chapter 2 on ESDP resources, pp. 93-95.

38. 'Inter-institutional Agreement between the European Parliament, the Council and the Commission on budgetary discipline and sound financial management', *Official Journal* C 139/01, 14 June 2006.

as foreseen in the 2006 IIA, the Council submits to the EP by June each year a report on CFSP, which should include both an evaluation of the measures undertaken in the previous year and a general presentation of upcoming priorities.[39]

In the course of 2006, Presidency and Council officials briefed the Members of the EP on CFSP/ESDP issues on about 230 occasions, including 20 interventions by Heads of State or Government, or ministers, and six by the High Representative.[40] In 2007, corresponding figures stood at almost 340 briefings overall, of which 20 from national political leaders and five from the HR. Roughly one third of these interventions are performed in plenary or mini-plenary sessions, while most take place in the AFET committee and in the numerous parliamentary delegations for relations with third countries. ESDP issues are addressed on many of these occasions but debates bearing specifically on this policy are less frequent and take place mainly in the SEDE committee. For example, the PSC representative from each Presidency presents to the SEDE the priorities and, at the end of the term, the achievements of the Presidency in the field of ESDP. Top Council officials are often involved in these exchanges. A range of other informal meetings are held, such as working lunches between the PSC and the chairs of the AFET, SEDE and of the Human Rights committees.

In addition to adopting a range of resolutions and own-initiative reports on CFSP/ESDP issues, the EP can address to the Council written and oral questions and express recommendations. The report by the Chairman of the AFET committee on the above-mentioned Council annual CFSP report is the reference document outlining the EP assessment of CFSP. In the specific context of ESDP, the SEDE committee has progressively developed a new practice, dispatching parliamentary delegations in crisis areas or at operational HQs. These visits can take place in the early planning phase, such as in the case of EULEX Kosovo, EUFOR Tchad/RCA and the British HQ of Northwood running the *Atalanta* operation, or during the conduct of an ESDP operation, such as in Bosnia-Herzegovina (*Althea*) or DRC (EUFOR). These field trips enable the members of the EP to acquire more awareness and specific data on the challenges met by ESDP on the ground, thereby paving the way for a better informed dialogue at the inter-institutional level. Furthermore, provision has been

---

39. Ibid., point G, paragraph 43.

40. Figures on the appearances by representatives of the Council in the European Parliament in the field of CFSP/ESDP are reported in successive notes from the Council. See for example Council document 7358/07, 14 March 2007 and Council document 6112/08, 5 February 2008.

made to allow a limited number of prominent members of the EP to have access to secret and confidential information pertinent to ESDP.[41]

The parliamentary dimension of CFSP/ESDP is enriched by the involvement of members of national parliaments in a multiplicity of formats. Every six months, the chairs of the foreign affairs committees of national parliaments come together in the presidency capital and their meetings are regularly addressed by the SG/HR. Likewise, the chairs of the defence committees have begun to meet twice a year, while the chairs of relevant committees from national parliaments and senior members of the EP hold joint meetings in Brussels. Alongside these and other meetings, the practice of national parliamentary delegations directly visiting the Council Secretariat and meeting the SG/HR and other senior CFSP/ESDP officials is growing. Needless to say, engaging the members of national parliaments in the debate on CFSP/ESDP is politically very important, considering the power of respective assemblies in scrutinising national foreign and security policy, allocating resources to expand military and civilian capabilities and, in some Member States, authorising the use of force.

The planning process

Having reviewed the main institutional actors of ESDP, this section addresses their interaction in the context of the planning of military and civilian operations – the core of ESDP decision-making. Like other aspects of the ESDP institutional and procedural framework, the planning process has evolved to include the contribution of newly established ESDP bodies such as the Civ-Mil Cell and to introduce the lessons drawn from operational experience. Likewise, the formulation of the concept of civil-military coordination (CMCO) has informed the evolution of planning procedures, notably between 2002 and 2005, with a growing emphasis on the notion of comprehensive planning.[42] Since the first ESDP military and civilian operations were envisaged in 2002, planning has entailed a lot of 'learning by doing' at the institutional level, and learning on the job for the individuals involved, notably for those on the civilian side.

---

41. 'Inter-institutional Agreement of 20 November 2002 between the European Parliament and the Council concerning access by the European Parliament to sensitive information of the Council in the field of security and defence policy', *Official Journal* C 298/1, 30 November 2002. The Chair of the AFET also chairs a special committee of five who can request and receive oral briefings by the Presidency or the SG/HR on sensitive issues and can consult secret documents within the premises of the Council, in so far as this is necessary for the exercise of the EP's attributions concerning ESDP.

42. On the genesis and features of the concept of CMCO, see Radek Khol, 'Civil-Military Coordination in EU crisis management', in Agnieszka Nowak (ed.), op. cit. in note 30.

Crisis response planning includes two main phases, namely strategic planning and operational planning. By and large, the former concerns the definition of the political objectives of the Union and of the military or civilian means required to fulfil those objectives. In other words, strategic planning provides the framework for operational planning. The latter addresses more specifically how to implement the political mandate through a military or civilian operation, including its organisation, the key operational tasks and how to fulfil them, while providing for all the enabling requirements such as logistics and communication and information systems.

A distinction should be drawn upfront between the planning of, respectively, military and civilian operations in the context of ESDP. With some simplification, in so far as the former are concerned, EU structures are responsible for carrying out planning and the political-strategic level. Following the Initiating Military Directive (IMD), responsibility for military planning at the operational level is transferred to the designated operational HQ, although the latter continues to be assisted by the EUMS and DGE VIII. On the other hand, the planning and conduct of civilian missions is carried our entirely at EU level, without recourse to national capacities. In other words, notably after the creation of the CPCC, the EU disposes in principle of the equivalent to an autonomous operational HQ for civilian missions, although the structure is still quite weak.

As noted above, the goal of devising a comprehensive approach to crisis management, including the planning dimension, has driven the development of the EU's planning procedures. At the incentive of the Danish Presidency in 2002, earlier work on CMCO resulted in a joint Council/Commission paper in 2003, where CMCO was described as addressing 'the need for effective coordination of the actions of all relevant EU actors involved in the planning and subsequent implementation of EU's response to crisis.'[43] In other words, CMCO is about the internal coordination of EU structures in crisis management. A preference was expressed to sustain and develop a 'culture of coordination' instead of establishing detailed structures and procedures.[44] While this was a sensible recommendation to avoid burdening the necessarily flexible crisis response process with a rigid set of rules, it also exposed the reluctance of relevant institutions to be constrained by specific commitments.

---

43. Council of the European Union, 'Civil Military Coordination (CMCO)', 14457/03, 7 November 2003.

44. See Ursula C. Schroeder, 'Governance of EU crisis-management', in Michael Emerson and Eva Gross (eds.), *Evaluating the EU Crisis Missions in the Balkans*, Centre for European Policy Studies, Brussels, September 2007, p. 26.

The operational experience of ESDP between 2003 and 2005 revealed serious short-comings in the implementation of CMCO, both in Brussels and in theatre. Based on this experience, the British Presidency in 2005 provided new momentum to foster civil-military coordination at all levels. With a view to planning, a new document was adopted in November 2005 which defined comprehensive planning as 'a systematic approach designed to address the need for effective intra-pillar and inter-pillar coordination of activity by all relevant EU actors in crisis management planning ... This approach applies to all phases of the planning process...'[45] It was restated that the Council and the Commission would work together to this end.

With hindsight, a gap can certainly be detected between the letter of these documents and the actual institutional practice. The detailed review of the ESDP operational experience included in the second part of this book shows that EU institutions have not consistently coordinated and cooperated to enhance the coherence and effectiveness of EU crisis management. It is clear that extensive inter-institutional coordination under time pressure, while various ESDP operations are being planned or conducted at the same time, can prove very demanding. However, while a positive trend can be observed, the record is very much uneven. In what follows, the analysis of the planning process highlights the requirements for CMCO and leads to further considerations on the implementation of comprehensive planning.

It is important to stress that, in practice, the planning process does not follow the linear sequence sketched out below, whether because of time pressure or gaps in the coordination and consultation among relevant bodies. Besides, some flexibility needs to be built into the system to adapt to specific circumstances. In particular, the distinction between strategic and operational planning is not as clear-cut as it appears on paper, as the institutions in charge of strategic planning actually contribute to the operational planning stage and to the conduct of the mission as well. That said, the review of the planning process as formally envisaged provides the basis for assessing the actual performance of EU planning structures.[46]

Planning at the strategic level comprises advance and crisis response planning. Advance planning entails considering potential crisis scenarios and devising basic planning documents (generic planning) and more detailed ones (contingency planning), so as to better support decision-makers with timely situation-assessments if and

---

45. Council of the European Union, 'Draft EU Concept for Comprehensive Planning', 13983/05, 3 November 2005.

46. While a number of documents have been subsequently produced on specific aspects of the planning process, the basic reference document outlining the crisis management procedures remains: Council of the European Union, 'Suggestions for procedures for coherent, comprehensive EU crisis management', 11127/03, 3 July 2003.

when an actual crisis erupts. In practice, advance planning has not been conducted on a permanent or consistent basis because of both limited human resources and the political sensitivities associated to the identification of potential crisis spots. Within the EUMS, the Civ-Mil Cell was initially charged with strategic contingency planning, which is now a prerogative of the MAP. So far, advance planning has not been accompanied by a noticeable comprehensive dimension: the range of EU crisis management bodies has not been consistently involved.

Once a crisis erupts, crisis response strategic planning kicks in. The functions of early warning and situation assessment are crucial at this stage. The documents on comprehensive planning insist on the need for a joint assessment of an emerging crisis so as to include the perspectives of all institutional actors and cover different areas of expertise. The creation of the SIAC in 2008, to which both the Joint Situation Centre and the intelligence division of the EUMS contribute, has reinforced the ability of the EU structures to collect and process relevant information early on. The SIAC is supposed to support both military and civilian planning and structures. At this initial stage of the planning process, the Commission can also feed information through its delegations on the ground and its crisis management department.

Once informed of a crisis that may require the intervention of the EU, the PSC becomes the central pillar of the planning process, responsible to ensure the coherence of the EU's crisis response. The PSC can request that joint Council/Commission fact finding missions (FFM) are dispatched in the field to collect information on the context of EU intervention. Joint FFMs have progressively become standard practice, which in principle improves CMCO at this level. All information and analysis, including policy option papers from the PU, converge towards the PSC, which decides whether, in principle, EU action is appropriate or not. If it considers that it is, a Crisis Response Coordination Team (CRCT) is set up to oversee the drafting of the Crisis Management Concept (CMC).[47]

Planning documents define the CRCT as a vehicle for inter-service coordination in crisis response. As such, CRCTs are not standing bodies but meet *ad hoc* and are responsible to prepare the draft CMC. Their composition is supposed to be flexible, so as to reflect the specific nature of the crisis at hand, but normally includes the crisis management departments of DG E, the EUMS, the CPCC, the Policy Unit, the SitCen, the legal service of the Council and the Commission. Meetings are held at

---

47. Ibid., pp. 33-34. See also Gourlay, op. cit. in note 30, p. 115 and Schroeder, op. cit. in note 44, pp. 26-28.

working level and chaired at Council Director level. Depending on the mission at hand, DGE VIII or DGE IX normally play a leading role in this phase.

The experience of CRCTs is mixed. On the one hand, they represent the only venue for inter-pillar coordination at an early stage in the planning process. As such, they are considered a useful platform to discuss the objectives and the options for EU intervention. However, CRCTs have been regarded more as a vehicle for exchanging information and for mutual consultation than as real planning bodies. On the whole, they have met on a rather discontinuous basis, although meetings have become more regular in the last year or so. In practice, in the run-up to the CMC, much of the political advice and military and civilian expertise is exchanged on an informal and not always systematic basis, with senior Council officials taking the lead in drafting the early versions of the CMC.

The CMC is the 'conceptual framework describing the overall approach of the EU to the management of a particular crisis.'[48] Documents on comprehensive planning stress that the CMC is meant to ensure the full coherence between different EU actors and to point out the interdependencies between their tasks. Besides, it should define what is the endstate that the envisaged ESDP operation wishes to achieve, the key objectives that need to be met and the steps that are necessary to deliver those objectives. After thorough consultation, if the PSC decides in favour of EU intervention, it agrees the final CMC and submits it to the Council.

Following the political approval of the Council, the PSC requests that either military or civilian strategic options (MSO or CSO) are developed. On the military side, the EUMC issues a military strategic option directive (MSOD) to the EUMS, tasking the latter to draw up and prioritise MSO, in cooperation with DGE VIII, describing in further detail what action is required to fulfil the political ends outlined in the CMC.

On the civilian side, the CPCC is responsible for the elaboration of the CSO, in co-operation with DGE IX and with the support of the Civ-Mil Cell. The EUMC and the CIVCOM assess, respectively, MSO and CSO and submit their advice to the PSC. The latter decides on the best course of action and forwards its recommendation to the Council. The approval of the Council, normally expressed in a joint action fleshing out the mandate and tasks of the envisaged ESDP operation, marks the end of the planning process at political-strategic level.

---

48. Ibid., p. 45.

EU military crisis response planning process at the political and strategic level

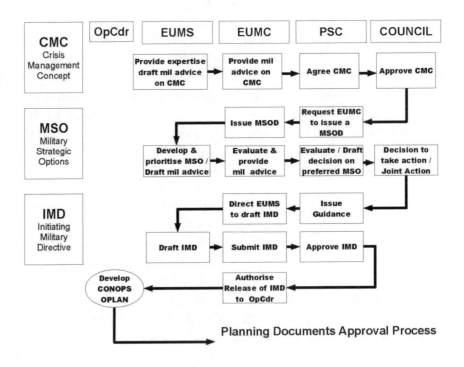

Source: EU Concept for Military Planning at the Political and Strategic Level, 10687/08, 16 June 2008.

The operational planning phase includes the drafting of the concept of operations (CONOPS) and of the operational plan (OPLAN), as well as the force generation process. As noted above, operational planning for military or civilian operations follows different tracks. On the civilian side, the CPCC is in charge of preparing the CONOPS and the OPLAN, in close cooperation with the designated Head of Mission and with the support of the Civ-Mil Cell. CIVCOM provides the PSC with advice on these planning documents and the PSC agrees them before submission to the Council for final approval. The CPCC, in permanent exchange with CIVCOM and with the Head of Mission, is responsible for generating the personnel required to conduct the envisaged civilian mission. Calls for contributions are sent out to Member States announcing the posts and functions to be filled.

On the military side, responsibility for operational planning shifts away from EU bodies to the designated operational HQ, whether NATO or a national one, and to the Operation Commander. So far, the Operation Centre within the EUMS has not been activated. In this context, the EUMS drafts the Initiating Military Directive (IMD) and the PSC instructs the EUMC to release the directive to the Operation Commander. The IMD should provide the Commander with a clear picture of the political objectives and of the military mandate of the operation, thereby framing the successive development of the CONOPS, the statement of requirements, the OPLAN and the rules of engagement.

This is a critical stage in the EU military planning process. The identification of the available operational HQ may take considerable time and, once a national HQ is identified, the process of augmenting and 'multinationalising' it with military personnel from contributing countries starts. This process is managed by the EUMS, which also sends liaison officers to the relevant HQ so as to ensure continuity and consistency between the phase of strategic planning and that of operational planning.

The parallel force generation process is triggered at the earliest possible stage, when planning assumptions and documents are specific enough to present Member States (and third countries) with clear force requirements as a basis to assess their national contributions. More often than not, the force generation process has proven very cumbersome due to a mix of inter-related factors including weak strategic planning, serious constraints on national capabilities and divergences between Member States on the mandate and scope of ESDP military operations.

The Lisbon Treaty: continuity and innovation

With a view to CFSP and ESDP, the Lisbon Treaty can be regarded as the output of years of institutional practice, strategic reflection and compromise between different national perspectives on EU foreign and security policy. Many of the CFSP/ESDP provisions translated from the rejected Constitutional Treaty to the Lisbon Treaty were negotiated between 2003 and 2004 in parallel to the development of ESDP structures, the drafting of the 2003 European Security Strategy, and the acquisition of early ESDP operational experience. The importance of the reforms envisaged under the Treaty concerning CFSP and ESDP and the close connection of these reforms with the institutional developments illustrated above call for an overview of the most salient aspects of envisaged innovation.[49]

The Lisbon Treaty sets important aspects of institutional innovation in the context of broad continuity.[50] The mix of continuity and innovation is a regular feature of all stages of Treaty reform. The aim to enhance the coherence of EU foreign policy and to foster the convergence of different national positions has driven Treaty reform since the launch of CFSP, although it remains largely unfulfilled. Against this background, however, the Lisbon Treaty does introduce considerable novelty. By way of general assessment, reform aims to create the conditions for more effective policy- making without affecting the formal rules for taking decisions in the field of CFSP and ESDP. Unanimity continues to apply to decisions in these areas, with very limited exceptions. Besides, the Declarations 13 and 14 annexed to the final act of the inter-governmental conference in December 2007 make clear that the envisaged CFSP and ESDP Treaty provisions do not affect the prerogatives of Member States concerning their national foreign and defence policies. The purpose of the reforms foreseen by the new Treaty, however, is not to constrain Member States but rather to better enable them to work together by upgrading the institutional bedrock of their cooperation at EU level.

The Treaty of Lisbon both thoroughly modifies the institutional context of ESDP and introduces more specific innovations pertaining to this policy area as such.[51] In extreme synthesis, the new Treaty frames for the first time all aspects of the EU's external action within a common set of principles and objectives. This is meant to enhance the overall coherence and consistency of EU external action in the pursuit of the principles of democracy, the rule of law and human rights that have inspired European integration and with a view to supporting international law, multilateral cooperation and the UN. In the context of CFSP, much stronger emphasis is put in the Lisbon Treaty than under current provisions on the requirements for mutual political solidarity, convergence and early consultation among Member States in devising a common foreign and security policy. The Lisbon Treaty also clarifies the respective roles of different EU institutions in CFSP policy-making, confirming the

49. See the Consolidated versions of the Treaty on the European Union and the Treaty on the Functioning of the European Union, *Official Journal* C 155, 9 May 2008.

50. For an analysis of the proceedings of the Convention and of the 2004 Inter-governmental Conference leading to institutional innovations in the area of CFSP/ESDP, see Giovanni Grevi, 'The Institutional Framework of External Action' and 'The Common Foreign, Security and Defence Policy', both chapters in G. Amato, H. Bribosia, B. de Witte (eds.), *Genesis and Destiny of the European Constitution* (Brussels: Bruylant 2007).

51. The innovations introduced by the Lisbon Treaty are outlined in Gerrard Quille, 'The Lisbon Treaty and its implications for CFSP/ESDP', Briefing Paper, Policy Department External Policies, European Parliament, February 2008; and Antonio Missiroli, 'The impact of the Lisbon Treaty on ESDP', Briefing Paper, Policy Department External Policies, European Parliament, January 2008.

key role of the European Council in providing strategic impulse and guidance and the centrality of the Foreign Affairs Council (separated from the General Affairs Council) in taking decisions and overseeing their implementation.

The keynote reform envisaged by the Treaty in the sphere of the EU foreign and security policy consists of the double-hatting of the new High Representative of the Union for Foreign Affairs and Security Policy, who would combine the functions of the existing SG/HR for CFSP and of the Vice-President of the Commission in charge of External Relations (RELEX).[52] This is a 'personal union' of two functions, which remain governed by different decision-making procedures, in the same post. In addition, the new HR would replace the rotating Presidency in chairing the Foreign Affairs Council and be attributed a formal right of initiative (proposal) in CFSP/ESDP matters, alongside Member States. Likewise, the rotating Presidency would give way to a permanent President of the European Council at the helm of this institution. The President would be responsible for the preparation and follow-up of summit meetings and also for representing the Union on CFSP issues at the level of Heads of State or Government. The relations between these two new positions and the President of the Commission are not the subject of detailed regulation under the Lisbon Treaty, which leaves scope for mutual adjustment on the job but also for potential tensions.

The job description of the envisaged double-hatted HR is vast and cannot be reviewed in detail here. By and large, in addition to the important role of policy initiative mentioned above, the prerogatives of the new HR post would include coordination across the range of EU external policies, external representation of the Union for CFSP matters, implementation of CFSP decisions, as well as specific responsibilities in the context of ESDP crisis management.[53] A complementary innovation to the establishment of the double-hatted HR post is the creation of the European External Action Service (EEAS), supposed to assist the HR in fulfilling his mandate. In a major departure from current institutional arrangements, the new EEAS would include officials form the relevant departments of the Council Secretariat and of the Commission, as well as staff seconded by national diplomatic services.[54]

---

52. The double-hatted HR would however relinquish the function of Secretary-General of the Council currently attributed to Javier Solana.

53. Giovanni Grevi, Daniela Manca and Gerrard Quille, 'The EU Foreign Minister: Beyond Double-Hatting', *The International Spectator*, vol. XL, no. 1, 2005.

54. The envisaged set up of the EEAS has triggered a rich debate in think tanks and academia. Among other contributions, see Julia Lieb and Andreas Maurer, 'Making EU Foreign Policy more effective, consistent and democratic. The options and variables for the European External Action Service', *Working Paper* FG 1, SWP Berlin, July 2007; Graham Avery, Antonio Missiroli et al., 'The EU Foreign Service: how to build a more effective common policy', *EPC Working Paper* no 28, Brussels, November 2007; and Julia Lieb and Andreas Maurer, 'Creating a European External Action Service. Preconditions for avoiding a rude awakening', *SWP Comments* 13, June 2008.

The size, composition, exact institutional position and policy remit of the new service remain subjects for negotiation and debate between the SG/HR, the Commission and the Member States, if the Treaty is ratified.[55] There is a certain consensus, however, that the service would at least include all the departments dealing with external political relations with all third countries and regions in the world, multilateral affairs, neighbourhood policy and the political-strategic dimension of crisis management through ESDP and other EU instruments. While not specified as such in the Lisbon Treaty, a combined reading of relevant provisions suggests that the envisaged Union delegations abroad (replacing the Commission delegations) would also be part of the EEAS.

On the whole, the reforms envisaged by the Lisbon Treaty point to overcoming the rigid distinction between the Community and the intergovernmental dimension of EU foreign policy and to providing more continuity to policy-making over time. In so far as ESDP is concerned, this evolution paves the way towards more structural synergy between ESDP operations and other EU instruments in crisis management and, notably, to a stronger connection between CFSP priorities and ESDP activities.

First, the Lisbon Treaty changes the denomination of ESDP into 'common security and defence policy' and describes this policy as providing the EU with '...an operational capacity drawing on civil and military assets ... using capabilities provided by the Member States.'[56] Second, the Treaty expands the range of the so-called Petersberg tasks which the common security and defence policy needs to fulfil to include joint disarmament operations, military advice and assistance tasks, conflict prevention and post-conflict stabilisation in addition to the tasks envisaged under the current Treaty, namely humanitarian and rescue tasks, peacekeeping tasks and tasks of combat forces in crisis management, including peacemaking.[57] All these tasks are supposed to contribute to the fight against terrorism.

Third, the new Treaty translates in the area of security and defence the stronger commitment to solidarity of EU Member States by introducing a clause of mutual assistance in case of armed aggression on the territory of one of them.[58] While not

---

55. Declaration 15 on Article 27 TEU, annexed to the final act of the Inter-governmental Conference that adopted the Treaty of Lisbon.

56. Article 42.1 TEU as amended by the Lisbon Treaty.

57. Article 43 TEU as amended by the Lisbon Treaty and Article 17.2 TEU, as currently in force.

58. Article 42.7 TEU, as amended by the Lisbon Treaty. In the event of an armed attack on one of them, the other Member States would be under the obligation to provide the country in question with aid and assistance by all the means in their power. In fact, however, such a clause is qualified by two other provisions in this article, whereby this commitment would not prejudice the specific policy of some Member States (neutrals) and would be consistent with the commitments of EU Member States that are also part of NATO. For them, NATO remains the foundation of their collective defence. It follows that the new clause has essentially a political significance.

set in the context of the common security and defence policy, the Treaty also introduces another clause, explicitly named 'solidarity clause', providing for the Union and its Member States to assist a Member State that is the object of a terrorist attack or victim of a natural or man-made disaster with all relevant means, including military ones.[59]

Fourth, the scope for flexibility under the common security and defence policy is much expanded by the Lisbon Treaty at three main levels. At the operational level, the new Treaty envisages that the Council may entrust the implementation of an operation to a group of willing and able Member States, which shall act in association with the HR and keep the Council regularly informed of their action.[60] Furthermore, the mechanism of enhanced cooperation, which allows under certain conditions a group of Member States to engage in closer cooperation in areas where not all EU countries may want to integrate further, extends to CFSP and the common security and defence policy.[61] Under the current Treaties, enhanced cooperation only applies to the implementation of CFSP joint actions or common positions and does not concern matters with military or defence implications. From this standpoint, however, the biggest innovation consists of the envisaged provisions on 'permanent structured cooperation'. The latter would involve those Member States with stronger military capabilities and willing to enter more binding commitments with a view to undertaking demanding crisis management tasks.[62] These provisions, as well as the related Protocol on permanent structured cooperation, should be read in conjunction with the envisaged Treaty commitment of Member States to progressively improve their military capabilities and with the definition at Treaty-level of the tasks of the European Defence Agency, set up in summer 2004 with the purpose of enhancing the military capabilities of EU countries.[63] This important set of Treaty reforms is addressed in Chapter Two, dealing with the military and civilian resources available to ESDP.

Fifth, the HR acquires a stronger profile in the field of the common security and defence policy as well. With a view to crisis management operations, this applies both to policy initiative and to policy direction and coordination. On the one hand, the

---

59. Article 222 Treaty on the functioning of the European Union, as renamed and amended by the Lisbon Treaty (current Treaty establishing the European Community).

60. Article 44 TEU, as amended by the Lisbon Treaty.

61. Article 329.2 Treaty on the functioning of the European Union, as renamed and amended by the Lisbon Treaty.

62. Articles 42.6 and 46 TEU, as amended by the Lisbon Treaty.

63. Articles 42.3 and 46 TEU, as amended by the Lisbon Treaty. See also the Council Joint Action 2004/551/CFSP on the establishment of the European Defence Agency, 12 July 2004.

HR can propose to the Council the use of both national and EU resources, together with the Commission where appropriate.[64] On the other hand, the PSC exercises the political control and strategic direction of crisis management operations under the responsibility of both the Council *and* the HR.[65] Finally, the HR is made responsible for coordinating the civilian and military aspects of crisis management operations and is involved in all forms of flexible cooperation in this policy area.

Conclusion

The analysis of the ESDP institutional framework and of its evolution over the last ten years delivers a mixed picture. Unquestionably, the sheer fact of having created in 2000-2002 and subsequently expanded and improved a complex crisis manage-ment architecture at EU level is a major accomplishment. Establishing the 'capacity to decide' is a basic precondition for progress with a view to both operations and capabilities. It is equally clear, however, that this achievement needs to be qualified with regard to three problems still affecting policy-making in the ESDP domain.

First, while they have grown considerably larger over the years, EU crisis manage-ment structures at the political, strategic and operational level remain relatively fragile and incomplete. In other words, they are unfinished business. The current framework does not empower the Union to fulfil the level of ambition that it has set for itself in terms of the quantity and intensity of crisis management opera-tions to be carried out simultaneously. In fact, notably on the civilian side, it is al-ready stretched to the limit. On the military side, in the absence of EU operational headquarters, the Union remains a non-autonomous actor and the availability of national HQs to plan and run ESDP operations has proven intermittent. Further issues concern the experience and expertise of the staff in Brussels-based bodies with a view to assuring the proper planning and conduct of ESDP operations, both civilian and military ones. Although progressively addressed, shortcomings in these respects constrain the ability of the Union to undertake more demanding tasks.

Second, the emphasis rightly put on the need to ensure more and better coordina-tion within and between EU institutions and to devise a comprehensive approach to crisis management has delivered modest results until quite recently. On the whole, little structural cooperation and coordination between the Council Secretariat and the Commission have accompanied the development of ESDP, undermining its out-put. That said, after years of debate and conceptual elaboration, there are grounds

---

64. Article 42.4 TEU, as amended by the Lisbon Treaty.
65. Article 38 TEU, as amended by the Lisbon Treaty.

for some optimism on progress towards an integrated, cross-pillar civil-military approach. Nobody seriously questions the need to strengthen synergies and coordination among EU actors and tools: a strong case has been made and comprehensiveness features at the core of the EU strategic culture. The envisaged setting up of the Crisis Management Planning Department, which would bring together the bodies responsible for strategic planning and important horizontal functions from both the military and the civilian side, provides strong evidence of renewed political will to set civil-military coordination on firmer foundations, drawing on all relevant resources. Furthermore, the entry into force of the Lisbon Treaty would provide a major boost to these efforts.

Third, the piecemeal reform of ESDP structures can be regarded as the substitute for political agreement on what ESDP is for in the first place. This owes both to enduring differences between Member States regarding the ambition and priorities of ESDP and to the difficulty of more effectively integrating CFSP strategies, often blurred, and ESDP action. As noted in the introduction, institutional reform has sought to address shortcomings concerning both the convergence of national positions and the coherence between crisis management and foreign policy at large. However, institutional engineering can only achieve so much if political consensus on making the Union a strong, autonomous international actor in the field of security and defence is not forthcoming. From this standpoint, the reforms envisaged by the Lisbon Treaty are of particular importance. They create the institutional conditions for much more joined up policy-making at EU level, bridging the intergovernmental and the Community dimension as well as the national and the European levels of decision-making. That said, ultimately, institutional reform cannot provide a conclusive answer to a political question.

In conclusion, when turning back to past developments and looking ahead to future reforms in the area of ESDP, three final considerations should inform the debate. First, understanding ESDP institutions and practice requires appreciation of their evolution over the years, instead of simply taking a snapshot of the institutional architecture at a given point in time. Second, individual institutions and bodies are part of a complex system of policy- and decision-making. Their ability, or inability, to fulfil their mandates largely depends on the quality of their interactions with other institutional actors at the EU and national level. Third, institutional practice and reform cannot be regarded in isolation from parallel developments at the political and operational level, including the elaboration of the strategic priorities of ESDP and the lessons drawn from experience in the field. The interaction of these different strands of policy-making shapes institutional outcomes in ways that no national government or EU institution can entirely foresee and control.

BIBLIOGRAPHY

Avery, Graham, Missiroli, Antonio et al. 'The EU Foreign Service: how to build a more effective common policy', *EPC Working Paper* no. 28, Brussels, November 2007.

Duke, Simon. 'The Lynchpin COPS. Assessing the workings and institutional relations of the Political and Security Committee', *Working Paper* 2005/W/05, European Institute of Public Administration, Maastricht, 2005.

Glière, Catherine (ed.). 'European security and defence: Core documents 2008, vol. IX', *Chaillot Paper* no. 117, EU Institute for Security Studies, Paris, July 2009.

Gourlay, Catriona. 'Civil-Civil Coordination in EU crisis management' in Agnieszka Nowak (ed.), 'Civilian crisis management: the EU way', *Chaillot Paper* no. 90, EU Institute for Security Studies, Paris, June 2006.

Grevi, Giovanni. 'The Institutional Framework of External Action' and 'The Common Foreign, Security and Defence Policy', both chapters in G. Amato, H. Bribosia, B. de Witte (eds.), *Genesis and Destiny of the European Constitution* (Brussels: Bruylant 2007).

Grevi, Giovanni, Manca, Daniela and Quille, Gerrard. 'The EU Foreign Minister: Beyond Double-Hatting', *The International Spectator*, vol. XL, no. 1, 2005.

Howorth, Jolyon. 'The Political and Security Committee: a case study in supranational inter-governmentalism', in Renaud Dehousse (ed.), *The Community Method in Perspective: New Approaches* (New York: Palgrave, 2009).

Khol, Radek. 'Civil-Military Coordination in EU crisis management', in Agnieszka Nowak (ed.), 'Civilian crisis management: the EU way', *Chaillot Paper* no. 90, EU Institute for Security Studies, Paris, June 2006.

Lieb, Julia and Maurer, Andreas. 'Making EU Foreign Policy more effective, consistent and democratic. The options and variables for the European External Action Service', *Working Paper* FG 1, 2007/07, SWP, Berlin.

Lieb, Julia Lieb and Maurer, Andreas. 'Creating a European External Action Service. Preconditions for avoiding a rude awakening', *SWP Comments* 13, June 2008.

Missiroli, Antonio (ed.). 'From Copenhagen to Brussels: European Defence: core documents', *Chaillot Paper* no. 67, EU Institute for Security Studies, Paris, December 2003.

Missiroli, Antonio. 'The impact of the Lisbon Treaty on ESDP', Briefing Paper, Policy Department External Policies, European parliament, January 2008.

Quille, Gerrard. 'The Lisbon Treaty and its implications for CFSP/ESDP', Briefing Paper, Policy Department External Policies, European Parliament, February 2008.

Quille, Gerrard, Gasparini, Giovanni, Menotti, Roberto, Pirozzi, Nicoletta and Pullinger, Stephen. 'Developing EU Civil Military Coordination: The Role of the new Civilian Military Cell', Joint Report by ISIS Europe and CeMISS, Brussels, June 2006.

Rutten, Maartje (ed.). 'From Saint Malo to Nice. European Defence: core documents', *Chaillot Paper* no. 47, EU Institute for Security Studies, Paris, May 2001.

Rutten, Maartje (ed.). 'From Nice to Laeken. European Defence: core documents', *Chaillot Paper* no. 51, EU Institute for Security Studies, Paris, April 2002.

de Schoutheete, Philippe. 'La cohérence par la défense. Une autre lecture de la PESD', *Chaillot Paper* no. 71, EU Institute for Security Studies, Paris, October 2004.

Schroeder, Ursula C. 'Governance of EU crisis-management', in Michael Emerson and Eva Gross (eds.), *Evaluating the EU Crisis Missions in the Balkans*, Centre for European Policy Studies, Brussels, September 2007.

Spence, David and Fluri, Philippe (eds.). *The European Union and Security Sector Reform*, Geneva Centre for the Democratic Control of Armed Forces (London: John Harper Publishing, 2008).

Thym, Daniel. 'Beyond Parliament's Reach? The Role of the European Parliament in the CFSP', *European Foreign Affairs Review*, vol. 11, no. 1, 2005.

2. ESDP resources

Giovanni Grevi and Daniel Keohane*

One of the biggest challenges for ESDP since 1999 has been finding adequate resources for it to perform effectively and contribute to international security. The experience gained from ESDP operations has helped to indicate which capability priorities should be pursued, and some progress has been made over the last ten years. However, ESDP has endured shortcomings in both the quantity and quality of available resources. This chapter analyses the civil, military and financial resources available to ESDP, and the constraints on those resources. It also looks at how EU governments and institutions have attempted to address gaps in resources, ranging from military transport planes to civil personnel such as judges and police.

The chapter begins with an analysis of EU military resources. The EU does not have its own army, or its own defence budget. Each Member State retains full sovereignty over their armed forces, and can choose to contribute (or not) to each ESDP operation as they see fit. The EU institutions cannot tell Member States how much money they should spend on defence, or how to spend their national defence budgets. Even so, the 27 EU governments collectively spend over €200 billion on defence, which is a lot of money, and should be enough to cover Europe's defence needs. Indeed, collectively the EU-27 is the largest spender on defence in the world after the United States.

But despite these hefty financial resources, Europeans do not have nearly enough soldiers with the necessary skills for international peacekeeping. Some EU Member States have not yet fully reformed their armed forces from a Cold War posture of defending national territory to participating in international peacekeeping operations. As a result, the EU-27 governments have roughly

* Giovanni Grevi is the author of the Civilian Resources part of this chapter, and Daniel Keohane is the author of the Military Resources part.

2 million personnel in their armed forces but they can barely deploy and sustain 100,000 soldiers around the globe. Almost 80% of those 100,000 were deployed in 2007, meaning that some European armed forces are already over-stretched because of EU, UN and NATO commitments in places such as Afghanistan, Bosnia, Chad, Congo, Kosovo and Lebanon.[1]

Apart from a lack of deployable soldiers, EU armed forces desperately need more useful military equipment. For example, one legacy of Cold War defence planning is that EU Member States own more than 10,000 main battle tanks, many more than are required for international peacekeeping missions, but have access to only 8 long-range transport planes (C-17s), to carry personnel, equipment and development aid (the US, in comparison, owns more than 200 C-17s). It took fully six months for EU governments to find only 16 helicopters and 10 short-range transport planes for their peacekeeping operation in Eastern Chad.

Serious constraints of available financial resources, personnel and equipment have also accompanied the development of ESDP civilian crisis management, which is analysed in the second part of this chapter. These limitations became particularly apparent as the early operational experience of ESDP unfolded in the Balkans and, subsequently, in Georgia, Indonesia (Aceh) and Africa.

From a budgetary standpoint, the problem has been twofold, concerning both the scarcity of the resources allocated to civilian ESDP under the Community budget and the cumbersome procedures established to mobilise them. For human resources, the crux has been deploying a sufficient number of highly skilled and adequately trained personnel within a short timeframe, and supporting the mission in the field. Another challenge has been procuring the necessary equipment to carry out a mission in a timely fashion, whether IT and communications infrastructure or vehicles.

Over the last ten years, much has been achieved to enable the launch of 17 civilian operations on three continents. Financial resources at EU level have significantly expanded, although they remain relatively small, while procedures have been streamlined to some extent, so that equipment can be procured more quickly. More importantly, considerable effort has been put into finding personnel with the relevant experience and expertise to serve in ESDP civilian missions. Turning to the Community dimension of civilian crisis management, the Instrument for Stability was

---

1. European Defence Agency, 'National Defence Expenditure in 2006 and 2007', 11 December 2008. http://www.eda.europa.eu/defencefacts/default.aspx?Year=2007.

devised in 2007 to rationalise different pre-existing Community instruments under one framework, creating scope for more synergy of EU civilian crisis management activities at the inter-institutional level. This chapter also assesses the size and allocation of the CFSP budget for civilian ESDP, and the priorities driving the civilian capability development process.

Military resources for ESDP

As noted above, the budgetary challenge faced by European defence ministries is considerable. European defence budgets have consistently fallen as a percentage of GDP in the last ten years. According to defence data from the European Defence Agency (EDA) the EU average for defence spending as a proportion of GDP fell from 1.81 percent in 2005[2] to 1.69 percent in 2007.[3] The cost of defence equipment is rising by six to eight percent a year, plus current missions are consuming money that had been set aside for buying new equipment – operation costs rose by 30.5 percent between 2006 and 2007 alone.[4] This is putting EU military establishments under enormous strain. However, the challenge of generating adequate European military capabilities for international peacekeeping is not new. From the beginning of ESDP in 1999, military reform has been widely recognised at the EU level as absolutely necessary if the EU is to fulfil its security aims.

The Helsinki Headline Goal

EU governments formally agreed to create the ESDP in June 1999 only weeks after the end of NATO's 78-day bombing campaign in Kosovo. The Kosovo war had exposed huge equipment gaps between US armed forces and European armies. Furthermore, the massive hikes in US defence spending – especially on new technologies – after 2001, exacerbated American concerns about the growing transatlantic military capability gap.[5] Some US officials and academics feared that ESDP would be more about demonstrating deeper European integration than developing useful military capabilities, which NATO would also need if it was to remain a relevant alliance in US plan-

---

2. European Defence Agency, 'European Defence Expenditure in 2005', 20 November 2006. http://www.eda.europa.eu/genericitem.aspx?area=Facts&id=170.

3. EDA, op. cit. in note 1.

4. Ibid.

5. Hans Binnendijk and Richard Kugler, 'Transforming European Forces', *Survival*, vol. 44, no. 3, 2002.

ning.[6] Some Americans questioned whether EU commitments would mean that Europeans would spend their much lower defence budgets on lower-end peacekeeping priorities rather than try to keep up with NATO or US capability plans.[7]

At the EU Helsinki summit of 1999, EU governments signed up to a number of military capability goals. EU governments committed themselves to a 'headline goal' (a force of 60,000 troops known as the European Rapid Reaction Force – ERRF), plus supporting naval, aerial and civilian capabilities, that were supposed to be ready by the end of 2003.[8] EU governments committed 100,000 troops, 400 combat planes, and 100 ships to the force. Although these figures looked impressive, all of those troops and assets already existed, and were also available for NATO or UN missions. What was more important – and more difficult to show – was what new equipment governments had purchased due to EU requirements. The former Chair of NATO's Military Committee, General Klaus Naumann, observed at the time that the EU would not have a real military intervention capability until at least 2010.[9] By 2001 the 'Helsinki headline goal' had produced only meagre results. To improve their performance, in 2002, EU governments agreed on a new implementation programme – the European Capabilities Action Plan (ECAP) – which aimed to focus European efforts on acquiring particular crucial assets.[10] Equally significantly, the EU's equipment goals complemented NATO's in most areas except for some advanced network-centric warfare capabilities.

NATO members had also agreed on a programme – a list of 58 priorities – in April 1999, called the Defence Capabilities Initiative (DCI), to focus European procurement efforts on particular needs.[11] By 2002, the DCI had proved to be a failure as less than half of the programmes were funded. At the NATO summit in Prague of November 2002, NATO governments agreed on a new, smaller, and more precise procurement programme – the Prague Capabilities Commitment (PCC).[12] The PCC – a list of 8 requirements – focused on critical areas such as secure communications, precision-guided weapons, air and sea transport, and air-to-air refuelling.

6. Philip Gordon, 'Their own army?', *Foreign Affairs*, vol. 79, no. 4, July/August 2000.

7. Kori Schake, 'Constructive duplication: Reducing EU reliance on US military assets', Working Paper, Centre for European Reform, London, January 2002.

8. Council of the European Union, Presidency Conclusions, Annex I to Annex IV, 'Presidency Progress Report to the Helsinki European Council on strengthening the common European policy on security and defence', Helsinki, 10-11 December, 1999.

9. Cited in Douglas Hamilton, 'European Rapid Reaction Force Unlikely by 2003' *Reuters*, 29 March 2000.

10. Council of the European Union, General Affairs Council, 'Statement on improving military capabilities', Brussels, 19-20 November 2001.

11. NATO, Washington Summit Ministerial Communiqué, NAC-S(99)69, Defence Capabilities Initiative, 25 April 1999.

12. NATO, Prague Summit Declaration, 21 November 2002.

The ECAP did introduce two important ideas that were later adopted by NATO members at the 2002 Prague summit. The first idea was the concept of a 'framework nation' to take the lead on procuring a particular common asset – the Netherlands, for example, led a collective effort to acquire precision-guided munitions, and Spain did the same for air-to-air refuelling planes. The second ECAP innovation was that governments must come up with interim arrangements to fill their capability gaps, if their products are scheduled to arrive years down the line. The first deliveries of the A400M transport plane were not due to arrive for some years, and in the meantime some EU defence ministries explored the option of leasing transport planes from other countries – the German Ministry of Defence used Ukrainian planes to take its troops to Afghanistan in 2002.

Headline Goal 2010

At NATO's 2002 Prague summit NATO members also agreed to increase their military might by creating a NATO response force (NRF) of 21,000 elite troops, backed by supporting air and sea components, which would be mainly European. However, given their scarce defence resources, some analysts argued that European governments may have to choose between the NRF and the ERRF agreed in the Helsinki headline goal in 1999.[13] There was some debate over whether Europeans could expect to get two sets of forces for the price of one. But the EU later decided to adopt the same shift in approach to capability priorities as NATO, from larger peacekeeping forces to smaller more capable military units able to carry out the most demanding types of military mission. At the Le Touquet summit in February 2003, the British and French governments proposed that the EU should be able to deploy nine 'battle groups', consisting each of 1,500 troops, and deployable within two weeks, and Germany publicly supported this plan in February 2004.

EU defence ministers agreed to the battle group initiative at their informal meeting in April 2004, with the first units to be established by 2007. The battle group plan was formally endorsed by EU heads of government at their summit in June 2004 as part of a new 'Headline Goal 2010' for EU military capabilities.[14] Each EU battle group should be able to draw on extensive air and naval assets, including transport and logistical support. This has been envisaged in three ways. First, a government could put together a national battle group. Only France and Britain could do

---

13. Barry Posen, 'Europe cannot advance on two fronts', *Financial Times*, 24 April 2003.

14. Council of the European Union, General Affairs and External Relations Council, Headline Goal 2010, Brussels, 17 May 2004, endorsed by the European Council, Brussels, 17-18 June 2004. http://www.consilium.europa.eu/uedocs/cmsUpload/2010%20Headline%20Goal.pdf.

this easily. Second, some larger or more capable countries – such as Germany, Italy, Spain and Sweden – could become lead or 'framework' nations for a battle group. Smaller countries would then supply some troops or equipment to plug gaps that the lead country could not fill. The third option would be for several countries to come together to form truly multinational units, similar to the Strasbourg-based Eurocorps, which unites soldiers from Belgium, France, Germany, Luxembourg and Spain. For a smaller country which did not want to 'plug into' a particular lead nation, a multinational unit might be a politically more appealing option.[15]

Since 2003, the EU has launched six military operations and, with each new mission, the task of military reform has become more evident. Europe's military operations to date have displayed some real weaknesses. For instance, in 2008 the EU had to delay its mission to Chad because Member States could not find enough working helicopters. The EU's missions have also provided valuable lessons in what types of equipment are useful, and what types of skills the troops need to adequately perform their missions. EU Member States are not in the business of fighting other nations; most of the time their peacekeepers have and will be intervening in civil wars or post-conflict societies to protect civilians. So Europe's soldiers will need to be able to build roads and hospitals, while at the same time, they need to remain fit to keep the peace at a moment's notice. This skill set is quite different from what armies were trained to do over the past few decades.

This realisation has led to a re-focusing of EU capability-generation efforts since the launch of the battle groups in 2007. In November 2007, the EU Council approved a Progress Catalogue 2007, the culmination of the process launched in the wake of the approval of the Headline Goal 2010.[16] The Catalogue identified quantitative and qualitative military capability shortfalls. On that basis, a Capability Development Plan (CDP) was submitted in July 2008 to the Steering Board of the European Defence Agency (EDA).[17] The Board endorsed the CDP conclusions and started work on an initial list of priority capability areas. The EDA, the Member States, the EU Military Committee (EUMC) the EU Military Staff (EUMS) and the General Secretariat of the Council have all worked together on the CDP.

---

15. Gustav Lindstrom, 'Enter the EU Battlegroups', *Chaillot Paper* no. 97, European Union Institute for Security Studies, Paris, February 2007.

16. Council of the European Union, Council Conclusions on ESDP, Brussels, 19-20 November 2007. Available at http://www.consilium.europa.eu/ueDocs/cms_Data/docs/pressData/en/esdp/97165.pdf.

17. European Defence Agency, 'EU governments endorse capability plan for future military needs, pledge joint efforts, Brussels, 8 July 2008. Available at http://www.consilium.europa.eu/uedocs/cmsUpload/080708-PR_Capability_plan.pdf. See also European Defence Agency, 'Background Note – Capability Development Plan' Brussels, 8 July 2008. Available at http://www.consilium.europa.eu/uedocs/cmsUpload/080708-CDP_Press_Background_brief%20.pdf.

The CDP process led to a new 'Declaration on strengthening capabilities' during the French presidency of the EU in December 2008. The declaration is honest about the EU's failure to meet previous headline goals, and ambitious for what EU governments should be able to do in the future:

'In order to rise to current security challenges and respond to new threats, in the years ahead Europe should actually be capable, in the framework of the level of ambition established, *inter alia* of deploying 60,000 troops within 60 days for a major operation, within the range of operations envisaged in the Headline Goal 2010 and in the Civilian Headline Goal 2010, of planning and conducting simultaneously a series of operations and missions, of varying scope: two major stabilisation and reconstruction operations, with a suitable civilian component, supported by up to 10,000 troops for at least two years; two rapid-response operations of limited duration using *inter alia* EU battle groups; an emergency operation for the evacuation of European nationals (in less than ten days)...; a maritime or air surveillance/interdiction mission; a civilian-military humanitarian assistance operation lasting up to 90 days; around a dozen ESDP civilian missions (*inter alia* police, rule-of-law, civilian administration, civil protection, security sector reform, and observation missions) of varying formats, including in rapid-response situations, together with a major mission (possibly up to 3,000 experts) which could last several years.'[18]

The 2008 declaration also launched a number of new multinational equipment projects to better equip Europeans for the types of operations described in the above quote. Different groups of Member States agreed to try to improve the availability of helicopters, collaborate on observation satellites, and pool some air transport assets. The EU-27 also agreed to investigate setting up joint aircraft carrier groups, share the development of maritime surveillance systems and set up new joint funds for defence research and technology.

The *Athena* Mechanism

The 2008 French presidency of the EU also completed a review of the *Athena* mechanism. In February 2004, the Council of the European Union established the *Athena* mechanism to administer the financing of the common costs of EU military operations.[19] According to the Treaty on European Union, civilian crisis-management

---

18. Council of the European Union, 'Declaration on strengthening capabilities', Brussels, 11 December 2008.

19. Council of the European Union, Council Decision 2004/197/CFSP of 23 February 2004 (*Official Journal* no L 63, 28 February 2004, p. 68), amended by Decisions 2004/925/CFSP of 22 December 2004, 2005/68/CFSP of 24 January 2005 and 2007/91/CFSP.

operations are funded from the European Communities budget (see section on civil financing below). Operations that have military or defence implications, however, cannot be financed from the Community budget. Previously, an ad hoc funding system had to be put in place at the beginning of each ESDP operation. However, in 2003, funding problems for operations *Concordia* in the former Yugoslav Republic of Macedonia and *Artemis* in the Democratic Republic of the Congo highlighted the need for a permanent funding mechanism for military operations that would cover the preparatory phase of missions and the common costs involved in such operations.

Common costs funded through *Athena* can include a number of items, such as the Operation Headquarters in Europe, the Force Headquarters in theatre and transport of forces, amongst other things. Funding for *Athena* must come from the Member States and is based on a GDP scale, unless otherwise decided by the EU Council. The amounts of money directed through the *Athena* mechanism usually cover only around ten percent of total operation costs. For example, *Athena* amounted to roughly €120 million for the EUFOR Tchad/CAR operation, out of an estimated total operational cost of around €1 billion.[20] In other words, the majority of costs for operations are covered by the contributing Member States, based on the "costs lie where they fall" concept. This places a large financial (as well as personnel and equipment) burden on those governments which contribute to each ESDP military operation.[21] The 2008 French presidency had hoped to increase the amounts of money contributed by all Member States to the *Athena* mechanism, but there was not a consensus amongst Member States. EU governments, however, did agree in December 2008 that the common costs administered through the *Athena* mechanism could cover a wider range of operational needs.[22]

Comparing EU military capabilities in 1999 and 2009

A comparison of EU governments' military capabilities between 1999 and 2009 shows that some success has been achieved in reforming Europe's armies, even if much more could be done. The Headline Goal 2010 contains six capability categories: (i) mobility and deployability; (ii) sustainability; (iii) engagement; (iv) strategic transport; (v) command, control and communications; (vi) intelligence and surveil-

---

20. See the chapter on EUFOR Tchad in Part Two of this book.

21. See Annex 1 for a table of the contributions of each Member State to ESDP military operations.

22. Council of the European Union, Council decision establishing a mechanism to administer the financing of the common costs of European Union operations having military or defence implications (Athena), Brussels, 16 December 2008. Available at http://register.consilium.europa.eu/pdf/en/08/st16/st16561.en08.pdf.

lance. In other words, the essential aim of EU military reform plans has been to develop more useful equipment programmes for international peacekeeping, such as transport planes and helicopters, and encourage a reform of national armies oriented away from territorial defence towards external deployments.

The table below, "Selected EU-27 military capabilities 1999-2009", which is based on estimates from 1999-2000 and 2009 editions of *The Military Balance* – published each year by the International Institute for Strategic Studies – shows a mixed picture. The table is not absolutely definitive. Since it is based on estimates and some national data remains classified, it is meant as a rough guide to the progress made on military capabilities since 1999. The table indicates that while military reform in Europe is a slow process, some concrete progress has been made by EU governments over the last decade – and this despite falling defence budgets combined with a constant growth in operational commitments.

The 27 EU governments spent just over €160 billion on defence in 1999, which has since risen to almost €210 billion in 2008. However, this apparent rise is misleading, since defence expenditure as a percentage of GDP has fallen in the last ten years, from 2.1 per cent in 1997 to 1.7 per cent in 2007. The figures for defence budgets – which should not be confused with defence expenditure – are even lower, having fallen from 1.8 per cent of GDP in 1998 to 1.4 per cent of GDP in 2008. Defence expenditure almost always exceeds planned budgets, not least because of operational pressures. Furthermore, four countries provide roughly 70 per cent of EU defence spending – the UK and France (43 per cent) and Germany and Italy. Add the Dutch and Spanish defence budgets to the four bigger countries, and those six account for around 80 per cent of EU spending. Add in Greece, Poland, Sweden and Belgium and only ten countries account for 90 per cent of EU defence spending. Even if the other 17 EU countries re-programme their defence spending and focus on 'niche' activities, how the largest and richest countries spend their defence budgets has an enormous impact on overall EU figures.

In 1999 the 27 EU governments had almost 2.5 million personnel in their collective armed forces, including more than 1.1 million conscripts, which are costly and much less preferable for international peacekeeping operations than professional soldiers. In 2008, the 27 EU governments had reduced their armed forces to 2 million personnel, and just over 200,000 conscripts. EDA defence data shows that in 2007 the 26 Member States of the EDA (Denmark is not a member) can deploy 444,000 soldiers, but can only sustain 110,000 on operations – which nevertheless represents an increase of 10 percent on the previous year.[23] This looks like progress, but according to the former Chief Executive of the EDA, a massive 70 percent of Europe's land forces remain unusable outside national territory.[24]

For different types of equipment, there are similar trends. In the land equipment sector, the total inventoried numbers of main battle tanks, armoured fighting vehicles and personnel carriers have all fallen, but their numbers are still high. For instance, although the number of tanks has almost halved since 1999, there are still close to 10,000 in total, many more than are generally needed for peacekeeping missions. For aircraft, the number of fighter jets has fallen from 3,800 to 2,400. Helicopters have also been reduced from 4,700 to 3,500, although the number of utility helicopters – a category which includes vital transport helicopters – has doubled. Even so, the problem is the quality and availability, not the quantity, of EU transport helicopters. Many of the EU's transport helicopters are not usable in certain types of conditions, such as in the desert. Javier Solana, the High Representative for CFSP, described the problem in the following terms: 'We are all aware that there is no shortage of helicopters in Europe. Inventories are high in numbers but the problem is that they are not deployable outside Europe in sufficient numbers.'[25]

One of the biggest equipment weaknesses identified by EU defence ministries in 1999 was that they needed more transport planes, a category including air-to-air refuelling planes, and they have increased their number by almost 50 percent since that time. However, EU armed forces still lack strategic transport planes which can carry the heaviest loads. Transport planes are crucial for most types of military operations, including humanitarian missions – one of the reasons EU governments could not get aid quickly to South East Asia after the 2004 tsunami was because they did not have enough long-range transport planes. They only have access to 8 C-17s, and are still waiting for the first deliveries of the A400M transport plane.

The December 2008 'Declaration on strengthening military capabilities' highlighted the need for greater cooperation between EU Member States in developing military capabilities together: "we undertake to seek new methods for developing and optimising our capabilities, and will accordingly explore the pooling of efforts, specialisation and sharing of costs."[26] Tentative efforts to encourage greater pool-

---

23. EDA, op. cit. in note 1.

24. Nick Witney, 'Re-energising Europe's security and defence policy', Policy Paper, European Council on Foreign Relations, London, July 2008, p. 20.

25. Opening Address by Javier Solana, EDA Conference: 'Helicopters – Key to Mobility', Brussels, 10 March 2009.

26. Council of the European Union, op. cit. in note 18.

ing of military resources have already started, such as the battle groups initiative. A number of Member States would also save money by pooling more of their military equipment, especially aircraft, which are very expensive to maintain. For example, France and Germany train their Tiger helicopter pilots together, and could use the same combat helicopter units. But pooling the support operations for fighter aircraft and transport planes could yield even more considerable savings The European Defence Agency is already drafting proposals for pooling some of the 180 A400M transport planes that six EU countries plan to buy. In order to achieve significant cost savings, a transport fleet would have to operate from one main base, using a single planning, servicing and logistics organisation to support the fleet. In a similar vein, ten EU countries own 136 Hercules C-130 transport aircraft; five smaller EU countries own 430 F-16 fighter aircraft between them; Germany, Italy and the UK operate 570 Tornadoes, and those three countries plus Spain have started deploying Eurofighters.

Until the EU initiated the EU NAVFOR (*Atalanta*) anti-piracy operation off the coast of Somalia in 2008, the maritime dimension of ESDP had generally been ignored. Military ships, like military aircraft, are expensive, and EU defence ministries have reduced their numbers of destroyers, frigates and mine warfare vessels. Conversely they have increased their numbers of aircraft carriers (by one), patrol boats and amphibious vehicles (some of which are vital for logistical support to operations). In the same way they could pool aircraft, defence ministries could save money by pooling some naval resources, or at least coordinating their naval deployments. At the Franco-British summit in February 2003, the two governments agreed to improve interoperability among their aircraft carriers and, in particular, harmonise activity cycles and training, so that one carrier is permanently available to support EU missions. One Member of the European Parliament (MEP) – and former head of UN forces in Bosnia – Phillipe Morillon, proposed going much further than the Franco-British aircraft carrier agreement. Morillon suggested that the EU should set itself 'the medium-term objective of providing support, with a European or even a Euro-Mediterranean fleet, for the US Sixth Fleet in the Mediterranean, until possibly taking over from it if the Americans so requested.'[27]

The ESDP military capabilities table below, comparing selected EU-27 military capabilities in 1999 and 2009, shows some progress, especially in cutting personnel and inventories of outdated equipment. Military reform is not easy, and it encompasses a number of areas, such as types of troops, equipment acquisition and development,

---

27. European Parliament, Draft Report on the new European security and defence architecture, 5 February 2003.

and doctrine. The EU has only slowly woken from the slumber of Cold war military thinking over the last decade, and some countries are more awake than others. As a result, there are still a number of key capability weaknesses, such as strategic transport assets. The good news is that in the coming years, based on their current procurement plans, EU countries should have a number of new strategic capabilities such as: A400M and more C-17 transport planes; A330 air tankers; Eurofighter, Rafale and Joint-Strike-Fighter jets; and Franco-British aircraft carriers. EU defence ministries will also be able to use Galileo – a satellite navigation system – to guide their equipment and define their positions. All this equipment would greatly add to the military prowess of Europe's armies in the future.

European defence equipment projects

No one country in the EU can afford to buy or produce the full range of military equipment available. Plus, as noted above, not only does ESDP need access to more useful types of military capabilities; governments also have to find ways to develop those capabilities during a period of shrinking defence budgets. As the 2008 'Declaration on strengthening capabilities' put it: "Strengthening available capabilities in Europe will therefore be the principal challenge ahead. In a tough budgetary environment, such a goal can only be achieved through a joint, sustained and shared effort which meets operational needs".[28] EU governments, therefore, have increasingly collaborated on multinational defence equipment programmes. Defence budgets across Europe are falling as a percentage of GDP, while the cost of equipment is rising, so it makes sense for governments to share the cost of developing and procuring defence capabilities. Plus, common equipment can help countries work together on international missions. Most EU Member States will only carry out military operations as part of a multinational coalition, and such 'inter-operability' is vital for the success of military coalitions.

However, national rather than European priorities have largely been reflected in equipment procurement programmes. In 2007, the EU Member States spent approximately €32 billion on investments in equipment procurement, but only €6 billion on collaborative programmes, less than a quarter of the total.[29] Of 41 large procurement programmes in Europe – those worth more than €1 billion – only 11 projects are multinational.[30] There is tremendous waste in European defence spend-

---

28. Council of the European Union, op. cit. in note 18.

29. EDA, op. cit. in note 1.

30. Bastian Giegerich and Alexander Nicoll, 'European Military Capabilities', Strategic Dossier, International Institute for Strategic Studies, June 2008.

SELECTED EU-27 MILITARY CAPABILITIES 1999-2009 *

	1999: EU15	1999: EU27		2009: EU27	change '99-'09
Defence Expenditure **					
Total Expenditure (1997/2007)	€156.2 Bn	€162.9 Bn		€209.7 Bn	+ 29%
Expenditure / GDP (1997/2007)	2.1 %	2.1 %		1.7 %	- 19%
Budget / GDP (1998/2008)	1.7 %	1.8 %		1.4 %	- 22%
Armed Forces					
Total Active Military ***	1,759,568	2,478,608		2,013,990	- 19%
Army	1,125,718	1,516,378		996,234	- 34%
Navy	281,450	327,400		222,313	- 32%
Air Force	381,605	538,925		345,153	- 36%
Conscripts	669,770	1,131,020		212,785	- 81%
Equipment					
Land					
Main Battle Tanks	10,827	17,814		9,823	- 45%
Armoured Fighting Vehicles	6,851	10,622		7,951	- 25%
Armoured Personnel Carriers	19,751	26,311		22,844	- 13%
Aviation					
Fixed Wing Aircraft	5,600	7,453		5,401	- 28%
Fighter Jets	2,684	3,835		2,410	- 37%
Transport (incl. tankers)	439	612		898	+ 47%
Helicopters	3,515	4,732		3,573	- 24%
Attack	1,000	1,312		826	- 37%
Combat Support	969	1,305		849	- 35%
Utility (incl. transport)	445	584		1,076	+ 84%
Naval					
Aircraft Carriers	6	6		7	+ 17%
Destroyers	29	31		26	- 16%
Frigates	145	155		108	- 30%
Patrol and Coastal	314	521		811	+ 56%
Mine Warfare	208	296		243	- 18%
Amphibious	267	274		494	+ 80%

* The estimates in this table above are taken from *The Military Balance 1999-2000* and *The Military Balance 2009*, both published by the International Institute for Strategic Studies (IISS). The 1999-2000 edition uses figures from November 1998, including for defence budgets – the exception is defence expenditure estimates which date from 1997. The 2009 edition uses figures from 2008, except for defence expenditure figures which date from 2007.

** To calculate defence expenditure in euro, the 1997 total defence expenditure figures were calculated using the European Central Bank (ECB) fixed rates to the euro in 1999 where possible, or the earliest available annual average exchange rate provided by the ECB. For 2007 figures, where necessary, the European Central Bank annual average exchange rates of the national currency to the euro were used.

*** This figure also includes military police and paramilitary forces such as *Gendarmerie*, *Carabinieri* etc. as well as army, navy and air force estimates.

The editors wish sincerely to thank Charlotte Blommestijn, Project Assistant at the EUISS for her help in compiling this table.

ing; for instance, there are 23 separate armoured-fighting-vehicle programmes for essentially the same type of equipment. The result of this national fragmentation is a duplication of development and production and different standards of equipment. This fragmentation also hinders the development of common logistic support systems and diminishes military interoperability.

Too many countries order essentially the same equipment from too many different suppliers. A European Commission study in 2005 compared US and European procurement programmes and demonstrated Europe's huge inefficiencies: EU governments were collectively spending roughly €30 billion a year on some 89 equipment programmes; the US was spending much more, €83 billion annually, on only 27 projects. In other words, EU governments were collectively spending just over a third what the US spends on equipment procurement – on three times as many programmes.[31]

One striking example of this redundant spending on major equipment programmes is combat aircraft. Despite heavy competition from the US, Europe has developed three parallel types, namely the Swedish Gripen, the French Rafale and the German-British-Italian-Spanish-built Eurofighter. A global market of approximately 3,000 units is predicted for the new US combat aircraft, the Joint-Strike-Fighter (JSF), but the order book for the European types is much lower: Gripen (204), Rafale (294) and Eurofighter (620). Furthermore, the collective research and development costs of the three European airplanes are comparable to the more advanced JSF: Eurofighter cost €19.48 billion, Gripen €1.84 billion and Rafale €8.61 billion – the cumulated R&D costs of the three European combat aircraft amounted to €29.93 billion, with 1,118 units in final production. R&D for the JSF is estimated at €31 billion and the market forecast is for production of 3,000 units.[32]

In general terms, those countries with a significant defence industry are much more likely to participate in a cooperative programme than those countries which do not have a large defence sector. The six major European arms-producing countries (Britain, France, Germany, Italy, Spain, and Sweden) account for more than 90 per cent of defence equipment production in the EU. This means that most European countries are primarily consumers rather than producers – although many smaller countries are major sub-contractors and component suppliers. Plus, the growing use of

31. European Commission, UNISYS, Final report of the study: 'Evaluation of the Common Initiative in the context of the Intra-EU Transfers of Defence Goods', Brussels, February 2005.

32. Jean-Pierre Darnis, Giovanni Gasparini, Christoph Grams, Daniel Keohane, Fabio Liberti, Jean-Pierre Maulny and May-Britt Stumbaum, 'Lessons learned from European defence equipment programmes', *Occasional Paper* no. 69, European Union Institute for Security Studies, Paris, October 2007.

new technologies by defence ministries, especially software, which are increasingly adapted from civil technology for military use (known as 'dual-use' technologies), means that there are likely to be more opportunities for 'consumer' countries to participate in future cooperative programmes. The trend towards network-centric warfare creates many new opportunities for countries with sophisticated civil technology industries, i.e. software and electronics, to participate in ongoing and future programmes.

In addition, further opportunities for 'consumer countries' are created due to the fact that defence ministries are increasingly turning to the 'through-life' approach to multinational programmes, cooperating on maintenance, training and logistics as well as development and procurement. The cost of in-service life support can be over twice the acquisition cost of a programme. For example, a study from the French Comité des Prix de Revient des Fabrications d'Armement shows that the cost of the French aircraft carrier Charles de Gaulle was €3.1 billion to render into service, but cost €7.7 billion over the period of its useful life.[33] The EDA's Armaments Directorate is already trying to help EU Member States identify the full range of collaborative opportunities.[34]

The large number of different defence equipment programmes in Europe shows that European governments do not yet coordinate much of their demand for defence products, despite their shared capability goals. The task for European governments in the future is to coordinate more of their demand and to spend their defence budgets more efficiently, if they wish to acquire the full range of required capabilities.

The European Defence Agency

At the Le Touquet summit in February 2003, British Prime Minister Tony Blair and French President Jacques Chirac proposed the creation of a new EU defence agency, tasked with encouraging Member States to boost their military capabilities.[35] Other EU leaders offered their support at the Thessaloniki summit in June 2003.[36] The new agency would have three main tasks: harmonising military requirements; co-

---

33. Comité des Prix de Revient des Fabrications d'Armement, 25ème rapport, Ministère de la Défense, Paris, April 2003.

34. For more see 'Armaments Cooperation' on the EDA website: http://www.eda.europa.eu/genericitem. aspx?area=28&id=108.

35. Franco-British Summit, Declaration on Franco-British cooperation on strengthening European cooperation in security and defence, Le Touquet, 4 February 2003. Available at http://www.ambafrance-uk.org/FRANCO-BRITISH-SUMMIT-All.html.

36. Council of the European Union, Presidency conclusions, Thessaloniki European Council, 19-20 June 2003.

ordinating defence research and development (R&D); and encouraging the convergence of national procurement procedures.

The idea of a European defence agency was not new. In 1978, Egon Klepsch MEP presented a report to the European Parliament that proposed the formation of a European armaments agency. The EU did not take up this proposal, because the more Atlanticist Member States were reluctant to set up a Europe-only armaments body. But in 1991 a declaration was attached to the EU's Maastricht Treaty, calling for the creation of such an agency. Again this proposal made no headway. Britain in particular feared that an armaments agency would create a 'Fortress Europe' that excluded American (and other non-European) suppliers from European defence contracts.

NATO and a multitude of other Europe-only bodies, such as the Western European Armaments Group (WEAG), had tried for decades to encourage governments to work together more closely in acquiring and developing tanks, ships and aircraft. But their Member States repeatedly failed to do so. Governments traditionally co-operated in armaments projects only on an *ad hoc* basis. They seldom gave much thought to what defence equipment might be most useful for Europe as a whole. This was mainly due to the fact that defence remained the most 'national' of all policy areas, in the sense that EU governments have been very reluctant to give up sovereignty in this domain to international organisations.

The hope was that the EU would have more success than NATO, WEAG and other bodies at convincing governments to work together more effectively in the field of armaments. The justification for this hope was that the EU is not just a defence organisation, and has far greater political momentum than NATO. And the EU has influence over a wide range of policy areas that affect the defence industry, such as competition policy, where NATO has no say. Furthermore, the difference between the EU agency proposed by Paris and London and earlier proposals was that it would not be similar to a traditional national 'armaments agency', that concentrated on procuring defence equipment. The new body was better described as a 'capabilities agency', since it would attempt to bring together the separate worlds of research, development, and procurement of defence equipment. In addition, the agency would have a political role: it would help to direct and then assess Member States' progress towards meeting their capability commitments. In other words, the agency would provide a more comprehensive political framework for European cross-border armaments cooperation and projects (such as the Eurofighter jet). For all these reasons, British officials reversed their traditional hostility to an EU role in armaments, and decided with the French to propose the agency in February 2003.[37]

EU governments, therefore, created the European Defence Agency (EDA) in 2004 to help them share more of the costs of developing, buying and using equipment.[38] But, as an inter-governmental agency, the EDA can only help coordinate Member State equipment plans so that – if they wish to – national defence ministries can find ways to share the cost of acquiring equipment. The EDA has no power to force Member States to spend more on equipment or to buy particular types of equipment.

By gaining the trust of its member governments, the EDA has achieved a lot in its first five years. Aside from its role over-seeing the Capability Development Plan described above, three achievements should be mentioned in particular: the Research & Technology Joint Investment Programme, the Long-Term Vision report, and the Code of Conduct on Defence Procurement (see next section on the European defence market). Research and technology spending indicates what new kinds of capabilities defence ministries will have in the future. Given that EU governments collectively spend only €9.5 billion on research and development (and only a little over €2.6 billion on research and technology), it is crucial that they eliminate duplication and collaborate as much as possible.[39] Currently, EU Member States only spend €347 million on collaborative research and technology projects.[40] The *Long-Term Vision* project is important because defence technology can take a decade or more to develop.[41] Therefore, if EU governments want to have the right types of missiles or aircraft in 2025, they should start thinking now about what types of equipment they would need.

The European defence market

In theory, a more integrated European defence market would allow free movement of most defence goods among EU Member States. Greater cross-border cooperation would allow larger economies of scale, increased industrial competition, and thus lower prices, particularly for more advanced equipment. Defence ministries would be able to purchase equipment from the company that offered the best financial and

---

37. Daniel Keohane, 'Europe's new defence agency', Policy Brief, Centre for European Reform, London, June 2004.
38. Council of the European Union, General Affairs and External Relations Council, Conclusions, Luxembourg, 14 June 2004.
39. EDA, op. cit. in note 1.
40. Ibid.
41. European Defence Agency, 'An Initial Long-Term Vision for European Defence Capability and Capacity Needs,' Brussels, 3 October 2006. Available at http://www.eda.europa.eu/genericitem.aspx?id=146.

technical package, regardless of its national origin. Keith Hartley of York University has estimated that a single defence market could save EU governments up to 20 percent of their procurement funds.[42] EU governments spend roughly €30 billion annually on purchasing defence equipment. Thus, a single defence market could save defence ministries up to €6 billion a year.

Defence goods related to the 'essential interests of security' – as stipulated in Article 296 of the EU treaties – have been one of the notable exclusions from the Commission's regulation of the single market. Article 296 is vague and difficult to interpret both legally and politically, making it a major obstacle to a more smoothly functioning European defence market. Members States and the European Commission have often disagreed on the exact scope of the Article, and they have increasingly needed the judgement of the European Court of Justice (ECJ) to resolve their differences.[43]

In different ways the European Defence Agency and the European Commission have been trying to break up a highly protectionist defence market, which should help improve many defence ministries' budgetary bottom lines. In 1997 the European Commission produced a report on the European defence sector that is often referred to as the Bangemann report (after the German Commissioner who wrote it). This included practical proposals for creating a common armaments market, including a simpler licensing system for internal transfers of defence goods in the EU; the promotion of open-tender procedures for defence equipment; and the abolition of customs duties on certain defence products. Other measures suggested in the report included amending the rules of EU competition policy, to allow the European Commission to supervise trade in all but the most sensitive types of defence equipment; standardising procurement procedures; and establishing clear 'dual-use' competences for the Commission.[44]

Europe's six main arms-producing states (France, Germany, Italy, Spain, Sweden and the UK) recognised the logic of harmonising some defence market rules more than a decade ago. In 1998 they signed an agreement known as the 'Letter of Intent', which unfortunately did not have a major impact on cross-border armaments regulations, partly because it only aimed to help transnational companies to operate across borders, and did not establish a common market among the signatories.

---

42. Keith Hartley, 'The future of European defence policy: an economic perspective', *Defence and Peace Economics*, vol. 14, no. 2, January 2003, p.107-15.

43. Erkki Aalto, 'Interpretations of Article 296', in Daniel Keohane (ed.), 'Towards a European Defence Market', *Chaillot Paper* no. 113, European Union Institute for Security Studies, Paris, November 2008.

44. European Commission, 'Implementing European Union strategy on defence-related industries', Brussels, 12 November 1997.

A July 2002 document from the European Commission, known as the STAR 21 report, suggested a new approach: the Letter of Intent could be used as a basis for an EU-wide agreement on defence market rules.[45] It recommended that the Letter of Intent signatory states should open a dialogue with the Commission. The aim of such a dialogue would be to extend the Letter of Intent to all EU Member States, while giving the Commission a regulatory role in the defence market, similar to that proposed in the Bangemann report.

Instead of embracing the proposals of the STAR 21 report, EU Member States explored another option with the creation of the EDA in 2004. In November 2005 the steering board of the EDA (which is made up of EU defence ministers) agreed that the EDA should introduce a defence procurement 'code of conduct' to open up the European defence market.[46] The EDA introduced the procurement code in July 2006. The basic idea behind the procurement code is to ensure that defence companies from any country could compete for most defence contracts across Europe, excluding multinational equipment programmes and the most sensitive items like encryption devices. The code works rather simply: countries that sign up to the code vow to open all non-essential defence contracts over €1 million to foreign bidders. And the EDA created a website where those contracts are advertised to potential suppliers.

However, the EDA's code is voluntary, and the Member States are not obliged to comply with it. In fact, they have so far shown very little enthusiasm for awarding contracts to outside suppliers. Two years after the adoption of the code, some 18 Member States had posted 320 tenders on the EDA's website, but only 26 of the 108 contracts awarded (collectively worth almost €2 billion) were cross-border.[47] But the importance of the code lies as much in its principle as its practice. The idea of more open European defence markets has been around for decades, but with little or no progress until the code. Never before had so many European governments agreed that they should open up their defence markets to each other.

The difficulty of adhering to a strictly inter-governmental approach is that it may prove inadequate, due to the limitations of agreements like the EDA's code of conduct and competing national interests. The European Commission had long wished to take on the task of regulating a European defence market, but its role was

---

45. European Commission, 'Strategic aerospace review for the 21st Century,' Brussels, July 2002.

46. European Defence Agency, 'The Code of Conduct on Defence Procurement,' Brussels, 21 November 2005. Available at http://www.eda.europa.eu/genericitem.aspx?area=Organisation&id=154.

47. European Defence Agency, 'Report on Implementation of EDA Code of Conduct on Defence Procurement,' Brussels, 11 July 2008. Available at http://www.eda.europa.eu/genericitem.aspx?area=Organisation&id=198.

confined to 'dual-use' products that are components of both civilian and military equipment. Given the sensitive nature of the defence market, some arms-producing countries have been reluctant to give much new regulatory power to the Commission. The main arms-producing countries in Europe have traditionally adhered to a strict interpretation of Article 296. This has prevented the Commission from having a meaningful involvement in the defence market, with the result that governments can protect their national companies from foreign competition.

To overcome national doubts, the Commission adopted a new approach to defence market rules. In December 2007 the Commission proposed a new legislative 'defence package'. Crucially, the Commission did not propose changing Article 296, as appeared to be the case with its past legislative initiatives. Instead the objective of the Commission's 'defence package' is to set up a new legal framework for security and defence-related procurement and intra-EU trade of defence equipment. The legislative aspects of the 'defence package' contained two proposals for directives: one on procurement, which would help streamline national procurement procedures; and another on trade to liberalise the trade of defence goods within the EU. The two directives were adopted in summer 2009.[48]

Pioneer groups for military capabilities

Europe's lack of useful military resources formed a major part of the inter-governmental discussion of the defence-related provisions of the Lisbon Treaty. The treaty aims to improve the way EU defence policy works and is resourced. The most important change is that the treaty would make it easier for a subset of EU countries to work together more closely on military matters, using a procedure known as 'permanent structured cooperation'.[49] Those Member States which meet a set of capability-based entry criteria can choose to cooperate more closely after securing a majority vote. This clause makes a lot of sense. Military capabilities and ambitions vary widely among the Member States. So the EU could rely on a smaller group of the most willing and best-prepared countries to run its more demanding military missions.

---

48. Directive 2009/43/EC of the European Parliament and of the Council, simplifying terms and conditions of transfers of defence-related products within the Community, 6 May 2009. At the time of writing (autumn 2009) the Defence and Security Procurement Directive had not yet been published in its adopted form. The proposed directive can be found at http://ec.europa.eu/enterprise/sectors/defence/documents/index_en.htm.

49. Article 28 A and 28 E TEU, as amended by the Lisbon Treaty.

At first glance, the defence group would seem, in some respects, to resemble the eurozone: some countries may stay outside because they choose to and some because they do not fulfil the entry criteria. EU defence ministries have yet to discuss what precisely the entry criteria should be, and some governments might worry that they might be left out, depending on the stringency of the criteria. The vague wording of the treaty suggests an achievable set of capabilities thresholds for participation in the defence vanguard.[50] For example, the treaty says that one of the basic criteria that EU Member States should meet is to supply a combat unit – a national unit or operating as part of a multinational formation – that can be deployed between five and thirty days. In fact, 25 out of 27 EU Member States already supply these combat units as part of a 'battle groups' plan that EU defence ministers approved in April 2004.

However, given the lack of useful military resources in the EU, the criteria for permanent structured cooperation should be ambitious and testing enough to encourage much closer and more effective cooperation on developing military capabilities. But the criteria should not be so stringent that most Member States are excluded, especially those who have contributed significant numbers of peacekeepers to ESDP military operations. Defining the entry criteria for the core group, therefore, may prove difficult, especially finding a balance between effectiveness and legitimacy. Various experts have offered models for how permanent structured cooperation could work in practice – if the Lisbon Treaty enters into force.[51] Most models contain smaller groups of Member States for specific capabilities. Those Member States participating in all (or most) of these capability groups would form a core pioneer group for permanent structured cooperation. In addition, if the Lisbon Treaty did not enter into force, Member States could develop the pioneer groups approach to developing military capabilities within the EDA – which already encourages smaller groups of Member States to cooperate on joint projects. As the former Chief Executive of the EDA, Nick Witney, has described it: "ESDP badly needs pioneer groups, and the basis for implementing the approach proposed already exists in the European Defence Agency."[52]

---

50. Protocol (No. 10) on permanent structured cooperation established by Article 28 A of the Treaty on European Union, as amended by the Lisbon treaty.

51. For example, see Nick Witney, op. cit. in note 24; Sven Biscop, 'Permanent Structured Cooperation and the future of ESDP,' *Egmont Paper* no. 20, The Royal Institute for International Relations – Egmont, April 2008; Véronique Roger-Lacan, 'Traité de Lisbonne et défense européenne,' *Défense Nationale et Sécurité Collective*, vol. 64, no. 2, février 2008, p. 55-62.

52. Witney, op. cit. in note 24, p. 27.

Civilian resources for ESDP

Financial resources

The CFSP budget in context

The Treaty on European Union (TEU) states that the operating expenditure incurred in implementing CFSP and ESDP decisions is charged to the budget of the European Communities (hereinafter referred to as the EU budget), 'except for such expenditure arising from operations having military or defence implications' (Article 28.3, TEU). It follows that the costs of civilian ESDP operations are charged to the EU budget, whereas the common costs of military ESDP operations are financed through a separate inter-governmental arrangement (*Athena*).[53]

Before describing the specific breakdown of the CFSP budget, it is important to situate it in the broader context of the financial resources allocated to external action ('the EU as a global player') under Heading Four of the EU budget. These resources have been fixed by the 2006 Inter-institutional Agreement, which outlined the financial framework 2007-2013 establishing ceilings for expenditure under all headings and chapters of the EU budget.[54] In so far as Heading Four is concerned, the table below sums up the yearly budgetary allocations for each of the main instruments of external action, including the CFSP budget. It also reports the total reference amounts by instrument (over the envisaged seven year period) and by year (concerning the overall external relations package).

The CFSP financial envelope amounts to around €2 billion, which results in an average annual budget of roughly €290 million between 2007 and 2013. While having grown at a fast pace over the last few years, the CFSP budget still only counts for a very small share of the budgetary allocations for EU external relations at large over 2007-2013 – about 3.5 percent. Against a commitment of €243 million for CFSP in 2009, the EU budget allocates almost €2.4 billion to the Development Cooperation Instrument (DCI) and over €1.6 billion to the European Neighbourhood and Partnership Instrument (ENPI).

---

53. As specified below, Member States cover the salaries of seconded personnel to ESDP civilian operations. The mechanism established by Member States to finance the common costs of military ESDP operations is illustrated above, see pp. 75-6.

54. Inter-institutional Agreement between the European Parliament, the Council and the Commission on budgetary discipline and sound financial management, Official Journal of the European Union, 2006/C 139/01, Brussels, 14 June 2006.

FINANCIAL FRAMEWORK 2007-2013 – HEADING FOUR

	2007	2008	2009	2010	2011	2012	2013	Total*
IPA	1.263	1.497	1.518	1.593	1.797	1.936	2.024	11.468/ 11.627
ENPI	1.653	1.675	1.617	1.553	1.704	1.917	2.089	11.181/ 12.210
DCI	2.179	2.250	2.375	2.416	2.506	2.574	2.723	16.897/ 17.024
EIDHR	140	147	157	156	163	169	176	1.104/ 1.108
CFSP	159	285	243	281	327	363	406	1.980/ 2.066
IfS	139	181	188	220	290	362	442	2.062/ 1.822
HUMA	732	931	777	800	825	850	875	5.614/ 5.790
Head 4 Total	6.626	7.550	7.860	7.921	8.277	8.844	9.441	56.170**

Source: The European Commission, 'Financial programming 2007-2013', April 2009.

Figures are in millions of euro. IPA = Instrument for Pre-accession Assistance; ENPI = European Neighbourhood and Partnership Instrument; DCI = Development Cooperation Instrument; EIDHR = European Instrument for Democracy and Human Rights; CFSP = Common Foreign and Security Policy; IfS = Instrument for Stability; HUMA = Humanitarian Aid. Only the figures for 2007 and 2008 are final budgets. Those for the other years are reported as planned in April 2009.

* Total reference amount as provided for in original legal basis or financial statement/Currently planned total amounts following transfers from other budget lines in response to new policy requirements.

** The total amount for Heading Four corresponds to that currently envisaged and includes budget lines that are not reported in this table, for example the Emergency Aid Reserve.

On the other hand, the CFSP budget is not the only resource relevant to EU security policy at large and to the EU intervention in crisis theatres in particular. On the Community side, the Commission has developed and manages a range of geographic and thematic instruments, such as those outlined in the table above, which address important dimensions of crisis prevention, crisis response and post-conflict peace-building. While a comprehensive review cannot be carried out here, action is taken on a regular basis to provide humanitarian assistance, to consolidate democratic institutions and promote human rights, to reform the security sector, to support the disarmament, demobilisation and reintegration of combatants as well as mediation and reconciliation processes, to monitor peace agreements, and to fund programmes in the specific domains of landmines and small arms and light weapons, among others.[55] When it comes to crisis response, the distinctive features of the

---

55. See Catriona Gourlay, 'Community instruments for civilian crisis management', in Agnieszka Novak, 'Civilian crisis management: the EU way', *Chaillot Paper* no. 90, European Union Institute for Security Studies, Paris, June 2006; and Catriona Gourlay, 'The emerging EU civilian crisis response capacity', in *Faster and more united? The debate about Europe's crisis reponse capacity*, (Luxembourg: Office for the Official Publications of the European Communities, 2006).

Instrument for Stability are illustrated in more detail below.

Framing the CFSP financial resources in the context of the much larger external action budget highlights the fact that CFSP and ESDP cannot be regarded in isolation from the other instruments of external action. Given the limited means allocated to civilian ESDP under the CFSP budget, the importance of adequately coordinating all EU activities relevant to crisis management across different policy areas stands out all the more clearly. However, as described in the second part of this book, the operational experience of the last six years has exposed the difficulty of ensuring coherence and continuity between long-term Community programmes and more circumscribed intervention under ESDP.

The CFSP budget at a glance

Under Heading Four on external action, Chapter 19.03 on CFSP is divided into seven articles addressing expenditure related to, respectively, the monitoring and implementation of peace and security (19.03.01), non-proliferation and disarmament (19.03.02), conflict resolution and other stabilisation measures (19.03.03), emergency measures (19.03.04), preparatory and follow-up measures (19.03.05), EU Special Representatives (19.03.06) and police missions (19.03.07). Articles one, three and seven of the CFSP budget are of direct relevance to civilian ESDP, as they cover the operational costs of monitoring and border control missions (19.03.01), rule-of-law missions (19.03.03) and police missions (19.03.07).

The CFSP budget in 2009 stands at about €243 million. The very fast growth of the CFSP budget since 2002 (when it stood at a mere €30 million) can be ascribed almost exclusively to the growth of the costs related to ESDP civilian operations, whose number and size have been constantly expanding. At the same time, the relatively much smaller budget of EU Special Representatives has expanded almost sixfold between 2004 and 2008 (as their number grew from six to 11), signalling the stronger involvement of the Union in crisis diplomacy. When assessing budgetary appropriations in CFSP (as well as in other policy areas), the distinction should be drawn between commitment appropriations and payment appropriations. The former concern the budgetary amounts committed, at the beginning of each budgetary year, for expenditure over one or more years. The latter regard the payments actually made over a given year. This distinction matters since the discrepancy between commitments and payments has been the source of inter-institutional tensions, as illustrated in what follows.

The table below outlines the evolution of commitment appropriations in the field of CFSP between 2003 and 2009, and singles out the budgetary amounts allocated to ESDP civilian crisis management as such (the sum of articles one, three and seven). Between 2007 and 2008, the notable expansion of the ESDP budget has been driven by the launch of large civilian crisis management operations in Afghanistan (EUPOL) and, above all, Kosovo (EULEX).

	2003	2004	2005	2006	2007	2008	2009
CFSP	46,3	62,6	62,6	102,6	159,2	285	243
Civilian ESDP*		44,2	58,6	79,7	135,6	250,5	210**

Source: Table based on data from the Council Secretariat. Figures are in millions of euro.

* Expenditure directly pertaining to civilian ESDP within the CFSP budget.

** Estimate for the current year.

Decision-making

Following a proposal from the Commission, the Council of Ministers and the European Parliament (EP) – the two branches of the EU budgetary authority – agree the exact size of the CFSP budget. The dialogue between the Council and the Parliament is crucial in this context, and it has not always been smooth. This is perhaps inherent to a policy area such as CFSP where, by Treaty, the EP has the last word on the budget but limited say on substantial political decisions.[56]

Tensions between the Council and the EP culminated in 2005/2006, over criticism that top Council officials did not provide sufficient information to relevant parliamentary bodies and that the annual CFSP report from the Council to the EP did not adequately envisage upcoming priorities for CFSP and ESDP. Besides, the Parliament objected to the sometimes considerable gaps between commitments and actual payments under the CFSP chapter. Whether for ESDP civilian operations or for EUSRs' offices, appropriations needed to be scaled up in the course of the budgetary year, which was taken by the EP as evidence of weak financial planning. On the other hand, it is clear that foreign policy and crisis management are by their own nature reactive to events and demand more flexibility than policy domains where expenditure is regulated by earlier legislation.

---

56. On the prerogatives of the European Parliament in the domain of CFSP, see pp. 51-3.

On balance, the dialogue between the Council and the EP on the budgetary profiles of CFSP has improved since the adoption of the new Inter-institutional Agreement of 2006.[57] The latter envisages that the Council submits to the EP a forward-looking document addressing the main aspects and basic choices of CFSP, and their budgetary implications, by 15 June each year. On the basis of this document and of other relevant information, at least five joint consultation meetings are held every year involving 10 members of the EP (the presidents and vice-presidents of the Foreign Affairs Committee and of the Budget Committee), the rotating Chairman of the Political and Security Committee (PSC) and officials from the Commission and the Council Secretariat. These meetings address the state of play of CFSP/ESDP action and the missions' requirements in terms of money, staff and equipment. They are also meant to look ahead and anticipate financial requirements for the following year. Debate in these meetings feeds into the so-called conciliation procedure, which accompanies the formal budgetary procedure in order to achieve agreement between EU institutions.

Once the CFSP budget is approved by the Council and the EP, the Commission is responsible for its implementation. In practice, the Commission authorises expenditure based on the legal acts adopted by the Council (joint actions, common positions and decisions). The Heads of ESDP civilian missions enter a contractual relationship with the Commission as the officials responsible for the management of the respective budgets. The Commission also has the authority to transfer funds between different articles of the CFSP chapter to meet emerging needs. In this context, the 'emergency measures' line under the CFSP budget can be used. If this is not sufficient, the Commission can also make a proposal to mobilise two instruments that are separate from the CFSP budget, namely the Emergency Aid Reserve under Heading Four on external action (€1.75 billion 2007-2013) and the Flexibility Instrument. In both cases, the approval of the Council and of the EP is required to make funds available. €70 million were drawn from the Flexibility Instrument in 2008 to finance the deployment of EULEX Kosovo, bringing the overall CFSP budget from €215 million to 285 million.

At the closure of accounts for each specific action undertaken in the context of CFSP, funds committed but not absorbed as payments are removed from the CFSP budget and redistributed in the EU budget. Over the last two years, somewhat paradoxically, this has posed an issue of over-allocation and consequent loss of funds for the purposes of CFSP. Among other factors, this is due to the fact that expenditure on the staff and equipment of civilian missions cannot go ahead due to delays in

57. Inter-institutional Agreement, 14 June 2006, op. cit. in note 53. See in particular points 42 and 43.

finding personnel to match calls for contributions or in using framework contracts to procure equipment.

When considering the financial resources available to civilian ESDP, overall EU budgetary allocations are not the only relevant indicator. Also important is what those figures do not cover and, in particular, how quickly the amounts are disbursed to enable speedy crisis response measures. As to the first issue, Member States cover the salaries of the national personnel seconded to ESDP civilian missions, whereas per diems are charged to the EU budget.[58]

Preparatory actions

Delays in funding early action to pave the way for civilian operations have been a familiar, and contentious, feature of the ESDP operational experience. This has been due to a mix of factors. Differences between the Commission and the Council Secretariat on the definition of respective competences in the area of non-military crisis management entailed that inter-institutional cooperation has been difficult at times, affecting the rapid financing of ESDP operations. Over and above these differences, however, the problem was that the financial regulations governing the work of the Commission in implementing the CFSP budget did not cater for crisis management situations where prompt reaction is of essence.

Specific provisions governing emergency response for humanitarian crises did not apply in the context of CFSP. The Commission services could only disburse funds based on the financial reference amount approved by the Committee of Permanent Representatives (COREPER) and included in the joint action establishing an ESDP civilian operation. Much work, however, needed to be carried out on the ground (and funded) before the mandate and tasks of a mission could be properly defined in the joint action itself. The problem was therefore structural and, while cooperation between the Council and the Commission could occasionally put a patch on legal gaps, it required structural solutions. Significant, if circumscribed, progress has been achieved in the last three years.

Between 2006 and 2007, relevant financial regulations were amended to enable the Commission to fund 'preparatory measures' from within the CFSP budget (19.03.05). In the context of ESDP crisis management, these measures are destined to support, among other actions, 'exploratory work to assess the operational requirements for an envisaged action, to provide for a rapid initial deployment of

---

58. The salaries of contracted mission staff are also charged to the EU budget.

personnel and resources...or to take necessary measures on the ground to prepare for the launching of the operation...'[59] In 2008, the Commission adopted a framework decision specifying what costs the preparatory measures for CFSP/ESDP operations can cover and the procedure to finance them.[60] The specificity of these measures is that they can make funds available before the relevant legal act (a joint action) is adopted. The priority is to make preparatory missions operational from day one, which requires that preparatory measures cover expenditure for essential equipment, high risk insurance, travel and accommodation, among other costs.

Almost €5 million were foreseen for preparatory and follow-up measures under the CFSP budget in 2008. Out of this amount, €470,000 were used to finance a preparatory measure in Georgia in September 2008. The objectives of this measure were to establish the conditions on the ground for the launch of a future ESDP mission (EUMM) and to rapidly dispatch a ten-strong core-team tasked with preparing the deployment of the envisaged operation.

The Instrument for Stability

The CFSP budget has been growing fast and new procedures have been devised to make funds more rapidly available for crisis response. However, ESDP civilian operations will deliver sustainable results and prove ultimately successful only if set in the broader context of the overall EU engagement on the ground. Synergy between expenditure under the CFSP budget and relevant Community instruments is therefore key to the effectiveness of EU foreign policy in crisis theatres.

In this context, the area of crisis response is where coherence between ESDP operations and Community instruments is most urgently required, with a view to shaping and implementing a comprehensive approach. Between 2001 and 2007, the Crisis Platform in the RELEX Directorate General of the Commission ran the Rapid Reaction Mechanism (RRM), which allowed a rapid disbursement of funds to support political stability in crisis scenarios.[61] However, the RRM was endowed with only €30 million per year and could fund actions for no longer than six months, which was sometimes not enough to allow for other financial instruments to take over and provide required assistance. Some of the measures adopted under this

---

59. Budgetary remarks as reported in Council Document 10238/07, 'Procedure for having recourse to "Preparatory measures" budget line within the CFSP budget,' 31 May 2007, point three.

60. Commission Decision of 8 August 2008, concerning the financing of Preparatory Missions of CFSP/ESDP Crisis Management Operations financed from the CFSP budget.

61. Regulation (EC) 381/2001 of the Council creating a Rapid Reaction Mechanism, 26 February 2001.

instrument preceded or accompanied ESDP operations. The RRM supported the peace process in Aceh, which created the conditions for deploying the Aceh Monitoring Mission; it funded confidence-building measures in FYROM and supported the demobilisation and reintegration of combatants in DRC, alongside ESDP police and SSR missions. In these and other cases, however, co-presence on the ground did not necessarily entail a sufficient degree of coordination across pillars.

A vast reform of the financial instruments for external action was adopted in 2006, which led to reducing their number and rationalising their remit. In particular, the creation of the Instrument for Stability (IfS) to replace the RRM and other tools represented an important innovation in order to improve the Commission's crisis response capacity and to foster cooperation between first and second pillar instruments.[62] The regulation establishing the new instrument expressly provided that relevant measures 'may be complementary to and should be consistent with measures adopted by the EU' in the context of CFSP and also under Title VI TEU on police and criminal justice cooperation.[63] The IfS includes two major components, namely assistance in response to situations of crisis and emerging crisis (Article 3) and assistance in the context of stable conditions for cooperation (Article 4). When it comes to crisis response, the IfS marks clear progress compared to the RRM in that it is endowed with much larger funds, it can support 'exceptional assistance measures' lasting up to 18 months, and it is deployed in close consultation with the Council bodies.

Out of an overall package of about €2 billion for the period 2007-2013, it is provided that 73% would be dedicated to crisis response, while the rest would be used for longer-term measures, including action against proliferation and trans-regional threats such as terrorism and organised crime. Commitments for crisis response measures amounted to over €90 million for 2007, 130 in 2008 and 135 committed for 2009.[64] Almost all of the available funds have been spent in 2007 and

62. The Instrument for Stability is managed by the Directorate A (crisis platform and policy coordination in CFSP) in DG RELEX. In particular, unit A2 (crisis response and peace building) manages crisis response measures and unit A4 (security policy) is responsible for long-term assistance.

63. Regulation (EC) 1717/2006 of the European Parliament and of the Council establishing an Instrument for Stability, 15 November 2006. The reference to Title VI TEU on police and criminal justice cooperation concerns the measures adopted under the Instrument for Stability to counter trans-national threats such as organised crime, trafficking and terrorism, among others.

64. See Commission staff working document, Report evaluating the implementation of the financial instruments for external actions, accompanying the Communication from the Commission to the European Parliament and the Council, Mid-term review of the financial instruments for external action (COM (2009) 196), 21 April 2009, pp.27-32. See also Report from the Commission to the Council and the European Parliament, Annual Report from the European Commission on the Instrument for Stability in 2007, Executive Summary, COM (2008) 181 final, 11 April 2008.

2008. Where more complex procedures (comitology) do not apply, namely for crisis response measures amounting to less than €20 million, the Commission needs to inform the Council and to take into account its views. In practice, this happens through regular exchanges in the PSC, based on Commission's information notes, before the finalisation of the relevant measure. Experience so far has been quite constructive with regard to both process, in terms of engagement of EU institutions and Member States, and substance, with a view to concrete crisis response initiatives.

Out of the measures adopted between 2007 and early 2009, many are complementary to ESDP engagement and the majority provide critical assistance in unstable areas in the proximity of the Union or in its outer neighbourhood. Of the €220 million committed for crisis response in 2007-2008, 29 percent of the funds went to Africa, 12 percent to the Middle East, over 10 percent to Kosovo and about 7 percent to Georgia.[65] As to synergies between the IfS and ESDP operations, interesting examples include, among others, Afghanistan (support to the rule of law and justice reform), Gaza (capacity-building for the Palestinian police), Chad (financing the MINURCAT programme of training and deployment of Chadian police in the East of the country), Somalia (support to both AMISOM planning and transitional Somali institutions), DRC (reintegration of combatants, police reform, support to the peace process in Eastern Congo), Guinea Bissau (security sector reform), Kenya (support to trials and treatment of suspected pirates), Georgia (post-conflict stabilisation) and Kosovo, where the IfS provides the bulk of the funding for the International Civilian Office headed by the International Civilian Representative/EUSR Peter Feith.[66]

Civilian capabilities

The early steps

The process of developing civilian capabilities for crisis management in the context of ESDP broke new ground. While the Commission had accumulated considerable experience in non-military crisis management and Member States had engaged, individually or in multilateral formats, in civilian operations, no capacity as such existed in the context of CFSP when ESDP was launched in 1999. The first priority

---

65. See Commission staff working document, op. cit in note 64, p.27.

66. For more specific information on these and other measures adopted under the Instrument for Stability, see Annual Report from the European Commission on the Instrument for Stability in 2007, op. cit. in note 64 and the Report from the Commission to the Council, the European Parliament, the Economic and Social Committee and the Committee of the Regions, Annual report from the European Commission on the Instrument for Stability in 2008, COM (2009) 341 final, 9 July 2009. See also European Commission, *From warning to action: Reportage on the EU's Instrument for Stability*, (Luxembourg: Office for Official Publications of the European Communities, 2008).

was therefore to map existing EU and national resources, as a step towards defining targets for generating collective capabilities.[67]

This was the primary objective of the Action Plan on non-military crisis management adopted at the Helsinki European Council in December 1999.[68] The Plan effectively established the working agenda for the years to come, envisaging three main steps. First, complete the inventory of the tools available to the Union and to Member States. Second, set up a database to collect and share information on pre-identified assets, capabilities and expertise. Third, conduct a study to define concrete targets in terms of both numbers of personnel and rapid deployability. The implementation of the Action Plan was entrusted to a new Coordinating Mechanism set up in the Council Secretariat and mandated to closely cooperate with the Commission.

The Helsinki Action plan unleashed a sustained dynamic in identifying priority areas for ESDP civilian crisis management, defining targets, registering national commitments and developing basic concept documents. The June 2000 European Council in Feira marked an important milestone by endorsing four priority areas for civilian crisis management.[69] These included police, strengthening the rule of law and strengthening civilian administration and civil protection. Across these four dimensions, emphasis was put on the ability to react quickly by deploying at short notice, and on the requirement for Member States to pre-select relevant officials or experts in the four priority areas and adequately train them. Police deployment was identified as central to civilian crisis management operations. Member States committed at Feira to strengthen their capabilities in this domain and make available on a voluntary basis, by 2003, 5,000 police officers, 1,000 of whom should be deployable within 30 days.

Subsequent work on the police dimension took special prominence in the ESDP civilian capability development process and anticipated methods and concepts that would apply to other priority areas as well. The Presidency Report on ESDP submitted to the Nice European Council in December 2000 outlined four steps for translating Member States' commitments to capability targets into practice, including

---

67. For a detailed overview of the civilian capability development process up to the launch of the Civilian Headline Goal 2008 in 2004, see Agnieszka Nowak, 'Civilian crisis management within ESDP', in Agnieszka Nowak (ed.), 'Civilian crisis management: the EU way', *Chaillot Paper* no. 90, EU Institute for Security Studies, Paris, June 2006.

68. Presidency Report on non-military crisis management of the European Union, Annex 2 to Annex IV to the Presidency Conclusions, European Council, Helsinki, 10-11 December 1999. In Maartje Rutten (ed.), 'From Saint Malo to Nice. European Defence: Core documents, vol. I', *Chaillot Paper* no. 47, EU Institute for Security Studies, Paris, May 2001, pp. 89-91.

69. Presidency Report on strengthening the Common European Security and Defence Policy, Annex I to the Presidency Conclusions, European Council, Santa Maria da Feira, 19-20 June 2000. Ibid., pp. 120-39.

preparing generic scenarios, describing the relevant missions under those scenarios, defining the capabilities required to fulfil those missions and calling upon Member States to identify available capabilities.[70] This would remain the basic framework for the civilian capability development process in the years ahead.

As to concepts, the Presidency Report drew the key distinction between the so-called 'strengthening' missions, essentially directed to monitor, advise and train local police, and 'substitution' missions, where the ESDP police operations would carry out executive tasks, from ensuring public order to investigative activities, in substitution for weak or collapsed local police structures. These two broad types of missions would inform scenario-building relevant to the rule of law and civilian administration dimensions of civilian ESDP as well. The Nice Report also put the accent on the synergy between police missions and rule-of-law ones, in so far as functioning criminal justice and prison systems are crucial both for police missions to attain their objectives and for establishing viable state structures more generally.

Targets for rule of law, civilian administration and civil protection were established at the Goteborg European Council in June 2001.[71] Member States committed to deliver 200 rule-of-law officials and civil protection intervention teams of up to 2,000 people by 2003.[72] Work on police was enhanced by adopting a specific Action Plan focusing on the need to develop a capacity for the (strategic and operational) planning and conduct of police operations. A new Police Unit was consequently set up in the Council Secretariat in 2001.

Following the first capability development conferences on, respectively, police and the rule of law in November 2001 and spring 2002, the ministerial capability conference held in November 2002 under the Danish Presidency concluded that the targets established in 2001 in the priority areas had been met and exceeded by national voluntary commitments.[73] The conference also stressed that more work was necessary to strengthen the planning structures for civilian crisis management within

70. Presidency Report on the European Security and Defence Policy, Annex VI to Presidency Conclusions, European Council, Nice, 7-9 December 2000. Ibid., pp. 168-211.

71. Presidency Report on the European Secuirty and Defence Policy, Annex to Presidency Conclusions, European Council, Göteborg, 15-16 June 2001. Maartje Rutten (ed.), 'From Nice to Laeken. European Defence: core documents', *Chaillot Paper* no. 51, EU Institute for Security Studies, Paris, April 2002, pp. 30-61.

72. No specific number was envisaged for pools of experts in the field of civilian administration, but priority functions were identified including general administrative functions (civil registration, elections, taxation and customs), social functions (education, health, social services) and infrastructure functions (water, energy, telecommunications).

73. Ministerial declaration adopted by the Civilian Crisis Management Capability Conference on 19 November 2002, in annex to the Conclusions of the General Affairs and External Relations Council, Brussels, 19 November 2002. In Jean-Yves Haine (ed.), 'From Laeken to Copenhagen. European defence: Core documents, vol. III,' *Chaillot Paper* no. 57, EU Institute for Security Studies, Paris, February 2003, pp. 145-146.

the Council Secretariat. This was especially urgent as ESDP was moving from words to deeds, with the EU police mission (EUPM) in Bosnia Herzegovina starting on 1 January 2003.[74]

In parallel to the launch of the EUPM and to the planning of the second ESDP civilian operation – EUPOL *Proxima* in FYROM[75] – incremental progress was achieved in 2003. Member States committed a pool of 248 experts in the field of civil administration. Besides, following the establishment in early 2002 of the Community Mechanism to facilitate cooperation in Civil Protection assistance interventions, the Council and the Commission adopted a joint declaration on the modalities for using such a mechanism (principally directed to respond to natural and manmade disasters) in crisis management situations under Title V TEU.[76] In the second part of 2003, ongoing dialogue with the UN and the OSCE on lessons learned, best practices and practical cooperation resulted under the Italian Presidency in a joint EU-UN declaration on cooperation in crisis management and in Council conclusions on EU-OSCE cooperation.[77] The principles guiding cooperation with other international organisations were added value, interoperability, visibility of the EU contribution and EU decision-making autonomy.

The step change

By the end of 2003, the preparatory groundwork for the development of civilian crisis management capabilities in the context of ESDP had been largely carried out. Following the Helsinki Action Plan, the *acquis* included, among other issues, the national commitments nominally fulfilling quantitative targets across the four priority areas identified in Feira, the Coordinating Mechanism running the databases on police and rule of law, the creation of the Police Unit in the Council Secretariat, the adoption by the PSC of concepts defining all the types of ESDP civilian missions, the establishment of modalities for cooperation with non-EU countries contributing to ESDP civilian operations, and regular dialogue and interaction with the UN and the OSCE.

---

74. See the chapter on EUPM in this book.

75. See the chapter on EUPOL *Proxima* in this book.

76. Council Decision 2001/792/EC, Euratom, establishing a Community mechanism to facilitate reinforced cooperation in civil protection assistance interventions, 23 October 2001. *Official Journal* L 297/7, 15 November 2001. See also the joint declaration of the Council and the Commission, of 29 September 2003, on the use of the Civil Protection Mechanism in crisis management referred to in Title V of the Treaty of the European Union.

77. Council of the European Union, 'Joint Declaration on UN-EU cooperation in crisis management', Council document 12510/03 (Presse 266), New York, 24 September 2003. As to EU-OSCE cooperation, see Presidency Conclusions, General Affairs and External Relations Council, Brussels, 17 November 2003. In Antonio Missiroli (ed.), 'From Copenhagen to Brussels: European Defence: core documents', *Chaillot Paper* no. 67, vol. IV,' EU Institute for Security Studies, Paris, December 2003, pp. 269-272.

The context of the civilian capabilities development process considerably shifted between 2003 and 2004. First, the ESDP police missions in the Western Balkans had been deployed and some lessons could be drawn from the serious challenges met in their planning and conduct. Second, the European Security Strategy (ESS) was adopted in December 2003 and became the reference document for successive developments, with a focus on synergy among all EU instruments, unity of command and the development of relevant capabilities. Third, the Union expanded to include ten new Member States, bringing with them not only additional capabilities but also their distinctive experience and expertise, as countries that had just completed a long process of political reform and institution-building.[78]

The conjunction of these events and of the expected increase in demand for civilian ESDP operations, from the South Caucasus to Africa, triggered a step change in the capability development process and led to the adoption of the Action Plan for the civilian aspects of ESDP in June 2004 and of the Civilian Headline Goal 2008 (CHG 2008) in December 2004.[79] Together with the Ministerial Declaration of the civilian capability commitment conference of November 2004, these documents identified the six priority issues that would drive the capability development process for the following three years and beyond.

First, drawing from the ESS, civilian crisis management under ESDP was presented as a key component of EU external policy in general and of the EU approach to crises in particular. Achieving stronger synergies with Community actors, including those active in the domain of Justice and Home Affairs (JHA), and with the military was therefore essential for the success of EU engagement. Second, and related, there was a need to expand the range of priority areas and expertise identified at Feira. The EU needed to be able to conduct monitoring missions and to provide adequate support to EUSR offices with experts in areas such as human rights, political affairs and gender issues. New national commitment to monitoring tasks and EUSR support amounted to, respectively, 505 and 391 officials by mid-2004. Furthermore, security sector reform (SSR) and disarmament, demobilisation and reintegration (DDR) were pointed out as domains where civilian ESDP would have to be increasingly involved.

---

78. Following the enlargement, national voluntary commitments were revised upwards to include 5,761 officials in the area of police, 631 for the rule of law, 562 for civilian administration and 4,988 for civil protection. See the Civilian Capabilities Commitment Conference, Ministerial Declaration, Brussels, 22 November 2004.

79. Action Plan for Civilian Aspects of ESDP, adopted by the European Council, Brussels, 17-18 June 2004. See European security and defence: Core documents 2004, vol. V, *Chaillot Paper* no. 75, EU Institute for Security Studies, Paris, February 2005, pp. 121-28. Civilian Headline Goal 2008, ibid., pp. 359-63.

Third, the EU needed to be able to deploy under ESDP multifunctional, integrated civilian crisis management packages, tailored to the needs on the ground and able to draw on a wide range of expertise. Fourth, the EU planning structures had to be urgently strengthened to enable the Union to conduct several civilian operations at the same time, including one large substitution mission at short notice in a non-benign environment. Fifth, given this level of ambition, rapid financing mechanisms, new procurement rules and adequate mission support structures were to be developed to enhance the ability of the Union to rapidly deploy and sustain ESDP civilian operations on the ground. Sixth, renewed effort was called for in the field of training civilian personnel, with a view to link the Commission-funded activities (the European Group on Training) more closely to national programmes, shape a common crisis management culture and improve interoperability.

The CHG 2008, adopted by the European Council in December 2004, was to be developed by a project team based in the Council Secretariat, with the full association of the Commission, under the oversight of the PSC supported by CIVCOM. The CHG process involved four main phases. First, the elaboration of planning assumptions and illustrative scenarios outlining what missions the EU could undertake and their context.[80] Second, a list of the capabilities required to carry out those missions was to be produced, including personnel, equipment, planning, logistics and mission support. Third, the voluntary contributions of Member States would be assessed against the list of required capabilities, with a view to identifying resulting shortfalls and designing a Capability Improvement Plan. Fourth, a system for the regular review of national contributions to meet the capability requirements and address the shortfalls would be established.

In a nutshell, the launch of the CHG 008 meant that the largely virtual, generic priority areas and national commitments agreed in the previous years needed to convert into a more specific description of required capabilities and into more stringent criteria for Member States to identify, recruit, train and make available personnel, including at short notice and in integrated packages. The uneven output of the CHG 2008 can be assessed with a view to the six issue areas indicated above, as outlined in the landmark documents of 2004.[81]

---

80. These scenarios, largely drawing from those elaborated in the context of the military capability development process, included a stabilisation and reconstruction scenario (envisaging both a substitution and a strengthening mission), a conflict prevention scenario, the targeted strengthening of institutions and support to humanitarian operations.

81. For an overall assessment of the output of the CHG 2008, see Council Document 14807/07, Final Report on the Civilian Headline Goal 2008, 9 November 2007, approved by the Ministerial Civilian Capabilities Improvement Conference and noted by the General Affairs and External Relations Council, Brussels, 19 November 2007.

First, as to the strategic requirement for more synergy and coherence between all EU actors involved in crisis management (notably ESDP operations, the Commission and the EUSRs) the added value of the CHG 2008 has been modest. Civil-civil and civil-military cooperation in the civilian capability development process has not spilled over to the operational dimension and has not proven very far-reaching in improving capabilities either.

Key areas of cooperation between the Commission and civilian ESDP concern of course financing and procurement, as illustrated above.[82] Continuity between short-term and long-term measures and coordination between ESDP missions and Community programmes has left much to be desired in all operational theatres during most of the CHG 2008 process. Some effort has gone into starting a dialogue between civilian ESDP and JHA actors, with the CIVCOM Presidency briefing the so-called Article 36 Committee twice.[83] However, engagement has remained piecemeal. As to civil-military coordination in developing ESDP capabilities, the civil and military processes have proceeded in parallel, with little exchanges between responsible officials. On a different level, however, the Civil-Military Cell within the EU Military Staff has often supported civilian structures in planning civilian ESDP operations.

Second, the CHG 2008 has made some strides in better specifying the required capabilities and in broadening the range of the operational tasks and professional profiles relevant to civilian ESDP. The list of civilian capabilities requirements based on the illustrative scenarios was central to this dimension of the CHG 2008. This list was completed in September 2005 and included a detailed breakdown of all the functions relevant to the civilian missions envisaged under the five scenarios. As such, the list provided the basis for more specific national commitments and for identifying shortfalls. These were registered, for example, concerning judges and prosecutors, prison personnel, police officers at junior and middle management level and border police officers at junior level.

The list was regarded as a living document, to be constantly updated based on real-life experience by inserting those profiles that had not been foreseen.[84] In the course of 2007, work on the list was taken a step further by starting the development of the so-called

---

82. See pp. 93-6.

83. The Committee, whose remit is outlined in Article 36 TEU, is in charge of coordinating the relevant working groups in the field of police and judicial cooperation in criminal matters.

84. Between 2005 and 2007 these included, among others, experts in monitoring and in particular aspects of DDR (based on the Aceh Monitoring Mission experience) as well as specialists in the prison sector and on property law (drawing from the planning of EULEX Kosovo).

Civilian Capabilities Management Tool (CCMT), which potentially allows for a better match between mission tasks, job descriptions, lessons learned and training needs.[85]

The development of integrated civilian crisis management packages for rapid deployment was a third, central driver of the CHG 2008. From this standpoint, conceptual work was largely completed by the end of 2005, fleshing out the new concept of the Civilian Response Teams (CRTs).[86] The CRTs are a multinational rapid response capability including pre-selected national experts with specific training. The aim was to set up a pool of 100 experts covering all relevant areas of expertise and deployable in five days, while sustainable for as much as three months, with autonomous logistical support. It was envisaged that CRTs could be deployed, as need be, at three stages, namely in the phase of early assessment and fact finding to provide input to the planning process, at the stage of mission build-up as a bridging tool to initiate key mission functions and, finally, by way of reinforcing an ongoing mission with specific expertise. As of 2006, identified CRT members went through a series of *ad hoc* training modules managed by the European Group on Training funded by the Commission.

Work on the rapid deployment of integrated units included progress to better define conceptually and make readily available Integrated Police Units (IPUs) and Formed Police Units (FPUs). The former are robust battalion- or company-sized units (gendarmerie units) which may or may not be placed under military command and are especially suited to intervene in non-stabilised situations to carry out executive police tasks such as patrolling, maintaining public order and fighting organised crime. FPUs, company-sized, cannot be placed under military command and may be used for lighter police tasks, including executive ones. IPUs and FPUs respond to a growing demand for deploying at short notice sizeable police forces which are interoperable with both the military and other civilian actors and are able to carry out a variety of tasks. Over the last few years, they have been used in the context of the ESDP missions in Bosnia Herzegovina and Kosovo.[87]

Reinforcing the planning structures for civilian crisis management was another important aspect of the capability development process (while not, strictly speaking,

---

85. See below p. 111.

86. Council Document 10462/05, Multifunctional Civilian Crisis Management Resources in an Integrated Format – Civilian Response Teams, 23 June 2005. See also Council Document 15406/05, CRT Generic Terms of Reference, 5 December 2005.

87. The development of police capabilities in the context of civilian ESDP is institutionally separate from the setting up of the European Gendarmerie Force (EGF) in 2004. The EGF is a multinational unit involving six EU Member States (France, Italy, the Netherlands, Portugal, Spain and Romania, which joined the EGF in 2008) and providing the capability for the rapid deployment of expeditionary and interoperable police missions, drawing on police forces with military status. While the EGF, based in Vicenza, Italy, is primarily at the disposal of the EU, it can also be made available for operations in the context of the UN, NATO, the OSCE or *ad hoc* coalitions.

part of the CHG 2008). The progressive expansion of DG IX in the Council Secretariat and the creation of the Civilian Planning and Conduct Capability (CPCC) in 2007/2008 are addressed in chapter one.[88]

Mission support – the fifth strand of capability development under the CHG 2008 as presented here – concerns the capacity to make readily available the human, financial and material resources necessary to the planning, implementation and termination of a civilian ESDP operation.[89] As such, mission support could be defined as a capability cutting across all others, aiming to facilitate their identification and management. Relevant expertise includes general support services (logistics, communication, medical care, mission security), financing, procurement, human resources and legal and financial control. These functions are crucial enabling factors for attaining operational and, ultimately, political objectives. Some progress has been achieved at the conceptual and practical level all along the CHG 2008 process, although more by way of *ad hoc* arrangement than of structural reforms. Expertise on the technical and procedural dimensions of mission support has been enhanced both at headquarters in Brussels and in the field, where the missions' administration offices play a central role.

Leaving aside the financial aspects as such, addressed earlier in this chapter, the Council Secretariat and the Commission worked in 2006 and 2007 on the development of the so-called framework contracts to streamline procurement procedures. Procuring the necessary equipment in due time to the first ESDP civilian missions proved extremely cumbersome.[90] Long delays seriously affected the early phases of some of them, from EUJUST *Themis* in Georgia to the Aceh Monitoring Mission.[91] The idea of establishing framework contracts aimed at streamlining the procedure by pre-identifying contractors who would be called upon to deliver equipment and services to different missions, as need be, without launching new tenders. Framework contracts were awarded in 2007 for armoured and 'soft-skin' (4x4) vehicles and more are envisaged for IT equipment as well as health and high-risk insurance cover for mission personnel. However, new problems have been met in practice, such as serious delays by 'framework contractors' and the difficulty of identifying new contractors for specific types of equipment.

88. See Chapter 1 on ESDP institutions, pp. 34-46.

89. Council Document 12457/06, 'Initial Concept of Mission Support for ESDP Civilian Crisis Management Missions,' 5 September 2006.

90. Calls for tender for a value above €10,000 had to be made anew for any successive mission and required the approval of Commission services at two stages, namely before the publication of the tender and before the awarding of the final contract. This could take as long as six months and remains the case today for most categories of equipment.

91. See the chapter on EUJUST *Themis* and the chapter on the AMM in this book.

Training was a key dimension of the CHG 2008. Early operational experience in Bosnia Herzegovina and the former Yugoslav Republic of Macedonia (FYROM) demonstrated the challenge of deploying personnel endowed with crisis management experience and with mission-specific training, for example in carrying out monitoring, mentoring and advising weak local institutions. This required different skills from standard police or rule-of-law activities and in-depth knowledge of the theatre of operation. Work on the quantity and quality of available personnel under the capability requirements list, effective recruitment procedures and training are closely linked aspects of the civilian capability development process. Training activities include generic (non mission- or task-specific) training, more targeted modules addressing distinctive areas of expertise or crisis management packages such as the CRTs, and mission-specific training, which itself may include pre-deployment, mission-induction and in-mission training.

National authorities are chiefly responsible for training activities, with EU institutions and funding playing a supporting and coordinating role. The Commission-funded European Group on Training has brought together a quite heterogeneous range of national training bodies and educational institutions supporting courses often open to experts or officials from more than one country. On the other hand, the European dimension has not always been prominent in national courses. Also, inevitably, some Member States have been more proactive than others, leading to an uneven level playing field for delivering properly trained personnel. From a different standpoint, much of the training has taken place at the generic level, including by the European Group on Training and by the European Security and Defence College. Much training-on-the-job was therefore required for the personnel of civilian missions, which affected the launching phase of these operations and their overall performance.

Two additional horizontal dimensions should be addressed when assessing the CHG 2008 process. First, the EU has pursued a dialogue with other international organisations involved in civilian crisis management, notably the UN and the OSCE, with a view to both drawing from their experience and best practices and paving the way for closer cooperation. Recurrent topics of mutual consultation included rapid deployment, the management of electronic platforms to facilitate the identification and recruitment of personnel, and options to speed up procurement including setting up warehouses and improving the transfer of equipment from one mission to the other.

Second, and crucially, the CHG 2008 process was meant to act as a platform to exchange information and best practices among Member States and as a catalyst to raise awareness of the growing requirements of civilian ESDP at the national level. Since most of the capabilities are in the hands of Member States, it was considered essential to engage all stakeholders within each country. They included not only the Ministries of Foreign Affairs but also relevant authorities from the Ministries of the Interior and Justice, functionally (and financially) responsible for police and rule-of- law personnel. Much of the initiative in this context could only be left to Member States themselves, with CIVCOM acting as a key interface and the EU services running the CHG 2008 acting as facilitators and providing constant input for progress.[92] By late 2007, it was clear that much remained to be done to improve the ability of Member States to make available the resources required, as the struggle to recruit personnel for the large ESDP missions in Afghanistan and Kosovo in 2007/2008 would demonstrate.

Two steps forward, one step back

The end of 2007 saw the conclusion of the CHG 2008 and the launch of the CHG 2010.[93] The latter was intended to end in the same year as the military headline goal 2010, which may create an opportunity for joining the two capabilities development processes, where appropriate. Over and above the transition from the CHG 2008 to the CHG 2010, however, in the last two years, the debate on the development of civilian capabilities has undergone a significant change of perspective. This has been triggered by the growing awareness of the urgent requirements stemming from operational experience. In other words, while the approach to the development of capabilities under the CHG 2008 was largely based on theoretical assumptions, illustrative scenarios and nominal commitments by Member States, the debate is now based on the real-life experience accumulated in the field and focuses on the quality of personnel required to fulfil specific tasks as opposed to quantitative targets.

From this standpoint, the 'scale' of civilian ESDP is a critical factor. When the CHG 2008 started in 2004, the EU was running three civilian ESDP operations (EUPM, EUPOL *Proxima* and EUJUST *Themis*). Today, it is running 11 of them, including one major strengthening/substitution integrated rule-of-law mission in Kosovo, while

---

92. For example, guidelines on the recruitment of personnel for EU civilian crisis management were agreed and addressed to Member States in October 2006. See Council Document 12687/1/06, Civilian headline Goal 2008 – Draft recommendations and guidelines on the raising of personnel for EU civilian crisis management, 9 October 2006.

93. Council Document 14823/07, New Civilian Headline Goal 2010, 9 November 2007.

four other missions were deployed in-between (EUPAT, AMM, EUPOL Kinshasa and EUPT Kosovo). Whether one thinks of available experts and officials, financial costs or adequate mission support, this difference of scale has not only quantitative but also qualitative implications. With a view to fulfilling what are, on paper, pretty much the same functions as five years ago, the system needs to be much more professional, efficient, effective and sustainable. To some extent, when turning back to the ground covered between 2004 and 2009, it has become so and the CHG 2010 aims to consolidate it further in all respects.

The problem is, however, that progress in the supply of civilian capabilities has been permanently outpaced by increase in demand, with much larger and more complex missions having been planned and deployed. If the level of ambition that has driven ESDP civilian crisis management in the last few years is sustained in future, the capability-expectations gap is liable to grow larger.

The main shift in the debate since the end of the CHG 2008 consists in the clear understanding that the solution to this serious problem lies at the national level. It is a question of enhancing the political commitment of Member States to make available more and better resources, some of which at short notice. Overall, progress at national level in the last few years has been slow at best, with most national rosters of civilian capabilities still to be completed, where they exist. The problem is compounded by the drastic budgetary cuts that are envisaged as a consequence of the current economic downturn and will affect the financing and availability of national capabilities.

In this perspective, EU structures can be of help in a number of ways but new political momentum has to be generated at the national level and through coordinated action, if the EU wants to continue to develop into a major crisis management actor. Hence the importance of exploring the scope for elaborating and implementing new national strategies to generate further civilian capabilities. In so doing, it is understood that no one-size-fits-all model can be applied to Member States given the diversity of their domestic legislative frameworks and institutional practices. For example, Finland has adopted a fully-fledged national strategy and formally established an inter-ministerial coordination mechanism managed by the Ministry of the Interior. Other countries, notably some small Member States, seem inclined to introduce elements of the Finnish model but the latter may not suit very large national administrations with deep-rooted bureaucratic cultures and more fragmented competences, including across different levels of government.

While, therefore, it is important to fix shared priorities and to monitor concrete progress at the national level, the measures adopted by individual countries may differ. Four priority areas have been identified in 2009 and broadly agreed by Member States to guide national efforts in this domain, namely national regulatory measures, budgetary arrangements, the development of national rosters and training.[94] When it comes to national regulations, it is a question of guaranteeing job security and providing opportunities for career advancement to those who are seconded to crisis management missions, and to ensure that at least some of them can be mobilised at short notice. Setting up national rosters following uniform or at least compatible formats would very much help identify the best qualified officials or experts in response to calls for contribution, while preserving the decision-making authority of separate ministries on the secondment of their personnel. Besides, training opportunities should be both multiplied, making training in one country available to nationals of other Member States and encouraging these exchanges, and more targeted, focusing for example on the specific tasks of mission administration and procurement.[95]

Having stressed the importance of the national dimension for the future development of civilian capabilities, many of the priorities outlined in the CHG 2010 help to focus the minds of practitioners and facilitate the convergence of national efforts. The main aspects of the work carried out under the CHG 2010 are presented in what follows. With a view to personnel requirements, the CHG 2010 broadly applies the same methodology as the CHG 2008 but updates it with a stronger emphasis on civ-mil cooperation. A new, pilot illustrative scenario was elaborated in early 2008 envisaging the simultaneous presence of civilian and military actors in a theatre of operation.[96] The scenario was produced in cooperation between the civilian capability planning task force and officials from the EUMS and highlights the requirements for a complex, integrated SSR operation. Based on that, a new list of required capabilities has been drawn up. The latter foresees the need for an additional 285 personnel, including new profiles such as experts on transitional justice, dialogue and mediation, and conflict analysis.

---

94. Interviews with EU and national officials, May to July 2009.

95. With a view to addressing shortages in these key areas of expertise, the Commission has provided training for ESDP mission staff in the areas of procurement and financial administration. See Richard Wright and Juha Auvinen, 'What ambitions for the civilian ESDP?', in Alvaro de Vasconcelos (ed.), *What ambitions for European Defence in 2020?*, EU Institute for Security Studies, Paris, July 2009, p. 112-14.

96. Council Document 15253/08, Civilian Headline Goal 2010: Progress Report 2008 (report on civilian preparedness), 5 November 2008.

With a view to integrated civilian crisis management packages, the CHG 2010 envisages the completion of the pool of 100 experts for CRTs. A call for the identification of additional experts was launched in 2008, with a focus on the rule of law, human rights and mission support. Besides, as is the case for other categories of personnel, the pool of experts needs to be updated on a regular basis to ensure their actual readiness for deployment at very short notice. A broader reflection is also ongoing on how to make CRTs more operational, given their limited use as teams so far. On the other hand, the deployment of small groups of experts drawn from the CRTs pool in the Palestinian Territories and in Georgia in 2008 in an assessment and fact-finding capacity signals potential for CRTs or equivalent packages to take over more tasks in the future.

Work on personnel resources is accompanied by the progressive development of the Civilian Capability Management Tool through a secure website empowered by a new software application called Goalkeeper.[97] The CCMT includes comprehensive and permanently updated catalogues of mission tasks, standard job descriptions, equipment (including framework contracts) and concepts, and is expected to serve different purposes. On the one hand, it supports the civilian capability development process by providing a clear overview of the different categories of personnel, as a basis to survey the availability of national resources and point at critical shortfalls. On the other hand, it aims to facilitate the planning of civilian missions and the recruitment of relevant personnel.[98]

More generally, the CCMT constitutes an enhanced database of required and available capabilities, accessible not only by EU institutions but also by national authorities and missions in the field, thereby contributing to a shared institutional memory, know-how, and sense of priority. The CCMT draws not only from the CHG 2008 list and from the CHG 2010 SSR scenario but also, and most importantly, from operational experience. As stressed above, following the launch of 17 civilian ESDP operations, virtual scenarios can only play a complementary role to the key lessons drawn from experience.

---

97. Council Document 8096/09, Civilian Headline Goal 2010: Outline of Goalkeeper software environment, 2 April 2009.

98. The Goalkeeper software should allow for a more rapid, precise and timely identification of the capabilities required for each mission, linking standard job descriptions to mission-specific ones with a view to publishing calls for contributions.

The establishment of a systematic process to identify and implement lessons and best practices based on operational experience is another important dimension of the CHG 2010. In a complex political and institutional environment as that of CFSP/ESDP, drawing up lessons learned is a sensitive exercise. In the past, this has been done on an *ad hoc* basis, very far from the public eye and with very little involvement of external expertise. As a result, lessons have been sometimes identified but not necessarily *learned*, meaning transposed in policies and practice.

New guidelines were adopted in November 2008 and envisage a quite structured process, moving from the collection and identification of relevant experience to the consequent revision, as needed, of policies and procedures.[99] The process of identification and analysis of lessons covers the entire lifetime of the missions including not only reports on the planning stage and final reports, but also the introduction of lessons identified in six-monthly reports. Besides, reports can address horizontal issues such as, among others, SSR, communication strategies and working with the UN.

Officials from DG IX and the CPCC carry out this process in Brussels, in cooperation with the Commission. In the field, the Heads of Mission are responsible for collecting and providing relevant information to headquarters. The appointment of best practices officers within each mission is also envisaged. Up until summer 2009, lessons have been identified and analysed concerning the planning phases of the SSR mission in Guinea Bissau and EUMM Georgia, and a new exercise concerning the planning of EULEX Kosovo has been launched. Clearly, the success of this process will depend on good cooperation within and between EU institutions, between Brussels and the field, as well as between the EU and Member States, who are the ultimate recipients of the output. As has been the case all along the civilian capability development process, the real challenge will lie in converting analytical findings into new policies and adequate capabilities.

BIBLIOGRAPHY

Aalto, Erkki. 'Interpretations of Article 296', in Daniel Keohane (ed.), 'Towards a European Defence Market', *Chaillot Paper* no. 113, European Union Institute for Security Studies, Paris, November 2008.

---

99. Council Document 15987/08, Guidelines for identification and implementation of lessons and best practices in civilian ESDP missions, 19 November 2008.

Binnendijk, Hans and Kugler, Richard. 'Transforming European Forces', *Survival*, vol. 44, no. 3, 2002.

Biscop, Sven. 'Permanent Structured Cooperation and the future of ESDP', *Egmont Paper* no. 20, The Royal Institute for International Relations, Brussels, April 2008.

Comité des Prix de Revient des Fabrications d'Armement, 25ème rapport, Ministère de la Défense, Paris, April 2003.

Darnis, Jean-Pierre, Gasparini, Giovanni, Grams, Christoph, Keohane, Daniel, Liberti, Fabio, Maulny, Jean-Pierre and Stumbaum, May-Britt. 'Lessons learned from European defence equipment programmes,' *Occasional Paper* no. 69, EU Institute for Security Studies, Paris, October 2007.

European Commission, *From warning to action: Reportage on the EU's Instrument for Stability* (Luxembourg: Office for Official Publications of the European Communities, 2008).

European Defence Agency. 'An Initial Long-Term Vision for European Defence Capability and Capacity Needs', Brussels, 3 October 2006.

'European security and defence: Core documents 2004, vol. V', *Chaillot Paper* no. 75, EU Institute for Security Studies, Paris, February 2005, pp. 121-28.

Giegerich, Bastian and Nicoll, Alexander. 'European Military Capabilities', Strategic Dossier, International Institute for Strategic Studies, London, June 2008.

Gordon, Philip. 'Their own army?', *Foreign Affairs*, vol. 79, no. 4, July/August 2000.

Gourlay, Catriona. 'Community instruments for civilian crisis management', in Agnieszka Nowak, 'Civilian crisis management: the EU way', *Chaillot Paper* no. 90, EU Institute for Security Studies, Paris, June 2006.

Gourlay, Catriona. 'The emerging EU civilian crisis response capacity', in *Faster and more united? The debate about Europe's crisis reponse capacity* (Luxembourg: Office for the Official Publications of the European Communities, 2006).

Haine, Jean-Yves Haine (ed.) 'From Laeken to Copenhagen. European defence: Core documents, vol. III', *Chaillot Paper* no. 57, EU Institute for Security Studies, Paris, February 2003, pp. 145-46.

Hamilton, Douglas. 'European Rapid Reaction Force Unlikely by 2003' *Reuters*, 29 March 2000.

Hartley, Keith. 'The future of European defence policy: an economic perspective', *Defence and Peace Economics*, vol. 14, no. 2, January 2003, pp.107-15.

Lindstrom, Gustav. 'Enter the EU Battlegroups', *Chaillot Paper* no. 97, EU Institute for Security Studies, Paris, February 2007.

Missiroli, Antonio (ed.). 'From Copenhagen to Brussels: European Defence: Core documents, vol. IV', *Chaillot Paper* no. 67, EU Institute for Security Studies, Paris, December 2003, pp. 269-72.

Nowak, Agnieszka. 'Civilian crisis management within ESDP', in Agnieszka Nowak (ed.), 'Civilian crisis management: the EU way', *Chaillot Paper* no. 90, EU Institute for Security Studies, Paris, June 2006.

Posen, Barry. 'Europe cannot advance on two fronts', *Financial Times*, 24 April 2003.

Roger-Lacan, Véronique. 'Traité de Lisbonne et défense européenne', *Défense Nationale et Sécurité Collective*, vol. 64, no. 2, février 2008, pp. 55-62.

Rutten, Maartje (ed.). 'From Saint Malo to Nice. European Defence: core documents, vol. I', *Chaillot Paper* no. 47, EU Institute for Security Studies, Paris, May 2001, pp. 89-91.

Rutten, Maartje (ed.). 'From Nice to Laeken. European Defence: Core documents, vol. II', *Chaillot Paper* no. 51, EU Institute for Security Studies, Paris, April 2002, pp. 30-61.

Schake, Kori. 'Constructive duplication: Reducing EU reliance on US military assets', Working Paper, Centre for European Reform, London, January 2002.

Witney, Nick. 'Re-energising Europe's security and defence policy', Policy Paper, European Council on Foreign Relations, London, July 2008.

Wright, Richard and Auvinen, Juha. 'What ambitions for the civilian ESDP?', in Alvaro de Vasconcelos (ed.), *What ambitions for European Defence in 2020?*, EU Institute for Security Studies, Paris, July 2009, pp. 112-14.

3. ESDP partnerships

Introduction

From its inception in 1999, ESDP has worked with other international organisations. This chapter looks at the relationship between ESDP and four of those organisations: the United Nations (UN); the North Atlantic Treaty Organisation (NATO); the Organisation for Security and Cooperation in Europe (OSCE); and the African Union (AU). ESDP has interacted with other international and regional organisations – for instance with ASEAN for its monitoring mission in Aceh in Indonesia. But over the last decade ESDP has worked most closely with the UN, NATO, the OSCE and the AU.

ESDP has worked with all four of these organisations on the ground in crisis theatres, to greater and lesser degrees, and with different levels of effectiveness. Each partnership has also been as much political as operational, and each relationship has been different, both operationally and politically. But each partnership has contributed greatly to the development of ESDP over the last decade.

Richard Gowan's essay on ESDP and the UN, explains how the UN has provided both legitimacy and a framework for most ESDP operations – especially the more politically contentious military missions. Furthermore, EU-UN cooperation on the ground has benefited both institutions, most notably for their operations carried out on the African continent. EU-UN cooperation has also brought new political challenges for ESDP; not only for the permanent (and non-permanent) EU members of the UN Security Council, but also to convince non-EU governments on the UNSC, such as Russia and China, to endorse ESDP operations.

The complexity of the relationship between ESDP and NATO relations has been well documented over the last decade, but it is no less interesting for that, as explored in the second essay in this chapter by Daniel Keohane. At times ESDP has struggled to establish its identity and credibility vis-à-vis NATO, a transatlantic military alliance which is a long established and central actor in international security. But over time, despite some turbulent political moments like the Iraq war in 2003, ESDP has developed both its own identity separate from NATO, and a close working relationship with NATO in Afghanistan, Bosnia, and Kosovo. Furthermore, while the EU and NATO cooperate closely today, their relationship also has its limits, pointing to an increasing need for closer EU-US cooperation.

In his essay, Dov Lynch describes how the relationship between ESDP and the OSCE has been crucial in "other Europe", or non-EU Europe, especially (but not only) in the Western Balkans and the Caucasus. For example, ESDP has worked with the OSCE on the ground in Kosovo and Georgia. Moreover, the OSCE is the only forum where the key questions for European security are debated by all members of wider Europe, including Russia. ESDP-OSCE cooperation, therefore, is crucial for stability in the EU's neighbourhood, and for developing the legal and political architecture of European security.

Finally, cooperation between ESDP and the African Union (and other African organisations) is a relatively new and exciting development, as Damien Helly explains in his essay. Africa has become a key theatre for ESDP missions, and the numerous ESDP operations in Africa are described in this book. But EU-AU cooperation is not only about ESDP operations; it is also about building up African capacities to tackle crises on that continent. Plus, ESDP can only have a constructive relationship with the AU if it complements other EU initiatives in Africa.

In 1999, ESDP was mainly about how to encourage Europeans to work more closely together on their security and defence policies. But the world has changed greatly over the last decade, and Europeans recognise that they can no longer afford to concentrate on their own interactions and institutions alone. It is a sign of the progress of ESDP that, in 2009, constructive partnerships with other international organisations have become so central to its contribution to global security.

ESDP and the United Nations

Richard Gowan*

Cooperation with the United Nations has been essential to the evolution of the European Security and Defence Policy. Of the 23 ESDP missions launched between 2003 and 2009, 15 have been deployed in countries where the UN has a peacekeeping or peacebuilding mission. All EU missions in Africa have involved direct or indirect cooperation with the UN, ranging from military support (as in the Democratic Republic of Congo) to parallel efforts to sustain the African Union (AU) in Darfur. The EU naval operation off the coast of Somalia (*Atalanta*) has taken place in parallel with UN support to AU peacekeepers in Mogadishu, and protected UN aid shipments. But EU-UN cooperation has also taken on unexpectedly complex forms in Kosovo and Georgia.

This degree of cooperation seemed unlikely at the birth of ESDP, although the new policy was explicitly 'in accordance with the principles of the UN Charter.'[1] The EU's desire for a stronger defence identity was driven in part by the humiliation of European troops under UN command in Rwanda and the former Yugoslavia in the 1990s. In June 1999, when the Cologne Council approved ESDP, there were only 12,084 uniformed UN peacekeepers deployed worldwide – the lowest figure since the end of the Cold War.[2]

Yet that summer, the figures started to climb again as the Security Council mandated a new generation of UN missions, starting with Kosovo and East Timor. The numbers have kept climbing: by June 2009, there were over 90,000 troops and police under UN command. They are deployed from Haiti to Lebanon (the latter accounting for the majority of European troops still under UN command) although

* The author would like to thank Renata Dwan, Jean-Marie Guéhenno, Ahmed Salim, Benjamin C. Tortolani, Teresa Whitfield and the staff of the EUISS for their advice and comments on this chapter.

1. Presidency Conclusions, Cologne European Council (3 and 4 June, 1999), Annex III, point 1. See also point 26 of the Presidency Conclusions, Helsinki European Council (10 and 11 December, 1999), which confirmed 'the primary responsibility of the UN Security Council for the maintenance of international peace and security' while endorsing ESDP.
2. UN figures are taken from the UN website (www.un.org) and Center on International Cooperation, Annual Review of Global Peace Operations 2009 (Boulder, CO: Lynne Rienner, 2009), unless otherwise indicated.

the main driver of growth has been operations in Africa. European governments – especially France and Britain in the Security Council – have been instrumental in mandating and funding these missions.[3] UN operations in south-east Europe, the Middle East and Africa have helped stabilise the EU's outer periphery, making a direct contribution to European security.

In contrast to the rapid development of UN operations, ESDP's evolution has been cautious, but the two have been intimately connected. There have been four phases of the ESDP-UN relationship. The first (from 1999-2002) was one of *inaction*. When Britain deployed troops to aid the UN in Sierra Leone in 2000 it floated the idea of including other EU forces. None were forthcoming.[4] The next phase (2002-3) was *experimental*, as the two institutions attempted their first overlapping operations in Bosnia and the Democratic Republic of Congo (DRC). Operation *Artemis*, the EU's reinforcement of the UN Mission in the Congo (MONUC), stimulated interest in cooperation in New York and European capitals alike.[5]

This led to a phase of *institutional convergence*, lasting from 2003 to 2006, as UN officials and their European counterparts attempted to define their relationship. This involved both the creation of formal mechanisms for inter-institutional dialogue (described in the next section) and operational steps such as the dispatch of EU police and security sector reform missions to DRC to complement MONUC. It culminated in a UN request for an ESDP military mission to deploy to the DRC during elections in 2006.[6]

The EU's (rather hesitant) decision to fulfil this request foreshadowed the third and most active phase of EU-UN engagement, lasting from late 2006 to date. The focus has been less on institutional relations than *hybrid operations* (cases where UN and EU missions have deployed in a coordinated manner). The theatres involved have included not only the DRC but also Chad and Kosovo. The reality of coordinating on the ground – not least in insecure environments such as eastern Chad – has inevitably involved frictions. But it has confirmed that EU-UN cooperation is more than a well-intentioned paper exercise.

---

3. EU Member States pay 40% of the UN peacekeeping budget.

4. Michael Mandelbaum, *The Case for Goliath: How America Acts as the World's Government in the 21st Century* (New York: Public Affairs, 2005), p. 267, note 39.

5. See the chapter on Operation *Artemis* in Part Two of this book.

6. Please see descriptions of all ESDP operations in the Democratic Republic of Congo in Part Two of this book.

The EU-UN relationship has benefited ESDP and UN peacekeeping in three ways. Institutionally, the UN and EU Council secretariats have proved willing albeit sometimes constrained partners. Operationally, UN missions have provided a strategic framework for ESDP operations that would have little purpose in isolation, as in DRC and Chad, while ESDP operations have provided significant military support to UN missions at critical junctures in difficult theatres. Politically, linking ESDP to the UN has let the EU present its defence identity as part of a global collective security strategy.

But, as the final section of this chapter underlines, these benefits come with challenges. Institutional cooperation does not always translate into effective operations. The EU's commitment to the UN risks creating false expectations: in 2008, the European Council decided not to meet a request from UN Secretary-General Ban Ki-moon for an ESDP mission to reinforce UN troops in the DRC. And working through the UN framework can limit the EU's choices, as in the protracted search for a UN-EU handover in Kosovo.

Institutional convergence: progress and limits

The institutional developments of ESDP and UN peacekeeping over the last decade have shared roots. Just as ESDP was a reaction to the Balkan disasters, the UN under Kofi Annan responded to its record of failures by overhauling it headquarters systems. The Annan-era reforms – set out in the 2000 Brahimi Report – aimed to expand and professionalise the UN's peacekeeping bureaucracy.[7] Post-Brahimi, the Department of Peacekeeping Operations (DPKO) in New York expanded from around 400 to 600 staff.[8]

The consolidation of the UN's headquarters capacities and the development of the bureaucratic machinery for ESDP laid the groundwork for an institutionalisation of relations between the two. In 2003 – after the initial experiments in cooperation in Bosnia and the DRC – the Italian EU presidency concluded a brief UN-EU Joint Declaration on crisis management, followed by a more detailed agreement the next year.[9] The 2003 declaration established a Steering Committee of officials from the UN and EU Council secretariats to coordinate on issues such as planning and training.

---

7. The 'Brahimi Report', named after the chair of its panel of authors, is formally *The Report of the Panel on United Nations Peace Operations*, UN Document A/55/305-S/2000/809, August 2000.

8. On the report's implementation, see William J. Durch, Victoria K. Holt, Caroline R. Earle and Moira K. Shanahan, *The Brahimi Report and the Future of UN Peace Operations* (Washington, DC: Henry L. Stimson Center, 2003).

9. See Council of the European Union, 'Joint Declaration on UN-EU Cooperation in Crisis Management' (19 September 2003) and 'EU-UN Cooperation in Military Crisis Management Operations' (17-18 June 2004).

These initiatives were intended to show that the EU could play a coherent role at the UN in spite of splits over Iraq. They implied an unusually structured inter-organisational relationship, in which EU and UN officials as well as national diplomats could develop the terms of engagement. Early meetings of the Steering Committee were positive, with high-level participation from both sides. In 2005, the EU Council posted its first military liaison officer to New York. Member States pursued the battlegroup concept, proposed by Britain, France and Germany to facilitate rapid EU support to the UN.[10]

Yet if 2003 to 2005 were hopeful years for EU-UN cooperation, many potential complications were left unresolved. These came to the fore in 2006 over the UN's request for another ESDP mission in support of its mission in DRC (MONUC). This was initially transmitted from Jean-Marie Guéhenno, the UN Under-Secretary General for Peacekeeping, to the outgoing British EU presidency in the last week of 2005.[11] While Javier Solana soon became an advocate of the mission, the routing of the request indicated the limits of secretariat-to-secretariat links. In the ensuing months the EU Military Staff assessed the potential for a mission with only limited reference to DPKO.[12] When EUFOR RD Congo deployed, its success owed in part to the good rapport between the French force commander and his Senegalese counterpart in MONUC.

The experience of EUFOR RD Congo caused frustration in Germany, which provided the second-largest contingent for the mission. Officials in Berlin felt that the UN had pushed them into an unnecessary operation and that the structures put in place in 2003-4 gave EU Member States too little oversight of relations with the UN.[13] Germany took over the EU presidency in the first half of 2007 intent on negotiating a new agreement with the UN.

Although DPKO officials questioned whether this initiative would genuinely ease further cooperation, Germany finally extracted a new joint statement that foresaw 'regular senior-level political dialogue between the UN Secretariat and EU-Troika on broader aspects of crisis management' in addition to the Steering Committee's work.[14]

---

10. On the battlegroups, see Gustav Lindstrom, 'Enter the EU Battlegroups' , *Chaillot Paper* no. 97, EUISS, Paris, February 2007.

11. Helmut Fritsch, 'EUFOR RD CONGO: A Misunderstood Operation', Queen's Center for International Relations *Martello Papers* no. 33, Kingston, Ontario: QCIR, 2008, p.27.

12. Ibid., pp.28-30.

13. Communication with former senior UN official, 17 July 2009.

14. Council of the European Union, 'Joint Statement on EU-UN Cooperation in Crisis Management', Brussels, 7 June 2007.

This dialogue has never taken off, although UN officials frequently brief EU committees and *vice versa*.[15] The Steering Committee has also lost momentum, in spite of suggestions by DPKO to promote joint frameworks with the EU in areas like logistics. However, the EU Council's office in New York has played an increasingly active role in coordinating with DPKO. Its staff are often better-informed on operational issues than their counterparts in Member States' missions, strengthening the wider 'EU identity' at the UN. The French EU presidency organised a series of seminars on EU-UN cooperation in crisis management in 2008, including a ministerial event in New York.

This high-level emphasis on cooperation has not always translated into smooth contacts in the field. In the DRC, for example, the EU's security sector reform mission (EUSEC RD Congo) has had an uneasy relationship with MONUC, with each side questioning the other's methods.[16] This has contributed to a 'fragmentation of military reform' that suits the DRC's government, which views any meaningful reform with great suspicion.[17]

But these low-level differences have been secondary to a series of high-profile tests of EU-UN ties since 2007 that have magnified the tensions revealed over EUFOR RD Congo in 2006. These have tended to involve military missions, which inevitably receive greater political attention. The controversial cases are addressed in what follows: the parallel EU-UN missions in Chad in 2008-9; the obstacles to a UN-EU transition in Kosovo in 2008; and the crisis in the DRC in 2008 that saw UN hopes for an ESDP mission frustrated. These cases reveal operational, political and institutional problems in the EU-UN relationship that may recur if left unaddressed by the two organisations.

Chad: a joint operation?

In some ways, the Chad case exemplifies how far EU-UN relations have come since 2003. In earlier crises, as in the DRC, EU missions in support of the UN had come together in an ad hoc fashion. By contrast, UN Security Council Resolution 1778 of 25 September 2007 mandated a UN police mission (MINURCAT) and an EU Force (EUFOR Tchad/RCA) simultaneously, laying out their duties and coordination structures in some detail. This implied a shared strategic vision between the EU

---

15. This paragraph is based on interviews with EU and UN officials, May 2009.

16. Center on International Cooperation, *Annual Review of Global Peace Operations 2009* (Boulder, CO: Lynne Reinner, 2009), p. 53.

17. Eirin Mobekk, 'Security Sector Reform and the UN Mission in the Democratic Republic of Congo: Protecting Civilians in the East', *International Peacekeeping*, vol. 16, no. 2, 2009, p. 278.

and the UN, and the Resolution stipulated that EUFOR would last a year – opening the way for UN-commanded troops.

In reality the planning process was less harmonious. In the Security Council, France and Britain had pressed the UN to send both troops and police to Chad since 2006, but the UN had resisted, arguing that the conditions were not ripe for peacekeeping.[18] When Ban Ki-Moon finally laid out plans for a robust force in February 2007, the Chadian government rejected them.[19] France formally floated the idea of an ESDP mission in May, and remained central to planning the mission thereafter.[20] Many other EU members did not want to risk involvement: even after the Security Council passed Resolution 1778, it was uncertain that enough helicopters could be found for EUFOR Tchad/RCA.

The net result was that EUFOR only deployed in March 2008, over a year after Ban had reluctantly proposed a UN force. But if the EU was slow to deploy, MINURCAT also struggled to get its personnel in place. In September 2008, one year after being mandated, it had recruited just 48 of a projected civilian staff of 542.[21] EUFOR tried to compensate for the UN's slow deployment by using military patrols in a policing deterrent role. EU-UN cooperation improved as the UN prepared to take over military duties in March 2009. Many EU contributors were keen to withdraw their forces after twelve months, but the UN found it hard to identify sufficient non-European forces to take over. European governments including Ireland, France and Poland agreed to 're-hat' their troops, averting a failed handover. The final transfer to the UN was smooth.

Nonetheless, the Chad experience highlights many of the operational limitations of the EU-UN relationship. While the Steering Committee allows for secretariat-level links, individual countries (France, in the case of Chad and elsewhere) set the agenda for missions. Planning cooperation tends to weaken in the face of political obstacles to deployments. The linkage between decision-making in the Security Council and the EU's General Affairs and External Relations Council (GAERC) is uncertain. These problems are striking because, politically, the EU's lead role in Chad was accepted by other governments at the UN, even if the UN Secretariat remained uneasy

18. See 'Report of the Secretary-General on Chad and the Central African Republic', UN Document S/2006/1019, 19 December 2006, especially paragraphs 83-85.

19. See 'Report of the Secretary-General on Chad and the Central African Republic', UN Document S/2007/97, 23 February 2007.

20. Alexander Mattelaer, 'The Strategic Planning of EU Military Operations – The Case of EUFOR Tchad/RCA ', *IES Working Paper* no. 5, Institute for European Studies, Vrije Universiteit Brussel, 2008, p.14.

21. Rahul Chandran, Jake Sherman and Bruce D. Jones, 'Rapid Deployment of Civilians for Peace Operations: Status, Gaps and Options', Center on International Cooperation, New York University, April 2009, p. 2.

about the UN operating there. France drove the agenda in the Security Council with British support – Russia offered helicopters to the ESDP mission. EU-UN cooperation is harder still where, as over Kosovo, there is no such consensus.

Kosovo: political limits to cooperation

If the EU and UN stumbled in Chad, they did so largely out of the public eye. Their difficulties in Kosovo gained much publicity in 2008.[22] Kosovo was meant to be an advertisement for good EU-UN relations. In 2006, as talks on the province's future got underway, the EU Council took the unprecedented step of setting up a full-time planning team in Pristina to prepare an ESDP mission. The general terms for the mission – to oversee policing and the rule of law – had already been set, but interactions with the UN Mission in Kosovo (UNMIK) shaped the concept. The EU had intended to deploy a light police presence, but UN officials persuaded the planners to propose a larger force.[23]

As of late 2007, EU and UN officials were generally happy with this field-based co-operation. UNMIK's leadership publicly emphasised the 'countdown to the EU.' But the lack of a political settlement, and Russia's ability to veto any alteration of Kosovo's status in the Security Council, meant that the two organisations were on weak ground.

Kosovo's unilateral declaration of independence in February 2008 revealed this weakness. UN officials were torn between the need not to alienate Russia – which sided with Serbia in declaring the declaration invalid – and their recognition that Kosovo's leaders and populace would not tolerate UNMIK indefinitely. The EU was split between those (in particular the UK) that wanted a full ESDP deployment as fast as possible and others (such as Spain) that were wary of any action without explicit UN approval.

These political tensions exacerbated practical problems over the transfer of UN assets to the EU – arising from simple differences over how to account for items like computers and vehicles – and souring personal relations between many international staff. UNMIK's leadership remained committed to a transfer, but mid-level officials (their jobs on the line) argued that the EU was ill-prepared to take on Kosovo. Some technical difficulties had to be resolved at the level of Ban Ki-Moon and Javier Solana.

---

22. See the chapter on EULEX Kosovo in Part Two of this book.

23. Interview by Benjamin C. Tortolani of the Center on International Cooperation with EU Planning Team, Pristina, 4 October 2007.

These tensions did not prevent a compromise on Kosovo's future that has allowed the EU to deploy while UNMIK has shrunk to a political mission that retains (if only in theory) formal authority over the territory. This reflected both pressure by the EU on Serbia and efforts by DPKO to create political space for a compromise through talks with Belgrade on a six-point plan including issues like justice and transport. By late 2008, most EU officials in Kosovo were complimentary about their UN counterparts, and *vice versa*.[24]

But the Kosovo case does point to a potentially recurring flaw in the EU-UN relationship. Although EU Member States are in a strong position on the Security Council (typically holding four or five of the fifteen seats), China and Russia have grown increasingly willing to block European initiatives at the UN in recent years.[25] If the EU wants to deploy an ESDP mission with a UN mandate or alongside a UN presence, it may have to compromise on the terms of its deployment – or risk rejection in the Security Council.

This dilemma was highlighted in 2008 not only in Kosovo but also in Georgia, where the EU chose to both support a long-standing UN monitoring mission after the August war and to deploy its own monitors without a UN mandate. This dual policy reflected the fact that the UN mission (limited to the secessionist province of Abkhazia) was subject to Russian approval in the Security Council. While Russia finally vetoed its continuation in June 2009, the EU was able to keep its monitors in place – a reminder that *not* working through the UN framework may sometimes be essential to an ESDP mission's credibility.

The DRC: false expectations?

Whatever the failings of EU-UN cooperation over Chad and Kosovo in 2008, the greatest setback came over the DRC. In the autumn of 2008, rebels in the east of the country defeated a government offensive supported logistically by the UN and counter-attacked, displacing 250,000 people and leaving MONUC largely unable to react. The crisis bore obvious similarities to that leading to Operation *Artemis* in 2003, and many influential figures in both Europe and the DRC called for another ESDP mission.[26]

---

24. Interviews with EU and UN officials, Kosovo, 1-3 August 2009.

25. See Richard Gowan and Franziska Brantner, *A Global Force for Human Rights? An Audit of European Power at the UN* (London: European Council on Foreign Relations, 2008), especially pp. 47-53.

26. See Richard Gowan, 'Good Intentions, Bad Outcomes,' *E!Sharp*, January/February 2009, pp.57-59.

France liaised with DPKO on a possible operation to open a humanitarian corridor in eastern DRC and a number of EU Member States (including Belgium, Finland, Ireland, the Netherlands and Sweden) lobbied for an ESDP mission.[27] But Britain and Germany opposed any operation. Britain, concerned that it might be required to deploy its battle group to DRC while struggling to sustain operations in Afghanistan, argued for an expansion of MONUC instead.[28] EU officials complained that they received mixed signals from their UN counterparts on the necessity and desirability of an ESDP deployment.[29] In December, Ban Ki-moon sent a formal request to the European Council arguing for a 'necessary', 'essential' and 'critical' ESDP operation in aid of MONUC.[30] But the European Council could not reach any agreement on this proposal.[31]

Whatever the merits of Ban's proposal, this episode provides three lessons about EU-UN cooperation. The first is that, in spite of progress towards a structured relationship between the two organisations since 2003, crisis decisions remain unpredictable and are driven by Member States. The second is that, receiving mixed signals from the EU, the UN Secretariat can develop false expectations of European support (a concern expressed by EU officials immediately prior to the Congo crisis).[32] The third is that – because of these limitations – the quality of EU-UN relations cannot only be measured in terms of institutionalisation. It is defined first and foremost by the quality of operational interactions.

Conclusion

This final observation points to an overarching trend in EU-UN cooperation – one that signals the maturation of ESDP. The shift from a phase of institutional cooperation to one of frequent if imperfect operational interaction between the EU and UN underlines that ESDP has moved from a 'paper policy' to concrete engagement in global security. The UN has been an important part of the framework for this transformation – without its large-scale presence in Africa, most small-scale ESDP missions there would be futile.

---

27. Communication between a UN official and the Center on International Cooperation, 26 February 2006; Helen Warrell and Harvey Morris, 'EU Sidesteps Urgent Appeal for Congo Force', *Financial Times*, 8 December 2008.

28. Julian Borger, 'Brown All Talk and No Action on Congo, Say Critics', *The Guardian*, 12 December 2008.

29. Discussion with EU official, 30 June 2009.

30. Toby Vogel, 'Why Europe is Split over Troops for Congo', *European Voice*, 11 December 2008. See: www.europeanvoice.com.

31. Warrell and Morris, op. cit. in note 27; Anand Menon, 'Empowering Paradise? ESDP at Ten', *International Affairs*, vol.85, no. 2, March 2009, p. 232.

32. Comments by senior EU official to the International Forum for the Challenges of Peace Operations, Paris, 20-22 October 2008.

The speed of change in EU-UN cooperation has revealed significant flaws. Operationally and politically, the EU needs to clarify the scale and limits of its support to the UN – and the UN needs to be realistic in what it asks for. Both institutions need to iron out the technical glitches that have complicated their previous interactions. Nonetheless, their unexpectedly complex relationship remains essential to sustaining security on Europe's periphery – and ESDP's developing reach and credibility.

BIBLIOGRAPHY

Bah, A. Sarjoh and Jones, Bruce D. 'Peace Operations Partnerships' in Center on International Cooperation, *Annual Review of Global Peace Operations 2008* (Boulder, CO: Lynne Rienner, 2008)

Gowan, Richard. 'The European Security Strategy's Global Objective: Effective Multilateralism', in Sven Biscop and Jan Joel Andersson (eds.), *The EU and the European Security Strategy: Forging a Global Europe* (New York: Routledge, 2008)

International Peacekeeping, vol. 16, no. 2, 2009 contains a section on the EU and the UN in the DRC (pp. 215-286) that also covers other cooperation in Africa.

Koops, Joachim A. 'Military Crisis Management – The Challenge of Effective Inter-Organizationalism', *Studia Diplomatica*, vol. 62, no. 3, forthcoming, 2009.

Major, Claudia. 'EU-UN Cooperation in Military Crisis Management: The Experience of EUFOR RD Congo in 2006' , *Occasional Paper* no. 72, EUISS, Paris, 2008.

Novosseloff, Alexandra. 'EU-UN Partnership in Crisis Management: Development and Prospects', International Peace Academy, June 2004.

Ojanen, Hanna (ed.) 'Peacekeeping-Peacebuilding: Preparing for the Future', Finnish Institute of International Affairs *Report* no. 14, September 2006.

Ortega, Martin (ed.) 'The European Union and the United Nations: Partners in Effective Multilateralism', *Chaillot Paper* no. 78, June 2005.

Tardy, Thierry. 'Limits and Opportunities of UN-EU Relations in Peace Operations: Implications for DPKO', UN Peacekeeping Best Practices Unit, New York, September 2003.

Tardy, Thierry. 'UN-EU Relations in Crisis Management. Taking Stock and Looking Ahead', International Forum for the Challenges of Peace Operations, October 2008.

ESDP and NATO

Daniel Keohane

In many ways the development of ESDP over the last decade has been defined by its relationship with NATO. It is stating the obvious to say that the EU-NATO relationship matters because of the strategic importance of the transatlantic relationship, not least because NATO remains the guarantor of European security for its Member States. This has made the EU's relationship with NATO a much more strategic and political challenge than the EU's interaction with other international organisations, such as the UN or the OSCE.

Over the last ten years, some observers have wondered if the development of ESDP might mean that NATO would eventually become irrelevant, if US and European strategic interests diverged?[1] So far, this has not been the case. NATO is still relevant, while ESDP has developed in its own direction over the last decade. ESDP defines itself as a broad and comprehensive international security policy, with access to both civil and military instruments. In other words, ESDP is potentially meant to do everything but collective defence – the *raison d'être* of NATO. Aside from the politics, this difference in approach to international security policy is one key reason why the EU-NATO relationship has been so interesting over the last decade.

Essentially there have been three phases in EU-NATO relations. The initial years, 1999-2003, were dominated by trying to find clear and compatible working methods between the two organisations. The middle period, 2003-2007, was marked by turbulence. This was mainly due to the splits in both the EU and NATO over the US invasion of Iraq, the aftershocks of which affected EU-NATO relations for many years. The current period, roughly from 2007 onwards, has been marked by a much more constructive approach on both sides, even if some difficulties have persisted.

1999-2003: getting to know each other

EU governments formally agreed to create the ESDP in June 1999 only weeks after the end of NATO's 78-day bombing campaign in Kosovo. Naturally, the lessons

---

1. For an analysis of that debate see Jolyon Howorth, *Security and Defence Policy in the European Union* (Basingstoke, Hampshire: Palgrave Macmillan, 2007).

from that war set a context for how ESDP would develop in its initial years. In particular, two issues stood out between 1999 and 2003. First, how to develop a close working relationship between the EU and NATO, in particular granting the EU access to NATO military assets. Second, based mainly on the experience of the Kosovo war and the apparent lack of useful military capabilities in Europe, how to ensure compatibility between EU and NATO capability plans.

These issues were not entirely new. The predecessor of ESDP, the Western European Union (WEU), had also tried to develop a working relationship with NATO. In 1996 negotiations started in Berlin on a WEU-NATO agreement, to give the WEU access to NATO military assets for WEU operations – these negotiations paved the way to arrangements that would subsequently be named the 'Berlin Plus' agreements. With the birth of ESDP at the EU Cologne summit in 1999, it was only a matter of time before the EU would replace the WEU as the negotiator with NATO on the Berlin Plus arrangements, and in January 2001 the EU and NATO initiated direct talks on Berlin Plus. In May 2001, the first formal meeting of EU-NATO foreign ministers took place in Budapest.

The difference from 1999 onwards was that the EU was not a military alliance like the WEU (or NATO), but a political Union which brought much more broad diplomatic, political and economic weight to the table. For example, at that time, the Union was about to launch its own currency (the euro), and was starting to plan to increase its membership from 15 to 25 Member States. At the same time, NATO, for its part, had conducted two successful interventions in the Balkans (in Bosnia and Kosovo), and had just taken in three new members from former Communist countries (Czech Republic, Hungary and Poland).

The key in the early years of the EU-NATO relationship was the US attitude to ESDP. The then US Secretary of State, Madeleine Albright, set the tone of American attitudes to ESDP, with her '3 Ds' statement, which outlined that the US welcomed an EU defence policy as long as it met three conditions: no de-coupling of the US from Europe; no discrimination against non-EU NATO members (such as Turkey); and no duplication of NATO assets (such as military planning headquarters).[2] From 2001 onwards, the Bush administration initially maintained essentially the same stance on ESDP as the Clinton administration. At that time, many Americans saw ESDP primarily as a defence (meaning military) project, not the broader security

---

2. Madeline K. Albright, 'The right balance will secure NATO's future', *Financial Times*, 7 December 1998.

and defence policy into which it would evolve.[3]

Between 1999 and 2003 both the Clinton and Bush administrations were especially concerned about how ESDP would affect European planning for military capabilities. The 1999 Kosovo war had exposed huge equipment gaps between US armed forces and European armies, one reason why the US initially spurned most European offers of military help for its operation in Afghanistan immediately after the terrorist attacks of 11 September 2001. Furthermore, the massive hikes in US defence spending – especially on new technologies – after 2001, exacerbated American concerns about the growing transatlantic military capability gap.[4]

Some US officials and academics feared that ESDP would be more about demonstrating deeper European integration than developing useful military capabilities, which NATO would also need if it was to remain a relevant alliance in US planning.[5] For example, the Helsinki Headline Goals agreed by EU governments in December 1999, did not exactly match the higher end equipment goals that NATO had agreed in April 1999 (known as the Defence Capabilities Initiative). Some Americans questioned whether EU commitments would mean that Europeans would spend their much lower defence budgets on lower-end peacekeeping priorities rather than try to keep up with US capability plans.[6]

Aside from capabilities, the other major issue was the so-called 'Berlin Plus' debate, namely how the principle of EU access to NATO military assets (including planning headquarters) would work in practice. After a year of negotiations, in December 2000, all NATO members, except Turkey, were willing to sign up to an EU-NATO agreement on EU access to NATO planning facilities and capabilities. Turkey wished to have the right to block autonomous EU operations in an area of strategic importance to Turkey. Ankara eventually backed down in return for assurances that the EU would not undertake a military operation against a non-EU NATO member (such as Turkey), and arrangements whereby the EU would consult Turkey in any crisis.

Turkey was willing to accept this deal in December 2001, but Greece then rejected it as too great a concession to Turkey. Negotiations were held up until late 2002, when

---

3. Robert E. Hunter, *The European Security and Defense Policy: NATO's Companion or Competitor?* (Santa Monica, CA: RAND 2002).

4. Hans Binnendijk and Richard Kugler, 'Transforming European Forces', *Survival*, vol. 44, no. 3, 2002.

5. Philip Gordon, 'Their own army?', *Foreign Affairs*, vol 79, no. 4, July/August 2000.

6. Kori Schake, 'Constructive duplication: Reducing EU reliance on US military assets', Working Paper, Centre for European Reform, London, January 2002.

Greek fears were assuaged.[7] At their summit in Prague in November 2002, NATO members declared their readiness to give the EU access to NATO assets and capabilities for operations in which NATO was not engaged militarily. This was followed by the EU-NATO declaration on ESDP in December 2002.[8]

2003-2007: The turbulent years

After the EU-NATO declaration on ESDP in December 2002, on 17 March 2003 the EU and NATO announced they had signed a 'framework for cooperation' which included an agreement on the Berlin Plus arrangements, most of which remains classified.[9] This quickly led to the EU initiating its first peacekeeping operation using the Berlin Plus mechanism in the Former Yugoslav Republic of Macedonia (FYROM), replacing the NATO operation in that country. All in all EU-NATO co-operation seemed to work very smoothly for the FYROM operation.[10] However, the constructive spirit that could have arisen from that experience had already been shattered by splits between EU Member States over the US invasion of Iraq, which began only three days after the EU-NATO framework was signed.

As a result, at the end of April 2003, four EU governments which had opposed the US-led invasion of Iraq – Belgium, France, Germany and Luxembourg – proposed that the EU should create its own operations planning staff in the Brussels suburb of Tervuren. Regardless of the technical pros and cons of the Tervuren proposal, the US and those EU governments which supported the Iraq war – such as Britain, Italy, Poland and Spain – saw it as a direct attempt to undermine NATO.

The Bush administration's attitude to ESDP further soured when EU governments sent an autonomous peacekeeping force to Bunia in the Democratic Republic of Congo in June 2003.[11] The Bush administration had assumed that NATO had the 'right of first refusal' on all potential EU peacekeeping missions, and was surprised when EU governments dispatched soldiers to the DRC without discussing their plans at NATO first. The Bush administration was also surprised that the draft EU

---

7. Fraser Cameron, 'The EU and International Organisations: Partners in Crisis Management', *EPC Issue Paper* no. 41, Brussels, 22 October 2005.

8. European Union – NATO declaration on ESDP, Brussels, December 16 2002 in Jean-Yves Haine (ed.), 'From Laeken to Copenhagen – European Defence: Core Documents Vol. III', *Chaillot Paper* no. 57, European Union Institute for Security Studies, Paris, February 2003, pp. 178-79.

9. Statement by NATO's Secretary General – Berlin-Plus, Brussels, 17 March 2003 in Antonio Missiroli (ed.), 'From Copenhagen to Brussels – European Defence: Core Documents, vol. IV', *Chaillot Paper* no. 67, European Union Institute for Security Studies, Paris, December 2003, pp.48-49.

10. See the chapter on Operation *Concordia* in Part Two of this book.

11. See the chapter on Operation *Artemis* in Part Two of this book.

constitutional treaty, which was presented in July 2003, included a mutual assistance clause, which implied the potential for the EU to become a collective defence organisation to rival NATO. [12]

In September 2003, the German Chancellor, Gerhard Schroeder, the French President, Jacques Chirac and the British Prime Minister, Tony Blair, met in Berlin to sketch out a new compromise on ESDP and its relationship with NATO. The deal was finalised in November 2003 and contained three elements. First, the EU would have a small unit of operational planners in the EU military staff to help with autonomous EU military operations (which are normally managed by national headquarters). Second, the EU would set up a small cell of operational planners at SHAPE, NATO's operational headquarters, to ensure that operations run through the Berlin Plus mechanism worked smoothly. Third, some of the articles dealing with defence policy in the draft constitutional treaty were amended. In particular, the so-called mutual assistance clause was watered down with new wording which clarified that the EU would not become a military alliance, and that NATO remained the foundation for collective defence in Europe and the forum for its implementation.

The Franco-British-German deal was endorsed by EU governments at their December 2003 summit. This in turn paved the way for NATO to agree at its summit in Istanbul in June 2004 that it would withdraw its peacekeeping force in Bosnia by the end of the same year, and it would be replaced by an EU force managed through the Berlin Plus mechanism.[13] However, even though the US was happy to withdraw its forces from Bosnia, given operational pressures in Iraq and Afghanistan, the political wounds opened up by the split over the Iraq war had not yet fully healed.

Between 2003 and 2007 many in the US remained suspicious that those EU Member States which had opposed the Iraq war, such as Belgium and France, wished to develop ESDP to undermine NATO. During discussions in 2005 on how the African Union (AU) could be helped with the problem of Darfur, there was something of a 'beauty contest' between those who argued that the EU or NATO should take the lead and the other should stay out (in the end both organisations decided to help the AU).[14] Some in the US also suggested that the 2006 EU peacekeeping operation in Congo should be run with NATO's help, rather than autonomously (as was the

---

12. Charles Grant, 'EU defence takes a step forward', Briefing Note, Centre for European Reform, London, December 2003.

13. See the chapter on EUFOR *Althea* in Part Two of this book.

14. Leo Michel, 'NATO and the European Union: Improving Practical Cooperation', Institute for National Strategic Studies, National Defense University, 2006.

case), and generally questioned the legitimacy of autonomous ESDP military operations.[15]

For their part, between 2003 and 2007 some Europeans worried that close EU-NATO cooperation could lead to the US gaining excessive influence over EU foreign and defence policy. They argued that the US might use NATO missions as a means for getting European troops to serve American strategic interests, which was also why Washington disliked autonomous ESDP military operations. They pointed to the example of Afghanistan – during 2006 the Taliban-led insurgency against NATO forces in Afghanistan revived and consolidated. Some Europeans felt that although their governments were providing a large number of the NATO peacekeepers, they apparently had very little influence over US policy in the country during this period.[16]

The enlargement of the EU in 2004 from 15 to 25 Member States further complicated the politics of EU-NATO relations. According to the December 2002 EU-NATO agreement, EU governments that are not members of NATO must be members of NATO's Partnership-for-Peace (PfP) to attend EU-NATO meetings. That arrangement worked well at first. It allowed the then four EU neutrals (Austria, Finland, Ireland and Sweden) to sit in on EU-NATO meetings since they are members of NATO's PfP. At that time the EU and NATO ambassadors were able to discuss a wide range of subjects, such as Afghanistan, Moldova and nuclear weapons proliferation.

However, all that changed after the enlargement of the EU (from 15 to 25 Member States) and NATO (from 19 to 26) in 2004. Two of the new EU members – Cyprus and Malta – are neutral but were not in the PfP (Malta joined the Pfp in April 2008). Turkey, annoyed that the Cypriots rejected a UN peace plan in a referendum in April 2004 referendum, started blocking Cypriot (and Maltese) participation in EU-NATO meetings. The Cypriots argued that they should be treated the same as other EU members, with the right to sit in EU-NATO meetings.

This meant that from 2004 onwards meetings between the EU and NATO ambassadors could take place with only 23 EU ambassadors. And they were only allowed to talk about joint operations (such as in Bosnia) and military capabilities. This was partly because some EU countries – like Belgium, France and Greece – understand-

---

15. Fran Burwell et al, 'Transatlantic Transformation: Building a NATO-EU Security Architecture', Policy Paper, Atlantic Council of the United States, March 2006.

16. Judy Dempsey, 'Mission impossible for NATO?', *Financial Times*, 24 June 2004; William Pfaff, 'A growing rift', *International Herald Tribune*, 1 November 2008.

ably said that the EU ambassadors should not discuss other issues, such as terrorism, the proliferation of weapons-of-mass-destruction or Afghanistan with only 23 EU representatives, since these issues should be dealt with among all the then 25 EU governments. The formal block in the EU-NATO relationship meant that useful discussions between the two organisations had to take place outside formal meetings. In September 2005 the EU and NATO foreign ministers held their first informal dinner, a practice which has continued since.[17]

Despite the extremely difficult political context between 2003 and 2007, informal political contact – along with pragmatism on the ground – did help to slowly develop EU-NATO cooperation in countries where both organisations were operating. The two organisations worked well in Bosnia, with NATO supporting the EU peacekeeping mission there, although less well in Africa. In 2005, the African Union asked both the EU and NATO to give logistical support to their peacekeeping mission in Darfur. Both the EU and NATO decided to use separate airlift commands in Europe, but EU and NATO personnel at the AU headquarters in Addis Ababa did try to coordinate their efforts.[18] In Afghanistan, during 2005 and 2006 the value of greater civil contributions from the EU, including a potential role for ESDP, was becoming increasingly apparent in the US and at NATO.[19] At their November 2006 summit in Riga, NATO governments asked for more help from other international organisations in Afghanistan.[20] During 2006, the European Commission had started funding some of the non-military activities (such as judges, aid workers and administrators) of the NATO provincial reconstruction teams, and in 2007 the EU deployed an ESDP police mission to Afghanistan.[21]

2007-2009: a new tone in transatlantic relations

The departures of Gerhard Schröder (in 2005), Tony Blair and Jacques Chirac (both in 2007) from their respective positions, changed the political context of EU-NATO relations. The new leaders in Britain, France and Germany – Gordon Brown, Nicolas Sarkozy and Angela Merkel – did not carry the same divisive baggage from the Iraq war and each has been perceived in Washington as constructive on transatlantic

---

17. David S. Yost, 'NATO and International Organisations', *Forum Paper* 3, NATO Defense College, Rome, September 2007.

18. Paul Cornish, 'EU and NATO: Co-operation or competition?', *Briefing Paper*, Policy department of external policies, European Parliament, October 2006; Leo Michel, 'NATO-EU cooperation in operations', NATO Defense College, *Research Paper* no. 31, February 2007.

19. James Dobbins, 'NATO peacekeepers need a partner', *International Herald Tribune*, 30 September 2005.

20. NATO, Riga Summit Declaration, 29 November 2006.

21. See the chapter on EUPOL Afghanistan in Part Two of this book.

relations. The May 2007 election of Nicolas Sarkozy in particular, was probably the most significant development. This is because President Sarkozy introduced a new transatlantic policy which has since helped transform the tone of the EU-NATO relationship.

President Sarkozy has argued that France (and Europe) cannot achieve much in the world without good relations with the United States. He announced that France would consider re-joining NATO's integrated military command, reversing more than 40 years of French resistance to American hegemony in NATO. In a speech to French Ambassadors in August 2007, he said he was 'convinced that it is in the vested interest of the United States for the European Union to assemble its forces, streamline its capabilities and independently organize its defence.'[22] In an interview with *The New York Times* in September 2007, he explained that in return for re-joining NATO's military command he wanted American acceptance of an independent EU defence policy.[23] To prove his intent, President Sarkozy deployed 700 more French soldiers to the NATO mission in Afghanistan during 2008.

The change in French attitudes towards NATO was soon matched by a change in US views of EU defence. The Bush administration had sometimes been hesitant about a military role for the EU, for fear that it would undermine NATO. But overtime, and mainly due to Sarkozy's overhaul of French NATO policy, it accepted that an effective EU defence policy was in the US interest. Victoria Nuland, the US ambassador to NATO, told an audience in Paris in February 2008 that the Bush administration supported a strong EU defence policy: 'we agree with France – Europe needs, the United States needs, NATO needs, the democratic world needs – a stronger, more capable European defense capacity.'[24] Since his 2008 election in the US, President Obama has continued with a constructive attitude towards ESDP, and France rejoined the NATO military command at the Strasbourg-Kehl NATO summit in April 2009. EU (and NATO) leaders understand that stronger cooperation between NATO and the EU would greatly help the Obama administration and Europeans work together more effectively in places such as Afghanistan and on key relationships such as with Russia.

22. Speech of M. Nicolas Sarkozy, President of the French Republic, at the French Ambassadors' Conference, Élysée Palace, Paris, 27 August 2007.

23. Elaine Sciolino and Alison Smale, 'Sarkozy, a Frenchman in a hurry, maps his path', *The New York Times*, 24 September 2007.

24. Ambassador Victoria Nuland, Speech to Press Club and American Chamber of Commerce, Paris, 22 February, 2008.

However, even though Franco-American tensions over the roles of the EU and NATO have rescinded, it is not yet clear how ESDP *per se* has benefited from the transatlantic *rapprochement* since 2007. There was some expectation during the French presidency in the second half of 2008, that France's *rapprochement* with the US and NATO would produce some concomitant progress on ESDP, in particular the idea of creating an EU operational planning headquarters – which France and others had long argued for.[25] However, although new capability plans were agreed by the 27 EU governments in December 2008, the UK government opposed the development of an outright EU operational headquarters for autonomous EU missions, arguing that existing national headquarters are perfectly adequate for the job (the EU can also use NATO headquarters for Berlin Plus operations). Instead EU governments agreed to set up a new civil-military strategic planning staff (at the time of writing in autumn 2009, this had yet to be created).[26]

Furthermore, it will be difficult to improve formal EU-NATO cooperation until a long-running dispute between Turkey and Cyprus is resolved. For example, that dispute means that NATO soldiers and EU police operating in Afghanistan or Kosovo cannot sign formal agreements covering practical measures such as sharing information and security guarantees. Therefore, despite the more constructive tone on both sides in Brussels, EU-NATO cooperation on the ground is not as effective as it could be. The same has so far held true for EU and NATO efforts on improving military capabilities, which could be better coordinated and reinforced.[27]

Conclusion

Looking to the future of transatlantic relations, for many Europeans (and some Americans), that will not only mean the EU and NATO working better together, it also means making EU-US cooperation more effective.[28] The US already works closely with the EU (rather than through NATO) on a whole host of issues. Some are well known, such as trade and climate change. But this cooperation now also includes key issues of foreign and security policy, like Iran's nuclear programme and counter-terrorism. Plus, there is growing interest in the US in how ESDP can

25. Tomas Valasek, 'France, NATO and European defence', Policy Brief, Centre for European Reform, London, May 2008.

26. Nick Witney, 'European Defence - now with added élan?', European Council on Foreign Relations, 19 December 2008.

27. Bastian Giegerich and Alexander Nicoll, 'European Military Capabilities', Strategic Dossier, International Institute for Strategic Studies, June 2008. Dan Hamilton *et al*, 'Alliance reborn: An Atlantic compact for the 21ˢᵗ century', Washington NATO Project, February 2009.

28. Jolyon Howorth, 'A new institutional architecture for the transatlantic relationship?', *Europe Visions* no. 5, Institut français des relations internationales (IFRI), June 2009.

contribute to international security, especially through its civil operations, rather than simply judging ESDP based on its relationship with NATO, as was the case in the past. For example, the US has contributed around 80 police and judges to the current ESDP operation in Kosovo (EULEX).[29] There is huge potential for the EU and the US to develop a broad strategic relationship covering many issues (both security and non-security, which sometimes overlap), which would further complement and reinforce EU-NATO cooperation.

BIBLIOGRAPHY

Albright, Madeline K. 'The right balance will secure NATO's future', *Financial Times,* 7 December 1998.

Binnendijk, Hans and Kugler, Richard. 'Transforming European Forces', *Survival*, vol. 44, no. 3, 2002.

Burwell, Fran et al, 'Transatlantic Transformation: Building a NATO-EU Security Architecture', Policy Paper, Atlantic Council of the United States, March 2006.

Cameron, Fraser. 'The EU and International Organisations: Partners in Crisis Management', *EPC Issue Paper* no. 41, Brussels, 22 October 2005.

Cornish, Paul. 'EU and NATO: Co-operation or competition?', Policy department of external policies, European Parliament, October 2006.

Dempsey, Judy. 'Mission impossible for NATO?', *Financial Times*, 24 June 2004

Dobbins, James, 'NATO peacekeepers need a partner', *International Herald Tribune*, 30 September 2005.

Giegerich, Bastian and Nicoll, Alexander. 'European Military Capabilities', Strategic Dossier, International Institute for Strategic Studies, June 2008.

Gordon, Philip. 'Their own army?', *Foreign Affairs*, vol 79, no. 4, July/August 2000.

---

29. See the chapter on EULEX Kosovo in Part Two of this book.

Grant, Charles. 'EU defence takes a step forward', Centre for European Reform Briefing Note, London, December 2003.

Haine, Jean-Yves (ed.) 'From Laeken to Copenhagen – European Defence: Core Documents Vol. III', *Chaillot Paper* no. 57, European Union Institute for Security Studies, Paris, February 2003.

Hamilton, Daniel et al, 'Alliance reborn: An Atlantic compact for the 21st century', Washington NATO Project, February 2009.

Howorth, Jolyon. *Security and Defence Policy in the European Union* (Basingstoke, Hampshire: Palgrave Macmillan, 2007).

Howorth, Jolyon. 'A new institutional architecture for the transatlantic relationship?', *Europe Visions* no. 5, Institut français des relations internationales (IFRI), June 2009.

Hunter, Robert E. *The European Security and Defense Policy: NATO's Companion or Competitor?* (Santa Monica, CA: RAND 2002).

Michel, Leo. 'NATO and the European Union: Improving Practical Cooperation', Institute for National Strategic Studies, National Defense University, 2006.

Michel, Leo. 'NATO-EU cooperation in operations', NATO Defense College, *Research Paper* no. 31, February 2007.

Missiroli, Antonio (ed.) 'From Copenhagen to Brussels – European Defence: Core Documents, vol. IV', *Chaillot Paper* no. 67, European Union Institute for Security Studies, Paris, December 2003.

Pfaff, William. 'A growing rift', *International Herald Tribune*, 1 November 2008

Schake, Kori. 'Constructive duplication: Reducing EU reliance on US military assets', Working Paper, Centre for European Reform, London, January 2002.

Sciolino, Elaine and Smale, Alison. 'Sarkozy, a Frenchman in a hurry, maps his path', *The New York Times*, 24 September 2007.

Valasek, Tomas. 'France, NATO and European defence', Policy Brief, Centre for European Reform, London, May 2008.

Witney, Nick. 'European Defence - now with added élan?', European Council on Foreign Relations, 19 December 2008.

Yost, David S. 'NATO and International Organisations', *Forum Paper* 3, NATO Defense College, Rome, September 2007.

ESDP and the OSCE

Dov Lynch*

The OSCE, and its predecessor the Conference on Security and Cooperation in Europe (CSCE), have always been testing grounds for EU foreign policy. The first European Political Cooperation (EPC) meeting of Foreign Ministers in November 1970 decided to handle the preparations for the CSCE within the EPC format.[1] Throughout the Helsinki process, the EU and Member States played a key, coordinated role in developing a framework for security dialogue despite the tensions of the Cold War.[2]

Since 1975, the EU, the OSCE and Europe have changed beyond recognition. Where do relations between the OSCE and the EU stand today? Ten years after the launch of ESDP, how does the OSCE matter for the EU? This essay starts by comparing 1999, the year of the Istanbul OSCE summit, and 2009 in terms of wider trends in Europe. It then reviews the evolution of relations between the EU and the OSCE since 1999. The essay concludes by underlining three immediate questions for the EU that are linked to the OSCE.

1999 and 2009

The contrast between 1999 and 2009 is striking. In 1999, the EU was composed of fifteen Member States. CFSP was taking off, and ESDP had just been launched during the Helsinki European Council. EU foreign policy remained focused on eastward enlargement. NATO had just completed a first wave of enlargement, bringing in Poland, Hungary and the Czech Republic. That year saw unprecedented NATO military engagement on European soil – embodied by the Kosovo Force (KFOR), deployed after an eleven week bombing campaign. The Russian Federation protested against both NATO enlargement and Operation *Allied Force*. Nonetheless, Moscow remained a close partner of the United States and the EU.

---

* The views expressed in this chapter are those of the author only, who writes in a personal capacity.

1. See Karen E. Smith, *The Making of EU Foreign Policy: the Case of Eastern Europe* (Basingstoke: Palgrave Macmillan, 2004), pp. 35-7.

2. For more information, see Jacques Andréani, *Le Piège: Helsinki et la chute du communisme* (Paris: Odile Jacob, 2005), and John J. Maresca, *To Helsinki: the Conference on Security and Co-operation in Europe*, 1973-1975 (Durham, NC: Duke University Press, 1985).

The comity of strategic perspectives produced impressive results during the 1999 Istanbul OSCE summit. The Summit saw agreement on the adaptation of the Treaty on Conventional Armed Forces in Europe (CFE) as well as the Vienna Document 1999.[3] The OSCE participating States agreed on a *Charter for European Security*, and on a *Platform for Cooperative Security* – the latter driven by EU Member States.[4]

The Istanbul agreements reflected the importance of the OSCE in 1999 as an inclusive pan-European forum and a key norm-setting agency. For good reason. In 1999, the OSCE was deployed throughout Eastern and South-Eastern Europe, the South Caucasus and Central Asia. In some countries, the Organisation was the only international presence on the ground. The OSCE led efforts to resolve the conflicts in Moldova and Georgia (the conflict in South Ossetia), and worked through field operations in the conflict zones. The OSCE provided the framework for talks to settle the conflict in Nagorno-Karabakh.

1999 was also a difficult year. A second war erupted in Chechnya, and stability was far from embedded in the Western Balkans. Nonetheless, 1999 closed a decade that opened with the *Paris Charter for a New Europe* and that had seen the OSCE play a prominent role on the international stage. Ten years on, the landscape has changed.

The continent's political geography has altered with EU enlargement. Starting with the EU Police Mission in Bosnia and Herzegovina in 2003, the EU has deployed some 23 civilian and military operations in the Western Balkans, the former Soviet Union, the Middle East, Africa and Asia. The Union has rolled out the European Neighbourhood Policy (2003) and developed an Eastern Partnership (2009). EU Member States have agreed a Strategy for Central Asia and framework for the Black Sea region. The EU has appointed Special Representatives to Moldova and Georgia, the South Caucasus and Central Asia as well as to Kosovo, FYROM and Bosnia, with mandates that include conflict prevention and crisis management.

The change of profile is most dramatic in Georgia. On 1 October 2008, the EU deployed a three-hundred strong EU Monitoring Mission in Georgia to contribute to the stabilisation and normalisation of the areas affected by the war in August.[5] The EU Special Representative to the crisis in Georgia acts as a Co-Chair of the Geneva

---

3. All documents may be found on the OSCE website: http://www.osce.org/documents/fsc/1999/11/4265_en.pdf.

4. The Platform may be found on the OSCE website: http://www.osce.org/mc/documents.html.

5. See the chapter on EUMM Georgia in Part Two of this book.

Discussions on security and stability in Georgia. Numerous meetings of the Geneva Discussions have been held since 15 October 2008, chaired by the EU, the OSCE and the UN, including the Georgian government, the South Ossetian and Abkhaz authorities, Russia and the United States.

The decade has been difficult for the OSCE. The OSCE has not held a summit-level meeting since Istanbul. Since 2002, the annual Ministerial Council meetings have failed to agree on a political declaration. OSCE budgets are routinely delayed because of political differences. Since 2003, the OSCE has been the subject of a re-curring debate about reform. In December 2008, the participating States failed to reach agreement on renewing the mandate of the OSCE Mission to Georgia, lead-ing to the discontinuation of OSCE activities on the ground. Compared to 1999, the OSCE has become a contested actor, and the theatre where wider divergences between states are played out.

Strategic relations have changed. The 2008 war in Georgia underlined the enduring utility of force in inter-state relations. The arms control regime created after the end of the Cold War is facing uncertainty, principally regarding the CFE Treaty. With all of this, political-military questions have returned to the mainstream of Euro-pean security. Russia's suspension of the CFE Treaty has underlined a wider trend in Moscow towards a more assertive foreign policy that seeks to revise agreements struck during and after the end of the Cold War because they are perceived as being unfair.

International relations and European politics have become more competitive also at the level of ideas. If in the 1990s democracy stood triumphant as the single most legitimate form of governance, this is no longer so clear. Other models of politics are gaining traction. Democratic transitions face difficult challenges throughout large parts of non-EU Europe.

These snapshots of 1999 and 2009 show that the places occupied by the EU and the OSCE in the European security architecture have changed. The hub role envisaged in the Platform for Cooperative Security has not materialised for the OSCE. The EU has emerged as a key power player on the continent. The last decade shows also that the importance of the OSCE for the EU has changed. The 2003 European Security Strategy set a rules-based international order as the key objective for EU foreign policy, with the pursuit of effective multilateralism as a means to build it.[6] In 2009,

6. *A Secure Europe in a Better World – The European Security Strategy*, Brussels, 12 December 2003.

as differences deepen across Europe, the EU must develop effective multilateralism across an increasingly divided continent. This is where the importance of the OSCE emerges.

EU-OSCE Interaction

The evolution of EU policy towards the OSCE reflected these wider trends. By the late 1990s, the EU and the OSCE had developed close cooperation in South-Eastern Europe and the former Soviet Union. Between 2003 and 2006, relations went into a higher gear with the aim of defining modalities for interaction. EU-OSCE relations have remained at a set level since then.

In the first instance, EU-OSCE relations were driven by cooperation between institutions on the ground. For instance, in 1999-2000, the European Commission was the main donor to the OSCE-led rehabilitation project in the areas affected by the Georgian-South Ossetian conflict. The Commission also provided routine support to OSCE election observation activities. The OSCE acted also as an instrument for when the EU could not act directly. For instance, the Commission was the largest donor to a number of OSCE projects in 2000 designed to strengthen institutions in Belarus.

The development of CFSP and ESDP catalysed sharper thinking in the Council. On 3 November 2003, the Political and Security Committee agreed on a set of Conclusions on EU-OSCE cooperation in conflict prevention, crisis management and post-conflict rehabilitation.[7] The Conclusions recognised the 'role of the OSCE as a valuable instrument for the promotion of peace and comprehensive security.' The Conclusions called for cooperation in the exchange of information, joint fact-finding missions, coordination of diplomatic activity and statements and enhanced consultations at all levels. The Conclusions noted the 'possible contribution by the EU to the OSCE's operational efforts in crisis management,' and the possibility of 'EU crisis management operations following a request from the OSCE.' Given the OSCE role in crisis management, such proposals made sense at the time.

The 2003 Council Conclusions also set out modalities for contacts between the two organisations – including twice-yearly meetings of the EU and the OSCE Troikas at ministerial and ambassadorial levels, twice-yearly presentations of priorities by the

---

7. See European Council, 'Draft Council Conclusions on EU-OSCE Cooperation in Conflict Prevention, Crisis Management and Post-Conflict Rehabilitation', doc. 14527/1/03 REV 1, Brussels, 10 November 2003.

EU presidency to the OSCE Permanent Council, briefings between EU and OSCE officials and mutual visits, as well as regular staff-level consultations. The idea of appointing a Council Secretariat liaison officer to Vienna was floated (the proposal was acted upon in April 2009). These modalities set the foundations for the close interaction between the EU and the OSCE today. Regular contacts have developed also between high-level OSCE officials and the Political and Security Committee, as well as with relevant Working Groups in the EU Council.

The next step occurred in December 2004, when the Committee of Permanent Representatives (COREPER) endorsed the Assessment Report on the EU's policy towards the OSCE.[8] The Assessment Report had a wider ambition than the 2003 Conclusions, and set out relations in a comprehensive manner. The Report developed suggestions for enhanced EU activity in the OSCE in the political-military, the humanitarian and the economic and environmental fields. It called for mainstreaming OSCE issues throughout EU foreign policy. The Report called on the EU to support OSCE crisis management, but the idea of contributing to OSCE operations had vanished, as had the idea of operating under OSCE mandate.

2006 saw a new attempt to strengthen relations by the Austrian EU Presidency and the Belgian OSCE Chairmanship working on a 'Joint Declaration on Cooperation between the EU and the OSCE.' The Declaration sought to codify interaction between the two organisations and provide impetus to enhanced cooperation. While benign in intent and content, the Declaration did not reach consensus, due to the objections of Eastern neighbours of the EU with which the Union had difficult relations.

In addition, significant cooperation developed on the ground. Interaction between EU and OSCE operations has not always occurred in easy circumstances, and has started sometimes with significant ambiguity. Relative to relations between headquarters, interaction on the ground has tended to be *ad hoc* and informal. Interaction between the OSCE Mission in Kosovo and EULEX is a case in point. With the downsizing of the UNMIK, the OSCE has worked alongside the EU mission in Kosovo. Areas of potential overlap in mandate between EULEX and the OSCE Mission in Kosovo (OMIK) have been worked out informally on the ground, for example on the monitoring of courts and aspects of police training.

---

8. European Council, 'Draft Assessment Report on the EU's Role *vis-à-vis* the OSCE', doc. 15387/1/04 REV1, Brussels, 10 December 2004.

The OSCE has been a crucial actor to which the EU has turned in situations where other venues for engagement are blocked. This was the case in Georgia in August 2008, when the OSCE deployed additional military monitoring officers in areas adjacent to the conflict zone almost immediately after the outbreak of hostilities.[9] This measure helped underpin the initiatives of the French EU presidency. It also set the ground for strong, if again informal, coordination between the OSCE Mission to Georgia and the EU Monitoring Mission deployed in October 2008. Since then, the EU and the OSCE, along with the UN, have worked together as Co-Chairs of the Geneva Discussions on security and stability in Georgia. In addition, a senior OSCE official and the head of the EUMM have co-chaired the meetings of the Incident Prevention and Response Mechanism that were held on the administrative border with South Ossetia.

By 2009, therefore, EU-OSCE interaction was regular between headquarters and the political leaderships. Cooperation was strong also in the field. These facts, however, should not obscure a deeper point.

On paper, the EU should have a leading role in the OSCE. In practice, the case is not clear. 27 of the 56 OSCE participating States are EU members. EU presidencies coordinate on a weekly basis to ensure joint statements on all OSCE issues, including current affairs. The number of states signing up to EU statements can reach up to forty two. EU Member States provide over seventy percent of the Organisation's budget. They also contribute over 65 percent of voluntary funds. EU Member States provide close to seventy percent of all seconded staff to the field operations, the Secretariat and Institutions, as well as fifty percent of all contracted staff. What is more, EU Member States have held most OSCE Chairmanships.

Despite all of this, the EU punches below its weight, leaving much of the political initiative within the OSCE to the United States and Russia. On key issues, the EU often finds itself dragged down by cumbersome procedures that dilute the Union's unity of purpose. There is often a disconnect between the EU in Brussels and the EU in Vienna.[10]

---

9. See OSCE, 'Permanent Council Decision 861 Increasing the Number of Military Monitoring Officers to the OSCE Mission to Georgia', PC.DEC/861, 19 August 2008. Available at: http://www.osce.org/documents/pc/2008/08/32615_en.pdf.

10. Note also that the European Commission has a Delegation to International Organizations in Vienna, with a section dedicated to the OSCE, headed by the experienced Ambassador Lars-Erik Lundin. For more information, see: http://www.delvie.ec.europa.eu/en/eu_osce/overview.htm.

Immediate issues

The EU faces three immediate questions that require a stronger voice in the OSCE.

The first concerns the need for the EU to maintain a united international effort in Georgia. The EU has a vital interest in ensuring strong, continuing OSCE and UN presences in Georgia – to bolster the activities of the EU Monitoring Mission and to underpin the Geneva Discussions. By summer 2009, the UN and the OSCE had withdrawn their operations on the ground but work has continued to reach agreement on new mission structures with new mandates. Building effective multilateralism in Georgia is vital for the Union. It will influence wider engagement in the former Soviet Union and set the tone in relations with Russia.

Second, the EU should make the most of the OSCE to take forward the call for a renewed European security dialogue. In June 2008, Russian President Dmitry Medvedev called for a renewed dialogue with the aim of agreeing on a legally-binding European security treaty. The Russian proposal reflected a sense of discomfort in Moscow with developments in the politico-military sphere occurring across wider Europe. Apart from Russian concerns, there are a range of questions that require collective responses, including the protracted conflicts, new threats and the future of arms control.

In 2009, the EU defined starting points for engaging in this dialogue – on the need for transatlantic unity, on revitalising rather than replacing existing institutions and on the need to fulfil commitments that have been agreed. The Union should set out its own positive agenda for a renewed dialogue – to address outstanding problems and revive the comprehensive approach to security. The OSCE is the natural forum in which to take forward this agenda.

The last question concerns the 2010 Kazakhstan OSCE chairmanship. This chairmanship breaks the tradition of EU leadership and announces the opening of a new era for the OSCE – with a first post-Soviet Chair and a new geographic centre of gravity. The Kazakh chairmanship is an opportunity to be seized by the EU – to continue supporting political reform in this country and to embed stability across Central Asia.

The Kazakhstan chairmanship makes the imperative of a stronger EU policy all the more important. With the EU not chairing the OSCE, the modalities for interaction between the EU and the OSCE must function more efficiently, more quickly and more sharply. In this respect, communication inside the EU – between Vienna and Brussels, between Member States and the Union – must become stronger. The presence of an official from the Council Secretariat with the Commission Delegation in Vienna is a welcome start, but it is only a first step.

Conclusion

With a competitive Europe emerging, the OSCE is becoming all the more important for the EU – as a forum for dialogue in a context of rising dissonance and as an actor for cooperative security, crisis prevention and crisis management. In Vienna and on the ground, the OSCE offers a framework to connect some of the dots of CFSP and ESDP. The Organisation remains the place where the strategic questions of European security are debated by *all* members of wider Europe – questions about the balance between sovereignty and self-determination, about the pursuit of tolerance, about preventing and settling conflicts. Europe needs this debate – as a pressure valve and thermometer, and as a part of the process necessary to develop common action. What is more, at a time when 'shared values' seem to be eroding across the continent, the OSCE body of shared commitments is a unique resource for the EU to draw upon to work through cooperation with non-EU Europe. The CSCE was one of the places where EU foreign policy was born. The EU needs to get its act together again to make the most of the OSCE.

BIBLIOGRAPHY

Andréani, Jacques. *Le Piège: Helsinki et la chute du communisme* (Paris: Odile Jacob, 2005).

Maresca, John J. *To Helsinki: the Conference on Security and Co-operation in Europe, 1973-1975* (Durham, NC: Duke University Press, 1985).

Smith, Karen E. *The Making of EU Foreign Policy: the Case of Eastern Europe* (Basingstoke: Palgrave Macmillan, 2004).

ESDP and the African Union

Damien Helly

Since 1999, ESDP has been used in Africa in two ways. First, and on an *ad hoc* basis, it has served as an essential tool to respond to immediate crisis management needs (DRC, Chad and Central African Republic, Somalia, Sudan). Secondly, in the framework of the 2007 Africa-EU strategic partnership, it has contributed to long-term capacity building efforts. Both approaches are pursued in coordination with a broad range of EU policies and agreements such as, among others, the Cotonou agreements and the European Development Fund (EDF) with its African Peace Facility (APF).[1] This dual approach is likely to remain a feature of the EU's engagement in Africa for the foreseeable future. While under pressure to respond and prevent crises, the African Peace and Security Architecture (APSA) is still in the making and thus is not ready yet to fill all security gaps on the continent. Africa-EU security relations are therefore still very much in a transition phase which could well last a decade or more. As long as African states or organisations are not fully willing, equipped and able to prevent or manage their own crises on the continent, outside interventions will be called for and partially outsourced to external powers.[2]

ESDP in the broader Africa-EU relations picture

ESDP is still in its early days; the African Union (AU) is an even younger organisation. Created in 2002 on the ashes of the Organisation for African Unity (OAU), it has a strong peace and security focus and was founded on three major principles: 'Africa must unite', 'responsibility to protect' and 'try Africa first.'[3]

---

1. Other instruments like the Development and Cooperation Instrument (DCI), the European Neighbourhood and Partnership Instrument (ENPI) and the Instrument for Stability (IfS) are used in Africa. For more details on these instruments and their interaction with ESDP, see chapter 1 on ESDP institutions. See also Nicoletta Pirozzi, 'EU support to the African security architecture: funding and training components', *Occasional Paper* no. 76, EUISS, Paris, February 2009, pp. 23-29.

2. Jean-François Bayart, 'Africa in the World, A History of Extraversion', *African Affairs*, vol. 99, no. 395, April 2000, pp. 217-67. Available at: afraf.oxfordjournals.org/cgi/reprint/99/395/217.pdf.

3. Pirozzi, op. cit in note 1.

EU Architecture for Peace and Security in Africa (EU APSA)

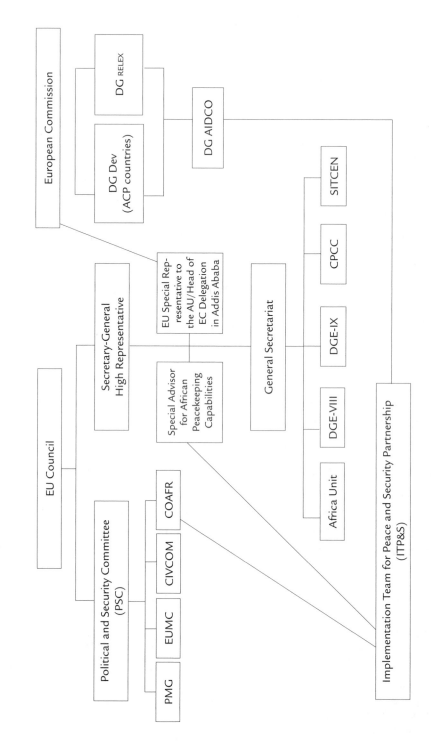

Source: Nicoletta Pirozzi, 'EU support to African security architecture: funding and training components', *Occasional Paper* no. 76, EUISS, February 2009.

While continental in nature, the AU has to coordinate with multi-decades-old su-bregional organisations (Regional Economic Communities – RECs – and Regional Mechanisms – RMs) which have already developed security and defence coopera-tion.[4] Through ESDP, the EU has therefore to take the decentralised nature of the APSA (African Peace and Security Architecture) into account.[5]

The adoption of the Joint Africa-EU strategy and of the Africa-EU strategic part-nership in December 2007 marked a turning point in the relationship between the two continents as established by the 2000 Africa-EU summit in Cairo. The joint strategy is supposed to be based on a more equal footing according to the principles of equality, partnership and ownership. The strategic partnership consists of eight thematic action plans implemented along a jointly agreed roadmap leading inter-locutors from both the AU and the EU to cooperate at all levels.[6] Progress achieved should be reviewed by the next AU-EU summit in 2010.[7] In the field of peace and security, three main priorities were identified: exchanging dialogue on challenges to peace and security, full operationalisation of the APSA and predictable funding for African-led peace support operations.

Key African and European actors and instruments

The African Union has to a large extent been inspired by the EU in the design of its institutions and particularly so in the field of peace and security. However, what distinguishes it from ESDP is the important role played by RECS/RMs.

Various documents underpin the development of APSA, namely the 2000 AU con-stitutional act, the 2004 Solemn Declaration of Common African Defence and Se-curity Policy (CADSP), and the protocol relating to the establishment of the Peace and Security Council. The latter document fleshes out the design of the APSA which entails a Peace and Security Council, a military staff committee, the African Standby Force, the panel of the wise and the Continental early warning system (CEWS) and a

---

4. For more information on RECs/RMs, see Alex Vines and Roger Middleton, Options for the EU to Support the African Peace and Security Architecture, Study for the European Parliament, February 2008, p. 21 and annex 2. For a map illustrating the overlapping of RECs/RMs, see Ludger Kühnhardt, 'African Regional Integration and the Role of the European Union,' *ZEI Discussion Paper* C184, 2008, p. 21.

5. Benedikt Franke, 'EU-AU cooperation in capacity building', in Joachim A. Koops (ed.), 'Military Crisis Manage-ment – The Challenge of Effective Inter-Organizationalism,' *Studia Diplomatica*, vol. 62, no. 3, Egmont, Royal Institute for International Relations, forthcoming, 2009.

6. See: http://africa-eu-partnership.org. The 8 themes are: (1) peace and security; (2) democratic governance and human rights; (3) trade, regional integration and infrastructure; (4) Millennium Development Goals – MDGs; (5) energy; (6) climate change; (7) migration, mobility and employment; (8) science, information society and space.

7. A mid-term review report was published in 2009 by the European Commission. Commission staff working docu-ment, 'Implementation of the Joint Africa-EU Strategy and its First Action Plan (2008-2010) – Input into the mid-term progress-report', SEC(2009) 1064 final, Brussels, July 2009.

peace fund.[8] The Commission of the AU, its administrative and executive body, also has a peace and security commissioner.

On the EU side, ESDP is one tool among many others. Bilateral cooperation from individual EU Member States plays a major role in security and defence.[9] The European Commission is a key partner for ESDP in its relationship with the African continent. It has developed a large range of programmes indirectly related to peace and security in the last 50 years in the framework of the Cotonou agreements. Its geographical financial instruments provide the lion's share of EU cooperation with Africa including for crisis management and conflict prevention. The creation in 2004 of the Africa Peace Facility – financed via the EDF managed by the Commission and the Member States – and its replenishment (€440 million spent under the 9th EDF and €300 million committed for 2008-2010) opened a new era in ESDP-AU cooperation. Since then and thanks to the APF, the AU has been able to finance its own peace operations in Darfur (AMIS – African Union Mission in the Sudan), Somalia (AMISOM – African Union Mission in Somalia), the Central African Republic (MICOPAX - Mission de consolidation de la paix en RCA) and Comoros (AMISEC - African Union Mission for Support to the Elections in the Comoros).[10]

Implementation and achievements

In practice, some ESDP initiatives were launched specifically to support AU peace operations in Somalia and Sudan. These contributions, though small in terms of the number of personnel, constituted a valuable test for the EU to assess the viability of practical cooperation with the AU in crisis situations. Significant EU support to AMIS and AMISOM troops and equipment have been funded mainly by the African Peace Facility.

Since 2008 ESDP has also contributed to the implementation of the Lisbon Partnership's three priorities. This work is being conducted by the special advisor to the SG/HR based in Brussels, Pierre-Michel Joana, together with the EU representations to the AU and to the UN. An implementation team composed of Member States'

8. For a more precise description of the various bodies and their role, see Alex Vines and Roger Middleton, op. cit. in note 4; Nicoletta Pirozzi, op. cit. in note 1, Veronika Tywuschik and Andrew Sherriff, 'Beyond Structures: Reflections on the implementation of the Joint Africa-EU strategy', *ECDPM Discussion Paper*, ECDPM, 2009; Jakkie Cilliers, 'The African Standby Force: an update on progress', *ISS paper* no. 160, Pretoria, March 2008.

9. Niagalé Bagayoko, 'The EU and the member states: African capabilities building programmes' in Christophe Cazelles (ed.), *Europe's activity in Africa in the field of security* (Paris: Centre d'analyse stratégique, 2007); Pirozzi, op. cit. in note 1, pp. 23-25.

10. More details on the use of the APF to support AU peace operations can be found on the European Commission's website at: http://ec.europa.eu/europeaid/where/acp/regional-cooperation/peace/peace-support-operations/index_en.htm.

representatives is also involved in this process. France and Italy have the lead on training, the EC and the UK on funding, and the EC and the EU presidency on political dialogue. Several recent initiatives and achievements in ESDP-AU relations are worth mentioning.

First, political relations between the AU and the EU, materialised by ministerial and Troika meetings, have intensified with the first meetings of the EU Political and Security Committee and AU Peace and Security Council taking place in 2009, all prepared upstream by EU and AU staff in Addis Ababa and Brussels.[11] The role of the double-hatted EUSR for the AU and Head of the EC delegation to the AU, Koen Vervaeke, has been crucial in this respect. Coordination efforts are also being carried out in New York by EU and AU representatives.[12]

Second, ESDP provided capacity-building support to the AU at headquarters level in Addis Ababa with a team of military advisers first based in the EC delegation to Ethiopia and then under the remit of the EU delegation to the AU. The staff of this team, sometimes complemented by seconded personnel to the AU Commission's Peace and Security Department (some of them funded by the Instrument for Stability or by individual Member States) contributed to the planning, deployment and conduct of AMIS, AMISOM and MICOPAX.

Third, ESDP engaged in support to African peacekeeping capabilities by developing the Amani Africa/Euro Recamp training programme consisting of various exercises and joint curricula for African troops, in coordination with RECs/RMs. Efforts were conducted so as to match African needs with European offers and to identify training gaps, particularly on the civilian side. The objective of the programme is to attract other donors so as to increase their participation in the project. The US, Japan, Canada, the UN and NATO have expressed some interest and some have already contributed to the programme's fund.[13]

Fourth, a new initiative for joint early warning between Situation Centres in the UK, France, the AU and the EU, known as the MIVAC (*Mécanisme interactif de Veille et d'Anticipation des Crises*), was launched in 2009. It follows efforts to maximise coop-

11. Uncoordinated initiatives from certain Member States like the one on mediation funded by Finland to support the Panel of the Wise were linked to the partnership afterwards.

12. One example of upgraded dialogue is the creation of the AU-EU expert group working on the principle of universal jurisdiction in relation to the International Criminal Court warrant against Sudanese President Al Bashir, which was contested by the AU and discussed with the EU at the 11th AU-EU Ministerial Troika meeting. See Council Secretariat, 'The AU-EU Expert Report on the Principle of Universal Jurisdiction', 16 April 2009.

13. 'Pierre-Michel Joana takes stock of EU aid to African peacekeeping and security efforts', *Europe Diplomacy & Defence - The Agence Europe Bulletin on ESDP and NATO*, 16 June 2009.

eration between ESDP/EC/Germany/the Joint Research Centre in Ispra with a view to fully equipping the AU situation room on the model of EU crisis rooms doing early warning on the basis of open source intelligence.

Finally, the adoption of a new €300 million funding package for the African Peace Facility in 2008 opened the door for new planning of the support to AU-led operations. This is being done in addition to some capacity-building projects funded by the first APF.

In July 2009, Pierre-Michel Joana was charged by the Council to explore options for further EU support to peace in Somalia, identify solutions to combat piracy and strengthen the security sector in this country, following the AU-UN-EU pledging conference organised in April 2009 in Brussels.

Existing challenges

The primacy of politics and its impact on peace and security matters

The official objective of the AU is to set up autonomous African peacekeeping capabilities. In practice, this will take time and will require a lot of capacity-building efforts from within as much as from the outside. African politics are as complicated, if not more, as EU politics. Reaching consensus and implementing collective decisions is a constant challenge in the AU. Summits have always been the occasion to discuss contentious topics. It is hard, as elsewhere on the planet, for African leaders to find agreement on sensitive questions such as the responsibility to protect (R2P), the International Criminal Court or specific crisis situations like Zimbabwe or Somalia. The multilevel and decentralised nature of the African security architecture, its overlapping regional and sub-regional structures and the ambitions of regional hegemons are all factors making the work of the AU a difficult political and diplomatic task. Powerful states do not necessarily want it to become a competitor.

Peace and security issues are particularly tricky. Security forces are both part of the problem of (when they contribute to repression, crime and coups) and of the solution to (as peace enforcers, peacekeepers, trainers or guarantors of democracy) insecurity and impunity on the continent. In this context, using African armies primarily in externally-funded peacekeeping exercises may suit several purposes quite alien to the implementation of collective political strategies:[14] e.g. sending threaten-

---

14. François Grignon and Daniela Kroslak, 'The Problem with Peacekeeping', *Current History*, April 2008, pp.186-87.

ing forces away to avoid their interference in internal politics, treating forces generously by providing them with higher salaries than usual, or displaying military strength to regional neighbours while training troops in new theatres.

However, the lack of clear collective political ambition has serious consequences for the very efficiency of the AU structures which face huge recruitment and human resources problems and therefore lack sufficient capacity to absorb external support. These shortcomings and realities must inform debates and decisions about the need to provide more equipment, logistics assets – like strategic transport – and direct material support as much as training.[15]

On the EU side, politics are just as problematic. Defence and political integration have been slow to deepen, thus hampering the design of ambitious foreign and security policy strategies. Member States have very uneven interests in Africa and some see them as divided into three groups: (i) the former – sometimes competing – colonial powers, (ii) the Nordics and (iii) the new Members States from Central Europe, with Germany playing a somewhat indecisive role in the middle of them.[16] EU structures are extremely complex and some consider that they need to be rationalised.[17]

Lessons learned

Several issues will require future ESDP-AU cooperation in theatre. ESDP staff need to be provided with diplomatic status to overcome basic obstacles when they operate in Africa. Although the negotiation of Status of Force Agreements (SOFAs) with hosting authorities may be a temporary solution, ad hocery is not enough. The example of difficulties experienced at border crossing points or delays in visa delivery from the Sudanese administration are cited as examples.[18] Second, lessons learned from AMIS showed that more clarity regarding the role of EU staff seconded to AU operations will be needed in the future. The EU's say and place in the chain of command and reporting channels, and the nature of its advisory role, have to be clarified early enough to maximise the cooperation in theatre. Third, the EU's influence as main donor of AU operations will have to be complemented by a high degree of political-military synergy between the two organisations. This is necessary to avoid

---

15. See the chapter on EU support AMIS and AMISOM in Part Two of this book.

16. Sébastien Bergeon, 'Le Partenariat stratégique « UE-Afrique » face aux « situations de fragilité »', *Studia Diplomatica*, vol. LXII, no. 2, 2009 ; Jérôme Spinoza, 'L'Afrique dans le regard allemand', *Revue Défense Nationale*, January 2007.

17. See chart 1 and Nicoletta Pirozzi, op. cit. in note 1, p. 12.

18. Pierre-Antoine Braud, 'Implementing ESDP Operations in Africa', in Anne Deighton and Victor Mauer (eds.), *Securing Europe ? Implementing the European Security Strategy* (Zurich: ETH Centre for Security Studies, 2006), pp.72-73.

past cases when changes in the conduct of AMIS recommended by the EU were not implemented.[19]

In the absence of strong African political will it is impossible for the EU to foster more African ownership in the spirit of the new EU-Africa partnership. Without strongly staffed structures enjoying political back-up on the African side, it is also hard to avoid the trap of the donor-recipient relationship that the Lisbon Summit was supposed to consign to the past.

The AU must convince RECs/RMs that it is able to give them some added value. For that purpose, RECs/RMs representation to the AU is being developed in Addis Ababa with the support of the EU. A legal framework to regulate AU-RECs/RM relations vis-à-vis the African Standby Force (ASF) is expected to be adopted in 2010. Similarly, given the differing levels of development reached by regional brigades, it is crucial to support the set-up of the ASF in a differentiated and targeted manner. Some have suggested prioritising the most advanced brigades.[20]

Suggestions were also made to increase cooperation and skills transfer between the AU and the UN in peacekeeping logistics management.[21] Finally, in the spirit of the partnerships, dialogue on peace and security would benefit from increased participation from non-state actors, including from the private sector, so as to stimulate progress and accountability.

Beyond the EU-AU partnerships, a myriad of actors have engaged the APSA. International organisations like the UN, NATO, the G8 or the Arab League have developed their own partnerships and support programmes. Brazil, China, India and Japan also are keen to cooperate more closely with Africans on peace and security. More coordination is needed to avoid divide and rule or 'aid auction' situations from those in Africa who have a long experience of donors' competition. The report of the AU-UN panel on modalities for support to AU peacekeeping operations has identified solutions to avoid overlapping and limit transaction costs. It remains to be seen how the EU will support and contribute to new funding mechanisms and in particular the suggested multi-donor trust fund for capacity building.[22] Decisions will also be influenced by debates on the definition of Official Development Aid

---

19. Ibid., p.76.
20. Vines and Middleton, op. cit. in note 4, p. 36.
21. Report of the African Union-United Nations Panel on modalities for support to AU peacekeeping operations, 26 December 2008.
22. Ibid.

(ODA) which so far, according to the criteria established by the OECD DAC (Organisation for Economic Co-operation and Development Assistance Committee), cannot be used to fund military activities.[23] Since the DAC criteria constrain the use of development budgets to fund peace and security efforts, some options should be considered to create or increase resources matching the hybrid nature of the security-development nexus. As for international coordination, various formats are being developed in the framework of the G8+, the trilateral EU-Africa-China partnership or the EU-AU cooperation at the UN.

Conclusion

After two years of implementation of the new EU-Africa partnership, qualitative steps have been made but 'the imbalance of benefits and commitments (political, financial and administrative) from the two partners gives the impression of a one-sided Partnership.'[24] A lot of emphasis so far has been put on crisis response and military assets. Civilian crisis management, conflict prevention and early warning efforts are lagging behind. More thought should also be given to linkages between peace and security and other EU-Africa partnerships, particularly in the field of post-conflict reconstruction and development and migration. Even though disagreements and divergences remain on the process and the method of cooperation, the EU has started to establish a new kind of relationship with African regional organisations and the AU in particular. What is required now is, based on a thorough understanding of political realities,[25] obstacles and opportunities, to identify and acknowledge the appropriate pace of progress and reform for all; to learn how to cooperate in the most productive manner by respecting each other, build up confidence steadily and promote win-win exchanges. ESDP is a complement to other EU and international tools and as such it has played its part. The new double-hatted representation of the EU in Addis Ababa prefigures what the much expected European External Action Service (EEAS) could be like and is seen as a very successful experience so far. How this service, if it is created, will interact with other cooperation instruments at the disposal of the EU in Africa will partly determine the future impact of ESDP on Africa's peace and security.

---

23. OECD DAC, 'Is it ODA?', Fact sheet, November 2008, available at: http://www.oecd.org/dataoecd/21/21/34086975.pdf

24. Commission staff working document, op. cit. in note 7, p.17.

25. Marc-Antoine Pérouse de Montclos. 'Les Occidentaux peuvent-ils sauver l'Afrique?', *Politique étrangère*, March 2006.

BIBLIOGRAPHY

Bagayoko, Niagalé. 'The EU and the member-states: African capabilities building pro-grammes' in Christophe Cazelles (ed.), *Europe's activity in Africa in the field of security* (Paris: Centre d'analyse stratégique, 2007).

Bayart, Jean-François. 'Africa in the World, A History of Extraversion', *African Affairs*, vol. 99, no. 395, April 2000, pp. 217-67.

Bergeon, Sébastien. 'Le Partenariat stratégique « UE-Afrique » face aux « situations de fragilité »', *Studia Diplomatica*, vol. LXII, no. 2, 2009.

Braud, Pierre-Antoine. 'Implementing ESDP Operations in Africa', in Anne Deighton and Victor Mauer (eds.), *Securing Europe ? Implementing the European Security Strategy* (Zurich: ETH Centre for Security Studies, 2006) pp. 72-73.

Cilliers, Jakkie. 'The African Standby Force: an update on progress', *ISS paper* no. 160, Pretoria, March 2008.

Franke, Benedikt. 'EU-AU cooperation in capacity building', in Joachim A. Koops (ed.), 'Military Crisis Management – The Challenge of Effective Inter-Organizationalism', *Studia Diplomatica*, vol. 62, no. 3, Egmont, Royal Institute for International Relations, forthcom-ing, 2009.

Grignon, François and Kroslak, Daniela. 'The Problem with Peacekeeping', *Current History*, April 2008, pp.186-87.

Kühnhardt, Ludger. 'African Regional Integration and the Role of the European Union', *ZEI Discussion Paper* C184, 2008, p. 21.

Pérouse de Montclos, Marc-Antoine. 'Les Occidentaux peuvent-ils sauver l'Afrique?', *Poli-tique étrangère*, March 2006.

Pirozzi, Nicoletta. 'EU support to the African security architecture: funding and training components', *Occasional Paper* no. 76, European Union Institute for Security Studies, Paris, February 2009.

Spinoza, Jérôme. 'L'Afrique dans le regard allemand', *Revue Défense Nationale*, January 2007.

Tywuschik, Veronika and Sherriff, Andrew. 'Beyond Structures: Reflections on the implementation of the Joint Africa-EU strategy', *ECDPM Discussion Paper*, The European Centre for Development Policy Management (ECDPM), 2009.

Vervaeke, Koen. 'EU-AU Cooperation in Military Crisis Management and Capacity-Building: A View From Practice', in Joachim A. Koops (ed.), 'Military Crisis Management – The Challenge of Effective Inter-Organizationalism', *Studia Diplomatica*, vol. 62, no. 3, Egmont, Royal Institute for International Relations, forthcoming, 2009.

Vines, Alex and Middleton, Roger. 'Options for the EU to Support the African Peace and Security Architecture', Study for the European Parliament, February 2008.

Part Two

4. EUPM (Bosnia and Herzegovina)

The EU Police Mission in Bosnia and Herzegovina (EUPM)

Michael Merlingen

Legal basis: Council Joint Action 2002/210/CFSP of 11 March 2002.

Highlights of the mission's mandate:

■ Mentoring, monitoring and inspecting, to establish in BiH a sustainable, professional and multiethnic police service operating in accordance with European and international standards.

■ Assist local authorities in planning and conducting major and organised crime investigations, in contributing to an improved functioning of the whole criminal justice system in general and enhancing police-prosecutor relations in particular.

■ Together with the European Commission, assist BiH authorities to identify remaining police development needs which could be addressed through Community assistance.

Duration: January 2003-December 2009.

Budget: 2003 €21.7 million (plus €14 million front-loaded in 2002); 2004 €17.5 million; 2005 €17.41 million; 2006 €12 million; 2007 €12.5 million; 2008 €14.8 million; 2009 €12.4 million; 2002-2009 €122.31 million.

> **Mission strength:** 540 international staff (peak capacity) and 175 international staff (March 2009).
>
> **Contributing states:** 27 Member States and 7 third states (Canada, Iceland, Norway, Russia, Switzerland, Turkey and Ukraine).

Introduction

The EU Police Mission (EUPM) in Bosnia was the first ESDP operation, and is still ongoing. This has made it both a trailblazer and a guinea pig. The mission can be credited with three main achievements. First, it demonstrated that the EU had succeeded in rendering the ESDP operational. Brussels could assemble a sizeable civilian mission, deploy it in the field and command and control it. Second, the EUPM has advanced the transformation of the Bosnian police from an instrument of ethnic warfare into a professional service. The process was initiated by the United Nations International Police Task Force (UN-IPTF, 1996-2002), which at its peak had about 2,000 international experts and enjoyed executive powers. Third, the EUPM has made significant headway in changing Bosnian policing mentalities, institutions and practices in line with European norms and standards. That said, law enforcement remains afflicted by some important shortcomings, and the obstacles that EUPM has confronted are illustrated below. Some of them have been successfully tackled. Others are such that they exceed the problem-solving capacity of the mission. These include the high politics of police restructuring and the fight against organised crime and corruption, which have manifold political, economic and cultural roots.

Bosnia-Herzegovina

Bosnia declared independence in March 1992. Within a few months, the country was embroiled in a brutal ethnic war that lasted until 1995. It pitted a coalition of Muslim and Croat Bosnians against Bosnian Serbs, who in turn were supported by Belgrade. The war was brought to an end by a NATO military intervention. In the ensuing Dayton peace negotiations brokered by Washington, a new constitution was hammered out. Prioritising a quick deal over careful negotiations, the Dayton constitution codified Bosnia's division into two powerful ethnic entities – the Muslim-Croat Federation and the Serbian Republika Srpska – and a weak central state. The Bosnian police remained legally, politically and ethnically divided. A High Representative (HR) was appointed to oversee the implementation of the civilian aspects of the peace settlement. At first, the position of HR was little more than that of a facilitator and coordinator of the country's post-war reconstruction. But the leaders of post-Dayton Bosnia proved less amenable to international guidance than assumed. In response, the international community transformed the country into a protectorate. In 1997, the Steering Board of the Peace Implementation Council, which was set up in the wake of the Dayton peace agreement, endowed the HR with far-reaching executive powers. Named after the town where the meeting took place, the 'Bonn powers' include the power to dismiss (elected) officials and impose laws. This has allowed the HR, who has been double-hatted as EU Special Representative (EUSR) since 2002, to persuade, cajole, pressure and force an often-reluctant political elite to reform the country in line with EU requirements. The downside is that his heavy footprint has fostered a culture of dependency among local authorities. The overall effect of these contradictory tendencies is that the country remains ethnically polarised and internationally mandated reforms have been obstructed and undermined by local actors at every opportunity.

Since the tenth anniversary of the Dayton accords in 2005, the international community has redoubled its efforts to overcome their legacy and push ahead with the Europeanisation of Bosnia. Constitutional reform aimed at strengthening the state at the expense of the ethnic entities has been at the top of the international agenda. The EU made the creation of a unified police structure which invests all legal and budgetary powers in the state one of the conditions for signing a Stabilisation and Association Agreement (SAA) with Bosnia. But the police is a key lever of governmental power, which the Republika Srpska in particular has been unwilling to give up. In the aftermath of the October 2006 elections, which reaffirmed the grip of nationalist politicians on the electorate, the political climate in the country deteriorated, making a fundamental overhaul of policing even more difficult. It required strong pressure by the HR/EUSR and the European Commission to get the coalition government at state level to agree finally to move ahead with police restructuring in order to meet the last outstanding condition for signing the SAA. The Mostar Declaration on police reform was followed up, in April 2008, by the approval of two new police laws by the country's parliamentary assembly.[1] However, the full implementation of key elements of these laws, and of the Mostar Declaration more generally, remains hostage to an overall constitutional settlement, which remains elusive.

---

1. The adoption of the laws paved the way for Bosnia to sign the SAA with the EU in June 2008.

The EUPM's evolving mandate

The EUPM is a non-executive police mission whose police officers are unarmed. It has been prolonged twice. EUPM 1 (January 2003-December 2005) had a broad mandate. Its international staff, which reached its peak at well over 500 people, was tasked to establish sustainable policing arrangements in line with best European and international practice. What these terms meant in practice was not clarified in the Joint Action. For instance, at the time the EUPM was launched, there was no agreed-upon catalogue of best European practices. To reach its imprecise mandate objectives – which were to be achieved within the existing fragmented structure of policing in Bosnia – the mission was to engage in mentoring, monitoring and inspecting activities. While 'mentoring' and 'monitoring' seemed clear enough assignments, it was unclear what was to be understood by 'inspections', not least because the mission had not been granted executive policing powers (such as arrest and prosecution powers). If the mandate had been formulated against the backdrop of an established *acquis sécuritaire*, its vagueness would not have been problematic. The head of mission and his planning team could have drawn on established practices in their elaboration of the Operation Plan (OPLAN). As it was, the OPLAN was far from being an exemplar of clarity, which meant that the mission failed to hit the ground running. Not long after the mission was up and running, EUFOR *Althea* arrived on the scene.[2] What followed had not been anticipated, neither by policy-makers in Brussels nor by the EUPM leadership. Interpreting its mandate liberally, *Althea* drew on its own armed police force (the Integrated Police Unit) as well as regular troops to carry out anti-organised crime operations, often without informing either the local police or the EUPM. This resulted in confusion both in the EU family and among Bosnian authorities over who was in charge of improving local law enforcement. Also, it created some bad blood between the *Althea* and EUPM leadership, with the latter complaining that the 'executive' approach of the military undermined its capacity-building approach based on local ownership. The disagreement was papered over first by a bottom-up agreement between the two ESDP operations and later by adjustments to their mandates, which designated the EUPM as the lead actor on this issue.

EUPM 2 (January 2006 to December 2007) and EUPM 3 (January 2008 to December 2009) have had a slimmed-down workforce of about 200 international police officers and civilian experts, and re-focused mandates. Their overall objectives, though

---

2. See the chapter on EUFOR *Althea* in this book.

slightly rephrased, have remained essentially the same – to establish a sustainable, professional and multiethnic police service. The mandates have been 'refocused' – they have zeroed in on the EUPM's role (coordination and assistance) in the fight against organised crime and on its contribution to police reform. The latter is basically code for the centralisation of the Bosnian police. The inclusion of the task of police reformin the mandate was premised on the expectation that the necessary laws would be passed by the parliamentary assembly early in the lifetime of EUPM 2. This did not happen. As a result, the mission mandate was *de facto* cut in half by the constitutional stalemate in Bosnia. EUPM 3 has been luckier. Though only a step, albeit a crucial one, towards creating a unified police system, new police laws were passed in April 2008 to strengthen state-level policing authority. Hence, EUPM 3 has been in a better position than EUPM 2 to act on its mandate to monitor and guide the centralisation of Bosnia's police.

A final point to be made about the mission mandate has to do with mission creep. EUPM 1 identified the strengthening of local capacities to combat organised crime as one of its four strategic priorities. When the mission was prolonged, the issue was elevated to one of the two principal mandate objectives. Under EUPM 2 & 3, therefore, a goal related to the external dimension of the area of freedom, security and justice, namely the protection of the EU against the negative externalities of organised crime in Bosnia, acquired central prominence.

Mission activities

EUPM 1 designed seven capacity-building programmes which together comprised about 120 reform projects. They covered institutional and operational police issues, ranging from the modernisation of the criminal police and the police administration to the improvement of public order policing.[3] EUPM staff were co-located with local police officers, mid- and senior level police managers and senior ministerial personnel throughout the country. Their tasks were manifold. They monitored the implementation of reform projects; mentored street police and mid-level management police in how to improve their work routines; advised senior police managers on how to overcome gaps in police operational capacity and improve police leadership and law enforcement strategies; and provided recommendations to political authorities on how to reform the security sector and the criminal justice system

---

3. Cf. Michael Merlingen, with Rasa Ostrauskaite, *European Union Peacebuilding and Policing: Governance and the European Security and Defence Policy* (London: Routledge, 2006); Thomas Mühlmann, 'The Police Mission EUPM in Bosnia, 2003-05', in Michael Merlingen and Rasa Ostrauskaite (eds.), (with a Preface by Javier Solana), *European Security and Defence Policy: An Implementation Perspective* (London: Routledge, 2008), pp. 43-60.

more broadly. EUPM 2 and 3 have focused on reforms that upgrade the capacity of the local police to combat organised crime. Mission crime advisors are co-located throughout the country. Their work is supported by criminal justice experts whose task is to develop the police-prosecutor interface. This link is crucial in Bosnia because prosecutors are the lead actors in crime investigations. Among other things, EUPM 2 and 3 have contributed to joint police-prosecutor training and provided advice on how to adjust legislation and procedures so as to enhance cooperation between law enforcement agents and the judiciary. Also, both missions have built on the work of EUPM 1 to further raise police accountability. Among other things, they have been monitoring and inspecting the exercise of political authority over the police and the conduct of officers during crime-busting operations.[4] These activities support the mission's anti-organised crime drive as police corruption, misconduct and political interference in operational policing decisions have been among those factors hampering the fight against organised crime.

Finally, EUPM 3 has benefited from long-awaited progress towards police reform. The two police laws passed in April 2008 establish a series of state-level institutions, notably a Directorate for Coordination of Police Bodies. Among the other new bodies are a police training agency and a public complaints bureau. The implementation of the laws has proved slow and difficult. The politicised context notwithstanding, the EUPM has eagerly jumped on the opportunity to monitor and assist in the further consolidation of the Bosnian police.

As to the relations of the EUPM with the HR/EUSR and the European Commission, they have generally been good. The HR has been one of the principal interlocutors of the EUPM, not least because many police reforms require changes to the laws and formal rules governing Bosnian policing. In such cases, the support and political clout of the HR have been crucial in bringing about the desired adjustments. The EUSR and the EUPM have closely cooperated from the beginning, both at the levels of principals and staff. The EUSR has provided the head of mission with local political guidance and on occasions played an important role in helping to 'deconflict' relations between the EUPM and EUFOR *Althea*. This happened for instance when the two ESDP missions disagreed about their respective policing roles in Bosnia. Finally, the European Commission has been crucial in facilitating EUPM mandate

---

4. Inspection powers came to be interpreted by the EUPM and the HR as meaning the right to full and unimpeded access by mission staff to Bosnian police documents, premises and personnel. The 'stick' behind this power is the ability of the EUPM to ask the HR to make use of his Bonn powers to sanction police officers who systematically fail to cooperate with the EUPM and are not disciplined through appropriate internal control procedures.

implementation. Community funding has supported many of the mission's police reforms as well as complementary projects targeting, among other things, the judiciary and customs services.

Implementation problems

The EUPM struggled with considerable growing pains, some of which continue to plague the mission even as it has matured.[5] First, the mission faced severe difficulties in the start-up phase even though it had benefited from an unduly long planning period – some nine months. Procurement of mission equipment and the development of a concrete reform agenda in the form of implementation plans proved particularly thorny issues. The latter was a challenge because of the absence of standardised mission management tools and the former was complicated by cumbersome Commission procedures. For instance, the final delivery of office computers for mission staff only took place about a year into the mission. During both the start-up and implementation phase, EUPM 1 received, according to its own assessment, insufficient support and directions from the Council General Secretariat.[6] Second, Member States did not always do their best to facilitate mandate implementation. After a good first batch, the quality of seconded police officers tended to decrease. On more than a few occasions, they lacked the experience and qualifications for mentoring and monitoring mid- and senior-level police managers. Third, EUPM 1 did not fully take on board lessons learned by the United Nations, notably that reforms of the police have to be part of an integrated rule-of-law approach that pays equal attention to the triad of law enforcement, the judiciary and the penitentiary. While this can partly be blamed on the imprecise mandate, the EUPM is not blameless. As *Proxima* would later demonstrate in the former Yugoslav Republic of Macedonia (FYROM), mandate gaps can be filled by innovative bottom-up approaches. Yet EUPM 1 did not develop its own version of *Proxima*'s holistic Law Enforcement Monitoring Programme.[7] Consequently, its policing reforms were hampered by the patchy interface between Bosnian police agencies and the court system. This shortcoming was remedied starting with EUPM 2, which set up a Criminal Justice Interface Unit within the mission to enable it to improve relations between prosecutors and the police. The mandate of EUPM 3 made better police-prosecutor relations an explicit mandate objective.

---

5. Cf. also Michael Merlingen and Rasa Ostrauskaite, 'ESDP Police Missions: Meaning, Context and Operational Challenges' in *European Foreign Affairs Review*, vol. 10, no. 2, 2005, pp. 215-35.

6. Interviews, EU Council General Secretariat and Sarajevo, 2005 and 2006.

7. See the chapter on EUPOL *Proxima* and EUPAT in this book.

Last but not least, the mission struggled to develop solutions to deal with the literally impossible mandate task to use non-existent best European and international practices as benchmarks for its reform programmes. After some false starts, project developers operationalised police-related SAA requirements, and the mission put nationals or national teams from EU countries in charge of certain reform projects. For instance, the mission deployed a 70-strong, mostly German co-location team – 'godfathers' as its members were referred to in mission jargon – to strengthen the capacity of the Border Police.[8] They were supported by bilateral assistance, notably by Berlin, which provided funds and equipment. Also, the German border guard agency – the *Bundesgrenzschutz* – entered into a twinning arrangement with the Border Police and provided, for instance, management training to the agency's leadership in Germany. The problem of how to benchmark ESDP policing reforms has been largely defused since the phase of EUPM 1. EUPM 2 ushered in a shift in emphasis from programme-driven reforms to assistance in the implementation of police restructuring and the fight against organised crime. Moreover, work has been ongoing in the Council Secretariat to come up with agreed-upon definitions of best practice.[9]

Challenges on the ground

Initially, there were some concerns about whether the EUPM would be considered legitimate by Bosniaks given the EU's less than impressive performance during the war. These worries turned out to be without substance. Bosnian politics has proved a more serious challenge. Somewhat unexpectedly, the domestic political environment has turned out not to be conducive to the statebuilding reforms the EUPM has been trying to advance. At least four closely linked challenges can be identified: the Dayton legacy with its weak central state institutions and ethnically divided governance structure; the continuing politico-ethnic polarisation and inter-ethnic distrust; the heavy footprint of the HR; and a combination of economic underdevelopment and donor fatigue.

The Dayton legacy bequeathed to Bosnia a highly fragmented police system. While organised crime freely operates across the country, law enforcement has been ham-

8. Interview, Sarajevo, 27 September 2005.

9. 'European and international standards of policing' were defined in Council planning documents as follows: First, the police are structured in accordance with criteria of effectiveness and efficiency; Second, their activities are based on the rule of law; Third, they are adequately protected from improper political interference; Fourth, they act in accordance with democratic values and human rights standards; Fifth, they see their task as protecting citizens' rights and properties.

pered by the existence of many separate police forces and jurisdictional boundaries. This problem has been aggravated by the staying power of nationalist politicians and the preponderant role played by the HR. The two factors feed on each other. The recalcitrance of nationalist leaders has persuaded the international community to support the HR's heavy-handed use of his powers. This, in turn, has weakened the incentives for reforms among local politicians. Instead of forging a consensus and making tough decisions in the interest of their country, they look to the international community as either a scapegoat for what is wrong in Bosnia or an ally in their domestic struggles for power and influence. Hence, despite the fact that the existing policing system is dysfunctional and a drag on scarce economic resources, politicians have so far been unable to fundamentally overhaul it.

The lack of progress towards the unification of the police was a major challenge for EUPM 2. Instead of contributing to successful police restructuring, it had to content itself with reinforcing the centripetal forces within the existing decentralised system. In so doing it focused on strengthening existing state-level police agencies. Ever since EUPM 1, the operationalisation of the State Investigation and Protection Agency (SIPA) and the Border Police has been a mission priority. However, to this day the two bodies remain understaffed and under-resourced. This is primarily due to donor fatigue and a state budget that is overstretched, not least because of the many demands related to the country's reconstruction and development. Moreover, inter-ethnic rivalries have led to the politicisation of senior police appointments. This has resulted in decision blockages, delays and even reversals of appointments in SIPA and the Border Police.

Conclusion: mission achievements and outlook

The Bosnian police has come a long way since the days of the civil war when many of its units were repressive instruments of ethnic violence. The EUPM has played an important role in this development. With a view to some of the most salient improvements, the mission has succeeded in making the local police more accountable (e.g. by setting up, training and mentoring internal control units, which investigate police misconduct); in professionalising police training (e.g. through curriculum development); in implanting modern human resource management in the Bosnian police apparatus (e.g. by elaborating a gender- and ethnicity-blind recruitment and promotion system); and in changing how the police deals with crime scene management (e.g. through capacity-building measures aimed at enabling detectives to rely on forensic evidence rather than confessions).[10] Also, the Bosnian police has a growing capacity to investigate organised crime and prosecutors have become better at successfully arguing their cases in the courts.[11] This said, law enforcement still faces serious structural problems. Police restructuring remains incomplete. Political interference in high-level organised crime cases remains a fact of life, especially in the Republika Srpska. And state-level institutions continue to be hampered by a lack of manpower and resources. Yet it would be unfair to blame these shortcomings on the EUPM. They have complex causes that are located outside the policing field in the political, economic and cultural realms. It would be unrealistic to expect the mission to solve these problems. They can only be tackled through the further political and economic development of Bosnia. This requires the long-term and comprehensive development assistance that is the strength of the European Commission.[12]

BIBLIOGRAPHY

Chandler, David. 'EU Statebuilding: Securing the Liberal Peace through EU Enlargement', in *Global Society: Journal of Interdisciplinary International Relations* (London: Routledge, 2007), pp. 593-607.

Collantes Celador, Gemma. 'The European Union Police Mission: The Beginning of a New Future for Bosnia and Herzegovina?', in *IBEI Working Paper*, no. 2007/9, Institut Barcelona d'Estudis Internacionals, Barcelona, October 2007.

Juncos, Ana E. 'Police Mission in Bosnia and Herzegovina', in Michael Emerson and Eva Gross (eds.), *Evaluating the EU's Crisis Missions in the Balkans*, Centre for European Policy Studies, Brussels, 2007, pp. 46-80.

Merlingen, Michael and Ostrauskaite, Rasa. 'ESDP Police Missions: Meaning, Context and Operational Challenges' in *European Foreign Affairs Review*, vol. 10, no. 2, 2005, pp. 215-35.

10. In addition to the literature referred to in footnote 2, see also Ana E. Juncos, 'Police Mission in Bosnia and Herzegovina', in Michael Emerson and Eva Gross (eds.), *Evaluating the EU's Crisis Missions in the Balkans* (Brussels: Centre for European Policy Studies, 2007), pp. 46-80.

11. This assessment is based on interviews held in 2008 and 2009 with staff from the EU Council General Secretariat.

12. Arguably, the potentially positive impact of the EU on Bosnia has been undermined by the fact that the Union's political development agenda is a form of tutelage that is not accountable to the country's domestic political process. Cf. David Chandler, 'EU Statebuilding: Securing the Liberal Peace through EU Enlargement', in *Global Society: Journal of Interdisciplinary International Relations* (London: Routledge, 2007), pp. 593-607.

Merlingen, Michael and Ostrauskaite, Rasa. 'Power/Knowledge in International Peace-building: The Case of the EU Police Mission in Bosnia', in *Alternatives: Global, Local, Political* (Boulder, CO: Lynne Rienner Publishers, 2005), pp. 297-323.

Merlingen, Michael and Ostrauskaite, Rasa. *European Union Peacebuilding and Policing: Governance and the European Security and Defence Policy* (London: Routledge, 2006).

Mühlmann, Thomas. 'The Police Mission EUPM in Bosnia, 2003-05', in Michael Merlingen and Rasa Ostrauskaite (eds.) (with a Preface by Javier Solana), *European Security and Defence Policy: An Implementation Perspective* (London: Routledge, 2008), pp. 43-60.

Mühlmann, Thomas. 'Police Restructuring in Bosnia-Herzegovina: Problems of Internationally-led Security Sector Reform', in *Journal of Intervention and Statebuilding* (London: Routledge, 2008), pp. 1-22.

Penska, Susan E. 'Policing Bosnia and Herzegovina 2003-05: Issues of Mandates and Management in ESDP Missions', in *CEPS Working Document*, no. 255, Centre for European Policy Studies, Brussels, 2006.

5. Operation CONCORDIA (fYROM)

EU military operation in the former Yugoslav Republic of Macedonia (*Concordia*)

Eva Gross

Legal basis: Council Joint Action 2003/92/CFSP of 27 January 2003

Highlights of the mission's mandate: to contribute to a stable, secure environment in which to implement the Ohrid Framework Agreement.

Duration: 31 March - 10 December 2003.

Budget: €6.2 million.

Mission strength: 350.

Contributing states: 13 (Austria, Belgium, Finland, Germany, Greece, Italy, Luxembourg, the Netherlands, Portugal, Spain, Sweden, the United Kingdom) and 14 third states (Bulgaria, Canada, Czech Republic, Estonia, Hungary, Iceland, Latvia, Lithuania, Norway, Poland, Romania, Slovakia, Slovenia, Turkey).

Introduction

Operation *Concordia*, the first-ever military mission undertaken by the EU, was a logical outcome of the EU's successful intervention in the conflict in the former Yugoslav Republic of Macedonia (FYROM), where the Union had for the first time made use of CFSP instruments created in the Treaty of Amsterdam in 1999, with SG/HR Javier Solana taking the lead in negotiating the resolution of a crisis on behalf of the EU. As with the EU's political intervention in the 2001 crisis, *Concordia* was high on symbolism for ESDP but also for the development of the EU as a comprehensive crisis manager. Perhaps most importantly at the time, the mission also signalled that the EU was ready to assume further security functions in the Balkans, and *Concordia* in many ways represents a prequel for operation EUFOR *Althea*, the mission in Bosnia and Herzegovina launched in 2004. In addition to the operational learning curve concerning the implementation of the mission mandate and the coordination of EU instruments, the running of Operation *Concordia* also illustrated the challenge of delineating the EU-NATO relationship in military crisis management. While *Concordia* was launched in a specific regional context, its conduct has revealed broader and enduring challenges for ESDP not only in the internal (intra-EU) but also the external (extra-EU) coordination of actors and instruments. *Concordia* made a successful contribution to consolidating the role of the EU as a security actor but the attainment of a working EU-NATO relationship and the implementation of a comprehensive approach to crisis management represented two challenges that the mission could not fully meet.

Context and mandate

Concordia was a take-over mission from NATO, which had maintained a military presence in the country since 2001 to ensure a secure and stable environment in order for the political reforms mandated by the Ohrid Framework Agreement to proceed. NATO Operation *Essential Harvest*, a thirty-day mission with 3,500 troops, was launched in August 2001 following the signature of the Ohrid Agreement in order to collect and destroy weapons and ammunition of ethnic Albanian groups. Two small follow-up missions, operations *Amber Fox* and *Allied Harmony*, were tasked with protecting OSCE and EU monitors in the country and, in the case of Operation *Allied Harmony*, also to assist the government in taking over security functions in FYROM.[1] Local conditions were such that a renewed outbreak of large-scale violence

---

1. See NATO's Role in the former Yugoslav Republic of Macedonia, 6 August 2004. http://www.nato.int/fyrom/home.htm (Accessed on 30 May 2009).

was unlikely: the government of FYROM had begun to push actively for EU but also NATO membership, while the ethnic Albanian minority continued working within rather than against the government. Although there was a continued need for a deterrent force, conditions thus enabled not only the ESDP takeover from NATO, but also a progressive reduction in troop size. At around 350 personnel *Concordia* was a slightly smaller mission than the NATO mission Operation *Allied Harmony* had been. Given the local security environment, the operational tasks of the mission included monitoring operations in former crisis areas as well as promoting stability and deterring the resurgence of ethnically motivated violence.[2]

In accordance with the provisions of the 'Berlin Plus' agreement, which gives the EU access to NATO assets in the planning of operations, NATO's Deputy SACEUR General Rainer Feist (Germany) was appointed EU Operational Commander. Operation Headquarters was located at SHAPE in Mons, Belgium with three regional headquarters in Skopje, Kumanovo and Tetovo.[3] Major General Pierre Marral (France) was EU Force Commander, with France acting as framework nation. General Luis Nelson Ferreira dos Santos (Portugal) assumed the post of Force Commander on 30 September 2003, and the European Operational Rapid Force (*Eurofor*) took over the command of Operation *Concordia* for the remainder of the operation.[4] 12 Member States and 14 non-Member States contributed to the mission with the biggest contingents provided by France (145) followed by Italy (27), Germany and Belgium (26 each). The budget for the mission was raised from an initial €4.7 million to €6.2 million, after *Concordia*'s mandate was extended beyond six months, as had been originally foreseen.[5] Operation *Concordia* terminated on 15 December 2003 and was followed by a civilian police operation, EUPOL *Proxima*.[6]

Mission implementation and performance

Although the EU declared its willingness to take over from NATO at the June 2002 Barcelona Council, Turkish opposition delayed the conclusion of the Berlin Plus agreement until December 2002. FYROM authorities formally invited the EU to assume responsibility for the follow-on to the NATO operation and the EU decided to

2. 'Putting "Berlin Plus" into Practice: Taking over from NATO in fYROM', *European Security Review* no. 16. Brussels, ISIS Europe, February 2003, pp. 2-4.

3. Gustav Lindstrom, 'On the ground: ESDP operations', in Nicole Gnesotto (ed.), *EU Security and Defence Policy: the first five years (1999-2004)* (Paris: EU Institute for Security Studies, 2004) pp. 111-30.

4. Council Joint Action 2003/563/CFSP of 29 July 2003, *Official Journal* L190/20, 29 July 2003. See also 'Eurofor: a peace force for Europe', available at: http://www.eurofor.it/index.htm (Accessed on 30 May 2009).

5. Council Decision 2003/563/CFSP of 29 July 2003.

6. See the chapter on EUPOL *Proxima* and EUPAT in this book.

launch the mission on 18 March 2003.[7] As the EU relied on NATO both for planning and logistical support, there was close EU-NATO coordination through the Political and Security Committee (PSC) and North Atlantic Council (NAC) throughout the conduct of the mission. The chain of command as set out in the mandate had the Force Commander work closely with NATO Headquarters while the PSC was to exercise political control and provide strategic direction.

Beyond the NATO presence in FYROM, Operation *Concordia* entered a theatre where other EU actors were already active. In addition to the office of the EUSR and the Commission delegation, the EU presence included the European Agency for Reconstruction (EAR), the EU Monitoring Mission (EUMM), as well as the EU Presidency. The office of the EU Special Representative (EUSR) held a pivotal position for the coordination of EU instruments.[8] EUSR Alexis Brouhns acted as an interface between the force commander and local political authorities, and was to ensure the coordination of the military operation with other EU policies in place.[9] *Concordia* worked in close cooperation with the office of the EUSR through daily briefing meetings and a joint security dialogue with FYROM authorities. In addition, weekly meetings of EU operational representatives took place in an effort to avoid duplication in contacts with Macedonian authorities.

In operational terms, the mission consisted of 22 light field liaison teams, whose tasks included patrolling, reconnaissance, surveillance, situational awareness, reporting and liaison activities. Eight heavy field liaison teams with access to wheeled armoured vehicles and helicopters provided troop support, and additional support was available through a helicopter detachment with light reconnaissance and MedEvac helicopters, an Explosive Ordnance Disposal (EOD) capability and a medical evacuation team.[10] At the behest of the EUSR, and in an attempt to link existing different EU instruments to *Concordia*, EAR funds were made available for limited civil-military cooperation (CIMIC) projects identified and implemented by liaison teams in the field.[11] Specific operational activities served both to collect information to assess the security situation on the ground and to raise the visibility of the EU mission. They included presence patrols and information-gathering patrols; re-

---

7. Council Decision 75307/03 relating to the launch of the EU Military Operation in the former Yugoslav Republic of Macedonia, Brussels, 18 March 2003.

8. Between 30 September 2002 and 26 January 2004, and therefore the duration of Operation *Concordia*, this position was held by the senior Belgian diplomat Alexis Brouhns.

9. Council Joint Action 2003/446/CFSP, 16 June 2003. Cited in Giovanni Grevi, 'Pioneering foreign policy: The EU Special Representatives', *Chaillot Paper* no. 106, EU Institute for Security Studies, Paris, October 2007.

10. Op. cit. in note 3, p. 118.

11. Interview with former EU official, 8 April 2009.

connaissance tasks; meetings with civilian and military authorities, international organisations and Macedonian civil society groups; and support to the OSCE and EUMM international observers in specific missions.[12] Given the largely stable situation on the ground, the mission size was sufficient for carrying out its mandated tasks.

Main challenges confronting the mission

While *Concordia* successfully tested the EU's ability to undertake a military mission and to develop operating procedures, in assuming its tasks the mission confronted a number of internal and external coordination challenges. External challenges predominately involved EU-NATO relations.[13] A cumbersome reporting chain in addition to issues over information sharing between the EU and NATO signalled not only problems over EU-NATO coordination but also the need for a more elaborate delineation of tasks between the EU and NATO in future operations. Intra-EU debates centered around the coordination of EU instruments in pursuit of a comprehensive approach and the degree to which the planning and conduct of Operation *Concordia* made use of synergies with other EU instruments already in place.

In addition to the use of NATO Headquarter at SHAPE and the joint appointment of *Concordia*'s Operation Commander as Deputy Supreme Allied Commander Europe (DSACEUR), coordination between EU and NATO elements was also required in the field. NATO maintained a presence in the country through a Senior Civilian Representative and a Senior Military representative in Skopje to help with Security Sector Reform (SSR) and adaptation to NATO standards in preparation for NATO membership. This caused some confusion, as the maintenance of a NATO military structure in FYROM and NATO advising FYROM authority on border security created some overlap between the two missions. The continued NATO presence also made it difficult for the EU to establish itself as the primary security provider but also the main political actor *vis-à-vis* Macedonian authorities.

More importantly for the mission itself, intelligence sharing between the EU and NATO had not been agreed upon before the launch of the mission and this presented a significant coordination challenge.[14] While NATO was eventually given full

---

12. See Colonel Pierre Augustin, 'Lessons learned: Operation *Concordia/Altaïr* in Macedonia', *Doctrine* no. 6, March 2005. See: http://www.cdef.terre.defense.gouv.fr/publications/doctrine/doctrine06/version_us/retex/art_22.pdf.

13. While the OSCE also maintained a mission on the ground, its operational mandate did not directly conflict with that of *Concordia*.

14. On this point, see also International Crisis Group, 'Macedonia: No Room for Complacency', *Europe Report* no. 149, 23 October 2003.

access to *Concordia* mission reports, the EU in turn never gained access to NATO reports on Kosovo. This had potential security implications for the operation. Villages close to the Kosovo border were involved in trafficking of arms and potentially vulnerable to general unrest, and frequent if minor incidents in the mountainous regions were also due to instability in Kosovo. Had there been a serious security incident during *Concordia*'s operational mandate, the EU presence would likely have been negatively impacted.[15] Differences between NATO and the EU also prevented the establishment of a direct contact between *Concordia* and KFOR, with the EU Force Commander having to go through Allied Forces Southern Europe (AF-SOUTH) in Naples to have contact with NATO rather than developing field-level contacts, which would have facilitated the running of the operation. The sharing of intelligence, but also broader (ideological) issues in the EU-NATO relationship thus became rather important.

With respect to intra-EU coordination, the chain of command structures that were established based on the Berlin Plus agreement and closely modelled on NATO structures were not ideal to promote the coordination of civilian and military instruments; nor were they conducive to delivering coordinated messages to FYROM authorities. The military chain of command had the Force Commander report to SHAPE via AFSOUTH. Although these chain of command structures were compatible with the Berlin Plus Agreement,[16] they were not efficient in ensuring the EU's political control of the mission. Rather, the fact that the Force Commander had to report to SHAPE through AFSOUTH created institutional distance between the Force Commander and SG/HR Solana as well as the PSC. As a result, the respective positions of *Concordia* and that of the Council in Brussels but also that of the EUSR *vis-à-vis* the FYROM authorities in the field were not always fully coordinated and were expressed separately – with predictable results in terms of the coherence of the message to local authorities. Beyond the matter of imperfect intra-EU coordination, the separation of military and political structures was unfortunate also because the military mission essentially constituted a supporting element in a broader political undertaking.

During the planning phase of the operation, the strict delineation between *Concordia* and the various EU instruments already in place meant that *Concordia* did not make use of the political input and the expertise of the diplomatic staff of the office of the EUSR. As such, there was also no serious review early on in the process of

---

15. Interview with former EU official, 8 April 2009.

16. See Annalisa Monaco, 'Operation *Concordia* and Berlin Plus: NATO and the EU take stock.', ISIS NATO notes, vol. 5, no. 8, International Security Information Service (ISIS), Brussels, December 2003.

the possible impact of the operation on existing EU engagement in FYROM. After the launch of the operation, a close relationship was established between the Force Commander and the EUSR that included guidance on the political climate in the country, but this was on an informal rather than a formal basis.[17] Given the post-conflict setting, but also the quest for EU candidate status on the part of FYROM, ideally the military mission should have been as closely aligned as possible to the EU's broader political objectives.[18] Close links to NATO, at the expense of a closer link between *Concordia* and other EU instruments, however, prevented the EU as a whole from gaining the political leverage it could have reasonably been expected to wield in FYROM.

Political leverage *vis-à-vis* the Macedonian authorities was also negatively affected by the incomplete coordination of EU instruments at large. The inter-pillar coordination that had worked quite well in the negotiation towards a resolution of the 2001 crisis, with Chris Patten and Javier Solana often travelling together, thereby reinforcing the EU political line, revealed structural coordination challenges between the Council and the Commission that undermined the effective implementation of EU policies. While the Commission Delegation through the Community Assistance for Reconstruction, Development and Stabilisation (CARDS) programme helped move along political and economic reforms, these programmes were not coordinated with the political objectives or priorities set by the EUSR. Weekly coordination meetings with all EU actors were held in the office of the EUSR in order to align positions and activities, and generally good interpersonal relations between the EUSR, Delegation and *Concordia* facilitated informal contacts and coordination. In the end, however, different operating mandates, bureaucratic procedures and political imperatives impeded a closer structural coordination of military, political and economic instruments.

Lessons learned: achievements and shortcomings

The EU's record as a crisis manager in FYROM is in many ways exemplary, in particular with regard to the linear application of instruments and the devolution from a military to a civilian ESDP mission followed by Community programmes in preparation for eventual EU candidate status, which was granted in 2005. With respect to military ESDP, *Concordia* was a credibility test for the EU and its successful conduct paved the way towards more missions in more challenging theatres. *Concordia* thus

---

17. Interview with former EU official, 8 April 2009.
18. Annalisa Monaco, op. cit. in note 16.

laid the groundwork for the EU's growing profile as a military security actor. However, the main achievements of *Concordia* go beyond signalling the EU's increasing role in international security. The mission not only tested operational procedures, it also fulfilled its mandate to contribute to a stable and secure environment. Both aspects count as achievements for the operation as well as for ESDP more broadly.

The operation's main shortcomings, on the other hand, stem from the mission's internal and external coordination challenges. These concerned in particular the structural linkages between the political and the military aspects of the operation, raising enduring questions as to the EU's ability to implement a comprehensive approach that links military, political and economic instruments. Arguably, the aim of comprehensiveness was even more important given the enlargement perspective at play in FYROM, which is one of the biggest foreign policy incentives the EU has at its disposal. Given that FYROM represented a relatively benign theatre in which to launch the first military ESDP operation, the fact that the launch of *Concordia* did not contribute to a stronger, in the sense of a more coordinated, EU political, military, and economic presence must be regarded as *Concordia*'s main shortcoming.

BIBLIOGRAPHY

Augustin, Col. Pierre. 'Lessons learned: Operation *Concordia/Altaïr* in Macedonia', *Doctrine* no. 6, March 2005.

International Crisis Group. 'Macedonia: No Room for Complacency', *Europe Report* no. 149, 23 October 2003.

Lindstrom, Gustav. 'On the ground: ESDP operations', in Nicole Gnesotto (ed.), *EU Security and Defence Policy. The first five years (1999-2004)* (Paris: EU Institute for Security Studies, 2004), pp. 111-30.

Monaco, Annalisa. 'Operation *Concordia* and Berlin Plus: NATO and the EU take stock', *NATO notes* vol. 5, no. 8, International Security Information Service (ISIS) Europe, Brussels, December 2003.

6. Operation ARTEMIS (RD Congo)

The EU military operation in DR Congo (*Artemis*)

Damien Helly

Legal basis: Council Joint Action 2003/423/CFSP of 5 June 2003.

Highlights of the mission's mandate:

■ To contribute to the stabilisation of the security conditions and the improvement of the humanitarian situation in Bunia.

■ To ensure the protection of the airport and of the internally displaced persons in the camps in Bunia.

■ If the situation so required, to contribute to the safety of the civilian population, United Nations personnel and the humanitarian presence in the town.

Duration: 12 June – 1 September 2003.

Budget: €7 million (common costs).

Mission strength: Approximately 2,000 troops.

Contributing states: 14 Member States (Austria, Belgium, France, Germany, Greece, Ireland, Italy, the Netherlands, Portugal, Spain, Sweden, UK. Hungary and Cyprus contributed but only became EU members in 2004) and 3 third countries (Brazil, Canada, South Africa).

Background

Since 1998 a civil war had been going on in the Democratic Republic of Congo (DRC) with the involvement of several neighbouring countries. A ceasefire was negotiated in July 1999 and UN-sponsored inter-Congolese dialogue started. In this context, the DRC and Ugandan governments signed an agreement in 2002 putting an end to the presence of Ugandan troops in the Eastern province of Ituri. Following the departure of Ugandan forces, fighting between the Union des patriotes congolais (UPC, dominated by the Lendu) and the Front de résistance patriotique de l'Ituri (FPRI, led by the Hema) started in February 2003, leading to a major humanitarian crisis with between 500,000 and 600,000 displaced persons. 700 UN Uruguayan MONUC troops were deployed in Bunia in April but were unable to address the situation properly. UNSG Kofi Annan therefore asked France to lead a multinational force to intervene before more UN troops were deployed on the ground. France attached minimal conditions to its intervention: a clear UN mandate with limited geographical range and timeframe and regional political support from Uganda and Rwanda. Once those conditions were fulfilled, Paris expressed its readiness to conduct the operation (codenamed Mamba) on 16 May 2003. The UN Security Council adopted its Resolution 1484 on 30 May 2003. At the initiative of France, EU Member States decided to launch the operation in the framework of ESDP. This would create an historical precedent, as the first European military operation deployed without NATO support.

The Europeanisation of an initially French-led operation made it possible to initiate ESDP operations outside the Berlin Plus framework. It also tested the 'framework nation' concept.

Mandate

The mandate was threefold and focused on the town of Bunia: it was therefore very limited in time and space although some flexibility was allowed to review the size of the area of operations if need be. The general objective was the stabilisation of the town and the improvement of the humanitarian situation. The second, more specific, objective was to ensure the protection of the airport and of those internally displaced persons (IDPs) stationed in camps in the town. Thirdly, the protection of the civilian population, UN personnel and humanitarian presence had to be ensured, if needed.

The force was under the command of two French officers (Operation Commander Major-General Bruno Neveux and Force Commander Brigadier-General Jean-Paul Thonier). France provided most of the force (1,785 of which 1,651 were deployed, 42 stationed in the OHQ and 92 in the FHQ). The OHQ (staffed with around 80 officers, 40 percent of whom were non-French) was located in Paris and the FHQ (approximately 400 troops) near the Entebbe airport in Uganda.

All in all 14 Member States contributed to *Artemis* including, among others, Belgium (23 medical staff and tactical and strategic aircrafts),[1] Germany (34 based in Entebbe for medical evacuation), Sweden (approximately 70 troops in special forces) and the UK (up to 85 staff among whom engineers and sappers in Bunia, support staff in Entebbe). Three non-EU countries joined the operation: Brazil (50 troops), Canada and South Africa (120 troops).

Implementation and achievements

The operation only lasted three months. Troops first secured Bunia airport on 6 June. Deterrence was prioritised over direct combat and militia casualties remained limited (2 killed on 16 June). On 21 June, the UPC militia was forced to withdraw. On 4 July, the 5 entry points to Bunia were under control and on 8 July security was restored in the town. A week later, following violence in the Miala camp and the consequent need to intervene there, the area of operation was extended so that the force could enter the camp and secure it.[2] Until the end of the operation, patrolling outside of the town was carried out to deter outbreaks of violence. As of 20 July, a gradual handover to the UN troops was put in place, leading to a full withdrawal from Bunia on 6 September and from Entebbe on 25 September 2003. A new UN contingent of about 5,000 troops from India, Pakistan, Bangladesh, Nepal and Indonesia took over in the area.

Achievements and lessons learned

Artemis operationalised some new concepts for military ESDP: autonomous action outside the NATO framework, at the request of the UN and with a UN mandate. Besides, *Artemis* fulfilled some key operational goals: rapid deployment in a very remote area; the capacity to protect the civilian population with a minimum

---

1. For Belgium, *Artemis* was the first time sending troops to Africa again after the loss of soldiers in Rwanda in 1994. See Niagalé Bagayoko, 'L'Opération Artémis, un tournant pour la politique européenne de sécurité et de défense?', *Revue Afrique contemporaine,* no. 209, 2004, p. 107.

2. Ministère de la Défense, Centre de Doctrine d'Emploi des Forces (CDEF), *Doctrine*, December 2006, p. 54. Available at: http://www.cdef.terre.defense.gouv.fr/default.htm.

number of casualties; coordination with humanitarian actors and other international organisations.

It also constituted an opportunity to test the functioning of the politico-military structures (the PSC, the EUMC and the EUMS) and it showed that quick decisions could be made by these institutions.[3] Thanks to its success, *Artemis* created a precedent for the ESDP and validated the concept of the 'framework nation' which, in this particular case, was France. It also created a strategic precedent by extending ESDP's remit to Africa and thus opening a new field of experimentation.

However, questions remained and challenges appeared. The mission was so limited in scope that some debates emerged about the difficulty of gauging its success, especially when new massacres erupted in the area shortly after the departure of the force.[4] Furthermore, since France was the main initiator, contributor and leader of this operation, doubts were raised about the real ability of the EU as such to do the same without a French contribution.

At the operational level, the *Artemis* experience demonstrated the military advantages of leaving considerable flexibility to the Force commander on the ground in a very violent and volatile context, even though this option may imply less control exerted by the PSC.[5] Various shortcomings were noted regarding strategic, political or operational intelligence gathering and sharing, the obsolescence of certain equipment and the lack of common and secured communications tools and channels. Shortfalls in secure communications channels and information technology were addressed in the course of the mission.[6]

As for UN-EU cooperation, one of the lessons learned by the operation was that both organisations were still 'discovering each other.' EU requests to use UN DPKO logistics assets (this did not match UN procedures) and to benefit from the legal agreement that MONUC had reached with the Congolese (which would have put

---

3. Niagalé Bagayoko, op. cit. in note 2.

4. 'Declaration by the Presidency on behalf of the European Union on the massacres in the province of Ituri in the Democratic Republic of the Congo', 13526/03 (Presse 301), Brussels, 13 October 2003. Criticism was also expressed by NGOs like the International Crisis Group and Médecins Sans Frontières. See Anand Menon, 'Empowering paradise? The ESDP at ten', *International Affairs*, vol. 85, no. 2, 2009, pp.227-46, p.230. See also Catherine Gégout, 'Causes and Consequences of the EU's Military Intervention in the Democratic Republic of Congo: A Realist Explanation', *European Foreign Affairs Review*, vol. 10, no. 3, Autumn 2005, pp. 427-43.

5. Niagalé Bagayoko, op. cit. in note 2, pp.111-12.

6. Kees Homan, 'Operation Artemis in the Democratic Republic of Congo', in European Commission (ed.), *Faster and more united ? the debate about Europe's crisis response capacity* (Luxembourg: OPOCE, May 2007), pages 151-55.

ESDP troops under UN command) could not be met.[7] However, *Artemis* was seen as 'a remarkably positive experiment in cooperation between the UN and a regional organisation, in the domain of peace and security.'[8] The operation created rather high expectations from the UN about the prospects of ESDP launching more operations in Africa.[9] At the end of the day though, European peacekeeping in Africa has remained limited. The rapid reaction scheme set up for *Artemis* later inspired the creation of the Battle Group Concept which came under question in late 2008 when the EU decided not to intervene in the Kivu region.

BIBLIOGRAPHY

Bagayoko, Niagalé. 'L'Opération Artémis, un tournant pour la politique européenne de sécurité et de défense?', *Revue Afrique contemporaine* , no. 209, 2004.

Braud, Pierre-Antoine Braud. 'Implementing ESDP Operations in Africa', in Anne Deighton and Victor Mauer (eds.), *Securing Europe ? Implementing the European Security Strategy* (Zurich: ETH Zurich, 2006).

Gégout, Catherine. 'Causes and Consequences of the EU's Military Intervention in the Democratic Republic of Congo: A Realist Explanation', *European Foreign Affairs Review*, vol. 10, no. 3, Autumn 2005, pp. 427-43.

Homan, Kees. 'Operation *Artemis* in the Democratic Republic of Congo', in European Commission (ed.), *Faster and more united ? The debate about Europe's crisis response capacity* (Luxembourg: OPOCE, May 2007), pages 151-55.

Lindstrom, Gustav. 'On the ground: ESDP operations', in Nicole Gnesotto (ed.), *EU Security and Defence Policy: the first five years* (1999-2004) (Paris: EUISS, 2004), pp. 111-29.

Menon, Anand. 'Empowering paradise? The ESDP at ten', *International Affairs*, vol. 85, no. 2, 2009, pp. 227-46.

Ulriksen, Ståle, Gourlay, Catriona and Mace, Catriona. 'Operation *Artemis*: The Shape of Things to Come?' in *International Peacekeeping*, vol. 11, no. 3, 2004, pp. 508-25.

---

7. Pierre-Antoine Braud, 'Implementing ESDP Operations in Africa', in Anne Deighton and Victor Mauer (eds.), *Securing Europe ? Implementing the European Security Strategy* (Zurich: ETH Zurich, 2006), p.77.

8. Kees Homan, op. cit. in note 7, p. 154.

9. Ståle Ulriksen, Catriona Gourlay and Catriona Mace, 'Operation Artemis: The Shape of Things to Come?' in *International Peacekeeping* vol. 11, no. 3, 2004, pp. 508-25.

7. EUPOL PROXIMA / EUPAT (fYROM)

The EU Police Mission (EUPOL *Proxima*) and the European Union Police Advisory Team (EUPAT) in the former Yugoslav Republic of Macedonia

Isabelle Ioannides

EUPOL *Proxima*

Legal Basis: Council Joint Action 2003/681/CFSP of 23 September 2003.

Highlights of the mission's mandate:

■ Monitoring, mentoring and advising on the consolidation of law and order, including the fight against organised crime.

■ The practical implementation of the comprehensive reform of the Ministry of Interior.

■ The operational transition and creation of a border police.

■ Building confidence between the local police and the population; and enhanced cooperation with neighbouring states in policing.

Duration: *Proxima I*: Dec. 2003-Dec. 2004, *Proxima II*: Dec. 2004-Dec. 2005.

Budget: *Proxima I*: €15 million; *Proxima II*: €15.95 million.

Mission strength: *Proxima I*: 186 international police officers; *Proxima II*: 169 international staff (138 international police officers, three civilian seconded personnel and 28 international experts).

Contributing states: *Proxima I*: 22 Member States and 4 third countries (Norway, Switzerland, Turkey, Ukraine); *Proxima II*: 24 Member States and 4 third countries (Norway, Switzerland, Turkey, Ukraine).

EUPAT

Legal basis: (Council Joint Action 2005/826/CFSP of 24 November 2005).

Highlights of the mission's mandate:

■ Monitoring, mentoring and advising on priority issues in the field of border police; public peace, order and accountability.

■ The fight against corruption and organised crime.

■ Special attention given to: overall implementation of police reform in the field.

■ Police-judiciary cooperation; and professional standards/ internal control.

Duration: 15 December 2005-14 June 2006.

Budget: €1.5 million.

Mission strength: 29 police advisors (including EU police officers and civilian experts).

Contributing states: 16 Member States (Austria, Belgium, Cyprus, Denmark, Finland, France, Germany, Greece, Hungary, Italy, Latvia, Slovakia, Slovenia, Spain, Sweden, and the United Kingdom).

EU efforts to tackle 'urgent needs' in police reform in the former Yugoslav Republic of Macedonia (FYROM) were undertaken within the framework of the Ohrid Framework Agreement (13 August 2001), which encompassed two important goals. First, it laid down clear objectives and benchmarks, addressing the issue of inequitable representation of minorities in the police, the redeployment of mixed police patrols in the crisis areas and the provision of technical assistance for institutional/procedural changes in public security institutions. Second, it provided the international community with a mandate to organise international assistance, including the police. An EU Special Representative (EUSR) was appointed to help ensure, *inter alia*, the coherence of the EU external action and coordination of the international community's efforts. In parallel, long-term efforts to assist the Macedonian government improve internal security – developing a capable, depoliticised, decentralised, community-based, multi-ethnic police service which is responsive to citizens' needs, accountable to the rule of law and transparent – have been ongoing since 2000. They were carried out under the Stabilisation and Association Agreement (SAA) (9 April 2001), which was further reinforced by the European Partnership for FYROM and the Council decision to grant candidate status to the country (17 December 2005).

EU Police Mission (EUPOL) *Proxima*

Despite European Commission contributions for the reconstruction of the country through the Rapid Reaction Mechanism (RRM) and CARDS programme and the presence of the NATO operation *Allied Harmony* followed by the EU military mission *Concordia*, the political and security situation in FYROM remained fragile in late 2002: arms in private possession proliferated; the coalition government was weak; law enforcement in ethnic Albanian-dominated areas was absent; and international human rights organisations criticised the situation on the ground.[1] Yet, as the country slowly progressed towards stability and the police was redeployed to the former crisis areas from which it had withdrawn during the interethnic crisis (February-August 2001), the EU's attention shifted to the qualitative improvement of the police. Improving relations between the police and ethnic minorities and ensuring the sustainability of institutional/procedural police reform were issues of primary concern. In this context, the first EU police mission in FYROM, code-named EUPOL *Proxima*, was launched on 15 December 2003 initially for a year and extended for another year to 14 December 2005, in line with the objectives of the

---

1. Anna Matveeva *et al.*, *Macedonia: Guns, Policing and Ethnic Division* (London/Bonn: Saferworld and Bonn International Centre for Conversion, 2003); International Crisis Group, 'Macedonia: No Room for Complacency', *Europe Report* no. 149, ICG Skopje/Brussels, 23 October 2003.

Ohrid Framework Agreement and in close partnership with the country's authorities. It followed on from the EU's first military operation *Concordia*, which had taken over from NATO to maintain a visible military presence and to support stability and confidence-building in areas of potential ethnic tension.[2]

Mandate and performance

EUPOL *Proxima* was the second police mission falling under ESDP, but unlike the EU Police Mission in Bosnia-Herzegovina (EUPM) that took over from the UN International Police Task Force (IPTF), it was the first one to start from scratch.[3] In line with the objectives of the Framework Agreement and the Stability and Association Process (SAP), the mission aimed at promoting the gradual stabilisation of the country. Unlike the European Commission, which acted at a strategic level through small teams co-located in the Ministry of Interior (MoI), *Proxima* deployed EU police officers and civilian experts at an operational level in the Macedonian MoI and police stations at central level in Skopje and at regional, sub-regional and local levels in the former crisis areas, where a majority of ethnic Albanians live.[4] Their objective was to mentor, monitor and advise middle and senior management police officers, assisting the implementation of the National Police Strategy and the Integrated Border Management Strategy, both of which had been adopted by the Macedonian government.

Proxima's mandate was primarily to provide support to the Macedonian authorities to consolidate law and order, including the fight against organised crime; to undertake the practical implementation of the reform of the MoI, police and border police; to build confidence with local populations; and to enhance cooperation with neighbouring countries. The mandate was translated into 28 activities covering all the functions of these five programmes: uniformed police; criminal police; department for state security and counter-intelligence; internal control; and border police. A team of EU border police officers was deployed at the border crossing points and the international airports of Skopje and Ohrid to support the strengthening of regional cooperation; assist the creation of a border police with decentralised structures; and facilitate the transfer of border control from the border brigade (army) to civilian surveillance. In the context of a broader rule of law perspective, law enforce-

2. See the chapter on Operation *Concordia* in this book.

3. Isabelle Ioannides, 'Police Mission in Macedonia', in Michael Emerson and Eva Gross (eds.), *Evaluating the EU's Crisis Missions in the Balkans* (Brussels: Centre for European Policy Studies, CEPS, 2007), p. 92. See also the chapter on EUPM Bosnia-Herzegovina in this book.

4. The national distribution of the *Proxima I* personnel was as follows: Germany (25); France (24); Netherlands (15); Italy (13); Sweden (11); Spain (10); Greece (9); Finland (8); Turkey (8); United Kingdom (7); Belgium (6); Denmark (6); Hungary (5); Norway (5); Slovenia (5); Ukraine (5); Cyprus (4); Austria (3); Czech Republic (3); Poland (3); Switzerland (3); Ireland (2); Latvia (2); Lithuania (2); Luxemburg (1); Portugal (1).

ment monitors assisted the development of cooperation between all bodies in the criminal justice system (the police, Public Prosecutor's Office, investigative officers, and courts). To enhance public confidence in the police, they supported *Proxima* co-locators in the investigation of police misconduct complaints and monitored the investigation carried out by the newly-established Internal Control and Professional Standards Unit in the MoI and the conditions and treatment of detainees in police stations.[5]

EUPOL *Proxima* was extended for a second year (informally code-named *Proxima II*), until 14 December 2005. It was the first-ever mission to be extended with a new mandate, therefore carrying out a major overhaul of its activities and procedures while in the field.[6] The mission continued to give particular attention to upper and middle management, but reduced the number of staff and focused functionally on specific challenges in the police reform process.[7] The five programmes of *Proxima I* were restructured and reduced to three programmes in *Proxima II* concentrating on organised crime, public peace and order, and border police. Simultaneously, *Proxima* expanded its geographical coverage to a countrywide deployment, though retaining a higher presence in the former crisis area.

During the extension of its mandate, *Proxima* concentrated on the more demanding facets of *Proxima*'s initial mandate, issues which it had been unable to tackle during the first year of its existence. Concretely, the mission aimed at improving leadership and crime scene management, border policing and the capacity of the department for state security and counter-intelliegence to plan and manage operations to counter terrorism and fight organised crime. For example, it organised 'in-service training' on handling informants, the legal framework of the department for state security and counter-intelligence, planning operations and personnel evaluation procedures. It also established a multidisciplinary working group on intelligence and a multi-ethnic Working Group in the MoI to develop the mission statement on organised crime. At an operational level, it monitored and advised the special police units dispatched to deal with the stand-off created in June 2005 by a heavily

5. Ioannides, Isabelle, 'EU Police Mission *Proxima*: Testing the "European" Approach to Building Peace', in Agnieszka Nowak (ed.), 'Civilian Crisis Management: The EU Way', *Chaillot Paper* no. 90 (Paris: European Institute for Security Studies, June 2006), p. 75; EUPOL *Proxima*, 'Internal Control/Law Enforcement Monitoring Programme', Factsheet (Skopje: EUPOL *Proxima*, June 2004).

6. Tobias Flessekemper, 'EUPOL *Proxima* in Macedonia, 2003-05', in Michael Merlingen and Rasa Ostrauskaite (eds.), *European Security and Defence Policy: An Implementation Perspective* (London: Routledge, 2008), p. 78.

7. Specifically, the national distribution of international staff in EUPOL *Proxima II* was as follows: France (25), Germany (21), the Netherlands (11), Sweden (11), Spain (11), Italy (11), Greece (8), Turkey (8), Finland (6), Denmark (5), Hungary (5), Norway (5), the UK (5), Slovenia (5), Cyprus (4), Belgium (4), Ukraine (3), Czech Republic (3), Austria (3), Poland (3), Switzerland (2), Lithuania (2), Latvia (2), Slovakia (2), Portugal (1), Ireland (1), Estonia (1) and Luxembourg (1).

armed ethnic Albanian group that emerged in the village of Kondovo near Skopje and which denied access to the area by the police. In the context of enhancing
confidence building in democratic policing (public peace and order programme),
Proxima supported the Community Advisory Groups (CAGs) bringing together the
police and community members to discuss and resolve local problems (e.g. garbage
collection, possession of small arms, etc.).

In order to fulfil the programme objectives, result-based activities tied to a specific
timeframe were developed and monitored on a weekly basis. Unlike the situation
during *Proxima*'s initial mandate when activities in field offices were organised on
an *ad hoc* basis in agreement with the chiefs of police, *Proxima*'s newly-established
'benchmarking system' enabled the mission to tackle very specific projects according to a benchmarking document that the MoI had endorsed *ex ante* at a strategic
level. This 'benchmarking system' was distinct from the one developed for the EU
Police Mission (EUPM) in Bosnia-Herzegovina, which was considered complicated
and unable to identify the objectives of activities. This political tool ensured the
implementation of reforms, therefore tackling local police's resistance to change
– a great impediment to *Proxima*'s work during the first year of its mandate – and
contributing to the end of mission evaluation. However, the benefits of this 'benchmarking system' were limited to assessing whether an activity was carried out; it
could not verify whether its objectives were attained.

European Union Police Advisory Team (*EUPAT*)

With the end of EUPOL *Proxima*, the Council felt that a continued EU presence
in the rural areas and outside Skopje was necessary. It was concerned about possible instability resulting from the opening of Kosovo status negotiations, and
wanted to ensure that police reform was sustainable and that the fragile progress
that the country had achieved in the past four years was consolidated. Simultaneously, the Council recognised that, as FYROM moved closer to the EU, assistance
on police reform should be pursued primarily through Community activities and
programmes. Accordingly, the European Commission was planning to launch a
project ('Local Implementation Component' – LIC)[8] focusing on the implementation of reform at field level and capacity-building within the MoI in April 2006. To
bridge the six-month time gap between the end of *Proxima* and the commencement
of the Commission field-level project, the Council decided to launch an EU Police

---

8. An EC Twinning project on police reform, which supported the Ministry of Interior at central level (Nov 2005-Nov 2007), featured seven resident Twinning advisors in different key areas of the police reform.

Advisory Team (EUPAT) from 15 December 2005 until 14 June 2006. The Macedonian government welcomed EUPAT 'under certain conditions' that ensured that its EU membership prospects would not be compromised; that EUPAT be presented as a reform-oriented effort rather than a stabilisation-oriented one; that it not be defined as 'a mission'; and that it be clearly linked to the CARDS-funded projects.[9]

Mandate and performance

EUPAT was similar to *Proxima* in its goals, mission and organisation. Building on Proxima's results and drawing from its staff and expertise, EUPAT monitored, advised and mentored the Macedonian police at local level on priority issues including border police; public peace and order; and the fight against corruption and organised crime. Its interim status translated into fewer staff (29 police experts) and resources (€1.5 million), which slowed the momentum *Proxima* had created. Its focus on organised crime was said to allow the 'advisory team' to act as an 'early warning mechanism in case things flare up in Kosovo'.[10] EUPAT focused on the implementation of police reforms, cooperation between the police and judiciary, professional standardisation, and internal control. It also actively contributed to establishing a human rights culture, though the mandate did not explicitly raise human rights tasks.[11] EUPAT acted to a great extent as an 'exit mission' and the restrictions put on it resulted from political considerations surrounding the political decision on FYROM's EU candidate status rather than functional issues regarding the organisation and structure of the actual mission.[12]

The new element of EUPAT was the creation of a 'consultation mechanism', designed to improve *Proxima*'s 'benchmarking system'. According to this new mechanism, EUPAT submitted a report on a monthly basis to the national authorities on the progress accomplished in its activities, the progress the national authorities made on the reforms, and the shortcomings in the Macedonian police (through monitoring performance, corruption and organised crime). This system aimed at creating openness and transparency between the two parties – the EU and the national authorities – but also acted as leverage on the authorities.[13] The reciproc-

---

9. Other conditions included that EUPAT have a clear mandate with a defined end-date; that it would not be presented as a follow-up to *Proxima*, but as a transitional measure until the CARDS-funded project was in place; and that international police officers would not wear a uniform. Interview with Council official in Brussels, May 2006.

10. Interview with Council official in Brussels, on 14 December 2005.

11. Jana Arloth and Frauke Seidensticker *The ESDP Crisis Management Operations of the European Union and Human Rights* (Berlin: German Institute for Human Rights, April 2007), p. 46.

12. Interview with EU Mission official, in Skopje, in June 2006.

13. Interview with Council official, in Brussels, on 14 December 2005.

ity created by the consultation mechanism implied that FYROM would honour its promises and ensure that reforms were implemented, not simply endorsed through legislation or in political declarations.

Challenges to EUPOL *Proxima* and EUPAT

Proxima and to a lesser degree EUPAT faced several challenges related both to internal EU procedures and coordination and to coordination with other international actors in the field. *Proxima*'s short planning phase and the slow and cumbersome EC procurement regulations meant that some of its field offices had not received computers and other essential office equipment three months after the launch of the mission. In fact, the OSCE's help was essential for the mission to commence on time. Furthermore, the inflexibility in the recruitment procedures in the Member States led to a high turnover, resulting in precious relations built with the local police having to be re-built from scratch. As a *Proxima* police officer explained, personal relationships created with local staff in the MoI were the only way to receive reliable information.[14]

Despite an elaborate system for political coordination among the EU institutions during weekly informal meetings, led by the EUSR, EU actors faced problems working out how to best complement each other and how to coordinate successfully. Competition between the EU missions resulted in an acrimonious relationship between the different parties. For example, the European Agency for Reconstruction withheld information from *Proxima*, waiting for the Council police mission to leave the country before launching its programmes. This 'turf war' between the European Commission and the Council was not only detrimental to the EU's image, but also compromised European policing. *Proxima* police officers felt that such infighting created a motivation problem within the local police service and a lack of confidence in the reforms.[15]

In addition, relations between the Head of the EC Delegation and the EUSR proved difficult.[16] It was not until 1 November 2005 when these two positions were combined with a 'double-hatting' arrangement that relations improved. However, while this arrangement enhanced inter-institutional coordination in Skopje, it did not

---

14. Interview with EUPOL *Proxima* official, in Skopje, on 15 June 2004.

15. Interviews with EUPOL *Proxima* officials, in Skopje, in June and July 2004.

16. While the permanent Delegation of the European Commission in Skopje was opened in February 2000, the EUSR was deployed after the signature of the Ohrid Framework Agreement (August 2001).

tackle contentions in Brussels.[17] Consequently, transition from the ESDP police mission EUPAT (intended as an 'exit mission' for the Council) to the Commission Twinning programme (LIC) was not smooth. In particular, insufficient coordination between the Commission and Council led to a limited number of ESDP police and civilian staff being retained by the implementing agency. Ensuring continuity of personnel would, however, have improved the transfer of lessons from the Council to the Commission.

Proxima and EUPAT were also challenged by the competition among, and ineffective coordination with other international and bilateral donors active in police reform in FYROM.[18] A formal coordination mechanism for police reform, the Police Experts Group, chaired by the EUSR's police adviser, regularly brought together international actors actively engaged in supporting the transformation of the national Macedonian police.[19] To promote a broader rule-of-law approach, donors supporting the judicial and penal systems were also associated with this group, but actors assisting regional policing were not invited. Participants in the Police Expert Group agreed that the forum was inefficient in coordinating activities, because of the formality of the event, which led actors to defend their mandate. It translated into a lack of exchange of information on the efforts underway, leading to programmes and initiatives being duplicated, while the required training of local personnel was not undertaken. For example, law enforcement monitors explained that there was much overlap in the monitoring of the legal process with the OSCE, but that no one was providing training to the armed court guards.[20]

Furthermore, international actors questioned *Proxima*'s presence and mandate because it was the last mission to arrive on an already very crowded scene with competing mandates. *Proxima*'s weak exit strategy further aggravated the situation: the decision to terminate the mission in December 2005 was largely predetermined for political reasons, namely the Macedonian government's perception that the presence of a crisis management mission in the country could jeopardise their chances of getting a positive *avis* from the European Commission on its prospects for EU membership.

17. Interview with Council official, in Brussels, 10 July 2006.

18. These included: the Organisation for Security and Cooperation in Europe (OSCE); the French, Dutch, Italian and Greek Embassies; the British Embassy; the US International Criminal Investigative Training Assistance Programme (ICITAP); the former Stability Pact for Southeastern Europe; the Council of Europe; the International Organisation for Migration (IOM); and the United States Agency for International Development (USAID). For an analysis of the role of these actors in police reform, see Isabelle Ioannides, 'Police Mission in Macedonia', op. cit. in note 2, pp. 99-105.

19. The post of police adviser was not renewed beyond July 2004; coordination of international police efforts was moved to the EC Delegation/ EU Mission, where an expert on JHA issues would be recruited. His recruitment was delayed resulting in coordination taking place in an *ad hoc* manner.

20. Interview with EUPOL *Proxima* official, in Kumanovo, on 15 and 18 June 2004.

In the absence of a common EU-wide view on policing conduct, *Proxima* police officers tasked with operationalising their mandate – i.e. translating it into concrete programmes and activities – were faced with implementing incoherent reforms. The mission pursued a 'laundry-list approach' to police reform: although each recommendation was useful *per se*, they did not amount to a coherent reform effort or fit into the overall strategic objectives of the mission.[21] The mission's work was also substantially hindered by the slow pace with which the Macedonian authorities adopted legal changes (e.g. the new selection criteria of the reformed police recruitment procedure were not introduced before *Proxima*'s deployment).

Lessons learned from EUPOL *Proxima* and EUPAT

The EU police missions in FYROM point to important lessons to be learned. First, it is necessary to organise joint European Commission-Council General Secretariat fact-finding missions, such as the one conducted before the deployment of *Proxima* to assess the state of the Macedonian police structures and understand the needs of the country. In order to learn from past missions and liaise with existing actors on the ground, the mission incorporated officers from the EUPM, informally consulted with *Concordia*, and sought the advice of the OSCE and bilateral actors. It was the first time a joint Commission-Council Secretariat fact-finding mission was carried out. This would become usual practice for future civilian operations.

Second, both *Proxima* and EUPAT highlighted the importance of ensuring that equipment and resources are sent to the field for setting up a mission in good time during the planning phase. The transfer of equipment from the EUPM in Bosnia-Herzegovina and *Proxima* in FYROM to the Aceh Monitoring Mission (AMM) helped reduce costs and the time needed to set up the mission. The transfer of equipment in support of other existing or future ESDP missions under Title V of the Treaty is increasingly exercised and is seen to contribute to the overall effectiveness and efficiency of the operations.

Third, shortcomings in the EUPOL *Proxima* operation point to the need to link the police, justice and prison reforms. The mission could have played a stronger role in strengthening the rule of law component in FYROM by making better use of its Law Enforcement Monitors, as admitted by monitors in the *Proxima* regional offices.

21. Michael Merlingen with Rasa Ostrauskaite, *European Union Peacebuilding and Policing: Governance and the European Security and Defence Policy* (London: Routledge, 2006), p. 90; Michael Merlingen and Rasa Ostrauskaite, 'ESDP Police Missions: Meaning, Context and Operational Challenges', *European Foreign Affairs Review* vol. 10, no. 2, 2005, pp. 215-35.

The number of monitors was too small, they were too dispersed, had loose links among each other, and their mandate was somewhat vague. A more clearly defined role, perhaps including specific aspects of transitional justice, such as support to the International Criminal Tribunal for the former Yugoslavia or monitoring the justice system itself in relation to existing ethnic minorities, would have made better use of this important part of the mission.[22]

Fourth, both EUPOL *Proxima* and EUPAT highlighted the benefits of having EU police advisers in the field alongside local police, thus enabling them to have a real sense of the situation. The police officers in the ESDP missions were more visible to the Macedonian public than EC assistance programmes – the mission had a human face. In fact, the visibility of the *Proxima* police officers among the population, especially during year one when the traffic police programme was active, played to the mission's advantage. A nationwide survey carried out by the Skopje-based Institute for Democracy, Solidarity and Civil Society in May 2004 found that 55.3 percent of Macedonians had a positive opinion of the mission's work, ahead of the European Agency for Reconstruction (EAR) and the EC Delegation. Even during the second year of its operation, 49.5 percent of Macedonians supported *Proxima*, as the 2005 UNDP *Early Warning Report* showed.[23]

Fifth, the obstacles to inter-institutional coordination that *Proxima* and EUPAT faced demonstrated that the combination of crisis management and institution-building tools and/or the transition between them should be part of a single overarching EU concept. A clear division of responsibilities and proper mechanisms to oversee the transition when an EU exit strategy for an ESDP mission foresees a handover to EC instruments – as with the transition from EUPAT to the CARDS-funded Twinning 'LIC' programme – is necessary. Regular reviews of the common planning documents, such as joint roadmaps, should be built into the transition process. If, for example, at an early stage of the ESDP mission (e.g. EUPAT), the local conditions have stabilised to the extent that an exit can be anticipated leading to a Commission handover, then the findings of the midterm review of the mission should be used to develop synchronised planning between the Council General Secretariat and the Commission. While learning across missions was limited, as pointed out above, some 'institutional memory' of EUPAT was transferred to the Twinning project start-up team in FYROM through relevant EUPAT documents

22. Maria Avello, 'European efforts in Transitional Justice', *Working Paper* no. 58 (Madrid: Fundación para las Relaciones Internacionales y el Diálogo Exterior, FRIDE, June 2008), p. 6.

23. Violeta Petroska-Beska *et al.*, *Early Warning Report FYR Macedonia* (Skopje: United Nations Development Programme, UNDP, June 2005), p. 16.

and an exchange of views and information in order to fine-tune the 'LIC' tasks.[24] Furthermore, similar to what was done during EUPAT, the development of joint Council-Commission 'master messages' should be used to convey a clear and consistent public message to local authorities and population.[25]

Sixth, the 'double-hatting' of a European Commission official who also acts as EUSR in Skopje has allowed increased EU coherence, coordination and visibility. The presence of an ESDP mission coupled with the perceived need for continued external support and mediation among the different ethnic groups, including on security issues, meant that the function of an EUSR was still necessary. These circumstances led to the 'double-hatting' of a single EU representative in FYROM so as to generate a push for better coordination, a situation that became a prelude and laboratory for enhancing coherence in EU external action. It has not resolved, however, the interinstitutional 'turf war' in Brussels.

Last, the two mechanisms developed – the 'benchmarking system' for *Proxima* and the 'consultation mechanism' for EUPAT, analysed in the previous sections – demonstrate the EU's ability to learn from past experience and to adjust rapidly to operational demands. Indeed, both systems were said to set a precedent, paving the way for better operating procedures and exchange of information in future EU crisis management operations.

BIBLIOGRAPHY

Arloth, Jana and Seidensticker, Frauke. *The ESDP Crisis Management Operations of the European Union and Human Rights* (Berlin: German Institute for Human Rights, April 2007).

Avello, María. 'European efforts in Transitional Justice', *Working Paper* no. 58, Fundación para las Relaciones Internacionales y el Diálogo Exterior, FRIDE, Madrid, June 2008.

Flessekemper, Tobias. 'EUPOL *Proxima* in Macedonia, 2003-05', in Michael Merlingen and Rasa Ostrauskaite (eds.), *European Security and Defence Policy: An Implementation Perspective* (London: Routledge, 2008), pp. 78-97.

---

24. Transition arrangements between EUPAT and the 'LIC' were organised both between the General Secretariat of the Council and the Commission services in Brussels, and at field level in Skopje where the EUSR/HoD played an important role, including through monthly police coordination meetings.

25. Joint Paper on Lessons Learned on the transition between the EU Police Advisory team in the former Yugoslav Republic of Macedonia and a European Community policing project, Ref. No.: 16516/06, EXT 1. Brussels: Council of the European Union, 17 December 2006.

International Crisis Group. 'Macedonia: No Room for Complacency', *Europe Report* no 149, Skopje/Brussels, 23 October 2003. Ioannides, Isabelle. 'Police Mission in Macedonia', in Michael Emerson and Eva Gross (eds.), *Evaluating the EU's Crisis Missions in the Balkans* (Brussels: Centre for European Policy Studies, CEPS, 2007), pp. 81-125.

Ioannides, Isabelle. 'EU Police Mission *Proxima*: Testing the "European" Approach to Building Peace', in Agnieszka Nowak (ed.), 'Civilian Crisis Management: The EU Way', *Chaillot Paper* no. 90, EU Institute for Security Studies, Paris, June 2006, pp. 69-86.

Jakobsen, Peter Vigo. 'The ESDP and Civilian Rapid Reaction: Adding Value is Harder than Expected', *European Security* vol. 15, no. 3, September 2006, pp. 299-321.

Matveeva, Anna et al. *Macedonia: Guns, Policing and Ethnic Division* (London/Bonn: Saferworld and Bonn International Centre for Conversion, 2003).

Merlingen, Michael and Ostrauskaite, Rasa. *European Union Peacebuilding and Policing: Governance and the European Security and Defence Policy* (London: Routledge, 2006).

Merlingen, Michael and Ostrauskaite, Rasa. 'ESDP Police Missions: Meaning, Context and Operational Challenges', *European Foreign Affairs Review,* vol. 10, no. 2, 2005, pp. 215-235.

Petroska-Beska, Violeta et al. *Early Warning Report FYR Macedonia* (Skopje: United Nations Development Programme, UNDP, June 2005).

8. EUJUST THEMIS (Georgia)

The rule-of-law mission in Georgia (EUJUST *Themis*)

Xymena Kurowska

Legal basis: Council Joint Action 2004/523/CFSP of 28 June 2004.

Highlights of the mission's mandate:

■ To assist in the development of a horizontal governmental strategy guiding the reform process for all relevant stakeholders within the criminal justice sector in full coordination with, and in complementarity to, EC programmes, as well as other donors' programmes.

■ To provide guidance for the new criminal justice reform strategy and support the planning for new legislation.

■ To help develop an overall policy and improve top-level planning and performance capabilities in the areas identified as requiring assistance.

Duration of the mission: 15 July 2004 – 15 July 2005.

Budget: €2,050 million.

Mission strength: 10 EU experts (plus local national legal assistants).

Contributing states: 10 (Lithuania, Latvia, Denmark, Sweden, the Netherlands, Poland, Italy, Germany, France, Estonia).

Introduction

Between July 2004 and July 2005, the EU deployed its first rule-of-law mission under ESDP. EUJUST *Themis* was also the first ever ESDP operation in the post-Soviet space. At the time of *Themis*'s deployment Georgia remained in social turmoil and was entangled in long-standing ethnic conflicts in Abkhazia and South Ossetia. Pre-Rose Revolution governments, headed by the former Soviet foreign minister Eduard Shevardnadze, failed to initiate significant institutional reforms. November 2003 saw thousands of Georgian citizens in the streets of Tbilisi protesting against rigged parliamentary elections. Under intense domestic and international pressure, Eduard Shevardnadze resigned and the pro-Western Mikheil Saakashvili came to power. While the West hailed these developments as a victory of the Georgian people, Moscow spoke of a *coup d'état*, financed and directed by Western state and non-state actors.[1] With hindsight, the aftermath of the Rose Revolution may be viewed with disappointment as it did not lead to the fully-fledged democratisation of the country. At the time, however, it provided a genuine opening up of the political climate in Georgia. The new administration revived local enthusiasm for reform, voiced the need to overhaul the country's corrupt institutions and echoed the popular desire to stand up to Russia and to re-integrate the breakaway territories.

Throughout the 1990s, the EU's approach to Georgia resembled its strategies in other post-Soviet republics. Brussels signed a Partnership and Co-operation Agreement with Georgia and the EC provided technical and financial assistance under its TACIS programme. The EC Country Strategy paper indicated the priority areas of cooperation: rule of law and good governance, human rights, poverty reduction, conflict prevention and resolution and post-conflict rehabilitation.[2] Between 2001 and 2008, the European Commission was an observer in the Joint Control Commission overseeing the Russian-led peacekeeping operation in South Ossetia. The region was initially left out of the ENP framework which further underscores the low key character of the EU's preliminary engagement.

The footprint of the EU Council in Georgia before 2003 was equally light. The Swedish presidency in the first half of 2001 declared the Southern Caucasus one of its priorities and produced a paper calling for a major review of the existing policy.[3] The External Relations Commissioner Chris Patten and Swedish foreign minister

---

1. Dov Lynch, 'Why Georgia Matters', *Chaillot Paper* no. 86, EU Institute for Security Studies, Paris, 2006, p. 24.
2. European Commission Country Strategy Paper 2003-2006 and TACIS, 'National Indicative Programme 2004-2006, Georgia', adopted 23 September 2003, pp.21-23.
3. Lynch, op. cit in note 1, p.61.

Anna Lindh made a case for a more assertive EU role in the region,[4] with the ensuing political deliberation culminating in the designation of an EUSR for the region. The EUSR is mandated to increase the EU's political profile in the area and support international efforts to secure regional cooperation and the settlement of the frozen conflicts.[5]

The mission and the mandate

The proposal for an ESDP rule-of-law mission was introduced to the Committee for the Civilian Aspects of Crisis Management (CIVCOM) in February 2004 by the representative of Lithuania – at the time still a candidate country with observer status in the Council machinery.[6] It was keenly supported by Estonia and enjoyed the backup of Luxemburg and the UK as well as Poland. Challenged by some as potentially antagonising Russia, the proposal was supported by the Secretariat General of the Council of the EU (Council Secretariat). At that time, the Directorate for Civilian Crisis Management (DGE IX) was finalising the doctrine for rule-of-law missions and it welcomed the opportunity to test its ideas in practice and to get the civilian ESDP 'out of the police box'.[7] The reputation of the eastern accession countries as experts on post-Soviet politics further gave credibility to the initiative. There was also a desire to widen the geographical scope of ESDP missions, until then largely confined to the Western Balkans. A mission in Georgia would signal that the EU was in the process of becoming politically more active in its immediate neighbourhood. The pro-Western political changes in Georgia were also viewed as calling for an enhancement of the EU's engagement in the country to assist the new government in carrying out its reforms. The government in Tbilisi appreciated a diplomatic gesture of political support from the EU and welcomed the proposition of a rule-of-law mission despite some lobbying in favour of a military ESDP operation that could be potentially extended to the conflict areas.

The EC initially perceived the idea to deploy an ESDP mission to Georgia as overstretching the notion of civilian ESDP.[8] Civilian missions were originally envisaged as accompanying military operations while *Themis* was to be a stand-alone endeavour.

---

4. 'Resolving a frozen conflict. Neither Russia nor the West should try to impose a settlement on the South Caucasus', *Financial Times*, 20 February 2001.

5. Council Joint Action 2003/496/CFSP of 7 July 2003 concerning the appointment of an EU Special Representative for the South Caucasus.

6. Lithuania promoted a reform strategy for Georgia that was inspired by its own experience of the mid-1990s when Vilnius designed and successfully implemented a comprehensive reform of the justice sector. Interview in Tbilisi with a deputy head of *Themis*, 9 June 2005.

7. Focus group at the DGE IX, Council Secretariat, Brussels, 16 November 2005.

8. Interview with DG Relex official, EC, Brussels, November 2005.

Moreover, Georgia could hardly be regarded as being in a crisis or post-crisis situation calling for an ESDP operation. The EC thus favoured enhancing the development-oriented activities of its delegation in Tbilisi. Traditionally concerned with the international promotion of legal reforms and EU's standards, the Commission was already engaged in important rule-of-law reforms in Georgia. The EC Delegation in Tbilisi assisted the justice ministry in modernising the prosecutor's office and the penitentiary system[9] and it provided technical assistance and policy advice to the interior ministry with regard to its transformation into a civilian institution.[10]

Arguments in favour of organising the project within the ESDP context were equally strong. An ESDP operation could ensure effective control over the endeavour: the EC does not hold its own operational capacities but instead outsources the implementation of international projects to third parties, notably international consultancy firms or NGOs.[11] An ESDP mission would also be able to carry out quick-impact measures and generate a higher political profile for the EU than a Commission action, which is more technical than political in character.

In March 2004, the Council sent an exploratory mission to Georgia to identify the scope for a possible ESDP action in the Georgian justice system. It concluded that international assistance was needed to render the system more coherent and effective. The exploratory team suggested including the reform of the penitentiary system in the brief of the mission.[12] On 3 June 2004, the Georgian prime minister Zurab Zhvania, in a letter to the SG/HR Javier Solana, invited the EU to deploy an EU rule-of-law mission in the context of ESDP in Georgia and assist the country in reforming its judiciary. The next step in the launch sequence was the deployment of a fact-finding mission to Georgia.

After the decision to establish *Themis* as an ESDP operation, the discussions focused on the modalities of the mandate. It would exclude the reforms of the penitentiary system as the EC Delegation was involved in this realm but one *Themis* expert would deal with this issue in co-operation with the Commission penitentiary experts. On 28 June 2004, the EU Council adopted a Joint Action on the deployment of *Themis*.[13]

---

9. The penitentiary reforms supported by the Commission centred on the establishment of a probation service, the strengthening of the penitentiary administration and the rehabilitation of penitentiary infrastructure.

10. Damien Helly, 'EUJUST *Themis* in Georgia: an ambitious bet on rule of law', in Agnieszka Nowak (ed.) 'Civilian crisis management: the EU way', *Chaillot Paper* no. 90, EU Institute for Security Studies, Paris, 2006.

11. Interviews at the Council Secretariat, Brussels, November 2005 and at the Polish MFA, Warsaw, January 2006.

12. Focus group at the DGE9, Council Secretariat, Brussels, 16 November 2005.

13. Council Joint Action 2004/523/CFSP of 28 June 2004 on the European Union Rule of Law Mission in Georgia, EUJUST *Themis*.

It envisaged an ambitious mandate, albeit one limited to one year. In close coordination with the Commission and international donors, *Themis* was to assist local authorities in developing an overarching criminal justice reform strategy based on the principle of local ownership.

Crafting the strategy: challenges on the ground

Two major problems affected the start-up of the mission. First, the political support of the Georgian post-revolutionary authorities was volatile. While it benefited from the backing of Prime Minister Zurab Zhvania and his successor Zurab Noghaideli, it was only in October 2004 that President Saakashvili gave his formal stamp of approval to the mission by issuing a decree creating the high-level working group. According to the *Themis* experts, this was evocative of the mission's overall convoluted position. *Themis* was hardly acknowledged in the Georgian administration, caught up as it was in the post-revolutionary turmoil, and barely endorsed by authorities disappointed in its relatively low political profile as a rule-of-law project. The mission had, therefore, to struggle to establish its credentials as a serious actor vis-à-vis its local counterparts and be granted high-level access to national experts in the institutions where it co-located its members. Second, with civilian ESDP operations financed via the CFSP budget, *Themis* further had to comply with the complex Community financial and procurement procedures. Due to delays in this regard, the mission did not have computers for the first three months of its deployment. More mundane hitches took their toll as well, e.g. *Themis* experts initially were not assigned any desks in their host institutions.

Once these challenges were overcome, *Themis* co-located eight senior European experts in a number of Georgian institutions (the Ministry of Justice, Ministry of Interior, General Prosecutor's Office, Council of Justice, Public Defender's Office, Supreme Court and Appeals Court) in order to provide assistance on a daily basis. They were accompanied by national legal assistants who provided language help, inside knowledge of the Georgian criminal code and an in-depth understanding of the local context.

Headed by Sylvie Pantz, a French judge with international field experience, *Themis* was made accountable via a benchmarking system geared towards a systematic evaluation of the mission. The benchmarks were laid out in the mission's operation plan (OPLAN), which divided the mission's activities into three consecutive phases: an assessment phase (2 to 4 months), a drafting phase (4 to 6 months) and an implementation-planning phase (2 to 4 months). Each phase was expected to end with the realisation of specific objectives – the comprehensive assessment of the Georgian criminal justice system by *Themis*; the drafting of a reform strategy by a high-level working group composed of local and *Themis* experts; and the formulation of a plan for the implementation of the reform strategy by a high-level strategy group again made up of local and *Themis* experts.[14]

In Tbilisi, the high-level working group in charge of putting together the judicial reform strategy barely met. The sub-groups formed at a later date to deal with specific issues experienced a similar fate. The slow pace of the reform process was largely due to developments outside the control of the mission. The latter was also handicapped by constant staff reshuffles in the judicial system and the appointment of inexperienced officials in the Georgian administration. These developments gave rise to concern about the independence of the judiciary. In addition, the mission objected to some legislative proposals by the Georgian counterparts, in particular plea bargaining, jury trials and the creation of an ombudsman with prosecutor-like prerogatives. *Themis* experts saw the former two as reflecting the position of the American Bar Association in Georgia and some local NGOs, which advocated adopting legal solutions based on the American model. *Themis* was not in favour of their implementation as potentially leaving too much room for fraud in a deeply corrupted and non-transparent legal system. The prosecutor profile of the ombudsman was in contrast considered to be the legacy of the sanction-oriented Soviet tradition. Likewise, it was feared that such far-reaching competences might be instrumentalised in political skirmishes and thus distort the message of impartiality and public service the ombudsman should convey. Similarly, *Themis* criticised the amendment of the constitution which strengthened the executive branch, thus exacerbating the existing flaws in the system of checks and balances.

The mission's efforts to negotiate the political and institutional obstacles floundered in April 2005 when, despite a clear deadline, the Georgian side failed to contribute to finalising the draft strategy. The mission thus decided to draft the police part of the strategy without the Georgian input.[15] In mid-May 2005, after the invitation of justice minister Konstantine Kemularia to the Political and Security Committee in Brussels, the Georgian authorities submitted their contribution to the criminal justice reform strategy. President Saakashvili adopted the revised draft – the National Strategy for Criminal Justice Reform – in July 2005 by decree.

---

14. Interviews with *Themis* members, Tbilisi, June 2005.
15. Interview with a *Themis* expert, Tbilisi, 16 June 2005.

Assessment and lessons identified

The assessment of *Themis* defies clear-cut criteria. Arguably, the mandate envisaged objectives that were too ambitious for a one-year mission, especially for one operating in a volatile post-revolutionary environment. *Themis* enjoyed at best the shaky political support of Tbilisi and the initial logistical difficulties aggravated the situation. Given the procrastination, the strategy was finalised belatedly, reflecting predominantly the input by *Themis*. Crucially, the mission made little progress towards the objective of the final phase of the OPLAN, i.e. the planning of the implementation of the strategy. Mission experts thus suggested that the mission's mandate be prolonged but this proposal did not find sufficient backing in Brussels. Instead, it was decided to place two former *Themis* experts in the office of the EUSR Border Support Team in Tbilisi. This modest solution raised fears that the mission's effort may be squandered. However, the Georgian side initiated the incorporation of the strategy implementation into the Georgian ENP Action Plan. The experts were accordingly tasked to work in cooperation with the EC Delegation from 1 September 2005 to the end of February 2006 in order to monitor and assist the work of the Steering Committee set up by local authorities to draft the implementation plan for the criminal law reforms, to be included in the Georgian ENP AP. At present, the EC Delegation assists with the update of the strategy and with implementing its elements.[16]

Four points marking the mission's achievements can be highlighted. First, a reform strategy was drafted as stipulated by the OPLAN. Second, the mission managed, in line with one of the premises of the mandate, to bring together the different local stakeholders of the fragmented criminal justice system and to entice them to cooperate on the reform plans. Third, its shortfalls notwithstanding, the strategy for the reform of the Georgian criminal justice system is a blueprint to nudge the country closer to European standards. Fourth, *Themis* allowed to demonstrate that ESDP is a larger project than one confined to the Western Balkans.

Still the broader political impact of *Themis* in the region was moderate. It did not herald a more assertive EU policy in this part of its neighbourhood and the EU's involvement only picked up again after the 5-day Georgian-Russian war in August 2008 with the deployment of EU Monitoring Mission (EUMM).[17] Besides, rooted in the early days of operational ESDP, *Themis* was the subject of inter-institutional

---

16. For details, see the website of the Ministry of Justice of Georgia: http://www.justice.gov.ge/Strategy_eng.html, last accessed on 24 April 2009.

17. See the chapter on EUMM Georgia in of this book

debates over competences and the appropriate tools to deliver the EU's message. It thus brought into sharp relief the role of institutional entrepreneurship[18] and the issue of coordination across the EU institutions involved in external policies. Although formal channels of cooperation to ensure coherence existed from the out-set, concrete practices of cooperation and cross-fertilisation have been developing incrementally in a largely non-codified and on occasion conflictual manner. The negotiations over the institutional ownership of *Themis* and the substance of its mandate reflect how the realm of civilian crisis management can offer political op-portunities potentially accessible to both the Council and the Commission.[19]

At a practical level, the logistical problems of *Themis* showed that even a small mis-sion needs an administration component, possibly including a financial officer who deals on a daily basis with EU financial provisions unfamiliar to mission experts. It also demonstrated the necessity to strengthen the mission-support capacities in the Council Secretariat, a lesson acted upon by soon establishing relevant bodies geared towards this end. One way of providing greater operational backing for the mis-sions on the ground is to involve the regional EUSR more profoundly. Formally the head of the mission speaks directly to the EUSR which facilitates quick mobilisa-tion at the political level. The possibility and scope for granting such support varies depending on individual EUSRs and their profile. *Themis* did not secure sufficient assistance from the EUSR in April 2005 when the timely submission of the draft strategy was at risk. The head of the mission chose instead to travel to Brussels and appeal there for nudging the Georgian authorities towards more tangible commit-ment to the project.

Crucially however, the mission represented an innovative and pragmatic way of re-sponding to the needs of countries in transition towards democracy. Flexible in its formula and substance which allowed for substantial accommodation to the cir-cumstances on the ground, the mission relied on the conceptual contribution of highly skilled experts to the formulation of a national reform strategy. Co-location has further become the principal tool of the civilian ESDP. Embedding European experts in the institutions to be reformed, it allows for developing relations of trust, and fosters home-grown solutions rather than imposing foreign ones. This requires that experts on EU missions are endowed with adequate knowledge of the local legal context. Besides, *Themis* clearly illustrated the importance of national legal

---

18. On the role of 'the Solana milieu' in this regard see Xymena Kurowska, '"Solana Milieu": Framing Security Policy', *Perspectives on European Politics and Society* vol. 10, issue 4 (Taylor & Francis, forthcoming December 2009).

19. More on this inter-institutional interaction development see Xymena Kurowska and Benjamin Tallis, 'EU Border Assistance Mission: Beyond Border Monitoring', *European Foreign Affairs Review* vol. 14, issue 1 (Kluwer Law Interna-tional, 2009).

assistants, working in close contact with *Themis* officials, who brought in the necessary familiarity with the system and how to operate within it.

Conclusion

Two broader conclusions flow from the *Themis* experience. While the political malleability of ESDP is one of its greatest strengths – each mission can be tailored to the situation at hand – Brussels has to make sure that its ESDP deployments enjoy sufficient authority on the ground. The Council has to engage the host governments and give the missions its full backing in their search for political leverage to achieve their objectives. Further, because institution-building activities are complex and politically sensitive tasks – which cannot be delegated to technical experts – generating political impact should be wedded with a sector-wide approach to reform. In this respect, the oft-repeated call for ESDP missions to coordinate with the EC's projects on the ground remains valid.

BIBLIOGRAPHY

Helly, Damien. 'EUJUST *Themis* in Georgia: an ambitious bet on rule of law', in Agnieszka Nowak (ed.) 'Civilian crisis management: the EU way', *Chaillot Paper* no. 90, EU Institute for Security Studies, Paris, June 2006.

Kurowska, Xymena. 'More than a Balkan Crisis Manager: The EUJUST *Themis* to Georgia', in Michael Merlingen and Rasa Ostrauskaite (eds.), *The European Security and Defence Policy: An Implementation Perspective* (London and New York: Routledge, 2008), pp. 97–110.

Kurowska, Xymena. '"Solana Milieu": Framing Security Policy', *Perspectives on European Politics and Society*, vol. 10, no. 4, Taylor & Francis, forthcoming, December 2009.

Kurowska, Xymena and Tallis, Benjamin. 'EU Border Assistance Mission: Beyond Border Monitoring', *European Foreign Affairs Review*, vol. 14, no. 1, Kluwer Law International, London, 2009, pp. 47–64.

Lynch, Dov. 'Why Georgia Matters', *Chaillot Paper* no. 86, EU Institute for Security Studies, Paris, 2006.

9. EUFOR ALTHEA (Bosnia and Herzegovina)

The European Union military operation in Bosnia and Herzegovina (*Althea*)

Daniel Keohane

Legal basis: Council Joint Action 2004/570/CFSP of 12 July 2004.

Highlights of the mission's mandate:

■ To ensure compliance with the 1995 Dayton-Paris peace agreement.

■ To support the international community's High Representative, who is also the EU Special Representative for Bosnia and Herzegovina.

■ To assist local authorities in a number of tasks, such as mine clearance and control of lower airspace.

Duration: December 2004 to date.

Mission strength: 7,000 in 2004; 2,200 in 2009.

Budget: The common costs of the operation are €71.7 million (common costs).

> **Contributing states:** 21 Member States in 2009 (Austria, Bulgaria, Estonia, Finland, France, Germany, Greece, Hungary, Ireland, Italy, Latvia, Lithuania, Luxembourg, Netherlands, Poland, Portugal, Romania, Slovakia, Slovenia, Spain, United Kingdom) and 5 third states in 2009 (Albania, Chile, Switzerland, Turkey, former Yugoslav Republic of Macedonia).

Background

Bosnia declared independence from Yugoslavia in March 1992. Within a few months, the country was embroiled in a brutal ethnic war that lasted until 1995. It pitted Bosnian Muslims, Croat Bosnians and Bosnian Serbs against one another. The war was brought to an end by a NATO military intervention. In the ensuing Dayton peace negotiations brokered by Washington, a new constitution was hammered out. The Dayton constitution codified Bosnia's division into two powerful ethnic entities – the Muslim-Croat Federation and the Serbian Republika Srpska – and a weak central State.

NATO had operated in the country since 1995, when it first deployed 60,000 troops under the Implementation Force (IFOR). In December 1996, IFOR was replaced by the 30,000-strong Stabilisation Force (SFOR), which was eventually downsized and replaced by EUFOR *Althea*.

At its summit in Istanbul in June 2004, NATO announced that an EU peacekeeping force (EUFOR) would replace SFOR in Bosnia, by the end of the same year. The idea of having an EU force replace SFOR had been mooted by the EU Council of Foreign Ministers in December 2002, and a decision had been expected during 2003. However, splits between NATO Member States over the Iraq war delayed that decision.

One reason for this decision was the belief that NATO had accomplished its mission of preventing a return to civil war in Bosnia.[1] It was generally felt that organised crime posed a more urgent threat to Bosnian security than rival combatants. Another reason was because the EU had already initiated five operations through its then nascent ESDP – a police mission in Bosnia, a peacekeeping mission in the Democratic Republic of Congo, a peacekeeping operation and a police mission in the Former Yugoslav Republic of Macedonia, and a rule-of-law mission in Georgia. In other words, since the United States wished to draw down its military presence in Bosnia, the time was right for the EU to take over from NATO.

---

1. Julie Kim, 'Bosnia and the European Union Military Force (EUFOR): Post-NATO peacekeeping', CRS Report for Congress RS21774, Congressional Research Service, 5 December 2006.

However, NATO also stated at the Istanbul summit that it would maintain a small headquarters in Bosnia to do four tasks: continue providing advice on defence reform to the Bosnian army; help with counter-terrorism efforts; continue to search for war criminals such as Radovan Karadzic and Ratko Mladic; and to share intelligence with the EU peacekeeping force. Strategic planning for the handover from SFOR to EUFOR took around six months, mainly due to political disagreements over the precise meaning of EU access to NATO assets and capabilities – especially for planning.[2] Once these issues were clarified, the operational planning phase was relatively smooth.

Mandate

The military operation *Althea* in Bosnia and Herzegovina (BiH) was launched on 2 December 2004. It is the third military operation launched by the EU, and has been its largest ESDP mission to date. The decision to launch Operation *Althea* followed the decision by NATO to conclude its SFOR-operation and the adoption by the UN Security Council of Resolution 1575 authorising the deployment of an EU force in BiH. In the framework of Operation *Althea* – named after the Greek goddess of healing – the EU deployed 7,000 troops, under Chapter VII of the UN Charter, to ensure continued compliance with the Dayton/Paris Agreement and to contribute to a safe and secure environment in BiH. Operation *Althea* is carried out with recourse to NATO assets and capabilities, under the 'Berlin Plus' arrangements.

EUFOR essentially inherited the same robust mandate as had been given to SFOR, the primary role being to ensure compliance with the 1995 Dayton accords. Even though the security situation had improved greatly since 1995, EU governments agreed that, like SFOR, EUFOR should be prepared to use force if necessary, to act as a deterrent to any potential return to civil war. In addition, in the same way that SFOR was answerable to the North Atlantic Council (where NATO foreign ministers meet), EUFOR had its own chain-of-command answerable ultimately to the EU Council of Foreign Ministers – although the operational chain-of-command was managed through NATO (see below).

Even though EUFOR had a robust mandate on paper, in practice many observers expected it to play more of a policing role – assisting the Bosnian authorities with countering organised crime for example – relative to the predominantly military

---

2. See 'ESDP and NATO' in Chapter 3 ('ESDP partnerships') in Part One of this book.

deterrence role played by SFOR.[3] For example, the then US Secretary of Defense, Donald Rumsfeld, said that EUFOR would have a 'distinctly different mission' from SFOR, one that would be 'less military and more police in its orientation.'[4] A particular challenge was how EUFOR would assimilate the Integrated Police Unit (IPU), the armed police unit of SFOR (previously named the Multinational Special-ised Unit – MSU).

There were different opinions in different Member States about what to do with the IPU, which was made up of around 500 police with military status – about half of which were Italian *Carabinieri*. Some Member States – such as Finland, France, Spain and Sweden – argued that the IPU should be transferred to the EU Police Mission (EUPM), which had been operating in Bosnia since January 2003.[5] There were three reasons for this argument. First, police on EU missions – like those serving on the EUPM operation – should be placed under civilian command. Second, the IPU would strengthen the contribution of the EUPM, and send a message to Bosnians that the EU wished to help them build up their civil institutions, especially those concerned with the rule of law. Third, the IPU could enhance the EUPM's efforts to develop Bosnian police capacities and operational experience.

However, not all EU governments were convinced of the merit of placing the IPU with the EUPM, and preferred to continue with the SFOR model. They argued that since the IPU had been crucial for SFOR's success, especially to help the Bosnian police handle civil disturbances and organised crime, it should continue to be part of EUFOR's capacity. Ultimately EU governments agreed that the IPU would remain part of EUFOR.

Implementation

EU governments agreed that EUFOR *Althea* should have the same force strength as SFOR, some 7,000 soldiers. That figure remains the largest number of peacekeepers deployed by the EU to date. However, force generation for EUFOR *Althea* proved easier than for other (and smaller) ESDP operations, mainly because 80 percent of SFOR peacekeepers were European, and their governments wished them to remain on in Bosnia as part of the EUFOR force. Thus, they simply changed their NATO/SFOR badges to EUFOR insignia.

---

3. International Crisis Group, 'EUFOR: Changing Bosnia's security arrangements', *Europe Briefing* no. 31, Sarajevo/Brussels, 29 June 2004.

4. US Department of Defense, Joint Press Conference, US Defence Secretary Donald Rumsfeld and Croatian Prime Minister Ivo Sanader, 8 February 2004.

5. Ana E. Juncos, 'Bosnia and Herzegovina: A Testing Ground for the ESDP?', *CFSP Forum*, vol.4 no.3, Fornet, May 2006.

The main force generation challenge was to replace the 1,000 American troops that had formed a large part of SFOR, but EU governments managed to supply the extra troops in time for the handover in December 2004. All of the then 25 EU Member States provided soldiers to EUFOR, with the exception of three countries: Denmark (which does not participate in ESDP military operations); and Cyprus and Malta which were not members of NATO's partnership for peace programme and therefore could not operate under the EU-NATO 'Berlin plus' system, since they did not have bilateral security agreements with NATO.

EUFOR *Althea* also included contributions from some twelve non-EU countries, with the largest non-EU contingent coming from Turkey (450 soldiers). Altogether, for its initial 7,000-strong deployment between December 2004 and May 2007, some 34 countries contributed to EUFOR *Althea*. Naturally, the force generation picture changed when EU governments decided to reduce the force from its initial strength of 7,000 to 2,500 soldiers in 2007.[6] Currently, 22 EU Member States and five third countries contribute soldiers to EUFOR *Althea* (see box at the beginning of the chapter).

On the ground, the EUFOR Force Headquarters co-located with NATO in the former SFOR headquarters, in part because EUFOR has used NATO's SHAPE headquarters for operational planning. NATO's DSACEUR (Deputy Supreme Allied Commander Europe) acts as operational commander of EUFOR. Having a three star General, who is an integral and senior part of the NATO planning system, has helped ensure that EU-NATO cooperation for EUFOR *Althea* has worked well at SHAPE, where the 19-strong EU operations headquarters is located. The force commander of EUFOR reports up the NATO chain-of-command to AFSOUTH in Naples, which has overall responsibility for the Balkans and where the EU has also set up its own EU Command Element, made up of eight personnel. Furthermore, if needed the EU can have access to other NATO assets in the Western Balkans – NATO assets currently committed to Kosovo can reinforce Bosnia if needed and *vice versa*.

SFOR had run its operations from a central force headquarters based in Sarajevo, and through three regional headquarters in other parts of the country, which hosted three task forces. The three task forces were based in the northwest (Banja Luka), the north (Tusla) and the southeast (Mostar). Under SFOR the regional task forces

---

6. The 2009 breakdown of personnel contributions from EU Member States is: Spain 323, Italy 288, Poland 203, Hungary 158, Germany 132, Bulgaria 120, Austria 106, the Netherlands 82, Romania 54, Portugal 53, Greece 44, Slovakia 40, Ireland 37, France 31, Slovenia 27, Finland 20, the United Kingdom 13, Estonia 2, Latvia 2, Lithuania 1, Luxembourg 1. The breakdown of personnel contributions from third states is: Turkey 208, Switzerland 25, Chile 21, Albania 13, the former Yugoslav Republic of Macedonia 12. All figures date from 10 June 2009. See: www.eurforbih.org .

had acquired a large degree of autonomy in their respective territories, although they remained subordinate to the Sarajevo headquarters. EUFOR inherited the central SFOR command in Sarajevo, as well as the task force commands.

The first EUFOR commander, General David Leakey, was keen to re-assert the control of the Sarajevo headquarters over the regional task forces, so that all EUFOR efforts in Bosnia would be well coordinated under his command. In addition, the US had been the lead country for the Task Force North (Tusla), and a replacement had to be found. Finland volunteered to take over the Task Force North from the US, which was one important reason EUFOR deployed on time in December 2004. After EUFOR *Althea* was reduced from 7,000 to 2,500 peacekeepers in 2007, most EUFOR soldiers were concentrated near Sarajevo.

Activities

Although EUFOR inherited SFOR's deterrence role, thankfully the need for that task was almost obsolete by the time EUFOR deployed. Even if the likelihood of a return to civil war was relatively absent, EUFOR's first main task was as much psychological as practical, to provide reassurance simply through its presence. This was a major challenge initially, since many citizens in Bosnia had bitter memories of 'Europe's failure' during the 1992-1995 war, and were not convinced that the EU could credibly replace the military role of NATO.

From the beginning of its deployment EUFOR, therefore, strived to establish its credibility with the local population. It did this in two ways in particular. First, by engaging in a high operational tempo (i.e. patrols, exercises) to show EUFOR strength and capabilities, and pro-actively communicating the positive results of EUFOR activities in the Bosnian media. Second, by emphasising that EUFOR was practically the same in terms of size, types of personnel and capability as the NATO-run SFOR had been.[7]

The tasks of EUFOR *Althea* were twofold: key military tasks and key supporting tasks. Key military tasks took priority over key supporting tasks, and EUFOR could use force to implement military tasks if necessary. Key military tasks have included so-called 'harvest' operations to collect weapons, patrolling and intelligence gathering. EUFOR also observed the activities of Bosnian defence ministry structures, in particular to ensure that ammunition storage and defence industrial factories com-

---

7. Thomas Bertin, 'The EU Military Operation in Bosnia', in Michael Merlingen and Rasa Ostrauskaite, *European Security and Defence Policy: An Implementation Perspective* (Abingdon: Routledge 2008).

plied with the conditions set in the Dayton peace agreement.

Key supporting tasks centred mainly on helping the Bosnian authorities do two things: capture war criminals and tackle organised crime. EUFOR and the remaining small NATO operation in Bosnia have worked together to try and track down war criminals. Tackling organised crime emerged as a significant task for EUFOR, working with the Bosnian authorities. This was because General Leakey, the first EUFOR commander, argued that organised crime was a real hindrance to peace and stability in Bosnia, not least because war criminals and their networks were thought to be sustained by illegal criminal activities such as drugs, people and weapons-smuggling.[8] Helping the Bosnian authorities to tackle these criminal networks was also a way for EUFOR to distinguish itself from SFOR.

General Leakey therefore, not only used the IPU, EUFOR's military police unit, but was also prepared to deploy the full range of EUFOR military assets on counter-criminal operations, including intelligence and surveillance assets. EUFOR peace-keepers carried out joint patrols with Bosnian border guards, and joint inspections with forestry inspectors to prevent illegal logging. Not all EU governments were comfortable with EU soldiers carrying out what are essentially police tasks. Some governments even imposed caveats that their units could not take part in certain types of operations, such as riot control, since they did not have the appropriate training.

Cooperation with others

Aside from uncertainty in some EU capitals, EUFOR's counter-criminal activities also created some tensions with the EU Police Mission (EUPM), which was also deployed in Bosnia.[9] Since EUFOR had been assisting Bosnian law enforcement authorities with their operations, there was some confusion in the initial years over its coordination with the EUPM police mission, which had been active in Bosnia since the beginning of 2003. The EUPM focused on building up Bosnian police capacities, but there was a lack of coordination between EUPM's capacity-building efforts and EUFOR's support to Bosnian anti-crime operations.[10] In response the EUFOR commander established some basic principles of engagement for EUFOR's role in

---

8. David Leakey, 'ESDP and Civil/Military Cooperation: Bosnia and Herzegovina, 2005', in Anne Deighton and Victor Mauer (eds.), 'Securing Europe? Implementing the European Security Strategy', *Zürcher Beiträge zur Sicherheitspolitik*, no. 77, 2006.

9. See the chapter on EUPM in this book.

10. Dominique Orsini, 'Future of ESDP: Lessons from Bosnia', *European Security Review* no. 29, ISIS Europe, Brussels, June 2006.

tackling organised crime. In particular EUFOR would only act to incite, embolden and enable Bosnian law enforcement agencies to go after organised criminal networks, rather than carry out specialised police work.

In 2006, the Political and Security Committee adjusted the mandates of the two operations, making the EUPM the lead operation for anti-crime measures with the Bosnian authorities. The coordinating role of the EU Special Representative was upgraded, giving him more say over the coherence of the two operations, and Common Operational Guidelines were agreed in summer 2006. These guidelines stipulated that the EUPM operation must endorse any operational support carried out by EUFOR with the Bosnian law enforcement agencies. EUFOR's counter-crime activities were greatly reduced in 2006, after the new operational agreement between EUFOR and EUPM, and the reduction in troop strength to 2,500.

EUFOR also worked very closely with the EUSR, even though the EUSR was not formally part of EUFOR's chain-of-command. Since EUFOR needed political advice and access to local politicians, a constructive relationship with the EUSR has been vital for its success. From the beginning of EUFOR's deployment in 2004, both the then EUSR Paddy Ashdown and EUFOR commander, General Leakey, who are both British, made efforts to brief each other daily on issues of common concern. And on occasion the EUSR has even asked EUFOR to carry out operations, for example in 2004 seizing underground military facilities in the Republika Srpska to prevent war criminals using them as a refuge. EUFOR has also worked with the European Commission delegation in Bosnia, especially on improving civil-military relations. For example, the Commission funded school rehabilitation projects, which were overseen by EUFOR engineers.[11]

Conclusion

EUFOR *Althea* has been a very successful peacekeeping operation.[12] It has fulfilled its mandate, and has been the largest ESDP operation to date. Undoubtedly EUFOR *Althea* benefited from the fact that it was a handover operation from NATO's SFOR mission. Bosnia was much more stable in December 2004, when EUFOR deployed, than when NATO initially deployed its soldiers in 1995. But taking over from a successful NATO peacekeeping force brought its own challenges. EUFOR had to establish its credibility with the local population. Since most of the initial EUFOR

---

11. Thomas Bertin, op. cit in note 7.

12. For an assessment see 'Chapter Seven: Bosnia', in James Dobbins et al, *Europe's Role in Nation-Building: from the Balkans to the Congo* (Santa Monica, CA: RAND 2008).

force had served with SFOR, this helped reassure locals that EUFOR would be able to keep the peace.[13]

EUFOR also had to differentiate itself from SFOR, and it did this primarily by working closely with the Bosnian authorities to counter organised crime. However, one clear lesson to be drawn from the experience of EUFOR *Althea* is that when different ESDP operations are active in the same country (or theatre), any potential overlap in their mandates should be clarified as soon as possible. Initially, there was some confusion between the mandate of EUFOR and the EUPM operation in Bosnia. Furthermore, it took around 18 months to find a workable solution. The respective roles of EUFOR and EUPM, and their relationship with the Bosnian law enforcement authorities should have been clarified before EUFOR was deployed in December 2004.

Another lesson is that the EUSR can play a crucial role, especially in explaining to local politicians and the population at large what an EU peacekeeping force is doing. In Bosnia, initially the relationship between EUFOR and the EUSR was not entirely clear, since the EUSR did not form part of EUFOR's chain-of-command. Fortunately, the EUSR, Paddy Ashdown, and the EUFOR force commander, General David Leakey, quickly developed a strong rapport and close working relationship. But planning for future EU peacekeeping missions should take into account – where relevant – what operational relationship an EUSR should have with the EU peacekeeping force.

During 2008 and 2009 there has been some debate whether EUFOR *Althea* should continue to operate in Bosnia.[14] Some Member States, such as Finland, France and Spain, have favoured a withdrawal for political, operational and financial reasons. Other Member States have been concerned that if EUFOR *Althea* were withdrawn, not only would the political authority of the EUSR in Bosnia suffer, it could also lead to instability in the country. Those Member States against withdrawal have included Austria, the Netherlands, Slovakia and the United Kingdom[15] (although the UK withdrew 600 peacekeepers from EUFOR *Althea* in 2007; the remaining UK personnel in Sarajevo are staff officers).

At the time of writing (autumn 2009), the EU Council has been considering the possible evolution of Operation *Althea* towards a non-executive capacity-building

13. Marco Overhaus, 'Bosnie-Herzégovine : les limites de la gestion de crise à l'européenne', *Politique étrangère*, no. 3, 2009.

14. 'Les ministres de la Défense de l'UE pour un retrait de Bosnie', *Le Nouvel Observateur*, 1 October 2008.

15. Assembly of the Western European Union, 'European Union Military Operations – reply to the annual report of the Council', Document A/2038, 4 June 2009.

and training operation, and some planning for this eventuality has already been carried out.[16] It is a sign of EUFOR's success, and Bosnia's relative stability, that the operation may evolve from mainly peacekeeping to non-executive capacity-building and training tasks. However, due to the ongoing lack of consensus among Member States, the EU Council has been keen to stress that a political decision on the possible evolution of Operation *Althea*, would need to take political developments into account, including the future role of the EU Special Representative.

BIBLIOGRAPHY

Bertin, Thomas. 'The EU Military Operation in Bosnia', in Michael Merlingen and Rasa Ostrauskaite (eds.), *European Security and Defence Policy: An Implementation Perspective* (Abingdon: Routledge 2008).

Dobbins, James et al. 'Chapter Seven: Bosnia', *Europe's Role in Nation-Building: from the Balkans to the Congo* (Santa Monica CA: RAND 2008).

International Crisis Group. 'EUFOR: Changing Bosnia's security arrangements', *Europe Briefing* no. 31, Sarajevo/Brussels, 29 June 2004.

Juncos, Ana E. 'Bosnia and Herzegovina: A Testing Ground for the ESDP?', *CFSP Forum*, vol. 4 no. 3, Fornet, May 2006.

Kim, Julie. 'Bosnia and the European Union Military Force (EUFOR): Post-NATO peacekeeping', CRS Report for Congress RS21774, Congressional Research Service, Washington D.C., 5 December 2006.

Leakey, David 'ESDP and Civil/Military Cooperation: Bosnia and Herzegovina, 2005', in Anne Deighton and Victor Mauer (eds.), 'Securing Europe? Implementing the European Security Strategy', *Zürcher Beiträge zur Sicherheitspolitik* no. 77, 2006.

Orsini, Dominique. 'Future of ESDP: Lessons from Bosnia', *European Security Review* no. 29, ISIS Europe, Brussels, June 2006.

Overhaus, Marco. 'Bosnie-Herzégovine : les limites de la gestion de crise à l'européenne', *Politique Étrangère* no. 3, 2009.

---

16. EU Council, Council Conclusions on *Althea*, Brussels, 18 May 2009.

10. EUPOL Kinshasa and EUPOL RD Congo

The EU police mission in Kinshasa - DRC (EUPOL Kinshasa) and the EU Police mission in RD Congo (EUPOL RD Congo)

Thierry Vircoulon

EUPOL Kinshasa

Legal basis: Council Joint Action 2004/847/CFSP of 9 December 2004.

Highlights of the mission's mandate: to monitor, mentor and advise the Integrated Police Unit.

Duration: 12 April 2005-June 2007.

Budget: €4,300,000.

Mission strength: 23 international staff.

Contributing states: Belgium, France, Italy, Netherlands, Portugal, Sweden.

EUPOL RD Congo

Legal basis: Council Joint Action 2007/405/CFSP of 12 June 2007.

Mission's mandate:

■ To provide assistance and advice on police reform.

■ To improve coordination between the police and criminal justice system.

■ To ensure consistency of all SSR efforts.

Duration: June 2007 to date.

Budget: €6,920,000 (From 1 July 2008 to 30 June 2009).

Mission strength: 53 international and 9 local staff.

Contributing states: Germany, Belgium, Spain, Finland, France, Italy, Portugal, Romania, Sweden.

Introduction

Since 2005, the European Union has deployed two police missions in the Democratic Republic of Congo (DRC). The DRC, a country the size of Europe, experienced massive turmoil between 1996 and 2002. The global and inclusive peace agreement signed in South Africa by the main fighting factions in 2003 created an interim government composed of one president (Joseph Kabila) and four vice-presidents. This peace agreement opened up a transitional period between 2003 and 2006 that was characterised by several violent events and eventually led to national elections in 2006. During this transitional period, following a request of the Congolese authorities, the EU set up its first police mission (EUPOL Kinshasa). The mandate of the first police mission reflected the priorities of the political transition: supporting the establishment of the Integrated Police Unit (IPU) in charge of the protection of state institutions and reinforcing the internal security apparatus. Given the fragile internal security situation after the national elections, EUPOL Kinshasa did not end but it was transformed into EUPOL RD Congo (2007) whose mandate has continued to evolve.

Mandate and implementation

The first police mission (EUPOL Kinshasa) deployed its first personnel in Kinshasa in February 2005 and was launched officially on 12 April 2005. This mission was part of the international effort to consolidate the volatile internal security of the DRC but focused on Kinshasa only. At this time, preparation for the elections was the political priority. Tensions were high in the capital due to the presence of several politicians' militias in the city centre (Jean-Pierre Bemba and Azarias Ruberwa's special guards and the Republican Guard of Joseph Kabila). Except for the rich businessmen who could afford private security, policing was non-existent, militiamen had a free hand and political factions could easily mobilise the population and launch massive demonstrations leading to riots and violence. This very volatile security situation in Kinshasa had the potential to jeopardise the whole election process.

In this context, the transitional government created the IPU by decree in 2003. Its main purpose was to protect state institutions (and therefore to replace militiamen – although factions remained) and to perform crowd management functions in a non-lethal way. Motivated by the risk of political unrest, this police unit was seen by the diplomatic community as a very important stabilising tool in Kinshasa and a test for the integration of the militiamen into the police service. From this perspective, the mission of EUPOL Kinshasa was 'to monitor, mentor and advise the setting up and the initial running of the IPU in order to ensure that the IPU acts following the training received in the Kasangulu Police Academy and according to international best practices'.[1] The support for the IPU was provided through a €10 million budget including contributions by the Commission (€7 million for technical assistance, the rehabilitation of the training centre and the provision of certain equipment for the IPU: cars, communication systems, uniforms and non-lethal weapons) and the Member States (€2.4 million for training and equipment). Placed under the political guidance of the EUSR (Aldo Ajello), EUPOL Kinshasa started working in February 2005 and was headed by the Superintendent Adilio Custodio from Portugal. In terms of staff, the mission was progressively reinforced (1 UK national, 1 from Denmark, and 1 from Romania) and enlarged to non-European States (1 from Canada, 1 from Turkey, 2 from Mali and 13 from Angola).

---

1. Council Joint Action 2004/847/CFSP on the European Union Police Mission in Kinshasa (DRC), Brussels, 9 December 2004.

Given the tense situation especially during the electoral campaign in 2006, there were intense exchanges of information between EUPOL Kinshasa and the ESDP military operation EUFOR RD Congo in order to monitor the security situation in the capital.[2] After the elections, the second police mission (EUPOL RD Congo) built on the experience of EUPOL Kinshasa. Launched in June 2007, EUPOL RD Congo aims at supporting the Congolese efforts to reform and restructure the whole police force, the *Police Nationale Congolaise* (PNC). The PNC, like other security services and the army, is a rundown institution which is very fragmented and disorganised. The Ministry of Interior was run by General Kalume during the Kabila government I and II. However, the PNC could not and still cannot be regarded as a unified force. Staff estimates vary between 75,000 and 114,000. The main units are the special police forces, the 'brigade de garde' (mainly in charge of securing businesses in Kinshasa), the IPU (this unit was suppressed by decree in June 2007 and its elements have been dispatched to other police units) and the PIR ('police d'intervention rapide', trained by the French and Angolan police cooperation scheme during the transition). In fact, the IPU, the PIR and the police special forces were the only operational units of the PNC. Even if there is a – sometimes very influential – chief of police (the General Inspector), in practice the commanders of these units run them as private fiefdoms and cultivate a range of connections providing political cover. In addition to this fragmentation, the Department of Justice has its own police (the 'police des parquets').

In this context, the mandate of EUPOL RD Congo is: to provide advice and assistance through the police reform committee set up by the Congolese authorities; to improve the interaction between the police and the justice criminal system; and to ensure coherence between the three pillars of Security Sector Reform (defence, justice and police).

EUPOL RD Congo therefore focuses on the institutional reform of the Congolese police: regulatory framework, internal organisation, human resources, training curriculum, etc. The deployment areas are Kinshasa, Bukavu and Goma. As a result of this focus and of security constraints, EUPOL RD Congo did not deploy to the provinces. Only in June 2008 the mandate of the police mission was enlarged to Eastern Congo following the signing of the Goma peace agreement in January 2008. This peace agreement for the Kivus was supposed to be implemented by the *Amani Programme* (peace support programme of the Congolese government) and the *Eastern Congo Stabilisation Plan* (elaborated by the UN). The re-establishment of law and

---

2. See the chapter on EUFOR RD Congo in this book.

order was one of the central objectives of these programmes and by implication required the improvement of police capacity in the Kivus. In order to support the Kivu peace process, the Council of the EU authorised EUPOL RD Congo to deploy personnel in Goma (North Kivu) and Bukavu (South Kivu). This extension was slowed down by the military developments at the end of 2008 in North Kivu (the offensive of the government against Nkunda's CNDP[3] backfired and resulted in a major defeat for the Congolese army) and only the first elements of EUPOL RD Congo have been deployed in Goma and Bukavu.

The Council also extended EUPOL RD Congo's mandate to provide support to the border police force and the police inspectorate. At present, EUPOL RD Congo has been authorised by the Council to operate until 30 June 2010.[4] In terms of non-European countries, EUPOL has received contributions from the Angolan police force, Turkey, Switzerland and Canada (one expert for each country).

Main challenges and performance

The two European police missions have been able to adjust to the fast-changing imperatives of the DRC political context. Such flexibility owed by and large to the continuity between EUPOL Kinshasa and EUPOL RD Congo: the Head of Mission and his political advisor have not changed since 2005 and there was no time gap between the two missions. This allowed for the coherence and continuity of the EU interventions in the field of policing over the medium term.

During the transitional period, EUPOL Kinshasa assisted the police (the IPU) in improving its capacity to deal with mass demonstrations and street protests. This proved to be very useful during several political rallies and demonstrations during the electoral campaign. Together with the UN police mission, EUPOL Kinshasa was also involved in the preparatory work for the reform of the Congolese police together with Member States (the UK and France), Angola and South Africa and the European Commission. It participated in the 'groupe mixte de réflexion sur la réforme et la réorganisation de la police nationale congolaise (GMRRR)' that formulated the guidelines of the reform and the draft organic law in 2006.

EUPOL RD Congo continues to focus on police reform as a whole and played an active role in the National Workshop on Police Reform (April 2007) and in the National Roundtable on Security Sector Reform (February 2008). These two workshops gave

---

3. Congrès National pour la Défense du Peuple.
4. Council Joint Action 2009/466/CFSP of 15 June 2009.

public visibility to the issue of security sector reform and helped to clarify concepts and to pave the way for further actions. Furthermore, EUPOL RD Congo seeks to cover all aspects of police reform (legal framework, structures, administration and management, etc.). In addition, the mission is also trying to develop more operational and visible activities such as the establishment of a research and intervention police unit in Kinshasa (through German funding of €500,000), and support to the border police and the police inspectorate. EUPOL RD Congo has tried to support the peace process in the Eastern Congo that was launched at the beginning of 2008, collapsed at the end of 2008, and allegedly re-started after the RDF/FARDC[5] collaboration against the FDLR.[6]

The absence of Congolese ownership of the reform process and the gap between the local demand and the actual assistance provided represent the biggest challenges that the EU police missions need to confront. Nevertheless it must be noted that these challenges are not limited to police reform but concern the full spectrum of development assistance in the DRC.

Despite the end of the transitional period, police reform is more an initiative of the donors than of the DRC government. The government delayed agreeing to the recommendations emanating from the police reform paper (final report of the 'groupe mixte de réflexion sur la réforme et la réorganisation de la police nationale congolaise' in 2006), in setting up the Police Reform Monitoring Committee (the CSRP[7] was created by decree in September 2007) and in appointing civil servants to working groups. The organic law for the police that was drafted by the working group on police reform in 2006 and concerned every aspect of the police service (values, organisation, missions, recruitment, equipment, discipline, rights and duties of the policeman, etc.) has not yet been examined by the Council of Ministers. The government even postponed the National Roundtable on Security Sector Reform (SSR) and eventually organised it in February 2008 after the signing of the Goma agreement. The police reform plan submitted to the donors during this roundtable was totally unrealistic (the Congolese government asked for more than $1 billion only for police reform) and, as a result, it was greeted with a lot of scepticism.

Despite being regarded as priorities in the police reform paper, the demilitarisation, reorganisation and the centralisation of the police forces have not taken place. Since

---

5. RDF = Rwandan Defence Forces; FARDC = Forces Armées de la République Démocratique du Congo.

6. FDLR = Forces Démocratiques de Libération du Rwanda.

7. French acronym = Comité de Suivi de la Réforme de la Police. The CSRP is presently composed of 7 working groups (human resources, legal framework, organisation, training, budget and finance, communication and information, logistics and infrastructures) and is busy elaborating a global action plan for the reform.

the establishment of the first EU police mission, the main challenge remains therefore the will of the Congolese authorities to reform their own police system and a lack of ownership undermining this reform process. It follows that the Congolese authorities are less interested in the advice or mentoring provided by European police services, than they are in more practical cooperation such as police equipment, infrastructures and training. Frustrated by the slow progress of the structural reform and also in response to the local demand, EUPOL RD Congo has sought to strike a new balance between support for structural reform and support for operational activities of the police, such as the creation of a research and intervention unit.

Lessons learned and problems

Coordination problems with both international partners and other EU actors on the ground have been hampering the performance of the two EU police missions in DRC.

First, coordination with UNPOL has been and still is wanting. EUPOL and UNPOL have been working in the very same fields, namely the training of the police (limited to the IPU for EUPOL Kinshasa, unlike UNPOL) and the formulation of the police reform. However, the mechanisms supposed to coordinate the activities of the UN, the EU and other countries in the field of SSR have never really worked properly. Turf wars, personal rivalries between heads of unit (sometimes from the same country) and donors' competition to get the attention of the Congolese authorities have hampered the sharing of information and have led to rather unproductive meetings. As a result, the overlap of the mandates of UNPOL and of the EU police missions has generated more competition than synergy.

Second, coordination between the EU institutions has proved to be difficult. Basically, the Council and the European Commission do not have the same perspective and timeframe: the European Commission has a development agenda and works within a five- year timeframe (European Development Fund programming) while the Council has a political agenda and works within a one-year timeframe, renewing the mandate of EUPOL every six months. However, most of the budget for material interventions in police reform comes from the European Commission (for example, it paid for the rehabilitation of the Kasangulu police academy and the CSRP building) while EUPOL RD Congo does not have a budget to finance material interventions. The disconnection between the budgetary resources and the specific expertise on police reform has led to serious differences between the policemen and the people in charge of development programmes, both in Brussels and in Kinshasa.

Despite formal consultation, the Commission has not been able to provide substantial input into the definition of EUPOL's mandate. Besides, EUPOL could have made better use of the considerable experience and expertise of civil society organisations such as human rights and lawyers' associations in the police reform process. At the core of the coordination problem lies the central question of how to integrate police reform into the broader state-building and development agenda. Efforts were undertaken in 2006 to frame a common concept and programme covering all aspects of SSR in the DRC but failed to overcome inter-institutional differences.

Third, some Member States have been developing their own police programmes independently from EUPOL (France trained the PIR, and the British Department for International Development elaborated a support programme for police reform). These countries therefore operate through both bilateral cooperation and EU structures (they second experts to the EUPOL mission). On the other hand, EUPOL has proven very useful for some like-minded Member States (Belgium, Germany, Spain and Sweden) that do not have the capacity or the willingness to develop their own police cooperation in the DRC. They have used EUPOL to channel their support to the police reform either through seconded experts or through funding. For instance, in late 2008, Germany financed the training of the research and intervention unit that is supposed to fight organised crime in Kinshasa. This new police unit is made of 50 persons who received training from EUPOL RD Congo in surveillance and pursuit, handling of information, investigation and arrest.

Finally, coordination with the non-European donors has also been difficult. The African countries involved in police cooperation (South Africa and Angola) have been reluctant to coordinate with the EU. Despite having seconded some policemen to EUPOL, Angola organised some police training without any consultation with the other actors and South Africa is exchanging information but it is not willing to go further. Equally uncoordinated has been the involvement of the International Organisation for Migration (IOM). The IOM started getting involved in police reform in 2007 through the issue of border policing. The Congolese authorities decided to create a border police unit and the IOM took this opportunity to mobilise some donors in support of the border police project.

The market for police reform in the DRC is indeed saturated with a lot of donors, international organisations, multilateral and bilateral interventions. This constitutes a real coordination challenge: EUPOL RD Congo is facing serious competition and, in this context, coordination turns into a very demanding exercise. The challenging relations with other international organisations also account for the constant expansion of EUPOL's mandate. This trend may be attributed to the positioning of the mission in the context of intricate donors' politics as much as to actual local needs.

On the other hand, the enlargement of the police mission's mandate poses an acute capacity problem. Most of the policemen are recruited on the basis of their experience (having served in another European police mission) and language skills (being able to speak French). Therefore they come mainly from France and Belgium and have often been posted in the Balkans, not in Africa (police experts with Congolese experience are definitely in short supply). EUPOL RD Congo must constantly adjust the skills of its personnel to the mandate and, given the fact that most of its personnel are recruited on a short-term basis, it can only do it by recruiting new people. With a view to matching its expanding mandate with relevant expertise, in 2007 EUPOL recruited a justice expert and it shares with EUSEC DRC expertise regarding human rights, children affected by armed conflicts and gender issues. However, the question of the relevant qualifications and expertise of the mission personnel remains open. Not all the policemen in EUPOL's staff are familiar with the constraints and problems of a developing country and, more especially, of an African country.

The geographical enlargement of the mission's mandate may also entail some risks: the deployment of EUPOL RD Congo staff in the Eastern Congo was disrupted by the violence in North Kivu in October 2008. Since then, security constraints have prevented the mission from deploying additional staff in Goma. As a result of this enlargement and of ongoing personnel constraints, some wonder whether the EU police mission is not losing its focus and is not extending beyond its capacity.[8]

Finally, while proving that the EU has been active and technically up to the job in the country, EUPOL RD Congo, is facing new difficulties at the political level linked to developments on the Congolese political scene. Feeling legitimised by the 2006 elections, the new government seems less keen to pursue a genuine police reform, thereby reducing opportunities for international cooperation and incentives for coordination among donors.

---

8. Interview with a EUPOL official, Kinshasa, 2008.

BIBLIOGRAPHY

Melmot, Sébastien. 'Candide in Congo, the Expected Failure of Security Sector Reform', *Focus Stratégique* no. 9 bis, IFRI, Paris, April 2009.

Memorandum de la Société Civile. 'Vision de la société civile sur la police nationale de la République démocratique du Congo', Kinshasa, November 2007.

Groupe Mixte de Réflexion et la Réorganisation de la Police Nationale Congolaise. *Travaux de réflexion sur la réforme de la police nationale congolaise* (Kinshasa: Ministère de l'Intérieur, 2007).

Vircoulon, Thierry. 'Reconstruire l'Etat de droit, le système de sécurité ou les forces de sécurité ? Dilemmes et paradoxes de la réforme du secteur de sécurité', in Jean-Marc Châtaigner et Hervé Magro (eds.), *Etats et sociétés fragiles* (Paris: Karthala, 2007).

11. EUJUST LEX (Iraq)

The integrated rule of law mission for Iraq (EUJUST LEX)

Daniel Korski

Legal basis: Council Joint Action 2005/190/CFSP of 7 March 2005.

Highlights of the mission's mandate:

■ To strengthen the rule of law and promote respect for human rights through training and providing professional development of the senior cadres in the Iraqi police, judiciary and penitentiary sectors, and by promoting cooperation between them.

■ Training courses are held in EU Member States.

Duration: 1 July 2005 to date.

Budget: €21.3 million until 2007. Around €8 million until June 2009.

Mission strength: 30.

Contributing states: 17 Member States (Austria, Belgium, Bulgaria, Denmark, Finland, Germany, Hungary, Ireland, Italy, Lithuania, Netherlands, Poland, Portugal, Romania, Spain, Sweden, United Kingdom). Jordan and Egypt played host to three conferences.

Introduction

In July 2005, a year after the European Union agreed on a new Iraq strategy, the then 25 member bloc deployed an ESDP mission to Iraq. Established to provide 'training for high and mid-level officials in senior management and criminal investigation',[1] the Integrated Rule-of-Law Mission for Iraq, EUJUST LEX, was initially set up for only one year on a budget of €10 million.[2]

In spite of the professed support for the mission from all EU governments, EUJUST LEX is one of the bloc's most politically contentious operations. Deployed only two years after the Iraq crisis, but before the wounds had time to heal, it was effectively hobbled at birth. As French scholar Fabien Terpan put it, 'EUJUST LEX is a testimony to the caution of the EU, which remains marked by the internal divisions of 2003.'[3] While those EU countries who fought alongside the US during the initial invasion, like the UK, Denmark and the Netherlands wanted the EU to engage robustly and saw rule of law reforms as a less controversial way in, others – like France and Spain – refused to allow the mission an in-country role, on grounds of the volatile security situation in Iraq.

The mission used a network of training facilities in Europe and held events in Jordan and Egypt, flying in senior Iraqi officials, police officers, judges and penitentiary officials to attend courses rather than conducting any work inside the war-torn country.

Launched in the midst of political controversy, EUJUST LEX has over the last four years achieved some successes, and provided some clear lessons for future ESDP missions. It also became what Xymena Kurowska describes as 'a form of therapy for member states' , which allowed them to demonstrate goodwill after the diplomatic fallout over the Iraq war.[4] In this light, the political significance of the mission mattered at least as much as the technical dimension of its mandate.

As discussions are underway on how to improve the EU's police role in Afghanistan, senior EU officials have begun to look at the lessons to be learnt from the out-of-country training run by EUJUST LEX. As such, EUJUST LEX provides relevant

---

1. Council Joint Action 2005/190/CFSP of 7 March 2005 on the European Union Rule of Law Mission for Iraq (EUJUST LEX), *Official Journal* L62/37, 9 March 2005.

2. The funds allocated cover the common costs of the mission while Members States funded any training that they hosted.

3. Fabien Terpan, 'The political dimension of ESDP', *Revue Défense Nationale* no. 2, February 2006.

4. Xymena Kurowska, , 'The transformative European Security and Defence Policy: between international refashioning and domestic rise of politics' in *Consent for Europe*, vol.3, 2007, p. 3.

guidance on how to shape any out-of-country component of future rule-of-law missions. On 26 March 2009 the Council agreed to extend and reinforce the EUJUST LEX mandate, authorising in-theatre pilot activities and holding out the promise of turning the mission into a more robust endeavour.[5]

Police reform in Iraq

The Coalition's focus on police reform grew out of concern about the deterioration of public order following the 2003 invasion. The outlawing of the Baath party, membership of which was ubiquitous in Saddam's Iraq, meant that many senior Iraqi police officers became outlaws overnight. Coupled with the freeing of criminals from jails by the crumbling Hussein regime and the tolerance of looting immediately after the invasion, Iraq had become almost lawless.

Even though police reform work had begun within weeks of the formation of the Coalition Provisional Authority (CPA), the resources and methodologies deployed were far from adequate for the complex task. It has been noted that, 'goals such as hiring 30,000 new policemen in 30 days were announced and implemented with little regard for the quality or vetting of recruits.'[6] By this stage, the remnants of the Iraqi police were struggling to deal with the spiralling crime and instability. The deteriorating situation prompted the Coalition in March 2004 to rethink the policy it had hitherto pursued, transferring responsibility for reforming the Ministry of Interior and training and equipping the Iraqi police from the State Department to the Department of Defense and the US military. Multi-National Security Transition Command (MNSTC-I) and its subordinate command, Civilian Police Advisory Training Team, were set up to take charge of the 'train and equip' programme.

EUJUST LEX takes shape

Meanwhile, a number of European governments began looking at ways to beef up their own contributions to police reform.[7] In the southern provinces, where British, Danish and Dutch and Italian soldiers were deployed, work had by then already begun. On 27 December 2003, UK and Danish police officers opened a police academy in Basra and in March 2004, the UK sent a group of 24 civilian police training officers

---

5. See Council Conclusions on the ESDP, 26 March 2009, Brussels. Available at: http://www.consilium.europa.eu/ uedocs/cms_Data/docs/pressdata/en/ec/104692.pdf

6. Robert Perito, 'Iraq's Interior Ministry: Frustrating Reform', United State Institute for Peace Briefing, May 2008.

7. In evidence to the House of Commons Defence Committee, Chief Superintendent Kevin Hurley, the Senior Police Adviser in southern Iraq said: 'immediately following and during the combat operations of March and April 2003 there was no plan for the maintenance of law and order amongst the civil population in Iraq.' See also Andrew Rathmell, 'Reforming Iraq's Security Sector: Our Exit Strategy from Iraq?', *RUSI Journal*, 1 February 2005.

into Basra while 50 British officers were stationed in Jordan to run out-of-country training. In the same month, Germany launched a training programme for Iraqi policemen in the United Arab Emirates. A number of troop-contributing countries, such as Italy and the Czech Republic, deployed military police contingents.

Given the multitude of European interventions, but the lack of any kind of coordination, a number of EU governments moved to consider how the EU could contribute to Iraq's development, including on police reform. The possibility of an EU police mission had been discussed after the invasion, and Sergio de Mello, the UN's representative, broached the idea of the EU sending police officers under UN command in a conversation with Javier Solana.[8] But, as Richard Youngs writes, most EU governments 'insisted that this should only take place after the end of the military occupation.'[9] Nor was the US, at this stage, particularly keen on the idea.[10]

In September 2004, however, an EU scoping mission recommended initiatives in the field of civil administration and the rule of law, in addition to police training and electoral support. At the same time, a number of reports and studies proposed that the EU build on its experiences from the Balkans and support police reforms.[11] To flesh out what could be done, the Council Secretariat deployed an 'Iraq Expert Team' (IET), drawing in experts from other ESDP missions as well as EU governments, to assess the needs of the Iraqi criminal justice system and to make recommendations for a possible ESDP mission.[12]

Given the extraordinary diplomatic sensitivities surrounding a possible ESDP mission for Iraq, the leadership of the IET was entrusted to a senior Council official, Pieter Feith, then Deputy Director General for Politico-Military Affairs. The team's report, drafted after visits to Iraq between December 2004 and January 2005, concluded that cooperation between the police, judges and prosecutors 'was lacking' while the police was seen to require 'major reforms', suffering 'from corruption and inefficiency, poor infrastructure.'[13] It recommended the deployment of a small ESDP mission to focus on training. The discussions in the PSC about the IET's

---

8. Referred to in Samantha Powers, *Chasing the Flame: Sergio Vieira de Mello and the Fight to Save the World* (Cambridge: Penguin Press, 2008). Refugees International, an NGO, issued a press release on 9 September 2003 calling for police reform to be run by the UN with 'EU support, given the EU's greater civilian police capacities.' See also Peter Gantz, 'The United Nations and Post-Conflict Iraq', Press Release, Refugees International, 9 September, 2003

9. Richard Youngs, *Europe and Iraq: From Stand-off to Engagement?*, The Foreign Policy Centre, London, October 2004.

10. See Powers, op. cit. in note 8.

11. See Youngs, op. cit. in note 9.

12. Report by the Expert Team for a possible integrated Police, Rule of Law and Civilian Administration Mission for Iraq, 21 January 2005.

13. Quoted in Stephen White, 'EUJUST LEX – The EU integrated rule of law mission for Iraq' in *Journal of Defense and Strategy*, vol.8, no. 2, Prague, December 2008, pp.97-103.

report exposed serious differences between Member States. But in February 2005 agreement was reached, in part because its roll-out was diplomatically useful both to those countries that had resisted the US-led invasion of Iraq and those who had joined the Coalition forces.

Implementation

After the Council approved the ESDP mission, a planning operation was set up led by Stephen White, who had been Senior Police Expert on the IET. In July 2005 EUJUST LEX became operational. With 21 staff from 15 different EU countries, EUJUST LEX set up two offices, a Coordination Office in Brussels and a Liaison Office housed in the British embassy in Baghdad (and a year later, alongside the European Commission office). EUJUST LEX relies on seconded and contracted staff and has grown to include in-house expertise in the fields of judicial, policing and penitentiary reform as well as human rights and training methods. Finally, EUJUST LEX has staff dedicated to mission support including security, administration and logistics, the last being particularly important given the complexity of transporting large numbers of Iraqi officials out of Iraq.

In the first phase of the mission from July 2005 until June 2006, EUJUST LEX delivered two types of courses: a Senior Management Course and a Management of Investigation Course. In the first and second extensions of EUJUST LEX specialist courses were developed including courses for police officers on leadership, investigations, incident management and human rights. For judicial personnel, EUJUST LEX offered courses in financial investigations, and forensic science while training for penitentiary staff focused on leadership, planning, and crisis management. All three professions received human rights training.

In spite of its constraints, since EUJUST LEX was set up it has trained 2,181 Iraqi officials through 99 different kinds of courses, using 18 facilities in as many European countries. Candidates are selected on the basis of applications submitted to the EUJUST LEX Mission by the Iraqi authorities. To date, 366 Iraqis have been trained or been on secondments in Britain; 255 in Germany; 155 in Italy; 98 in the Netherlands; and 350 in France. In addition, EUJUST LEX has organised three large events in the Middle East. The mission has also sought to develop its programme in response to requests from course-goers, a key recommendation of the IET, which stated that 'Iraqi experts would participate in the design of curricula for the courses'. EUJUST LEX also runs a series of 'Work Experience Secondments' where Iraqi senior officials are afforded the opportunity to work alongside European counterparts for short periods. To date, thirty-four such secondments have taken place in Ireland, Finland, Lithuania, Romania, Hungary, Estonia and Britain. Two Iraqi prison officials and a Probation Services researcher, for example, visited Wandsworth and Downview, two British prisons.

The number of Iraqi personnel trained by individual EU Member States from June 2005 to April 2009

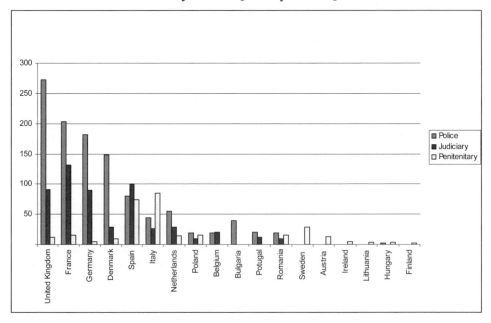

Source: EUJUST LEX[14]
See: http://www.consilium.europa.eu.

Given EUJUST LEX's narrow mandate and limited in-country presence, cooperation with the European Commission, the US and European bilateral programmes was crucial. The main vehicle for international cooperation has been the Rule of Law Sector Working Group, chaired by the Iraqi Chief Justice. Three EU institutions are represented at the group's meetings: EUJUST LEX, the Commission Delegation and the EU Presidency. An initial member of the mission's Baghdad office was also a Commission official. Yet with the Commission itself only having a limited presence in Baghdad, most of the coordination took place in Brussels.

---

14. Figures taken from: EUJUST LEX Activity List: Course Table, available at: http://91.194.202.11/uedocs/cmsUpload/ACTIVITY_LIST_0904.pdf

Lessons learned: achievements and shortcomings

From 2005, the mission has operated in a particularly difficult political context, in which several EU governments were not willing to allow the establishment of an extensive in-country presence.[15] As recently as in late 2008, Denmark and the Netherlands circulated a proposal suggesting that the mission be significantly beefed up, which faced resistance from a number of staff-contributing countries.[16]

Political constraints led EUJUST LEX to develop an innovative and cost-efficient mission concept, creating from scratch a network of training providers across Europe. However, the mission has not been able to test for the usefulness of the training offered or provide hands-on, post-training mentoring.[17] EUJUST LEX leaders maintain that 'participants in EUJUST LEX courses are required to share their knowledge about new investigative techniques with colleagues in Iraq'.[18] But the mission has no systematic way of knowing whether this takes place. EUJUST LEX has sought to develop a range of proxy indicators, including events with course-goers and their superiors, self-assessments, questionnaires and group discussions. But evaluations are still largely anecdotal.

Nor could the mission ensure that its training became an integral part of the Iraqi police's own training plan. The Iraqi Interior Ministry did have an extensive training prospectus, dating from before the 2003 invasion. Though many of the courses were out-of-date and the teaching methods archaic, the content of its training programmes was set out in documentation and course curricula, and was, crucially, authorised for teaching.

It is hardly surprising that given the lack of access to Iraqi training establishments, an assessment of training needs and other consultation on course design was limited, and that training did not take into account what Iraqi training had been developed between 2003 and 2005, or actual pre-2003 operational procedures within the Iraqi police. Being aware of these pre-existing rules, even if they would have to be amended, would have been important. For example Iraq's legal system, where an Investigating Magistrate plays as central role in investigating crime, is not well understood by police professionals in countries with common law systems. EUJUST LEX was by no means unique in this regard – most US training after 2003 was developed

---

15. Edward Burke, 'The Case for a New European Engagement in Iraq,' *Working Paper* no. 74, Fundación para las Relaciones Internacionales y el Diálogo Exterior, FRIDE, Madrid, January 2009.

16. Unpublished 'Danish-Dutch Non-Paper on The Future of Eujust Lex in Iraq', October 2008.

17. Personal interview with European diplomat, in June 2009.

18. Press Briefing by Stephen White, Head of the EUJUST LEX Mission for Iraq Brussels, 26 November 2008.

with little knowledge of Iraqi procedural realities. However, the EU mission's inability to operate in-country further hampered direct connectivity between the training delivered and the actual Iraqi legal or police processes.

Finally, by failing to implement a key recommendation of the IET – to develop a common and detailed curriculum that all the training had to follow rather than only have a loose framework for EU governments to interpret – the mission could not ensure that Iraqi officials were given compatible instruction.[19]

If EUJUST LEX had been able to operate in-country, however, it is not certain it could have achieved much more. Until early 2007, when the US 'surge' began changing security conditions, the Iraqi police barely existed as such, was corrupt and confronted with a well-equipped and seemingly undefeatable insurgency. Police stations were attacked by insurgents who were often better armed than the police. Between September 2005 and October 2006, a total of 2,842 police were killed and 5,792 wounded while many others fled in droves. According to the Ministry of Interior, 12,000 police were killed between May 2003 and December 2006. Had the conditions been right inside the EU for EUJUST LEX to deploy a larger mission from the beginning, it would probably still have struggled to make an impact. [20]

But the fact that the EUJUST LEX could only deploy four out of its 30-odd staff inside Iraq and therefore could not undertake systematic assessment of training needs or evaluation of the impact of its training programme, let alone engage in hands-on follow-up training, meant it came to be seen by the US military, which runs the majority of police training activities, as a professional, but ultimately tokenistic contribution. As late as spring 2009, few people in the office of the Commanding General, Multi-National Force-Iraq (MNF-I) were even aware of the EU's police mission. The so-called 'Jones Commission', mandated by Congress to study the Coalition's assistance to the Iraqi security forces, including the police, made only scant mention of the EU's mission. Its report, written two years after EUJUST LEX was established, says: 'most if not all Iraqi police leaders ... have no formal training nor experience in civil policing.'[21] The implication being that the US clearly did not think the EU mission had achieved much.

---

19. The IET clearly stated: 'A common curriculum would be designed by the mission planning team, with Iraqi participation'. See Report by the Expert Team, op. cit. in note 12.

20. Personal interviews, Council General Secretariat in Brussels, May, 2009.

21. See General James L. Jones et al, *Report by the Independent Commission on the Security Forces of Iraq*, 6 September 2007.

Though successive Iraqi governments welcomed EUJUST LEX, they too came to see the mission's value mainly as a political one, an important sign of Europe's' overall Iraq engagement.[22] As for the more than 2,000 course-goers, no doubt many benefited from the training offered by EUJUST LEX. However, because responsibility for selecting delegates was left in the hands of the Interior Ministry there was no certainty that the right officers, or even ones working in positions relevant to the training, attended. Corruption and mismanagement in the ministry meant it was also impossible to ensure selection was not made on the basis of patronage.[23]

Mission progress has been measured by such proxy indicators as the Iraqi government's willingness to continue the programme, the pronouncements of course-goers in occasional e-mail correspondence or third parties' evaluations. Only one survey was conducted. There is limited data on how many of the course-goers are alive, remain in their jobs or have been promoted, let alone whether they are applying their skills.

The anecdotal nature of the evaluation process is perhaps best summed up by the constant references to individual cases.[24] Admitting that monitoring had been a problem, a non-paper circulated in October 2008 noted that in future 'more emphasis should be put on follow-up activities, including monitoring, course-evaluation, and mentoring of former course participants.'[25]

Conclusion

On balance, EUJUST LEX can be considered as a 'useful, albeit limited training intervention.'[26] As such, the importance of EUJUST LEX lies not only in what it has done to date, but also and above all in the extent to which its four-year effort forms a foundation for the EU's future work reforming and modernising the Iraqi police and in the lessons that can be drawn from the mission for future ESDP operations. For example, consideration should be given to using the network of training providers across Europe that EUJUST LEX has created to fulfil its mandate to support other interventions. In the future, now that the Council has authorised pilot

22. Personal interview, Iraqi diplomat in London, March, 2009.

23. Personal correspondence with British officials, May 2009.

24. In this regard, Stephen White's remarks in late 2008 are typical: 'I can give you many examples where I met people or heard of people who were in our courses that have been promoted.' Press Briefing by Stephen White, Head of the EUJUST LEX Mission for Iraq Brussels, 26 November 2008. Available at: http://consilium.europa.eu/uedocs/cmsUpload/081126TranscriptPressBriefStephenWhite.pdf.

25. Unpublished Danish-Dutch Non-Paper, op. cit. in note 16.

26. Kurowska, op. cit. in note 4.

activities inside Iraq, EUJUST LEX has a real opportunity to make a wholesale evaluation of its training programme and create a new assistance package, which ties out-of-country training much more closely in with in-country activities (and, crucially, with the Iraqi Police Service and Interior Ministry's own training and development strategies).

BIBLIOGRAPHY

Burke, Edward. 'The Case for a New European Engagement in Iraq,' *Working Paper* no. 4, Fundación para las Relaciones Internacionales y el Diálogo Exterior, FRIDE, Madrid, January 2009.

Collantes Celador, Gemma. 'The European Union Police Mission: The Beginning of a New Future for Bosnia and Herzegovina?', *Working Paper* no. 9, Institut Barcelona d'Estudis Internacionals, Barcelona, October 2007, pp. 1-23.

Dodge, Toby, Luciani, Giacomo and Neugart, Felix. 'The European Union and Iraq: Present Dilemmas and Recommendations for Future Action', Bertelsmann Stiftung Foundation, Mediterranean Programme and Robert Schuman Centre for Advanced Studies, London/Florence/Munich, June 2004.

Jones, James L. Report by the Independent Commission on the Security Forces of Iraq, September 2007.

Kurowska, Xymena. 'The Role of ESDP Operations' in Michael Merlingen and Rasa Ostrauskaite (eds.), *The European Security and Defence Policy: An Implementation Perspective* (Abingdon, Oxon/New York: Routledge, 2008).

Kurowska, Xymena. 'The transformative European Security and Defence Policy: between international refashioning and domestic rise of politics', in *Consent for Europe*, vol. 3, 2007.

Perito, Robert. 'Iraq's Interior Ministry: Frustrating Reform', United States Institute for Peace Briefing, USIP, Washington D.C., May 2008.

Powers, Samantha. *Chasing the Flame: Sergio Vieira de Mello and the Fight to Save the World* (Cambridge: Penguin Press, 2008).

Rathmell, Andrew. 'Reforming Iraq's Security Sector', *RUSI Journal*, February 2005, pp. 8-11.

Terpan, Fabien. 'The political dimension of ESDP', *Revue Défense Nationale* no. 2, February 2006.

Youngs, Richard. *Europe and Iraq: From Stand-off to Engagement?*, The Foreign Policy Centre, London, October 2004.

White, Stephen. 'EUJUST LEX – The EU integrated rule of law mission for Iraq' in *Journal of Defense and Strategy* vol. 8, no. 2, December 2008, pp. 97-103.

12. EUSEC RD Congo

The EU mission to provide advice and assistance to security sector reform in the Democratic Republic of Congo (EUSEC RD Congo)

Caty Clément

Legal basis: Council Joint Action 2005/355/CFSP of 2 May 2005.

Highlights of the mission's mandate:

■ To support the integration of the Congolese army and good governance in the field of security.

■ To identify and contribute to the development of various projects and options that the EU and/or its Member States may decide to support in this area. In particular: separating the chain of payment from the chain of command; census of Congolese Army; advisory support to the 2009 Revised Strategic Plan for Army Reform and a multilateral approach to SSR.

Duration: May 2005 to date.

Budget: From March 2005 till December 2005: €1.6 million. From 1 December 2005 till 15 February 2006: €900,000. From 16 February 2006 until 2 May 2006: €940,000. From 3 May 2006 until 30 June 2007: €4.75 million. From 1 July 2007 until 30 June 2008: €9.7 million. From 1 July 2008 until 30 September 2009: €8.45 million. From 1 October 2009 until 30 September 2010: €10.9 million.

> **Mission strength:** Planned: 60 planned personnel. By March 2009, about 50.
>
> **Contributing states:** Belgium, France, Germany, Italy, Portugal, the United Kingdom.

Introduction

Army reform efforts in the Democratic Republic of Congo (DRC) were initiated in a highly inauspicious context. In the 1990s, during President Mobutu's final years, the army had suffered considerable neglect with the result that it was in an unprofessional and undisciplined state. Two successive regional wars had taken a heavy toll on the Congolese population, with 5.4 million 'excess deaths', and damaged the unified army structure.[1] The second Congo war came to an end after the signature of the Global and Inclusive Agreement in Pretoria in December 2002, which devotes an entire chapter to Security Sector Reform (SSR). The President became the head of the Superior Council of Defence, a body in charge of army integration and defence policy.[2] In 2005, the Congolese government developed a Strategic Plan on Army Reform. In this context, the DRC government requested the help of the international community (bilateral donors, the UN, as well as the EU).

By mid-2005, as part of its emerging ESDP policy, the EU deployed two relatively small missions: EUSEC RD Congo was to advise the military branch on army integration, and EUPOL Kinshasa to train police units in charge of securing the transitional institutions.[3] With regard to EU's foreign and security policy, the EUSEC mission was groundbreaking in at least three ways. First, this mission was the first of its kind; a 'civilian' mission designed to provide 'military' advice. In 2005, the mission proved an experimental laboratory where the lack of precedent and of clear guidelines was both a challenge and an opportunity. Second, the EU's desire to set up an SSR mission reflects its recognition of the importance of army reform in peacebuilding. EUSEC therefore embodies a shift whereby SSR is no longer regarded as an exclusive sovereign and bilateral issue, but as a challenge requiring a

---

1. The number of excess deaths refers to the number of people dying in excess of the average mortality rate in the region for similar income levels. See International Rescue Committee, 'Mortality in the Democratic Republic of Congo: an ongoing crisis', January 2008.

2. Army integration referred to a process whereby different fighting factions agreed to merge in a single unified army. The priority was to severe parallel chains of command. Interviews with senior military officials, Kinshasa, 2005.

3. See the chapter on EUPOL Kinshasa and EUPOL RD Congo in this book.

coordinated and multilateral response. Third, security sector challenges in a post-conflict environment, such as the DRC, require political savviness as much as technical expertise; and this was perhaps EUSEC's weakest point.

Mandate

EUSEC's mandate evolved over time. Originally, the aim was to provide advice and support for army integration in a way that was compatible with principles of good governance, human rights, international humanitarian law, democratic standards, transparency and the respect of the rule of law. This would have to be done in cooperation and coordination with other donors.

By April 2008, the mandate had evolved in the light of the ambitious objectives the EU sought to achieve in SSR. At least four new strands of activity were added. First, the follow-up and maintenance of two key achievements of the mission: the new chain of payment scheme for military salaries, as well as the census of the army. Second, operationally, the mission's support was to shift from army integration, now 'formally' completed, to the new aim of developing a Rapid Reaction Force. Third, the format of the army had to be consistent with available resources. Realism was required as other ambitious SSR efforts in the DRC had proved unmanageable (e.g., the country's National Commission for Demobilisation and Reintegration ran out of funds). Finally, a gender focus and the protection of children affected by armed conflict were explicitly added to the mandate.

Achievements

EUSEC can be credited with a number of notable achievements. Most prominent among these are (i) its expertise in SSR as well as the ability to understand the enormously complex set of security-related Congolese institutions; (ii) its coordination capacities; (iii) the famous chain of payment scheme; (iv) the census of the Congolese army, (v) a capacity assessment of the Congolese army, as well as (vi) smaller projects. These include issues such training (human rights, computer literacy, or the setting up of an administration school), gender-related activities (e.g. the rehabilitation of the Maluku social foyer to improve the living conditions of soldiers' families), IT projects (notably a network linking all regional military headquarters), and advisory support (e.g., on the general status of military personnel).

EUSEC started as a modest 8-strong mission in a private Kinshasa residence. All members were active or retired military and many had previous experience of dealing with SSR in the region. Therefore, although the mission was new and limited to Kinshasa, EUSEC's staff had a good grasp of the challenges involved in DRC's SSR. The pooling of information gathered from the Congolese officers they were advising was key to mission's success.[4]

The mission became one of the best informed actors in town, no small achievement given the hyper-fragmentation of SSR efforts in 2005 both within the Congolese state and among bilateral donors (Belgium, France, South Africa, Angola, etc). To coordinate with and advise their Congolese counterparts, some members of the mission were assigned to positions within the following national offices: Ministry of Defence private office, Combined General Staff, Army General Staff, National Committee for Disarmament, Demobilisation and Reintegration (CONADER), and the Joint Operational Committee. Today, EUSEC not only provides support to the General Headquarters in Kinshasa, but has also allocated personnel to the DRC's military regions.

Multinational in nature, EUSEC represented a new kind of actor. The EU mission had limited personnel, provided no training or equipment, was a 'civilian' mission, and most strikingly, was a coordinated effort to engage all relevant DRC authorities. SSR had so far largely been considered a sovereign state prerogative and assistance was provided on a bilateral basis. Donor countries operated with little or partial knowledge of what other countries were doing. Lack of coordination in the early days of SSR translated into non-compatible equipment (e.g. communication systems) or uneven training standards or doctrines among Congolese brigades.

European bilateral donors already active in the country, such as Belgium, decided to engage in a dual track strategy contributing both to bilateral projects and to the EU mission. The early supporters of the mission included Belgium, France, Luxembourg, the Netherlands, the United Kingdom, and Sweden. The successes of the mission would in time make it attractive to new SSR players, such as Germany and Italy. In terms of EUSEC's relationship with non-European actors, the good relations with Angola never materialised in Angolan officers formally joining EUSEC. Formal coordination with the US and South Africa are also under consideration.[5]

---

4. International Crisis Group, 'Security Sector Reform in the Congo', *Africa Report* no.14, 13 February 2006. See in particular the graph on p. 27.

5. Council of the European Union, 15834/08, Brussels, 17 November 2008.

EUSEC successfully tackled the serious and delicate question of the Congolese soldiers' pay – a key stepping stone to undertake broader SSR programmes. In 2005, Congolese foot soldiers received a salary of 10 US dollars (USD) per month, well below the world's absolute poverty line of 1 USD per day. They did not have proper barracks, shelter, transportation (they deployed on foot covering hundreds of kilometres), equipment or medical support. Many died of cholera, tuberculosis or sheer starvation.[6] In fact, the incentive for the best and brightest combatants at the time was to leave the army. Former combatants choosing to demobilise received a 410 USD package over the span of a few months, while those opting for a military career were paid a mere 10 USD per month.[7]

As a result, corruption became widespread in the Congolese army. One of the most notable schemes was known as 'Opération Retour' (Operation Return).[8] Senior officers ordered the soldiers' pay to be sent from Kinshasa to the commanders in the field, who took their cut and returned the remainder to their commander in Kinshasa instead of paying the soldiers. To ensure that foot soldiers would be paid their due, in late 2005, EUSEC suggested separating the chain of command from the chain of payment. The former remained within Congolese hands, while the EU mission delivered salaries directly to the newly 'integrated' brigades. Although efficient in the short term, this solution raises the question of sustainability and ownership in the long term. Once soldiers' pay could no longer be siphoned off via 'Opération Retour', however, two other budgetary lines, the 'fonds de ménage' and logistical support to the brigades, were soon diverted.

EUSEC attempted to improve the soldiers' pay again by tackling another corruption scheme as well, suppressing the army's numerous 'ghost soldiers'. In early 2006, officials estimated that 340,000 soldiers had to be integrated in the army. Many observers suspected this was a gross overestimate. There was a dual incentive for commanders in charge of army integration to provide inflated numbers. First, the more men an armed group counted, the more senior rank that group's chief would attain in the Congolese army. Second, once integrated, commanders often pocketed the pay of their ghost soldiers. A first census attempt was criticised by experts as it was ill conceived and allowed soldiers to record under multiple identities.

6. International Crisis Group, op. cit. in note 4; interviews with Congolese and international military in North and South Kivu, December 2005.

7. International Crisis Group, op.cit. in note 4, Executive Summary.

8. In March 2006, former Vice-President Jean-Pierre Bemba revealed that the military headquarters in Kinshasa diverted about US$5 million per month. See Sébastien Melmot, 'Candide au Congo. L'échec annoncé de la réforme du secteur de la sécurité –RSS' Focus Stratégique no. 9, IFRI, Laboratoire de Recherche sur la Défense, Paris, September 2008, p. 12.

Therefore, EUSEC undertook to biometrically record all soldiers in a central database. Each soldier received a military identity card with his/her biometric data which was necessary to receive their pay. The census not only solved the ghost soldier issue, but the precise tally of the Congolese army also allowed a sound management of human resources. The project was completed in December 2008, counting a total of 129,394 soldiers, much less than the original account. As a result, savings allowed an increase of the soldiers' pay up to 60 USD per month (still only 2 USD per day).[9]

EUSEC's latest and most considerable achievement relates to the mission's strategic advise on army reform. In 2007, under the leadership of the army's chief of staff, Congolese, UN and EUSEC officers had developed a strategic level plan for army reform. For political reasons (explained below) the plan was shelved until it was finally unearthed again and finally adopted by President Kabila in late May 2009 as the 'Revised Plan of Army Reform'.

Finally, EUSEC also undertook a number of other smaller projects which are currently at various stages of completion: human rights training, flanking measures, training, an IT network, and a school of military administration. Flanking measures were designed to improve the life of the military and their dependents, such as providing sanitation facilities and drinking water or tented barracks (from the British DFID). A pilot project designed to help military families, particularly women, was developed with the 7th Brigade whereby EUSEC helped provide soldiers' wives with a social foyer, and training in agriculture, finance and women's rights. The gender programme, however, did not address sexual abuses committed by the Congolese armed forces, nor did it address the situation (and promotion) of female soldiers. An IT network of Kinshasa's military administration was completed, but technicians are still undergoing training on how to use and maintain the system. EUSEC has also provided training to Congolese officers at the GESM (Grouping of Superior Military Schools) in Kinshasa in human rights and international humanitarian law, among other issues.

Main challenges

EUSEC faced essentially five types of challenges relating to: (i) the EU's internal organisation, (ii) the mission's ability to engage non-military actors, (iii) gender mainstreaming both within EUSEC and within the army, (iv) the coordination with

---

9. Council doc. 15834/08, op. cit. in note 5.

non-EU donors, and (v) the difficulties of implementing SSR when security forces are fighting a protracted conflict.

EUSEC was caught up in Brussels' inter-institutional rivalry from its inception. In late 2004, France and Belgium developed the concept of an EU SSR advisory mission in a joint non-paper to the Political and Security Commitee (PSC).[10] While a single EU mission for all SSR-related activities would have facilitated coordination, in the end three separate budget lines and two different missions were set up. Military activities were EUSEC's realm; police activities fell under the responsibility of EUPOL under a separate ESDP mission; and the justice sector was addressed by a Community programme for judicial reform, REJUSCO, under the responsibility of the Directorate General for Development.[11]

The mission's initial budget allocation to support activities related to the defence sector was rather limited. Although Congolese police estimates (70-80,000 men) were dwarfed by the army's (340,000 troops),[12] EUPOL's budget amounted to €4.37 million, while EUSEC was endowed with a mere €1.6 million.[13] The 'Athena mechanism', meant to finance military missions, had to be used to cover EUSEC's financial shortfall.[14]

The unclear division of labour between different EU actors in SSR gave rise to considerable political squabbling between the Council and the Commission. For example, when Solana's office asked the head of EUSEC's mission to develop an SSR strategy for the DRC, the Commission was affronted for it saw the Council as overstepping its responsibility. Indeed, the proposal formulated by EUSEC included the police, justice and penitentiary fields as well, which the Commission regarded as falling by and large within its remit.[15]

These differences are meant to be overcome in the future. The EU, which repeatedly called for improved coordination between ever-flourishing SSR institutions,

---

10. Hans Hoebeke, Stéphanie Carette and Koen Vlassenroot, 'EU Support to the Democratic Republic of the Congo', (IRRI-KIIB, Brussels), in *L'action de l'Europe en Afrique*, Centre d'analyse stratégique, Paris, 2007, p. 10.

11. Laura Davis, 'Small Steps, Large Hurdles. The EU's Role in Promoting Justice in Peacemaking in the DRC', New York, International Center for Transitional Justice, May 2009.

12. International Crisis Group, op. cit. in note 4, pp. 6 and 26.

13. Dietmar Nickel and Gerrard Quille, 'In the Shadow of the Constitution: Adapting to a Changing External Environment', paper presented at EUSA Tenth Biennial International Conference, Montreal, 17-19 May 2007.

14. Quentin Weiler, 'The European Union and Security Sector Reform in Africa: a Leader in Theory, a Laggard in Reality?', United Nations University CRIS, Bruges Regional Integration & Global Governance Papers, January 2009, p. 19. Contributing countries included Belgium, France, Luxembourg, the Netherlands, the United Kingdom, and Sweden.

15. Interview with EU officials, Kinshasa, June 2006.

seems to have grasped that its own internal disagreements not only impaired its efficiency, but also seriously affected its credibility towards its Congolese partners.[16] Since 2009, the mandates of both EUSEC and EUPOL include the ultimate aim of uniting police and military advisory activities under a single umbrella. If and when such a merger will eventually take place remains anyone's guess.

EUSEC's most serious setback with local authorities occurred in late 2007 when it got caught up in a Congolese political struggle around the drafting of a Strategic Plan of Army Reform. Two competing plans were put forward: one by the army's Chief of Staff and one by the Minister of Defence. The plan for a professional defensive army proposed by the Army's Chief of Staff, General Kisempia, with the support of EUSEC's head of mission and of MONUC's Chief of Staff, was not adopted by the Congolese leadership. The alternative plan presented by the Minister of Defence, Chikez, pushing for a development-oriented army whose remit would involve agricultural activities, eventually prevailed, but was welcomed by donors with lukewarm support. EUSEC's head of mission found himself in a difficult political position and eventually had to leave the mission. Since a new Congolese Minister of Defence and Chief of Staff took office in 2008, they have been working together with the international community on a Revised Plan for Army Reform based on the Kisempia plan, which was finally endorsed by the President in May 2009.

One of EUSEC's main weaknesses resides in its lack of political expertise. Its staff members are hired for their technical (military) expertise, not their ability to work the political system, which led to the political deadlock over the Strategic Plan. Most of the mission's members are military, not necessarily the best qualified to engage SSR's political (parliamentary commissions) and judicial (military courts) institutions. For example, although multiple UN reports and NGOs documented ghastly abuses (ranging from extra-judicial killings, widespread sexual abuse, forced labour, and extortion) committed by the armed forces and their subsequent impunity, strategies to curb abuses, namely strengthening military justice, ensuring

---

16. Quentin Weiler, op. cit. in note 14, p. 18.

parliamentary oversight, and vetting, have made little to no progress.[17] Two EUSEC proposals concerning the soldiers' statutes and the terms of reference of the Committee for the Follow-up of Army Reform (CSRA – Comité de Suivi de la Réforme de l'Armée) have also been shelved, but could gain new traction in the wake of the 2008 governmental reshuffle. The statutes proposal is core to army reform, because it outlines under what conditions prospective soldiers may join the army. To date, no vetting has ever taken place. As a result numerous unsavoury characters joined the new integrated army, sometimes in senior positions.

In terms of gender mainstreaming, EUSEC and ESDP missions in general are lagging behind international standards. In a damning October 2008 report, the United Nations Development Fund for Women (UNIFEM) highlighted the question of human resources, with an overburdened gender advisor shared by EUSEC and EUPOL in Kinshasa, the absence of a specific budget line, the lack of gender mainstreaming in the mission's recruitment process, no pre-deployment gender sensitisation of mission members, and more importantly a complete absence of sexual behaviour standards for mission members.[18] Gender initiatives have so far focused on small projects to help army dependents, but none tackled the promotion of gender issues within the Congolese army both in terms of recruitment and discipline towards civilians.

Coordination with non-EU actors, notably the UN mission (MONUC) and China, proved difficult. EUSEC has attempted to liaise with most donors, including non-European ones. This strategy appeared to work with Angola, but never formally materialised into joint coordination meetings. The mission never made much headway with China, one of Congo's most longstanding military partners. China has long invited officers for training and provided military material ranging from trucks to armaments. In the case of the UN, cohabitation proved difficult as a competition developed between the two missions, reflecting fundamental disagreements on how

---

17. UN reports and NGOs (Human Rights Watch, the International Crisis Group) have often referred to the armed forces' gruesome track record. The most recent reports include: United Nations Mission in DRC and Office of the High Commisioner of Human Rights, 'Rapport d'enquète consolidé du bureau conjoint des Nations-Unies pour les Droits de l'Homme (BCNUDH) suite aux vastes pillages et sérieuses violations des droits de l'homme commis par les FARDC à Goma et à Kanyabayonga en Octobre et Novembre 2008', Geneva, 7 Septembre 2009; Global Witness, 'Faced With a Gun, What Can You Do ?', London, July 2009; United Nations Security Council, 'Interim Report of the Group of Experts on the Democratic Republic of the Congo', New York, 18 May 2009 ; OXFAM International: 'Security Forces? The Security Services and Protection. Community Testimonies from DRC', March 2009. Concerning oversight mechanisms, see Quentin Weiler, op. cit. in note 14, p. 18 and Laura Davis, 'Justice-Sensitive Security System Reform in the Democratic Republic of Congo,' New York, International Center for Transitional Justice, February 2009.

18. Giji Gya, Charlotte Isaksson and Marta Martinelli, 'Report on ESDP Missions in the Democratic Republic of the Congo. Background Paper', UNIFEM, Brussels, October 2008.

and who should lead SSR in the DRC. However, in UN Resolution 1856 of 19 December 2008, the Security Council has for the first time tasked MONUC to coordinate its SSR activities with 'international partners, including the European Union operations EUSEC and EUPOL.'

In the DRC, SSR has been especially challenging because reform is being implemented in a context of a protracted conflict. The sustainability of two of EUSEC's main projects (chain of payment and census) was put to the test after numerous brigades were locally reshuffled in 2008 as a result of the casualties suffered in fighting against the National Congress for the Defence of the People (CNDP) rebellion. As fighting continues in the East where numerous armed groups remain active, other re-organisations may occur. The problem increased in early 2009, when the majority of the CNDP joined the Congolese army under a process of 'accelerated integration'[19] without being fully recorded in the central army database. The situation became even more complicated, when the salaries of the integrated brigades were diverted to pay the former rebels, thereby creating resentment among 'loyalists'.[20]

Lessons learned

There is a discrepancy between the modest means available to EUSEC and the role the EU wishes to play. A close observer has spoken of the 'politique de la canonnière verbale', as the EU's willingness to offer advice and take a leading role in SSR in DRC is not matched by the relatively small budget available to the two missions (EUPOL and EUSEC).[21] Still, EUSEC's smart projects and its ability to coordinate Western donors have allowed it to play a significant and innovative role in the field of SSR.

Due to its innovative approach, EUSEC appears to have won a vote of confidence. From the outset, the EU mission took a different SSR approach than most donors. Instead of focusing on training and equipment as bilateral and UN actors were doing, EUSEC tackled two main issues: management of resources and personnel as well as developing a strategic vision. The mission has developed good working relations with the numerous relevant military institutions. One of its main assets lies in

---

19. International Crisis Group, 'Congo: Five Priorities for a Peacebuilding Strategy', *Africa Report* no. 150, Brussels, 11 May 2009, pp. 10-13.

20. Interview with international official, April 2009.

21. In 2005, the CFSP's budget was 65% of that of MSF France. See Pierre-Antoine Braud, 'Enjeux de Stabilité : vers l'émancipation sécuritaire', presentation at the conference on 'Stratégies Africaines, Stratégies en Afrique. Quels Futurs?', Délégation aux Affaires Stratégiques, the French Ministry of Defence, 21 January 2009.

its common EU policy less likely to be perceived as linked to the partisan interests of a particular country. As a result, even reluctant Member States have agreed to increase EUSEC funding. However, when attempting to facilitate donor cooperation, EUSEC has sometimes run into a turf war with MONUC, the UN mission. EUSEC also reached its limit at the political level. Perhaps due to the background of the mission's members (former or active military), there has been a gap in its ability to liaise with and 'sell' its strategic plan to the relevant political actors, such as former Minister of Defence Chikez.

As the mission expands and personnel rotate, it is important that it does not lose its edge: its strategic approach. EUSEC members were also valued by their Congolese counterparts for their professionalism and their knowledge of the region. The different nationalities and backgrounds of the various members of the EU mission were instrumental in connecting with other SSR actors (for example the Portuguese team members and Angolan military). Likewise, the common experience of some EUSEC and Congolese military at the French military academy of Saint Cyr helped forge ties between them. A larger mission needs to retain personal contacts and deep knowledge of the Congolese strategic and institutional challenges, if it wants to remain relevant.

The mission will have to face further, important political challenges to SSR, such as the adoption of a code of conduct within the Congolese security forces, the improvement of their internal coherence and a thorough assessment of their true relevance. From this standpoint, the goal is not so much to increase the mission's technical expertise as its political *savoir faire*. On a separate matter, there is an equally urgent need to address the sexual conduct of Congolese soldiers.

Internally, the EU appears to have endorsed the rationale for a common institutional approach as it aims to merge EUSEC and EUPOL. As SSR becomes codified and more and more aspects can be accounted for as overseas development aid under the OECD-DAC rules, a European multilateral approach may prove increasingly attractive for European countries with less experience of operational involvement in the region (e.g., Italy and Germany). Finally, the EU must be realistic about its own capacities and the role it can play. A small team with limited means, EUSEC was not in a position to train or equip the Congolese army on any significant scale. Due to its limited resources, EUSEC must coordinate with larger actors, particularly the UN mission, and with representatives from non-EU countries, such as the US and potentially other African actors, notably Angola and South Africa.

BIBLIOGRAPHY

Braud, Pierre-Antoine. 'Enjeux de Stabilité: vers l'émancipation sécuritaire', presentation at the conference on 'Stratégies Africaines, Stratégies en Afrique. Quels Futurs?', Délégation aux Affaires stratégiques, the French Ministry of Defence, 21 January 2009.

Davis, Laura. 'Justice-Sensitive Security Sector Reform in the Democratic Republic of Congo', International Center for Transitional Justice, New York, February 2009.

Davis, Laura. 'Small Steps, Large Hurdles: the EU's role in Promoting Justice in Peacemaking in the DRC', International Center for Transitional Justice, New York, May 2009.

Gya, Giji, Isaksson, Charlotte, and Martinelli, Marta. 'Report on ESDP Missions in the Democratic Republic of the Congo. Background paper', UNIFEM, Brussels, October 2008.

Hoebeke Hans, Carette, Stéphanie and Vlassenroot, Koen. 'EU Support to the Democratic Republic of the Congo', (IRRI-KIIB, Brussels), in 'L'action de l'Europe en Afrique', Centre d'analyse stratégique, Paris, 2007, p. 10.

International Crisis Group. 'Security Sector Reform in the Congo', *Africa Report* no. 14, 13 February 2006.

International Crisis Group. 'Congo: Five Priorities for a Peacebuilding Strategy', *Africa Report* no. 150, 11 May 2009.

International Rescue Committee. 'Mortality in the Democratic Republic of Congo: an ongoing crisis', New York, January 2008.

Melmot, Sébastien. 'Candide au Congo. L'échec annoncé de la réforme du secteur de la sécurité –RSS', *Focus Stratégique* no. 9, Laboratoire de Recherche sur la Défense, Paris, Septembre 2008.

Nickel, Dietmar and Quille, Gerrard. 'In the Shadow of the Constitution : Adapting to a Changing External Environment', paper presented at the EUSA Tenth Biennial International Conference, Montreal, 17-19 May 2007.

Weiler, Quentin. 'The European Union and Security Sector Reform in Africa: a Leader in Theory, a Laggard in Reality?', United Nations University CRIS, Bruges Regional Integration & Global Governance Papers, January 2009.

13. Support to AMIS and AMISOM (Sudan and Somalia)

The European Union supporting actions to the African Union missions in Sudan (AMIS) and Somalia (AMISOM)*

Benedikt Franke

Legal basis: Council Joint Action 2005/557/CFSP of 18 July 2005 and Council Joint Action 2007/245/CFSP of 23 April 2007.

Highlights of the missions' mandates:

■ For AMIS: Ensure timely and effective EU assistance to the enhancement of AMIS II.

■ For AMISOM: Support setting up of a Strategic Planning and Management Unit (SPMU)

Duration: for EU support to AMIS: 18 July 2005-31 December 2007. For EU support to AMISOM: 23 April 2007-31 December 2007.

Mission strength: for support to AMIS: 30 civilian police, 15 military experts and 2 military observers; for support to AMISOM: 4 experts situated in the Strategic Planning Management Unit (SPMU).

* The full titles of the Council Joint Actions are, respectively: the EU civilian-military supporting action to the African Union mission in the Darfur region of Sudan (AMIS) and the EU military support element providing assistance to the setting up of the African Union Mission in Somalia (AMISOM).

Contributing states: for AMIS: 15 Member States (Austria, Belgium, Cyprus, Denmark, Germany, Finland, France, Hungary, Ireland, Italy, Netherlands, Portugal, Spain, Sweden, United Kingdom). For AMISOM: 9 Member States (Denmark, Germany, France, Italy, Netherlands, Portugal, Spain, Sweden, United Kingdom).

The African Union's ambition to seek a greater role for itself in the area of peace and security is clearly visible in the establishment of an elaborate security architecture and in its willingness to conduct its own peace operations. In the seven years since its foundation, the African Union (AU) has undertaken such operations in Burundi, Darfur, the Comoros and Somalia. The EU's support measures for the African Union Mission in Sudan (AMIS) and the African Union Mission in Somalia (AMISOM) not only afford an important insight into the development of ESDP, but also serve to highlight a series of contradictions and constraints in the EU's approach to security assistance that continues to limit its effectiveness.

EU support to the African Union Mission in Sudan

AMIS has been the AU's most ambitious operation to date. It has its origins in a series of African attempts to put an end to the long-running conflict in Sudan's eastern province of Darfur. As part of a much larger conflict network, the crisis in Darfur defies easy historical analysis.[1] Its most recent episode began in February 2003 when two rebel groups, the Justice and Equality Movement and the Sudan Liberation Movement/Army, attacked government installations in El-Fasher to protest against the social and economic marginalisation of Darfurians by the ruling regime in Khartoum. When the Sudanese government retaliated with a combination of its own military offensive and a proxy fighting force that became known as the *Janjaweed*, the escalating violence quickly left tens of thousands dead and millions displaced from their homes.

As Sudan's government at the time did not consent to a UN peace operation on its territory, the African Union was left to play the leading role when the parties to the conflict signed a ceasefire agreement in N'Djamena in April 2004 and called for an international body to monitor its implementation. Eager to sharpen its emerging

---

1. For a good overview of the conflict see Alex de Waal (ed.), *War in Darfur and the Search for Peace* (Cambridge, MA: Harvard University Press, 2007).

conflict management profile, the AU agreed to deploy 80 observers and a small protection force of 300 Nigerian and Rwandan troops (later referred to as AMIS I) to monitor, verify, investigate and report transgressions of the ceasefire agreement. When the latter broke down and international pressure to respond to the worsening violence mounted, the AU's Peace and Security Council first increased the number of AMIS personnel to 3,320 in October 2004 (AMIS II) and then to 7,730 in April 2005 (AMIS II-Enhanced). While the growing presence of AMIS personnel did bring some measure of security to the vulnerable civilian populations in selected camp areas and helped to achieve 'a semblance of stability in parts of Darfur,'[2] a combination of structural conditions, misguided politics, and a lack of peacekeeping experience seriously hampered the operation's overall effectiveness and eventually led to its replacement by the United Nations African Mission in Darfur (UNAMID) in December 2007, the first hybrid UN/AU operation.[3]

The European Union supported the AU's involvement in the Darfur conflict from the very beginning. As this involvement grew between January 2004 and December 2007, so did the EU's support for it. In accordance with the Action Plan for ESDP in Africa (adopted in November 2004), the EU Strategy for Africa entitled 'Towards a Strategic Partnership' (adopted in December 2005) and the EU Concept for Strengthening African Capabilities for the Prevention, Management and Resolution of Conflicts (adopted in November 2006), this support fell into three categories, namely, diplomatic support, operational assistance and financial aid.

On the diplomatic side, the EU began its involvement in Darfur by funding experts from the Geneva-based Centre for Humanitarian Dialogue to assist the AU in the N'Djamena negotiations and supporting subsequent political initiatives like the Darfur-Darfur Dialogue and Consultation Process, the Darfur Assessment and Evaluation Commission and the AU Cease-Fire Commission with the provision of more than €4 million through the Instrument for Stability and a limited number of military personnel. The EU also assigned two senior diplomats to assist with and coordinate its support to the peace process. Sten Rylander from Sweden, who was acting as Special Envoy for Darfur between early 2004 and December 2005, and Pekka Haavisto, who was appointed as the EU's first Special Representative (EUSR) for Sudan in July 2005, were responsible for ensuring the coherence of EU measures and the effective coordination with other international partners such as NATO and

---

2. Seth Appiah-Mensah, 'The African Mission in Sudan: Darfur Dilemmas', *African Security Review* vol. 15, no. 1, 2006, p. 19.

3. See UN Security Council Resolution 1769, 31 July 2007.

the US.[4] The EUSR also represented the Union at the Abuja Peace Talks and other high-level meetings in and around Sudan.

Operationally, the EU provided what it called a consolidated package of civilian and military measures to support AMIS from July 2005 to December 2007 (EU support to AMIS). During its two and a half year term, this package provided the AU mission with urgently needed equipment like vehicles, mobile generators and water tankers, but also with technical assistance, media support, police training, aerial observation capacity as well as strategic and tactical air transport for more than 2,000 troops. The EU also provided several dozen military and civilian personnel in support of AMIS. Averaging 30 police officers of the European Union Police Advisory Team (EUPAT), 15 military experts and two military observers, this personnel was deployed in the AU's Darfur Integrated Task Force (DITF) in Addis Ababa as well as the AMIS force headquarters in Khartoum and its forward and sectoral headquarters in Darfur, particularly in El-Fasher, Nyala and El-Geneina. In addition, military staff, a police officer and a political advisor were made available to support the EUSR in his contacts and cooperation with the AU.

The most visible support, however, was financial in nature. The EU dedicated more than one billion euro to the crisis in Darfur. While of this €691 million went to humanitarian aid via the European Commission's Humanitarian Aid Office, more than €300 million was dispensed directly to AMIS via the EU's newly created African Peace Facility (APF), a special funding instrument for capacity-building and operational support financed out of the 9th and 10th European Development Fund.[5] These amounts were used to pay for personnel costs including salaries, allowances, insurance, travel, food rations and medical costs. In addition to the APF funds, EU Member States such as the United Kingdom, France and Germany made substantial bilateral contributions taking the overall EU contribution to AMIS to more than €500 million.

Despite this extraordinary level of European support, AMIS proved unable to bring peace to Darfur. While the reasons for this failure were manifold and mostly related to the AU's meagre capacities and lack of peacekeeping experience, the EU's engagement was also not devoid of problems. For one, it was lacking in strategic coordi-

---

4. See Council Joint Action 2005/556/CFSP Article 7. Torben Brylle was appointed as the second EUSR in April 2007.

5. Nicoletta Pirozzi, 'EU support to African security architecture: funding and training components', *Occasional Paper* no. 76, EU Institute for Security Studies, Paris, February 2009.

nation with the initiatives of other actors like the UN and NATO.[6] Despite multi-lateral initiatives for information exchange on security assistance and cooperation programmes like the Africa Clearing House and the AU Partners Technical Support Group in Addis Ababa, possible synergies were not always utilised and donor efforts often overlapped leading to unnecessary duplications, which increased the transaction costs for the AU and further strained its absorption capacity. A good example is the fact that even though both NATO's Strategic Airlift Coordination Centre and the EU's European Airlift Centre are co-located in Eindhoven each dispatched its own liaison team to the DITF in Addis Ababa, thereby unnecessarily multiplying demands on AU staff and facilities.

A much more important shortcoming, however, was that even though it recognised the Darfur crisis from the beginning as a major challenge, the EU failed to fully appreciate the extent to which the AU's nascent capabilities would be stretched by the mission's growing requirements. As a result, it did not provide the operational and financial support necessary to ensure the mission's effectiveness. While adjustments were made as the mission evolved, the levels of support were always below the requirements of the moment. The EU has made a considerable contribution to the mission, yet even when taking into account the argument that the AU's absorption capacity for outside support may already have been overstretched, it is a fact that AMIS never had enough critical force enablers like vehicles, helicopters and communication equipment to fulfil its objectives. Admittedly, the crisis erupted at a moment when neither the EU's Africa policy nor the CFSP or ESDP had been consolidated, but it is hard not to share Jolyon Howorth's conclusion that 'the EU has ultimately proven unable to contribute to AMIS in a manner consistent with its future ambitions and historical responsibilities for Africa'.[7]

EU support to the African Union Mission in Somalia

Even more so than its support to AMIS, the half-hearted assistance the European Union provides to the AU's ongoing mission in Somalia (AMISOM) illustrates the discrepancy between its pro-Africanisation rhetoric contained in key documents like the Joint EU-Africa Strategy of December 2007 and its reluctance to commit sufficient resources to AU-led missions.

---

6. Markus Derblom, Eva Hagström Frisell and Jennifer Schmidt, 'UN-EU-AU Coordination in Peace Operations in Africa', *Swedish Defence Research Agency Report* no. 2602, Stockholm, November 2008.

7. Jolyon Howorth, *Security and Defence Policy in the European Union* (Basingstoke: Palgrave, 2007), p. 217.

While it was officially launched in January 2007, AMISOM had its roots in the 2005 attempt by the Intergovernmental Authority on Development (IGAD) to assemble a 10,500 strong regional peace-building force in support of Somalia's Transitional Federal Government. However, the reluctance of IGAD member states to contribute troops to the operation, disagreements over the composition of the force and the military advances of the Union of Islamic Courts (UIC) inside Somalia meant that the mission never materialised. When Ethiopia intervened in Somalia to prevent a spillover of the conflict into its notoriously unstable Ogaden province in December 2007, the AU agreed to step in and deploy a peacekeeping force to fill the security vacuum that was opening up with the retreat of UIC forces.

Initially, the EU and other partners were hesitant to pledge support to AMISOM. The controversial US-backed Ethiopian invasion, the apparent lack of African interest in the operation as well as the difficult political and humanitarian situation in Somalia made failure seem inevitable. Determined to foster its emerging conflict management profile and encouraged by the United States, which feared the spread of terrorist safe havens throughout Somalia, the AU, however, decided to launch the operation in spite of these adverse conditions. Bound by its commitment to African-led peace efforts and following a formal request for assistance by the AU, the EU Council on 23 April 2007 amended its Joint Action on the EU civilian-military supporting action to AMIS to include a military support element for the setting up of AMISOM.[8] Since then the EU has put together a set of diplomatic, operational and financial initiatives that are similar in type, but not in scale, to those provided to AMIS.

On the diplomatic side, the EU supported the Djibouti Peace Process and the efforts of the International Contact Group for Somalia through a variety of instruments. It also engaged in discreet diplomacy with international partners and regional organisations like IGAD to support a national reconciliation conference and extended diplomatic assistance to the Somali Unity Government elected on 30 January 2009. On the operational side, it has seconded four experts on civil engineering, human resources, budgeting and communications to AMISOM's Strategic Planning and Management Unit (SPMU) in Addis Ababa. Together with seven UN experts, two NATO officers and a US liaison officer, they continue to make up the bulk of the SPMU and provide crucial strategic and technical advice to the AMISOM commanders. The EU's anti-piracy Operation *Atalanta* also provides operational support by

---

8. Council Joint Action 2007/245/CFSP, 23 April 2007.

securing the mission's maritime supply lines into Mogadishu harbour and providing protection at sea to the vessels delivering the UN's logistical support package.[9]

As with AMIS, the EU's most important contribution to AMISOM has been financial in nature. Since March 2008, the European Commission has been supporting the deployment of AMISOM with €35 million from the African Peace Facility which is mainly used to pay troop allowances. It has also pledged €5 million from the Instrument for Stability to the establishment of the SPMU, €500,000 to cover some of the mission's insurance costs and €4 million to Somalia's transititional institutions. In December 2008, another €20 million was made available from the APF and at an international donors' conference held in April 2009, the EU pledged an additional €60 million to the operation. Several EU Member States have also made substantial bilateral contributions to AMISOM, including Italy (€10 million in direct funding as well as €32 million in the form of an extra-budgetary grant), the UK (£8.5 million for deployment-related expenses), and Sweden.

For reasons ranging from a lack of personnel – of the planned 8,000 troops only 3,450 have been deployed thus far – to the absence of critical force enablers, AMISOM has had only a very limited impact on the situation in Somalia over the last two years. Most of the mission's problems come down to a simple lack of funds. With less than ten percent of the overall budget covered, the AU cannot guarantee reimbursement to troop contributing countries (thus 'losing' them to well-funded missions like UNAMID) nor can it provide the necessary levels of mission support, thus essentially limiting the operation's coverage to a few streets in central Mogadishu. With partners reluctant to increase their commitments and the plans for an international stabilisation force dead in the water, it looks like AMISOM is bound to suffer the same fate as the AU's erstwhile flagship operation in Darfur.

Conclusion

The European Defence and Security Policy has undoubtedly come a long way in the last ten years, particularly so in Africa. However, the conclusion to be drawn from the two case studies above is that there is still a long way to go. If the EU is serious about its partnership with the African Union and its support to the process of Africanising the responsibility for peacekeeping on the continent, it must change the way in which it supports operations like AMIS and AMISOM. Three issues in particular must be addressed.

---

9. Council Joint Action 2008/851/CFSP, 10 November 2008. See the chapter on NAVFOR *Atalanta* in this book.

First and foremost, the EU must increase its level of support. While the EU has made available considerable financial resources (well over €300 million for AMIS and around €120 million for AMISOM), these contributions pale in comparison to the overall costs of these missions which are amounting to billions. With the annual costs of AMISOM set to rise to over €560 million, the need for sustainable and predictable funding from the EU is greater than ever.

Second, the EU should loosen the overly restrictive conditions on the funding it provides to AU operations or find alternative, more flexible channels to provide its assistance. For even though the lack of military equipment remains one of the key impediments to the success of such operations, the nature of the EU's financial support mechanisms prevents the provision of military hardware to the troop-contributing countries. The APF, for example, is financed through the European Development Fund, which does allow the use of funds for conflict prevention, but in accordance with the OECD criteria for Official Development Assistance explicitly prohibits the provision of material with 'potentially lethal implications'.[10] However, given the crucial importance of military hardware such as armoured personnel carriers and transport helicopters to mission success, a way needs to be found for the EU to extend its assistance to in-theatre loaning of selected material.

Third, the provision of peacekeeping training was overemphasised. The fact that such training is easy to sell to domestic constituencies because of its perceived harmlessness has led many actors, including the EU, to focus their support on its provision regardless of the actual needs for it. Even though initiatives like the Europeanisation of the French peacekeeping training programme RECAMP (*Renforcement des capacités africaines au maintien de la paix*) are certainly useful in the long-run, peacekeeping training simply is not perceived by Africans as being the requirement of the moment, especially so as the relevant experience of many African soldiers is often fresher and more substantial than that of their European trainers (after all, African countries are among the most frequent contributors to UN peace operations).[11]

Lastly, the EU needs to improve its coordination with actors like the UN and NATO, but also with its own Member States in order to avoid the unnecessary duplication of efforts and the divisive impact of mal-coordinated measures that has characterised European support to AU operations thus far. The establishment of a separate

---

10. Organisation for Economic Co-operation and Development (OECD), Development Assistance Committee (DAC), Official Guidelines for Development Assistance. Available at www.oecd.org.

11. This widely-held sentiment was reiterated throughout most of the author's interviews over the last two years at the AU Headquarters and several field missions, including AMISOM and AMISEC.

EU delegation to the AU in early 2008 was an important step in the right direction, but more should be done to make the most of Europe's potential.

At the same time, none of the above changes will have any lasting impact if adequate measures to increase the AU's institutional and absorption capacities are not implemented soon. Strengthening the African Union as an organisation is a prerequisite for improving the effectiveness of its peace operations, guaranteeing African ownership thereof and thereby reviving the enthusiasm for continental security cooperation that characterised the early years of the AU. Only if Africa's states are able to take pride in and identify with the AU's operations will they be willing to commit the necessary financial and political resources. In the meantime, the EU is likely to remain the most important supporter of these operations.

BIBLIOGRAPHY

Appiah-Mensah, Seth. 'The African Mission in Sudan: DarfurDilemmas', *African Security Review*, vol. 15, no. 1, 2006.

Assanvo, William and Pout, Christian. 'The European Union: African Peace and Security Environment's Champion?' (Paris: Fondation pour la Recherche Stratégique, 2007).

Bogland, Karin, Egnell, Robert and Lagerström, Maria. 'The African Union – A Study Focusing on Conflict Management', *Swedish Defence Research Agency Report* no. 2475, Stockholm, 2008.

Cazelles, Christophe. 'The EU as an international organization: the case of Darfur' (Paris: Centre d'analyse stratégique, 2007).

Derblom, Markus, Hagström Frisell, Eva and Schmidt, Jennifer. 'UN-EU-AU Coordination in Peace Operations in Africa', *Swedish Defence Research Agency Report* no. 2602, Stockholm, 2008.

Franke, Benedikt. *Security Cooperation in Africa: A Reappraisal* (Boulder, CO: Lynne Rienner, 2009).

Howorth, Jolyon. *Security and Defence Policy in the European Union* (Basingstoke: Palgrave, 2007).

Hull, Cecilia and Svensson, Emma. 'The African Union Mission in Somalia (AMISOM): Exemplifying African Union Peacekeeping Challenges', *Swedish Defence Research Agency Report* no. 2596, Stockholm, 2008.

Pirozzi, Nicoletta. 'EU support to African security architecture: funding and training components', *Occasional Paper* no. 76,, EU Institute for Security Studies, Paris, 2009.

Tardy, Thierry. 'The European Union, a regional security actor with global aspirations' in Thierry Tardy (ed.), *European security in a global context: Internal and external dynamics* (London: Routledge, 2009), pp. 17-36.

de Waal, Alex (ed.) *War in Darfur and the Search for Peace* (Cambridge, MA: Harvard University Press, 2007).

14. AMM (Aceh, Indonesia)

The Aceh Monitoring Mission

Kirsten E. Schulze

Legal basis: Council Joint Action 2005/643/CFSP of 9 September 2005.

Highlights of the mission's mandate:

■ To monitor the demobilisation of GAM and monitor and monitor and assist the decommissioning and destruction of its weapons.

■ To monitor the redeployment of non-organic Indonesian military (TNI) and police.

■ To monitor the reintegration of active GAM members into society.

■ To monitor the human rights situation in the context of the tasks above.

■ To monitor the process of legislation change in Aceh.

■ To rule on disputed amnesty cases.

■ To investigate and rule on violations of the MOU.

■ To establish and maintain liaison and good cooperation with the parties.

Duration: 15 September 2005–15 December 2006.

Budget: €15 million (€9 million from the CFSP budget and €6 million from the Member States taking part in the mission).

> **Mission strength:** 125 EU personnel and 93 ASEAN personnel.
>
> **Contributing states:** 12 Member States (Austria, Belgium, Denmark, Finland, France, Germany, Ireland, Lithuania, Netherlands, Spain, Sweden, United Kingdom) and 7 third countries (Norway and Switzerland. ASEAN states: Thailand, Malaysia, Brunei, Singapore and the Philippines).

Introduction: background and context of the mission

From October 1976 until August 2005 the Indonesian province of Aceh was wracked by armed conflict between the Free Aceh Movement (GAM) which sought Acehnese independence and the Indonesian security forces which sought to prevent such separation. At the heart of the conflict were fractious centre-periphery relations revolving around the degree of Acehnese autonomy, revenue-sharing, and human rights abuses. Until the fall of President Suharto in May 1998, the Aceh conflict was fought purely by military means. In 2000 peace negotiations were started. However, in May 2003 negotiations broke down and Aceh was placed under martial law.[1] After a year of Indonesian counter-insurgency operations and the election of a new Indonesian president, Susilo Bambang Yudhoyono, secret backchannel talks between GAM's exiled leadership and Jakarta were opened.[2] In the wake of the December 2004 Asian Tsunami, these contacts were turned into formal negotiations, facilitated by the Finnish Crisis Management Initiative (CMI) with backing from the European Union (EU). On 15 August 2005, GAM and the Indonesian Government concluded a Memorandum of Understanding (MOU) that granted Aceh wide-ranging autonomy. It also stipulated the establishment of an Aceh Monitoring Mission (AMM) to oversee the MOU's implementation.[3]

---

1. For a full discussion of GAM's negotiating position in the Geneva peace process see Kirsten E. Schulze, 'The Free Aceh Movement (GAM): Anatomy of a Separatist Organization' *East-West Center Policy Studies* no. 2, East West Center, Washington, September 2004. See also Edward Aspinall and Harold Crouch, 'The Aceh Peace Process: Why it Failed', *East-West Center Policy Studies* no. 1, Washington, November 2003.

2. For a discussion of the Helsinki peace process, see Michael Morfit, 'Staying on the Road to Helsinki: Why the Aceh Agreement was possible in August 2005', paper for the international conference on Building a Permanent Peace in Aceh: One Year After the Helsinki Accord, sponsored by the Indonesian Council for World Affairs, Jakarta, 14 August 2006. See also Edward Aspinall, 'The Helsinki Agreement', *Policy Paper* no. 20, East West Center, Washington, 2006. See also Kirsten E. Schulze, 'From the battlefield to the negotiating table: GAM and the Indonesian government, 1999-2005', *Asian Security*, Special Issue on Internal Conflicts in Southeast Asia: The Nature, Legitimacy, and (Changing) Role of the State, vol. 3, no. 2, July 2007.

3. Kirsten E. Schulze, 'The AMM, and the Transition from Conflict to Peace in Aceh, 2005-2006' in Mary Martin and Mary Kaldor (eds.), *A European Way of Security: The European Union and Human Security* (London: Routledge, 2009).

The AMM's size, composition, and mandate

The AMM, headed by Peter Feith and headquartered in Banda Aceh, comprised monitors from the EU and Norway and Switzerland as well as five ASEAN countries: Thailand, Malaysia, Brunei, the Philippines and Singapore. This was the first such cooperation between the EU and another regional organisation and it was as successful as it was groundbreaking. During its first mandate period from 15 September to 31 December 2005 the AMM had 125 EU and 93 ASEAN monitors on the ground, including four specially trained decommissioning teams, plus a logistics component provided by the Swedish government. The number of EU and ASEAN monitors progressively decreased over 2006, as the bulk of the mission's mandate was accomplished.[4]

The AMM's objective was to assist GAM and the Indonesian government with the implementation of the MOU and 'to contribute to a peaceful, comprehensive and sustainable solution to the conflict in Aceh.'[5] Its mandate, as specified in the MOU, comprised eight areas. First, to monitor the demobilisation of GAM and the decommissioning and destruction of its weapons. Second, to monitor the redeployment of the Indonesian military (TNI) and police. Third, to monitor the reintegration of active GAM members into society. Fourth, to monitor the human rights situation related to these tasks. Fifth, to monitor the legislation change agreed in the MoU, which included the Law on Governing Aceh, the establishment of a human rights commission and a human rights court as well as bringing legislation in line with internationally accepted human rights norms. Sixth, to rule on disputed amnesty cases. Seventh, to investigate and rule on complaints and alleged violations of the MOU.[6] And, eighth, to establish and maintain liaison and good cooperation with the parties.

The AMM's personnel comprised both civilians and military, located at the mission's HQ and in eleven District Offices with mixed civil-military teams. The decommissioning teams were predominantly military. The military personnel were tasked primarily with monitoring the security aspects of the MOU such as decommissioning, demobilisation and redeployment. They were well-trained, highly skilled and some had experience of other processes of disarmament. Besides, the ASEAN members

---

4. From 31 December 2005 to 15 March 2006, there were 100 EU and 93 ASEAN monitors. During the third period from 15 March to 15 June 2006, the number was reduced to 54 EU and 32 ASEAN monitors. From 15 June to 15 September, there were 54 EU and 32 monitors and from 15 September to 15 December there were only 29 EU and 7 ASEAN monitors left on the ground.

5. Aceh Monitoring Mission leaflet, Banda Aceh, 2006.

6. The MoU, section 5, 'Establishment of the Aceh Monitoring Mission'. See: www.aceh-mm.org/download/english/Helsinki%20MoU.pdf.

of the mission who were exclusively from a military background, had familiarity with the Indonesian military. The civilian personnel of the AMM were more mixed in terms of expertise and previous experience. At the top leadership level, the head of mission had excellent diplomatic and managerial skills as well as expertise and experience. On the other hand, the rapid establishment of the mission meant that mission personnel received little training and the level of experience of recruited officials was uneven. Furthermore, given the remoteness of the region and the fact that it had been the theatre of a civil war for decades, most of the mission personnel had little familiarity with Aceh.

Main challenges confronting the mission

The AMM faced a number of challenges both at the level of internal EU decision-making and on the ground. The most important internal challenge was funding. Part of the problem consisted of divisions within the EU, both among Member States and between institutions. Finland, Sweden, the Netherlands, France, and later the UK were in favour of an EU engagement while other Member States felt that the EU should concentrate on areas closer to Europe, where ESDP deployments had already occurred, such as the Balkans and Africa. This lack of unity was further complicated by the EU's 'complicated and cumbersome procedures and budgetary processes' which would not allow for the deployment of a fully-fledged AMM on 15 August.[7] And last, but certainly not least, proposals for funding quickly became the victim of a power-struggle between the EU Commission and the EU Council. Javier Solana's personal intervention helped swing the debate in favour of EU deployment and financing it from the CFSP budget. However, out of a total budget of €15 million, the CFSP could only cover €9 million. The rest had to be provided by 'willing and able' Member States.[8] In particular, the small Technical Assistance Mission deployed in early August to pave the way for the larger monitoring mission was partially financed by the UK, then holding the Presidency of the EU, while Finland, Sweden and the UK bore the brunt of the costs of the Initial Monitoring Presence, active as of the signing of the MoU – on 15 August – until the AMM was launched on 15 September.[9]

---

7. Pierre-Antoine Braud and Giovanni Grevi, 'The EU mission in Aceh: implementing peace', *Occasional Paper* no. 61, European Union Institute for Security Studies, Paris, December 2005, p.27.

8. Ibid, p.27.

9. The British Embassy in Jakarta provided £7,500 for the Technical Assessment Mission, another £7,500 for office space, office facilities, local mobile phones, and car and driver hire as well as $23,774.91 for the health insurance for the Interim Monitoring Presence and the AMM. For a detailed discussion, see Schulze, op. cit. in note 3.

The most important external challenge on the ground was the highly sensitive Indonesian domestic political environment. At the heart of the problem was the uneasy relationship between Indonesia and the international community since the violence that had followed the 1999 East Timor referendum. International concern for human rights was perceived by Indonesia as a stick with which to beat the government and the security forces. It was perceived as a deliberate political tool to keep Indonesia weak. This view was particularly prevalent in the military and in the Indonesian parliament. While the AMM was able to overcome the military's suspicions during the decommissioning process, it was viewed as a foreign intrusion by the parliamentarians. This made it extremely difficult for the AMM to push for the implementation of the human rights elements of the MOU, such as bringing Aceh's legislation in line with internationally accepted human rights standards. While the Indonesian government did ratify the human rights covenants required by the MoU, the new Law on the Governance of Aceh (LoGA) included Islamic *Sharia* Law with corporal *hudud* punishments. However, an excessive focus on this dimension of the mandate could have jeopardised the mission as a whole.

The AMM's implementation and performance

The AMM aimed to create the conditions for the peace process to take hold and make progress. In this context, the mission focused on pressing security issues first, namely monitoring the amnesty for GAM prisoners, the decommissioning and destruction of GAM weapons, the redeployment of the Indonesian security forces, and the reintegration of former combatants. In order to build GAM's confidence in the peace process the amnesty had to be implemented early and quickly. The AMM's key function was to monitor the releases and keep up the pressure on Jakarta to ensure that the amnesties were carried out speedily and completely. The first 298 persons were amnestied only two days into the agreement on 17 August to celebrate Indonesia's Independence Day. Following presidential decree 22/2005 on 30 August another 1,424 were released. Thus the majority of the approximately 2,000 prisoners were released quickly. There were some disputed cases which caused the completion of the amnesty process to drag on. At the heart of the dispute was whether certain prisoners had been criminally involved and thus did not qualify. By the end of the mission, all disputed amnesty cases had been resolved.

The amnesty was followed by the parallel decommissioning of GAM weapons and the redeployment of the Indonesian military and police. Both processes were divided into four stages to be completed by the end of December 2005. The first phase of decommissioning lasted from 15-18 September with 279 GAM weapons handed over, of which 243 were accepted by the AMM.[10] The second round of decommissioning took place in mid-October and resulted in a total of 291 weapons handed over, of which 58 were rejected as faulty. During the third round of decommissioning in November the process almost collapsed, due to troubled internal GAM politics. GAM's representative on the decommissioning team was replaced and the new representative all of a sudden said that there were no weapons left. Yet, the EU monitors had seen more weapons.[11] Eventually, a total of 1,018 weapons were handed in and destroyed. While there were some challenges throughout the decommissioning process as a whole, such as how to transport GAM weapons to the collection points and the lesser commitment of some GAM areas like East Aceh,[12] the overall process was a resounding success according to all parties involved.

In parallel with the rounds of decommissioning were four rounds of Indonesian troop redeployment from September to December 2005. The first phase of redeployment began on 14 September with the withdrawal of 1,300 mobile police (*Brimob*). This was followed by the redeployment of two military units of the TNI. By the end of the redeployment process 25,890 TNI and 5,791 *Brimob* had been withdrawn, bringing the total up to 31,681 non-organic security forces redeployed. While the process as a whole went smoothly, there were two issues raised by the AMM during the early period. The first was that the TNI continued aggressive patrolling and there were continuing allegations of harassment, beatings and extortion by *Brimob*.[13] The second was the repeated reports of intimidation of ex-GAM by members of the TNI intelligence (SGI) in the form of questioning, monitoring and photographing. Both issues had the potential to undermine the peace process, but ceased to be a problem once they had been brought to the attention of the TNI's liaison with the AMM. The troop redeployments were verified by the AMM and GAM was informed at each Commission on Security Arrangements (COSA) meeting. This was followed by an overall verification from 14 January to 15 February 2006 in which the AMM monitored the remaining troops in the various districts and concluded that the Indonesian government had fully complied with the MOU.

Once the decommissioning had been completed, the reintegration of former GAM combatants became a key priority. The AMM's role was to monitor the reintegration of GAM ex-combatants into society. However, implementing the actual re-

---

10. AMM Daily Report, Banda Aceh, 18 September 2005. In order to qualify, weapons had to have a steel barrel, a steel chamber, and be capable of firing lethal ordnance.

11. Interview with AMM head of decommissioning, Brussels, 5 September 2006.

12. See Monthly Report 001, HQ AMM, Banda Aceh, 15 September–21 October 2005, p.1.

13. Weekly Report 002, HQ AMM, Banda Aceh, 28 September-11October 2005, p.3.

integration programmes was not part of the AMM's mandate. These programmes were carried out by international agencies, local government, and the government agency Badan Reintegrasi Damai Aceh (BRA). The challenge of reintegration was first addressed by establishing financial reintegration packages, which were released in three rounds between October 2005 and January 2006. The money was issued to GAM regional commanders as GAM was reluctant to provide names. They received Rp[14]1 million (€74) per fighter based on a list of 3,000 GAM combatants detailed by district. As feared by the AMM, it soon became apparent that guerrillas in some areas were not included at all and others received significantly less than envisaged. Local GAM commanders explained that this was the result of having to share the money among a greater number of former combatants. However, 'there were hints of luxury cars and new houses for commanders at the expense of the rank-and-file.'[15]

The Indonesian government through the governor of Aceh then proceeded to establish the BRA on 15 February 2006. It comprised representatives from GAM, the Indonesian government, and civil society and cooperated with international agencies such as the International Organisation for Migration (IOM). The BRA changed the approach from a combatant-driven disbursement to a project-driven disbursement of reintegration funds. It developed two reintegration schemes. The first was for small projects proposed by groups of ex-GAM combatants. The second reintegration scheme was for civilians affected by the conflict. While the former was successful, the latter did not work well as the criteria were so broad that virtually everyone could put in a claim.

In addition to monitoring the reintegration of former combatants, the AMM also monitored the political process: the drafting of the LoGA followed by the first direct elections. The AMM was further responsible for monitoring the human rights situation and the establishment of the Human Rights Court and Commission for Truth and Reconciliation. The LoGA was finally passed on 12 July. According to Indonesian Justice Minister Hamid Awaluddin the AMM 'played a significant role in pushing [the parties] to keep to the timeframe but without interfering in the substance.'[16] The AMM welcomed the passing of the legislation. However, there was criticism from GAM, human rights organisations, women's organisations, civil society, moderate Muslims, and non-Muslim minorities. Critics thought that the role of the central government was still too great and that the LoGA and especially

---

14. Rp = rupiah (Indonesian unit of currency).
15. International Crisis Group, 'Aceh's Local Elections: The Role of the Free Aceh Movement (GAM)', *Asia Briefing* no. 57, Jakarta/Brussels, 29 November 2006, p. 10.
16. Interview with Hamid Awaluddin, Indonesian negotiator and Justice Minister, Jakarta, 15 July 2006.

its provision for *Shariah* Law, was contrary to the MOU which stipulated that 'the legislature of Aceh will redraft the legal code for Aceh on the basis of the universal principles of human rights.'

After the LoGA was passed the date for the first direct elections for governor and vice-governor as well as 19 regents (senior executive positions) and mayors was set for 11 December 2006. Around 2.6 million Acehnese were eligible to vote. GAM had decided against formally endorsing particular candidates for these elections because a rift had emerged between the 'old guard' leadership in Sweden and the 'young Turks' who had fought on the battlefield. The split was over perceptions of what Aceh is and should become and perceptions over who did what during the conflict. Eventually, a prominent former GAM member (Irwandi Yusuf), representing the younger wing of the movement, prevailed in the vote.

Lessons learned: achievements and shortcomings

The greatest achievements of the AMM were the decommissioning of GAM weapons, the demobilisation of GAM, the redeployment of the Indonesian security forces, and the facilitation of the transition from conflict to peace in Aceh – a peace that still holds today. One of the greatest shortcomings was the lack of progress on the human rights elements of the MOU. By the time the AMM ended neither the Human Rights Court nor the Truth and Reconciliation Commission had been established. Instead the Indonesian government decided that human rights cases could be tried in the human rights court in Medan in the neighbouring province of North Sumatra, which was established in 2000. However, so far no case has been brought to trial. Moreover, in Acehnese eyes, the failure to establish a human rights court in Aceh and to refer any case to North Sumatra, which is ethnically different and has had mixed relations with Aceh throughout history, is seen as proof that the Indonesian government is not seriously committed to the human rights elements of the MoU. Many human rights activists believe that the AMM had an opportunity to push the Indonesian government on human rights and that this opportunity has now been lost. Yet, somewhat ironically it was exactly the AMM's reluctance to do so that ultimately enabled it to achieve its overall aims. A too early or too overzealous focus on human rights would have jeopardised the mission. Some lessons can be learned from this. In environments where human rights have become highly politicised it may be worth considering a more limited human rights mandate. Another possibility is a sequenced implementation schedule, which in effect means prioritising the immediate stabilisation.

BIBLIOGRAPHY

Aspinall, Edward and Crouch, Harold. 'The Aceh Peace Process: Why it Failed', *East-West Center Policy Studies* no. 1, East West Center, Washington, November 2003.

Aspinall, Edward. 'The Helsinki Agreement', *Policy Paper* no. 20, East West Center, Washington D.C., 2006.

Braud, Pierre-Antoine and Grevi, Giovanni. 'The EU mission in Aceh: implementing peace', *Occasional Paper* no. 61, European Union Institute for Security Studies, Paris, December 2005.

International Crisis Group, 'Aceh's Local Elections: The Role of the Free Aceh Movement (GAM)', *Asia Briefing* no. 57, Jakarta/Brussels, 29 November 2006.

Morfit, Michael. 'Staying on the Road to Helsinki: Why the Aceh Agreement was possible in August 2005', paper for the international conference on Building a Permanent Peace in Aceh: One Year After the Helsinki Accord, sponsored by the Indonesian Council for World Affairs, Jakarta, 14 August 2006.

Schulze, Kirsten E. 'The Free Aceh Movement (GAM): Anatomy of a Separatist Organization', *East-West Center Policy Studies* no. 2, East West Center, Washington, September 2004.

Schulze, Kirsten E. 'From the battlefield to the negotiating table: GAM and the Indonesian government, 1999-2005', *Asian Security*, Special Issue on Internal Conflicts in Southeast Asia: The Nature, Legitimacy, and (Changing) Role of the State, vol. 3, no. 2, July 2007.

Schulze, Kirsten E. 'The AMM, and the Transition from Conflict to Peace in Aceh, 2005-2006' in Mary Martin and Mary Kaldor (eds.), *A European Way of Security: The European Union and Human Security* (London: Routledge, 2009).

15. EUBAM Moldova-Ukraine

The EU Border Assistance Mission to the Republic of Moldova and Ukraine

George Dura

Legal basis: Council Joint Action 2005/776/CFSP of 7 November 2005.

Highlights of the mission's mandate:

■ Assists and advises Moldovan and Ukrainian border guards and customs officials in areas involving border, customs and fiscal matters.

■ Sets up a system of exchange of information on customs data and border traffic between Moldova and Ukraine.

■ No executive authority to enforce the laws of Moldova or Ukraine, but has an advisory role.

■ Right to make unannounced visits to any location on the Ukrainian-Moldovan border.

■ Right to be present and to observe customs clearance in progress, to examine and copy customs import documents and other official books and records.

■ Right to order the re-examination or re-assessment of any consignment of goods.

■ Provide assistance in preventing smuggling of persons and goods.

Duration: 1 December 2005 to date.

Budget: December 2005 – November 2007: €20.2 million (Rapid Reaction Mechanism and Tacis). December 2007 – November 2009: €24 million (European Neighbourhood and Partnership Instrument).

Mission strength: 233 staff in January 2008 (122 international staff and 111 local staff).

Contributing states: all Member States (except Ireland, Luxembourg, Malta, Spain and Sweden) and 3 third states (Georgia, Kazakhstan, Tajikistan).

Introduction

The EU Border Assistance Mission (EUBAM) to Moldova and Ukraine was established at the end of 2005, a period when the EU was in the process of strengthening its relations with its eastern neighbours through the European Neighbourhood Policy (ENP). Both countries signed an ENP Action Plan with the EU in February 2005. In the course of the same year the EU also strengthened its presence in Moldova through the appointment of an EU Special Representative and the establishment of an EC Delegation in Chisinau. Reports of lucrative smuggling deals and trafficking activities (drugs, weapons and human beings) across Moldova's eastern border with Ukraine, particularly along the section controlled by the separatist authorities of the Transnistria region of Moldova, led to the swift deployment of the EUBAM. The imminent accession of Romania in 2007 also made it imperative for the EU to ensure that a lawful, orderly and effective control of goods, vehicles and people existed at the common border between two of its new neighbours, Moldova and Ukraine. The EUBAM has contributed to bring transparency and respect of internationally accepted customs procedures to the Moldovan-Ukrainian border. In addition, there are hopes that the EUBAM can also contribute to the peaceful settlement of the Transnistria conflict by reducing the illegal revenue which Transnistrian (but also Moldovan, Ukrainian and Russian) political and business elites derive from these illicit activities, and by creating the conditions for Transnistria to reintegrate Moldova's customs space. Whilst the EUBAM is not a pure ESDP mission since it is primarily managed by the European Commission, it plays an important role by way of stabilising the region and increasing security on the EU's eastern border.

Background and aims of the mission

Background

The 2005 joint Moldova-Ukraine initiative for requesting a EUBAM was preceded by Moldova-Ukraine negotiations in which the EU was also involved at the later stages. Moldova had long been complaining of the fact that Ukrainian border services were turning a blind eye (or even prospering) from the illicit cross-border activities. Chisinau insisted that Ukrainian authorities only recognise official Moldovan customs documents (and not the Transnistrian ones) and proposed to hold joint checks on the Ukrainian side of the common border along the Transnistrian segment, where Moldovan border services had no access. These unsuccessful attempts led Moldova to request the EU Commission's involvement and an initial trilateral meeting was held in Brussels on 11 March 2003. The meeting focused on the organisation of joint border control on the Ukraine-Moldova border, including on the Transnistrian segment, and on the introduction of a ban on the export of Transnistrian goods which did not carry the official customs stamps and documents issued by Moldova. Bilaterally, a Protocol between the Customs Services of Moldova and Ukraine was signed in Kyiv on 15 May 2003 on 'Mutual recognition of shipping, commercial and customs documents supply'.[1]

On 2 June 2005, the Moldovan and Ukrainian presidents addressed a joint letter to the President of the European Commission, Jose Manuel Barroso and to the EU High Representative for CFSP, Javier Solana. The letter was the result of a meeting between both presidents at Odessa in Ukraine where consultations on the Transnistrian issue were held and an agreement on mutual access to the markets of both countries and another agreement on implementing joint border control were signed. The joint letter requested EU technical assistance in establishing an 'international customs control arrangement and an effective border monitoring mechanism on the Transnistrian segment of the Moldova-Ukraine border'.[2]

The EU replied promptly to the joint Moldovan-Ukrainian request by sending a joint EU Council Secretariat/EU Commission Fact-Finding Mission (FFM) to Moldova and Ukraine between 23 and 29 August 2005. The FFM strongly backed an earlier

1. The Protocol stipulates amongst others (art. 5, §2) that 'movement in both directions of goods and cargo ... may take place exclusively if it has the customs seals and stamps of the Contracting Parties', implying the recognition of Ukraine from now on of the Moldovan stamps exclusively, whereby it would turn back Transnistrian goods or cargo not carrying such documents. Document available at: http://www.eubam.org/files/300-399/304/PROTOCOL-150506-eng.pdf.
2. EU Factsheet, 'EU Border Assistance Mission to Moldova and Ukraine', European Council, Brussels, December 2007.

EU Commission proposal to put in place the EUBAM as an EC-funded project and recommended that the newly appointed EU Special Representative[3] have his team expanded with four advisors on issues related to border control. The FFM also underlined that a formal agreement between Moldova and Ukraine on the mission's mandate and tasks was necessary before an EUBAM could be deployed. Such an agreement was soon reached in the form of a 'Memorandum of Understanding on the European Commission Border Assistance Mission to Moldova and Ukraine'.[4] The Memorandum removed any lingering diplomatic hurdles and the mission was officially launched in Odessa, Ukraine on 30 November 2005.

Aims

The EUBAM aims to bring transparency to the Moldova-Ukraine border by allowing both countries to better control their common border and thereby to combat smuggling and trafficking activities as well as customs fraud and corruption more effectively. The EUBAM seeks to improve the capacity of Moldovan and Ukrainian border and customs services, to provide them with technical assistance and training and to reach European 'best-practice' standards. Javier Solana felt that the mission was 'particularly significant in relation to our [the EU's] joint efforts to find a viable settlement to the Transnistrian conflict' and noted that it contributed with 'technical assistance and deep political co-operation'.[5]

More specifically, the mission is tasked to cooperate with the host countries to harmonise their border management standards and procedures with those prevalent in EU Member States; to assist with capacity-building of their customs and border guard services at operational level; to develop risk analysis capacities; to improve cooperation and complementarity between the border guard and customs services and with other law enforcement agencies; and to promote cross-border cooperation.

While EUBAM defined its objectives in rather technical terms, the mission has been operating in a difficult political context due to the unresolved conflict in Transnistria and was established to provide a contribution towards its resolution. As such, the mission fitted a broader range of EU initiatives, including the launch of the ENP

---

3. Adriaan Jacobovits de Szeged was the first EU Special Representative for Moldova, appointed on 23 March 2005.

4. The Memorandum was signed by the EU Commission and by the Moldovan and Ukrainian foreign affairs ministers on 7 October 2005 at the Palanca border crossing. Available at: http://www.eubam.org/files/0-99/73/memorandum_of_understanding_en.pdf.

5. Remarks of Javier Solana, EU High Representative for CFSP, at the launch of the EU Border Mission for Moldova – Ukraine , Odessa, 30 November 2005, EU Council press release, 2 December 2005. Available at http://www.consilium.europa.eu/uedocs/cms_data/docs/pressdata/EN/discours/87379.pdf.

and the signature of the EU-Moldova Action Plan February 2005, which committed the EU to a greater involvement in solving the conflict and in helping Moldova with its border management. The EU eventually became directly involved as an observer in the '5+2' talks on settling the conflict in September 2005.

The structure and financing of the mission

Structure and powers

Once the need was identified and the consensus within the EU reached to deploy the mission, it was necessary to determine the institution in charge of the mission. This was complicated due to the dual nature of the mission (involving both technical assistance *and* political and security concerns related to the Transnistria conflict). The EU Commission had been involved in the trilateral talks on the border question with Moldova and Ukraine since 2003 and it also monitors the implementation of the EU-Moldova and EU-Ukraine Action Plans which cover issues of border management. On the other hand, the political and security dimension of the mission was evident and required the involvement of the EU Council. As a result, the Commission took charge of the financing, management and implementation of the mission, but with close cooperation and political oversight by the EU Council and with input from EU Member States.

In addition, the EUSR to Moldova has been assigned new functions related to the EUBAM, thereby strengthening the Council's role. While the EUSR's mandate first and foremost focuses on strengthening the EU's contribution to the resolution of the Transnistria conflict, it has been modified in order to take into account a number of new functions related to assuming political oversight of the EUBAM.[6] This also allowed linking the mission's objectives to the EU's broader purpose of achieving pre-conditions for the peaceful settlement of the Transnistrian conflict.[7] In essence, a support team of four advisors, led by a Senior Political Advisor, was set up under the EUSR's supervision in order to deal exclusively with border-related issues. Moreover, the EU Member States contribute to the financing of the mission by providing the majority of the mission's personnel through the secondment of border guards or customs officials. The EU's implementing partner on the ground is the UN Development Programme (UNDP). Based on this distinctive articulation

---

6. Giovanni Grevi, 'Pioneering foreign policy: The EU Special Representatives,' *Chaillot Paper* no. 106, EU Institute for Security Studies, Paris, October 2007, pp. 63-70.

7. Council Joint Action 2005/776/CFSP of 7 November 2005 amending the mandate of the European Union Special Representative for Moldova, Official Journal of the European Union, 8 November 2005.

between the roles and contributions of EU institutions and Member States, the EUBAM can be viewed as an institutionally 'hybrid' mission.

The mission's head is the Hungarian Major-General Ferenc Banfi and its headquarters are located in Odessa, Ukraine. There are five other field offices located on the Moldo-Ukrainian border and one in Odessa Port. Major-General Banfi has a double-hatted function by being simultaneously also a Senior Political Advisor to the EUSR and leading the EUSR's support team on border issues.

Initially the EU Commission proposal on the EUBAM foresaw the deployment of up to 50 field staff in addition to other HQ staff and advisors for the first year of the mission. At the height of the mission's activities (in January 2008) the mission consisted of 233 staff, of which 122 were international staff from 22 EU Member States[8] and 3 CIS countries (Georgia, Kazakhstan, Tajikistan) and 111 local staff (from Moldova and Ukraine). By December 2008, the mission numbered three less international staff.[9]

The EUBAM provides training, advice, risk analysis, and can also carry out unannounced visits along the land border on any border crossing point and observe the customs clearance and border checks. If not fully satisfied with the quality of the checks, the EUBAM can request the re-examination of a cargo. However, the EUBAM as such does not have executive powers. Additionally, while the request for assistance initially only concerned the Transnistrian segment of the Moldovan-Ukrainian border (470 km), the mission's mandate extends to cover the entire 1,222 km long Moldova-Ukraine border.

Financing the mission

In order to get the mission deployed as fast as possible, due to a number of political factors offering a brief window of opportunity for action, the EU Commission made use of the EU's Rapid Reaction Mechanism (RRM) established by Council Regulation (EC) No 381/2001 which allowed 'the Community to respond in a rapid, efficient and flexible manner, to situations of urgency or crisis or to the emergence of crisis'. As such the Commission proposed €4 million to be committed to EUBAM under the RRM. The mission would subsequently be financed from TACIS funds and from contributions by EU Member States.

---

8. The following EU Member States have not contributed to EUBAM: Ireland, Luxembourg, Malta, Spain and Sweden.

9. See the various background notes on the mission, produced by EUBAM. Available on the website of EUBAM, www.eubam.org.

Combined funding under the RRM and the TACIS programme over the period December 2005 to November 2007 amounted to €20.2 million.[10] The budget for the mission from December 2007 until November 2009 is €24 million and is provided by the European Neighbourhood and Partnership Instrument (ENPI). As noted above, EU Member States also provide direct contributions by funding the secondment of national border professionals.

The EUBAM Advisory Board also endorsed an EC-funded project called BOMMOLUK (Improving Management on the Moldovan-Ukrainian State Border) which provides an additional €9.9 million in technical assistance for the procurement of equipment[11] and communication systems (allowing to share information instantly on the goods and vehicles transiting the border), risk analysis development and the training for officers placed at jointly controlled border crossing points. BOMMOLUK 1, with a budget of €3.3 million, ran until the end of December 2007 and was replaced by BOMMOLUK 2, with a budget of €6.6 million, which runs until the end of 2009.

Implementation record

In the planning stages of the mission, the EU Commission believed it was imperative to get the mission off the ground as fast as possible, owing to a 'window of opportunity to make headway in resolving the frozen Transnistrian conflict'[12] which had arisen after the election of President Yushchenko following the Orange revolution in Ukraine. Yushchenko's election opened the prospect for better cooperation on border questions with Moldova. The Commission therefore sought to capitalise on the favourable conjuncture (the signature of the Action Plan with Moldova and Ukraine in February 2005, the appointment of an EUSR for Moldova in March 2005, the planned opening of an EU Commission delegation in Chisinau in October 2005 and the involvement of the EU as an observer in the negotiations on the Transnistria conflict).

---

10. EU Factsheet, 'EU Border Assistance Mission to Moldova and Ukraine', December 2007. Available at: http://www.consilium.europa.eu/uedocs/cmsUpload/071205_Factsheet_BM_Moldova_Ukraine-update.pdf.

11. Equipment was predominantly handed over to the Moldovan border guard service and included 28 personal computers, 4 laser printers, 4 switches and 1 server optical binoculars, portable thermal imagers and three mini-buses. BOMMOLUK technical assistance has also provided for the improvement of the border infrastructure on both sides of the Ukrianian-Moldovan border.

12. Draft Commission Decision regarding a programme of measures to support the establishment of a European Community Border Assistance Mission to Moldova and Ukraine under the Rapid Reaction Mechanism, October 2005.

The mission is neither a distinct ESDP mission (although the EU Council exercises political oversight), nor is it an exclusively EC-managed operation (due to the participation of EU Member States). The implementation of the mission provides a good example of the exhaustive use by the EU of its instruments (joint actions, technical assistance, training, secondment, etc.). The coordination between the EU's institutions in running the mission and in ensuring the advancement of concrete EU foreign policy interests in the region (i.e. that of bringing security and stability on the EU's eastern border) has been remarkable, notably through the excellent cooperation between the EUSR, Kalman Mizsei, and the head of the mission on the ground, Major-General Banfi, both Hungarian nationals.

The mission can be hailed as a success for the EU, but also for the Moldovan and Ukrainian border services. Firstly, the EU succeeded in sending a civilian mission right on the border of a conflict zone, thereby contributing to the stabilisation of the region through the mere presence of its border guards. Secondly, the EUBAM contributed to the introduction of a new customs regime between Moldova and Ukraine. This allowed Transnistrian businesses to register with Moldova's official agencies and to receive the official customs documents (their number reached 539 by mid-April 2009).[13]

Indeed, one of the aims of the mission was to legalise the external trade activities of Transnistrian businesses by allowing them to register with the Moldovan authorities. To this effect on 30 December 2005, the prime ministers of Moldova and Ukraine issued a joint declaration in which the Moldovan side committed to reintroduce by 25 January 2006 the 'mechanism for the simplified registration system for businesses in the Transnistrian region according to resolution no. 815 of 2 August 2005, which stipulates the collection of duties from economic agents of the Transnistrian region only for performing customs procedures'. In other words, aside from allowing the registration of Transnistrian businesses with the authorities in Chisinau using a fast-track procedure, Moldova also guaranteed that if the Transnistrian businesses registered in Chisinau, they would not be subjected to double taxation (i.e. once in Tiraspol and a second time in Chisinau). This move was followed by Ukraine's introduction of new customs rules in March 2006, leading to accusations by the Transnistrian leadership about attempts to install an 'economic blockade' around Transnistria.[14] Much of Transnistria's economy is in the hands of its political elite, who resented the direct oversight of their businesses by Chisinau.

---

13. 'The State Chamber of Registration has registered another 31 economic agents from the Transnistria region', *The News – Business Media Assistance*, 14 April 2009.

14. Jan Maksymiuk, 'Ukraine: Kyiv tightens customs controls on Transdniester', *Radio Free Europe*, 9 March 2006.

Russia also has sizeable economic interests and investments in the Transnistrian economy and 'many Russian businessmen profit from [Transnistria's] illegal trade and re-export economy'.[15] This eventually led Russia to join those accusations. The reticence among some of Moldova and Ukraine's business and political elites with economic interests in the region was, however, overcome by the political leaders in both countries.

With clearer customs procedures from Moldova and Ukraine and with the action of EUBAM, it was expected that the illegal revenue pocketed by the Transnistrian regime would decrease and that this would ultimately make Transnistria more co-operative in conflict settlement talks and more prone to democratisation. Evidence of such evolution remains weak, but those Transnistrian companies which have registered are exporting legally to the EU and to the rest of the world.

Furthermore, EUBAM technical assistance and advice has contributed to a number of spectacular busts involving large-scale meat-smuggling, but also the smuggling of cigarettes and alcohol and the dismantling of human trafficking networks. In one case of meat-smuggling the potential loss to the Ukrainian budget was estimated at €43 million. On the other hand, there has been no substantial seizure of weapons over the years, which may suggest that concerns related to weapons' trafficking were excessive. The fact that the mission was extended for another two years in November 2007, points to the fact that the EU and its partners countries in the region still perceived a need for continued training and technical assistance leading to yet more effective border controls.

EUBAM also held Joint Border Control Operations, such as 'FOCUS' and 'FOCUS 2'. In the latter operation FRONTEX, OLAF and the SECI Centre were also involved.[16] This allowed Moldovan and Ukrainian border guards to work alongside and learn new techniques from their EU colleagues. Besides, EUBAM contributed in setting up a system of data exchange between the Moldovan and Ukrainian customs services resulting in the level of shared data to reach 85 to 90 per cent. Data-sharing has also led to raising the level of trust between respective customs services and to reducing corruption levels. Finally, through the BOMMOLUK 1 and 2 projects, the Moldovan and Ukrainian border services have received much-needed IT and

---

15. International Crisis Group, 'Moldova: Regional tensions over Trandniestria', *Europe Report* no. 157, 17 June 2004, p. 14. The 're-export' economy worked as follows: large amounts of goods were being brought into Transnistria through Ukraine and then re-exported to Moldova. This resulted in a very lucrative re-export scheme exploiting the different tax and customs regimes between Transnistria and Moldova.

16. FRONTEX is an EU agency based in Warsaw, responsible for coordinating cooperation between Member States in the field of border security. OLAF is the EU's anti-fraud office. The SECI Centre is an operational regional organisation bringing together police and customs authorities from 13 member countries in Southeast Europe.

sophisticated detection equipment as well as relevant training and have been involved in exchanges throughout the EU. All these initiatives were instrumental in improving the quality and effectiveness of the controls on both sides of the border.

Conclusion

The EUBAM has in 2009 entered in its fourth year of operation and has largely yielded the expected results. Many Transnistrian companies continue to register with the Moldovan authorities and the lawlessness on the Transnistrian segment of the Moldovan-Ukrainian border is increasingly a thing of the past. The lack of executive powers has been compensated by a quite wide array of advisory powers which have allowed the EUBAM to be very effective on the ground. However, it is the political will in Chisinau and Ukraine which has played a decisive role in ensuring the success of the mission. In fact, Ukraine has been the more reluctant partner of the two, particularly in the early stages, expressing concerns over territorial sovereignty and pointing to the fact that the EUBAM was questioning the quality of its border services. Over the years though, cooperation between the EUBAM and the Moldovan and Ukrainian border services has much improved and this has fostered mutual confidence.

The violent crackdown on protestors in Moldova following the parliamentary elections on 5 April 2009 has not visibly affected EU-Moldova relations. While Moldova has somewhat tarnished its image in Brussels regarding democratic reform and the respect for the rule of law and human rights, it was nevertheless invited to take part in the launch of the Eastern Partnership, a new EU initiative designed to strengthen relations with its Eastern neighbours. Additionally, the EU is not planning to withhold any technical assistance earmarked for Moldova and the EUBAM is likely to continue unhindered under Moldova's next government.

EUBAM has successfully focused on issues of a rather technical nature. To what extent EUBAM has contributed to pave the way for a political solution of the Transnistrian conflict is, however, questionable. The Transnistrian regime, while having lost some of its illegal revenue, does not seem more willing to engage in negotiations with Moldova on the resolution of the conflict. Instead, it seems to rely more heavily on Russia's generosity in the form of loans, investments, gas supplies and 'humanitarian assistance'. The EUBAM's deployment has actually coincided with an indefinite pause in the conflict negotiation talks. Provided that the EUBAM's mandate is extended for another two years at the end of 2009, its effectiveness and political relevance may be strengthened in two ways. First, EUBAM's activities should be paralleled by greater EU efforts towards solving the Transnistrian conflict in the '5+2' negotiation format and by stronger EU engagement in supporting the democratisation of Transnistrian society. Second, EUBAM could reach out to the Transnistrian border services and hold joint Moldova-Ukraine-Transnistria checks under EUBAM oversight. This may prove feasible if a majority of the more important Transnistrian businesses register with the Moldovan authorities. Such a step would represent significant progress towards unifying Moldova's customs and fiscal territory and may further contribute to solving the Transnistrian conflict.

BIBLIOGRAPHY

Dura, George. 'EU border guards set to ensure Moldova's economic reintegration', *Eurojournal*, April 2004.

Grevi, Giovanni. 'Pioneering foreign policy: the EU Special Representatives', *Chaillot Paper* no. 106, EU Institute for Security Studies, Paris, October 2007.

International Crisis Group. 'Moldova: Regional Tensions Over Transdniestria', *ICG Europe Report* no. 157, 17 June 2004.

Lynch, Dov. 'Russia faces Europe', *Chaillot Paper* no. 60, EU Institute for Security Studies, Paris, May 2003.

'Mission Eubam Moldavie/Ukraine', *EUROPOLITIQUE*, 23 April 2008, no. 3516, Dossier Spécial, pp. 9-16.

Popov, Andrei. 'Tiraspol softens its stance on new customs regulations: a first or a Pyrrhic victory?', *Eurojournal*, June 2006.

Rácz, András. 'EU border assistance mission to Ukraine and Moldova: a preliminary analysis', *Eurojournal*, October 2005.

Spruds, Andris et al. 'Analysis of the EU's Assistance to Moldova', European Parliament, Committee on Foreign Affairs, Briefing Paper, November 2008.

16. EUPOL COPPS (Palestinian territories)

The EU Police Mission for the Palestinian Territories – EU Coordinating Office for Palestinian Police Support (EUPOL COPPS)

Esra Bulut*

Legal basis: Council Joint Action 2005/797/CFSP of 14 November 2005.

Highlights of the mission's mandate:

■ Contribute to the establishment of sustainable and effective policing arrangements under Palestinian ownership in accordance with best international standards, in cooperation with the Community's institution building programmes as well as other international efforts in the wider context of Security Sector including Criminal Justice Reform.

■ Assist the Palestinian Civil Police (PCP) in implementation of the Police Development Programme by advising and closely mentoring PCP, and specifically senior officials at District, Headquarters and Ministerial level.

■ Coordinate and facilitate EU and Member State assistance, and where requested, international assistance to PCP.

---

*The author would like to thank Pol Morillas for research assistance, and participants of a March 2009 EUISS task force on the EU and Middle East Peace Process for comments on an earlier version of this chapter.

■   Advice, programme planning and project facilitation for the Palestinian Criminal Justice elements.

Duration: November 2005 to date.

Budget: 2005: €2.5 million; 2006: €6.1 million; 1 January 2007- 29 February 2008: €2.8 million; 1 March 2008-31 December 2008: €6 million ; 1 January-31 December 2009: €6.2 million.

Mission strength: 42 international staff and 19 local staff (September 2009).

Contributing states: 17 Member States (Austria, Belgium, Czech Republic, Denmark, Estonia, Finland, France, Germany, Greece, Hungary, Ireland, Italy, Netherlands, Portugal, Spain, Sweden, United Kingdom) and 2 third states (Norway and Canada).

Introduction: background and context

The EU Police Mission for the Palestinian Territories – EU Coordinating Office for Palestinian Police Support (EUPOL COPPS) was established in late 2005, against a backdrop of decades of European and EU involvement in the Arab-Israeli conflict. From the 1993 Oslo Accords until the outbreak of the second *intifada* in 2000, the fate of Palestinian security forces and security in the Occupied Palestinian Territory (OPT) were key issues in the internationally-supported development of the Palestinian Authority (PA) in the OPT. This period saw evolving international support to policing development and reform, with Europeans, notably a number of EU Member States, including the UK, Sweden, Germany, Netherlands and Denmark, increasingly active.[1]

The second *intifada* interrupted this process, with substantial destruction of the nascent security sector infrastructure during Israeli-Palestinian and intra-Palestinian violence, and Israel's tightening of its control over the OPT and reoccupation of Palestinian cities. The subsequent 2003 international quartet roadmap required 're-structured and effective Palestinian security services' as part of the immediate and longer term benchmarks it set for the parties, placing the Palestinian security sec-

---

1. For detailed information on Palestinian policing and international police assistance, see Brynjar Lia, *A Police Force Without a State: A History of the Palestinian Security Forces in the West Bank And Gaza.* (London: Ithaca Press, 2006); Brynjar Lia, *Building Arafat's Police: The Politics of International Police Assistance in the Palestinian Territories after the Oslo Agreement.* (London: Ithaca Press, 2007).

tor at the centre of international attention and assistance to the PA.[2] In June 2004, European leaders reiterated the EU's 'readiness to support the Palestinian Authority in taking responsibility for law and order and, in particular, in improving its civil police and law enforcement capacity.'[3]

Most immediately, the deployment of an ESDP mission built on British-led efforts to identify areas for support to Palestinian civil policing, and on the establishment in early 2005 of an EU Coordinating Office for Palestinian Police Support (EU COPPS).[4] Based within the office of the EU Special Representative Marc Otte, and located in the PA Ministry of Interior and in the Civil Police Headquarters in Gaza through a satellite office, EU COPPS worked closely with the PA in the development of the Palestinian Civil Police Development Programme 2005-8 (PCPDP). The PCPDP aimed to produce a 'transparent and accountable police organisation with a clearly identified role, operating within a sound legal framework, capable of delivering an effective and robust policing service, responsive to the needs of the society and able to manage effectively its human and physical resources.'[5] Rule-of-law work builds on the substantial support of, and projects developed by, the European Commission.

Both EUPOL COPPS, and the other ESDP mission for the OPT, EUBAM Rafah, constitute noteworthy but cautionary undertakings that have raised the profile of the EU in relation to the sensitive policing, rule-of-law and border dimensions of the conflict.[6] Overall, the security domain is defined by the ongoing power struggle between Israel, the PA and Palestinian factions; and shaped by a number of other international actors, most notably the US. European policies are guided by the long-term objective of an independent, democratic and viable Palestinian state living in peace and security alongside Israel, as well as by more immediate, sometimes apparently contradictory, conflict management and counter-terrorism objectives.

Mission and mandate

EUPOL COPPS is a civilian mission, specifically a police and rule-of-law mission. The mission was launched by the Council on 14 November 2005, shortly after a

---

2. US Department of State, 'A Performance-based Roadmap to a Permanent Two-State Solution to the Israeli-Palestinian Conflict', Washington DC, 30 April 2003.

3. Presidency Conclusions, European Council, Brussels, 17-18 June 2004.

4. The office consisted of four EU police experts and two locally recruited staff. 'EU Assistance to the Palestinian Police', EU Council Secretariat Factsheet, 8 July 2005.

5. EU COPPS and Palestinian Civil Police Development Programme 2005-8 Factsheet, undated.

6. See the chapter on EUBAM Rafah in this book.

letter of invitation from the PA.[7] The mission has enjoyed wide support among

Member States. Israel's acceptance of such a mission was also essential for its deployment, although it is not formally accredited with Israel.[8] The stated aim of the mission 'is to contribute to the establishment of sustainable and effective policing arrangements under Palestinian ownership in accordance with best international standards, in cooperation with the Community's institution building programmes as well as other international efforts in the wider context of Security Sector including Criminal Justice Reform.'[9]

There are four dimensions to its mandated work: (i) assisting the PCP in implementation of the PCPDP by advising and closely mentoring PCP, and specifically senior officials at District, Headquarters and Ministerial level; (ii) coordinating and facilitating EU and Member State assistance, and where requested, international assistance to PCP; (iii) advising on police-related Criminal Justice elements; and from 2008 (iv) strengthened action in the area of rule of law through advice, programme planning and project facilitation for the Criminal Justice sector. After an initial 3-year mandate running to the end of 2008, the mandate was extended for another 2 years to the end of 2010.[10] Its financial reference budget for 2008 was raised to over €6 million to allow for the reinforcement of its activities, while the 2009 budget is set at €6.3 million.[11]

The mission is currently headed by Chief Constable Paul Kernaghan, the third Head of Mission. He follows Assistant Chief Constable Jonathan McIvor, who helped set up the mission and headed it until the end of 2006, and his successor Deputy Chief Constable Colin Smith who served until the end of 2008. All three are British and have served in Northern Ireland. International staff stood at 42 in September 2009, drawn from sixteen Member States plus Norway and Canada. There are 19 local staff.

The mission's headquarters are in Ramallah, with a satellite office at Jericho, and staff move around the West Bank in the course of their work. The mission consists of an advisory section, programme coordination section, administration section, and from 2007, a rule of law section. The Head of Mission reports to the Civilian Operations Commander in Brussels. The High Representative and Special Representative for the

---

7. Council Joint Action 2005/797/CFSP, 14 November 2005.

8. Israeli acceptance of the mission came after prolonged high-level EU diplomacy and a shift in Israeli perceptions of third party involvement in the security sector. For further discussion of Israeli attitudes towards third party involvement, see the chapter on EUBAM-Rafah in this book.

9. Council Joint Action 2005/797/CFSP, 14 November 2005.

10. Council Joint Action 2008/958/CFSP, 16 December 2008.

11. Council Decision 2008/482/CFSP, 23 June 2008. Council Joint Action 2008/958/CFSP, 16 December 2008.

Middle East Peace Process, Marc Otte, provide guidance, while the Political and Security Committee (PSC) provides political control and strategic direction.

Implementation, achievements and challenges

Implementation and achievements

The operational phase of the mission commenced on 1 January 2006. However, Hamas' victory in Palestinian legislative elections, held the same month, led to the mission halting work with the Hamas-controlled PA Interior Ministry and the withholding of donor funds in line with EU policy towards the Hamas government. The mission only resumed its operations in earnest, and then only in the West Bank, after the establishment of the Salam Fayyad-led emergency government in June 2007 in the wake of Hamas' violent takeover of the Gaza Strip. The Palestinian Reform and Development Plan 2008-10 (PRDP) devised by the emergency government with international support, identified the strengthening of civil policing as one of seven main elements of its Security Sector Reform and Transformation (SSRT) Plan.[12]

The mission has made tangible contributions to civilian policing in the West Bank. Operations span advice, training, equipment, infrastructure and assessment. Field and specialist advisers work with PCP in different parts of the West Bank to provide relevant assistance and identify training and equipment needs. Field advisers, seven at the time of writing, visit police stations in a specified area of the West Bank regularly. Specialist advisers work in a number of specific areas, including criminal investigation and crime scene management, command and control, public order including visible policing, community policing, traffic policing, human resources management, police administration, communications and information storage, and training development.[13] The mission has also supported cooperation between Palestinian and Israeli police, with joint training workshops in areas such as traffic policing and criminal investigation.

The mission has also been involved in the provision and refurbishment of equipment and infrastructure, working as a bridge between Member State and third-state donors, the European Commission, the PA, and implementing agencies such as the

---

12. Palestinian National Authority, 'Palestinian Reform and Development Plan 2008-10', 2007. Civil policing prospects are closely related to the fate of the other six elements of the SSRT plan: establishing a clear legal framework for the security sector; policy management and capacity building; restructuring; rightsizing; security infrastructure; equipping and training the security services. In turn, developments here are closely related to PRDP objectives in the field of justice, spanning infrastructure, justice police, technology, and training facilities. The EU and its Member States seek to support capacity-building and reform in practically all these areas.

13. EUPOL COPPS brochure, undated.

United Nations Office for Project Services (UNOPS). The mission has attempted to streamline, consolidate and render sustainable previous and current assistance, from introducing a fleet policy for police vehicles to ensure sustainable maintenance, to designing an upgrade of radio communications to allow for maximal use of existing infrastructure, to ensuring that the Jericho Training Centre has the necessary basic safe infrastructure for use.[14] Train and equip operations have gone hand in hand, with new equipment necessitating relevant training.

The mission has extended its work into the area of rule of law, reflecting acknowledgement of, and emphasis on, the continuum between policing and justice. In October 2007, a rule of law section was set up within the mission. The section aims to support the development of the Civilian Police Law and guidelines, the prison sector, the judicial police, and work related to domestic violence and honour crimes by drawing in experts from new areas, including prosecution, defence counsel, criminal justice, court administration, human rights and policy drafting.

The mission has established an important precedent in terms of EU involvement in the sensitive security sector. It constitutes a formal, coordinated and visible commitment and presence of the EU, after many years of European involvement in the security sector. In particular, its status as an *ESDP mission* as such is noteworthy given clashing Israeli and Palestinian perceived interests, objectives and sensitivities regarding formal third party presence in the security realm in the OPT.[15] Mission staff and EU officials cite further achievements.[16] They deem the relations the mission has with the PCP at all levels and mission staff presence on the ground (albeit only in the West Bank) an important achievement, especially when compared with the staff of the US Security Coordinator, perceived as having been largely confined to 'a monastery in Jerusalem' due to security constraints. The diversity of European policing traditions and judicial systems from which the mission draws its personnel, a division of labour within the mission that invites bottom-up solutions in working with PCP counterparts at different levels, and efforts to draw Palestinians into training as instructors and with on-the-beat learning, all appear to demonstrate a distinctly European approach. This presence also provides a visibility that other examples of extensive EU assistance to the OPT have not generated.

---

14. Interviews, Mission Staff, Ramallah, November 2008; Ari Kerkkanen *et al*, 'Building Capacity for the Palestinian Civil Police: EUPOL COPPS and Communications Project', *CMC Finland Civilian Crisis Management Centre Report*, 2008.

15. The unsuccessful negotiations regarding deployment of a police observer mission in the OPT in the mid-1990s had demonstrated the sensitivities and diverging objectives of the parties and potential third parties. Lia 2007: 221-243, op. cit. in note 2.

16. This paragraph draws on interviews with mission staff, EU officials, Ramallah & Jerusalem, November 2008; Brussels, April 2009.

Challenges

The mission faces a number of challenges in a complex political and security domain. First, the mission faces the challenge of marrying short-term impact with long-term effect, in an attempt to defy the tendency to simply resort to 'transmitting resources, hardware and new technical skills.'[17] The mission's mandate directly draws on the PCPDP, which comprises a transformational plan, 'concerned with fundamental long-term organisation change', and an operational plan, 'concerned with raising operational capacity and performance in the short-term.'[18] By definition, it is too early to assess long-term transformational impact after just two years of operations.[19] However, the mission has already been subject to criticism that a quick impact and project-based focus has limited the policy impact of the assistance, with a perceived absence at the 'strategic planning level.'[20] Some observers have related this to a lack of political will to engage strategically, others to a lack of capacity and propensity to interact with policymakers among personnel. Given that the mission is unusual among ESDP missions in having a project cell with the aim of quick impact projects, the European Commission is additionally concerned about a possible loss of oversight over procedures and its traditional project management role.[21] An early emphasis on providing equipment at the expense of capacity-building and reform has also been noted.[22] The mission appears to have responded to criticism through wider attention to transformational issues and a more ambitious approach to the policing-justice continuum.[23]

Yet, most fundamentally, the mission faces the challenge of operating in a 'political minefield.'[24] In addition to the basic question of whether conditions of ongoing conflict are an appropriate environment for SSR, and the day-to-day challenges arising from the deep distrust between Palestinians and Israelis, the ambiguous

---

17. Lia 2007, op. cit. in note 1, p. 17.

18. EUPOL COPPS brochure, undated.

19. A ten-year period is regularly cited as the required period of support for sustainable police reform. See Nicole Ball et al, 'Squaring the Circle: Security-Sector Reform and Transformation and Fiscal Stabilisation in Palestine', Report prepared for DFID, 16 January 2006.

20. Interview with EU and Palestinian officials, Jerusalem & Ramallah, November 2008; interview with EU official, Brussels, March 2009.

21. Ibid. EUPOL COPPS is one of two ESDP missions to have such a unit within the mission; the other being EUSEC RD Congo. Marie Derks and Sylvie More, 'The European Union and Internal Challenges for Effectively Supporting Security Sector Reform', Clingendael, June 2009, p. 26.

22. House of Lords European Union Committee Report, 'The EU and the Middle East Peace Process', July 2007, p. 48.

23. Interviews, mission staff, Ramallah, November 2008.

24. Lia 2007, op.cit. in note 1, p. 321.

nature of the PA raises questions.[25] With 'little indication that the OPT is evolving beyond a permanently sub-sovereign status', some observers argue that the PA has in practice 'principally acted as a service and job provider for the non-refugee population of the OPT and as a *sub-contractor of security* for the Israelis within the interim arrangements of self-rule.'[26] EU and Member State officials maintain that EUPOL COPPS principally derives its legitimacy from the peace process and the objective of a Palestinian state.[27] Yet in the period since 2005, both the process and the objective have been marginalised by events on the ground, most notably Israel's 2005 unilateral disengagement from Gaza; Hamas' 2006 victory in Palestinian legislative elections; US and Israeli-led efforts to undermine the Hamas government politically and militarily;[28] and the 2007 West Bank-Gaza Split between two *de facto* Palestinian governments. The challenge is ensuring that the legitimacy and utility of the mission is achieved through its positioning within a coherent and realistic diplomatic and assistance policy for ending the conflict. This would require the resuscitation of the PA not just as a services provider but as the basis for a viable inclusive democratic Palestinian state.

This challenge is made all the more Herculean by the fact that the security sector has been a prime site of competition over the fate and functions of the PA. Among varying visions of the purposes of SSR in the OPT, two broad approaches have been identified. The first is a more 'reformist' approach aiming to transform security institutions into more effective and democratically accountable institutions for the security of the Palestinian people. The second is a more 'restructurist' agenda to reorganise security forces to address Israeli security concerns and suppress Palestinian violence.[29] Hamas' 2006 victory brought both approaches into direct confrontation, given the 'restructurist' objective of excluding and eliminating Hamas and associated elements from Palestinian politics and society. The EU and the US sought to undermine the Hamas government through aid policy, factional support

25. For more on the conflict conditions and fiscal constraints under 'highly unfavourable economic conditions', see Nicole Ball et al, 'Appendix D: HMG GCPP Work in Occupied Palestinian Territories' in *Promoting Conflict Prevention Through Security Sector Reform: Review of Spending on Security Sector Reform through the Global Conflict Prevention Pool*, April 2008, p. 38.

26. Anne Le More, *International Assistance to the Palestinians after Oslo: Political Guilt, Wasted Money* (London: Taylor & Francis, 2008), pp.168-9. (Italics added).

27. Interviews, EU and Member State officials. Ramallah; Jerusalem, November 2008; London, December 2008; Brussels, January; April 2009; Paris, May 2009.

28. One observer has described this as attempting to induce '"controlled" state failure'. Yezid Sayigh, 'Inducing a Failed State in Palestine', *Survival* vol. 49, no. 3, 2007, p. 8.

29. Bonn International Center for Conversion, (BICC), 'Inventory of Security Sector Reform (SSR) Efforts in Partner Countries of German Development Assistance – Palestine', citing Roland Friedrich, 2005; Gemma Collantes Celador et al, 'Fostering an EU Strategy for Security Sector Reform in the Mediterranean: Learning from Turkish and Palestinian Police Reform Experiences', *EuroMeSCo Paper* no. 66, 2008, p. 17.

and a bolstering of the Presidential Guard under PA President Abbas's control.[30] Since the June 2007 West Bank-Gaza Strip split, the US, the EU and a number of other donors have followed a 'West Bank First' strategy of supporting President Abbas and his appointed governments' efforts in the West Bank, while isolating the Hamas-controlled Gaza Strip.

EUPOL COPPS' aims with regard to the PCP still aspire to uphold a reformist logic, while being situated within a wider restructurist 'West Bank First' diplomatic and aid strategy.[31] While Europeans stress the continued reformist spirit of the mission, in practice the restructurist framework impacts on many aspects of the mission's work. Most basically, operations are restricted to the West Bank, raising important questions about the trajectory of the two thirds of the PCP based in the Gaza Strip and its potential reintegration.[32] The restructurist approach also impacts on the legitimacy of the mission and its objectives, given the heightened politicisation of the security sector, doubts over the neutrality of the Palestinian police, and European involvement in more controversial aspects of US-led SSR.[33] While the PCP has been documented as one of the least abusive forces amidst 'a marked deterioration in respect for human rights and the rule of law' in the OPT,[34] police handling of protests has been controversial.[35] EUPOL COPPS has been active in public order training and equipment for the PCP, and while officials and police cite progress in using non-violent and non-lethal techniques during protests in the West Bank, the wider conflict context and crackdown on Hamas supporters in the West Bank has made this an inherently sensitive area.

Through EUPOL COPPS' focus on the PCP, and more recently criminal justice, the EU has focused on a manageable and relatively less controversial component of the Palestinian security sector. Yet this strategy, and the wider international donor approach, arguably moves away from rather than towards a whole-of-government

30. Richard Youngs describes the shift from earlier efforts to bring security forces under the control of the prime minister's office in 2003-4 to later international bolstering of the presidential guard as a '180 degree turnaround' based on 'short term expediency rather than a well-thought approach to enhancing democratic accountability over security forces'. Richard Youngs, 'The European Union and Palestine: A New Engagement', *OpenDemocracy*, 28 March 2007.

31. For further assessment of the shift, see Gemma Collantes Celador et al, op. cit. in note 29.

32. The PCP in the Gaza Strip has been emasculated by a lack of resources, squeezed between orders from Ramallah and Gaza, sidelined by Hamas's executive Force in 2006-7 and radically altered by the integration of the Executive Force in PCP structures in late 2007. See Beverley Milton-Edwards, 'Order Without Law? An Anatomy of Hamas Security: The Executive Force (Tanfithya)', *International Peacekeeping*, vol. 15, no. 5, 2008, pp. 663-76.

33. Only 32% of Palestinians polled in 2006 trusted European SSR assistance. 'Politics, Security and the Barrier: Palestinian Public Perceptions', IUED/Geneva Centre for the Democratic Control of Armed Forces, November 2006, p. 44.

34. Human Rights Watch Report, 'Internal Fight: Palestinian Abuses in Gaza and the West Bank', July 2008, p. 3.

35. See International Crisis Group Report, 'Ruling Palestine II: The West Bank Model?', *Middle East Report* no. 79, 17 July 2008.

approach to SSR, undermining stated objectives to conform to best international standards.[36] It has also invited criticism that the mission has 'done little to address the most prominent problems in the Palestinian security apparatus,' such as 'politicization, human rights abuses, overlap between official structures and militias, security forces' involvement in criminal activities, and lack of control and accountability.'[37] The challenge would appear to be to consolidate the principles of the mission, and more forcefully argue for their prioritisation across international involvement in the security sector using the leverage the EU holds as the largest donor to the OPT.

This depends on political will, as well as relations with other actors, notably the US. At the practical level there are provisions in place such as the presence of a US liaison officer within EUPOL COPPS, and strong inter-personal ties with the US Security Coordinator's office. At the level of official declared strategy too, an effective division of labour has been sought, with the declaration of a 'blue-green' division of leadership roles between the EU and US at a high-level conference in June 2008.[38] This 'blue-green' division means that the EU should lead on supporting civil security structures, while the US should lead on assisting national security forces and the presidential guard. However, in between, at the level of objectives, tactics and strategies a number of different, and arguably incompatible, agendas are at work. Attaining the standards of best international practice in SSR and donor coordination is unlikely without a radical change at this intermediary level.

Looking inwards, the EU faces the challenge of achieving coherence across the technical, political and economic aspects of its assistance in pursuit of a whole-of-government approach to SSR. Relations between EUPOL COPPS and the European Commission Technical Assistance Office in Jerusalem, as well as the wider involvement of the Commission in the mission, demonstrate the interconnectedness of ESDP and Community objectives with regard to Palestinian security and justice. In the area of rule of law, EUPOL COPPS activities are officially designated as enhancing synergies with Community action in this field, yet efforts to establish a commonly shared and effective understanding of the precise nature of this synergy were inconclusive at the time of writing.[39]

---

36. Interview, Geneva Centre for the Democratic Control of Armed Forces, Ramallah, November 2008.

37. Muriel Asseburg, 'European Conflict Management in the Middle East: Towards a More Effective Approach', *Carnegie Endowment/SWP Working Paper*, February 2009, p. 40.

38. Berlin Conference in Support of Palestinian Civil Security and Rule of Law, 24 June 2008. Summary of the Chair.

39. Interviews, EU officials, Jerusalem, November 2008; Brussels, March, May 2009.

Conclusion

A number of sobering lessons emerge from the experience of EUPOL COPPS. First, the EU does have value-added and much potential as a distinctive, diverse and coherent actor in Palestinian security sector reform efforts, and EUPOL COPPS's deployment was a symbolically important step in highlighting this role. Second, ESDP missions cannot defy diplomatic circumstances and are dependent on them, from the facilitation of delivery of equipment to ensuring the basic legitimacy of the mission; in that sense they cannot replace but require diplomacy at all levels. Third, the decision to deploy and expand EUPOL COPPS in such a politically complex situation must be understood as rendering the mission political and not merely technical. Yet the aim of supporting a depoliticised Palestinian police force must be of utmost priority. In other words, while acknowledging the mission's own politically charged status, it must nevertheless strive to help reform the security sector so that, according to international standards, the PCP is not politicised – an intrinsically tricky endeavour. Fourth, the promising precedent set by the mission's deployment is offset by its containment within a problematic and contradictory international approach to the fate and function of the PA. Finally, as a result, no amount of mission success is likely to compensate for, or override, the disintegration of the PA and of prospects for peace. Under such conditions, the mission could be reduced to the thankless task of efficiently and professionally helping rearrange civilian policing and criminal justice on a sinking ship.

BIBLIOGRAPHY

Asseburg, Muriel. 'European Conflict Management in the Middle East: Towards a More Effective Approach', Carnegie Endowment/SWP Working Paper, February 2009.

Ball, Nicole et al. 'Squaring the Circle: Security-Sector Reform and Transformation and Fiscal Stabilisation in Palestine', Report prepared for DFID, 16 January 2006.

Centro Internacional de Toledo Para la Paz. 'EU Civil Missions in the Palestinian Territories: Frustrated Reform and Suspended Security', *Middle East Special Report* 1, Summer 2006.

Collantes Celador, Gemma et al. 'Fostering an EU Strategy for Security Sector Reform in the Mediterranean: Learning from Turkish and Palestinian Police Reform Experiences', *EuroMeSCo Paper* no. 66, 2008.

Derks, Marie and More, Sylvie. 'The European Union and Internal Challenges for Effectively Supporting Security Sector Reform', the Clingendael Institute, June 2009.

Friedrich, Roland and Luethold, Arnold (eds.) *Entry Points to Palestinian Security Sector Reform* (Geneva/Ramallah: DCAF, 2007).

House of Lords European Union Committee. 'The EU and the Middle East Peace Process', July 2007.

Human Rights Watch. 'Internal Fight: Palestinian abuses in Gaza and the West Bank', New York, July 2008.

International Crisis Group. 'Ruling Palestine II: The West Bank Model?', *Middle East Report* no. 79, 17 July 2008.

Kerkkanen, Ari et al. 'Building Capacity for the Palestinian Civil Police: EUPOL COPPS and Communications Project', *Finland Civilian Crisis Management Centre Report*, 2008.

Le More, Anne. *International Assistance to the Palestinians after Oslo: Political Guilt, Wasted Money* (London: Taylor & Francis, 2008).

Lia, Brynjar. *A Police Force Without a State: A History of the Palestinian Security Forces in the West Bank And Gaza* (London: Ithaca Press, 2006).

Lia, Brynjar. *Building Arafat's Police: The Politics of International Police Assistance in the Palestinian Territories after the Oslo Agreement* (London: Ithaca Press, 2007).

Milton-Edwards, Beverley. 'Order Without Law? An Anatomy of Hamas Security: The Executive Force (Tanfithya)', *International Peacekeeping*, vol. 15, no. 5, 2008, pp. 663-76.

Sayigh, Yezid. 'Inducing a Failed State in Palestine', *Survival*, vol. 49, no. 3, 2007.

Youngs, Richard. 'The European Union and Palestine: A New Engagement', OpenDemocracy, 28 March 2007.

17. EUBAM Rafah (Palestinian territories)

The EU Border Assistance Mission at the Rafah Border Crossing Point (EUBAM Rafah)

Esra Bulut*

Legal Basis: Council Joint Action 2005/889/CFSP of 12 December 2005.

Highlights of the mission's mandate:

■ Provide a third party presence at the Rafah Crossing Point in order to contribute, in cooperation with the Community's institution-building efforts, to the opening of the Rafah Crossing Point and to build up confidence between the Government of Israel and the Palestinian Authority.

■ Actively monitor, verify and evaluate the Palestinian Authority's performance with regard to the implementation of the Framework, Security and Customs Agreements concluded between the parties on the operation of the Rafah terminal.

■ Contribute, through mentoring, to building up the Palestinian capacity in all aspects of border management at Rafah.

■ Contribute to the liaison between the Palestinian, Israeli and Egyptian authorities in all aspects regarding the management of the Rafah Crossing Point.

* The author would like to thank Pol Morillas for research assistance and participants of a March 2009 EUISS task force on the EU and Middle-East Peace Process for comments on an earlier version of this chapter.

Duration of the mission: November 2005 to date. Operations suspended since June 2007.

Budget: 2005: €1.7 million; 2006-mid 2007: €5.9 million; mid-2007-24 November 2008: €7 million; 25 November 2008-24 November 2009: €2.5 million.

Mission strength: 24 international staff and 8 local staff (August 2009); 72 international staff and 11 local staff (June 2007).

Contributing states: 21 (Austria, Belgium, Cyprus, Denmark, Estonia, Finland, France, Germany, Greece, Hungary, Ireland, Italy, Luxembourg, Malta, Netherlands, Poland, Portugal, Romania, Spain, Sweden, United Kingdom).

Introduction: background and context

The EU Border Assistance Mission at the Rafah Border Crossing Point (EUBAM Rafah) was established in late 2005 against the wider backdrop of decades of European and EU involvement in the Arab-Israeli conflict. The EU and its Member States have been the largest donor to the Palestinian Authority (PA), with the stated objective of support for the building of an independent, democratic and viable Palestinian state existing in peace and security alongside Israel. Europeans have expressed their willingness to contribute to security and confidence-building arrangements on the way to, and in the event of, a permanent settlement. Both EUBAM Rafah and the other ESDP mission for the Occupied Palestinian Territory (OPT), EUPOL COPPS, constitute noteworthy but cautionary undertakings that have raised the profile of the EU in relation to the sensitive border, policing and rule-of-law dimensions of the conflict.[1] The definition and control of the borders of the OPT has been on the diplomatic and security agenda for many years. The borders of the Gaza Strip, today marked by an Israeli-built barrier, separate the densely populated 360 km² coastal strip, which is home to over 1.5 million Palestinians, from Israel to the northeast, east and south and Egypt to the southwest. In the absence of a functioning airport and seaport, land crossing points at Erez, Karni, Sufa, Kerem Shalom and Rafah serve as the sole conduit for people and goods between the Gaza Strip and its neighbours, and onwards to the rest of the OPT and wider world.

The specific impetus for an EU border assistance mission at the Rafah Crossing Point (RCP) came in 2005 after the Israeli unilateral decision to withdraw troops

---

1. See the chapter on EUPOL COPPS in this book.

and settlers from the Gaza Strip.[2] The US brokered an agreement between the PA and Israel to duly adjust the terms and conditions of movement to and from the Gaza Strip, between the Gaza Strip and West Bank, and within the West Bank. The 15 November 2005 Agreement on Movement and Access (AMA) sought, among other measures, to establish a mechanism for re-opening the RCP between Gaza and Egypt without an Israeli presence at the crossing point. The EU, while not party to the agreement, was invited to play a third party role, and its mandate is derived from further agreed principles and a protocol arrangement on the European Border Assistance Mission. The EU would monitor PA officials on the Palestinian side of the crossing point, while Israelis would monitor the crossing point indirectly from Kerem Shalom, by means of closed-circuit television. The EU would lead a liaison office of Israelis and Palestinians at Kerem Shalom to address any disputes regarding implementation of the AMA.

Mission and mandate

EUBAM Rafah aims to provide a third party presence at the RCP to facilitate the opening of the border crossing point and to build up confidence between the Israeli government and the PA. There are three dimensions to its mandated work: (i) actively monitoring, verifying and evaluating PA performance with regard to the implementation of agreements concluded between the parties; (ii) contributing, through mentoring, to building up the Palestinian capacity in all aspects of border management at Rafah; (iii) contributing to the liaison between the Palestinian, Israeli and Egyptian authorities regarding the management of the RCP. The mission's border control assistance and monitoring mandate is restricted to the RCP and it has not had, nor sought, an executive role at the border.

After an initial one-year mandate from November 2005, the mission's mandate has been extended four times, most recently until 24 November 2009.[3] The current reference budget is €2.5 million from November 2008 for a year. The December 2008-January 2009 Gaza conflict prompted renewed interest in the mission, heightened discussion of its possible reactivation, and a boosting of capabilities to allow for immediate reactivation. Since then, prospects of an imminent reactivation appear to have once again receded. The mission is currently headed by Colonel Alain Faugeras, from the French *Gendarmerie*, who took over in November 2008 from his Italian predecessor, Major General Pietro Pistolese who led the mission for its first

---

2. There are varying views on whether this ended Israeli occupation of the Gaza Strip. See, for example, Iain Scobbie, 'Is Gaza still occupied territory?', *Forced Migration Review* no. 26, August 2006.

3. Council Joint Actions 2006/773/CFSP; 2007/359/CFSP; 2008/379/CFSP; 2008/862/CFSP.

three years. The Head of Mission reports to the Civilian Operations Commander, head of the CPCC, in Brussels and receives local political guidance from the EU Special Representative for the Middle East Peace Process Marc Otte. International staff, drawn from 13 Member States, stood at 24 and local staff at 8 in August 2009, less than half that of the summer of 2007 when personnel stood at 83.[4]

Plans for the mission to be based in the Gaza Strip at RCP in a specially-built compound, and have mission headquarters in Gaza City, have not materialised. Based at a hotel in the Israeli coastal town of Ashkelon, mission staff travelled around the Gaza Strip and through Kerem Shalom Crossing Point on the southern tip of the Gaza Strip to reach RCP, returning to Ashkelon at night. Since the suspension of the mission's operations in June 2007, a small office in Gaza City staffed with locally contracted Palestinian language support staff has been the only regular presence of the mission in OPT, and for much of this period no other mission staff entered the Gaza Strip. Planning for a possible reactivation of the mission has included discussion of a number of alternative locations for mission, or forward, headquarters, including El Arish in Egypt.

Implementation and challenges

Implementation

EUBAM Rafah began its operational phase on 25 November 2005, just days after Member States formally decided to launch it, and after just three weeks of preparation.[5] The RCP re-opened under AMA terms the same day. During the period from 26 November 2005 until late June 2006 when the crossing point was regularly operational, 279,436 passengers crossed through the terminal with EU monitoring. The number of passengers crossing in spring 2006, represented a doubling in monthly figures from the two previous years when RCP was controlled by Israeli authorities.[6] Mission staff monitored and advised Palestinian border and customs officials at different stages of border control of passengers and baggage. They assessed PA capacity and required re-examination and re-assessment of any passenger or luggage in case of doubt about compliance with the applicable rules and regulations of the border guard or customs official.

---

4. Centro Internacional de Toledo Para la Paz, 'EU Civil Missions in the Palestinian Territories: Frustrated Reform and Suspended Security', *Middle East Special Report* no. 1, Summer 2006.

5. General Affairs & External Relations Council Conclusions 21-22 November 2005; Nicoletta Pirozzi, 'Building Security in the Palestinian Territories,' *European Security Review* no. 28, February 2006.

6. 'The Gaza Strip: Access Report April 2006', UN Office for the Coordination of Humanitarian Affairs (OCHA), 30 April 2006.

Israeli unease with the agreed RCP arrangements after Hamas' January 2006 electoral victory, reluctance to use agreed mechanisms for halting those deemed security threats, and calls for a more executive EU role appear to have brought arrangements to crisis point by June 2006, which saw closures of the RCP due to Israeli army security alerts on 21-23 June. After the 25 June abduction of Israeli Corporal Gilad Shalit from the Israeli side of Kerem Shalom by Gaza-based militants including Hamas, the RCP was regularly closed. From 25 June 2006 until June 2007 the RCP was open only exceptionally, for 83 days altogether with a total of 163,632 crossings in both directions.[7] Notwithstanding the terms of the AMA, the mission was only able to take up its monitoring positions irregularly, and often at short notice, with the Israeli authorities blocking access to the RCP, citing security concerns and refusing to take up their position at the liaison office.[8] In this period large numbers of Palestinians, including medical patients, were trapped on either side of the border, sometimes for weeks on end, between rare openings, usually announced only briefly beforehand.[9] In December 2006, on one of the small number of days the border was open, the mission suspended RCP operations temporarily due to the expected arrival of Palestinian Prime Minister Haniyeh alleged to be carrying $35 million in cash. The mission eventually monitored his crossing later that day without the money, but withdrew after the outbreak of inter-factional Palestinian fighting near and in the RCP terminal causing injuries and damage.

Meanwhile, tensions between Palestinian factions Hamas and Fatah mounted, and after intense inter-factional fighting, Hamas took over the Gaza Strip in June 2007, ousting Fatah-affiliated security forces. EUBAM Rafah's operations were suspended in the light of the departure of the PA Presidential Guard working at the RCP, security concerns and the EU's policy of not engaging with Hamas which it has designated a terrorist organisation. The mission has been on standby in Ashkelon since. During this period, there has been a flurry of diplomatic and technical activity around the possible reactivation of the mission. In particular during and immediately after the Israeli military operation Cast Lead and the Gaza conflict of December 2008-January 2009, the possible reactivation of EUBAM Rafah was a central theme of EU diplomacy. Study teams were dispatched from Brussels to examine different options and readiness for reactivation of the mission.

---

7. 'Rafah Crossing: Who Holds the Keys?', GISHA: Legal Center for Freedom of Movement and Physicians for Human Rights–Israel report, March 2009, citing OCHA.

8. The AMA protocol states 'the EUBAM will have unrestricted access to all operations and locations at the RCP, including all Border Units and Customs Posts, along access, exit and transit itineraries to and from the outer perimeter of the RCP including the road leading to and up to Kerem Shalom'.

9. 'Humanitarian Update November 2006', Office for the Coordination of Humanitarian Affairs (OCHA), 18 December 2006.

The mission also sought to contribute to capacity building, comprised of training, equipment and technical assistance, in cooperation with the European Commission and EUPOL COPPS. Capacity building efforts aimed to improve efficiency and effective control of persons and luggage, and cooperation between Israel, Egypt and the PA in cross-border information sharing and joint operations.[10] This included customs training in 2007 and security training in 2006 at RCP. Efforts to extend training beyond RCP, especially in the face of closures, were hampered by Israeli insistence on mission staff restricting their work to Rafah. The mission has assisted in EU provision of equipment for RCP, after much of the existing equipment was removed during the Israeli disengagement. By spring 2007, the European Commission had provided €1.3 million of equipment for RCP, including x-ray machines, metal detectors, communications equipment, baggage equipment and vehicles.[11] The mission has also provided uniforms to PA officers.

Challenges

The mission's primary challenge has been that of its staff taking up their monitoring positions at the RCP amidst adverse local political conditions. In the words of a member of the mission, 'all operational issues had political problems behind them.'[12] Essentially, the challenge of playing a confidence-building role between Israelis and Palestinians was substantially augmented by Hamas's victory in Palestinian legislative elections less than two months after the mission's deployment. EUBAM Rafah continued to work with the Presidential Guard at Rafah because of their affiliation with PA President Abbas rather than the Hamas-led government. However, the stakes changed for all parties involved. The opening of the RCP became a highly contentious issue to be bartered vis-à-vis other demands and concessions in the manoeuvring between Hamas and Israel, among Palestinian factions, between Israel and Egypt, and between Egypt and the Palestinians.

Two further challenges have emerged out of this messy political context. On the one hand, establishing and maintaining EU credibility as an impartial, reliable and capable third party. On the other, ensuring that the mission is compatible with wider obligations under international law. As to the first challenge, the mission's functioning has depended on the will of all concerned parties to honour AMA commit-

---

10. Capacity building was envisaged to include in a later phase effective control and search of vehicles, and use of vehicle search equipment in parallel with the planned expansion of RCP operations, which has not materialised.

11. European Commission Technical Assistance Office for the West Bank & Gaza Strip Press Release, 'European Commission Launches Training for Palestinian Customs Officers at Rafah', 29 April 2007.

12. Interview, EUBAM Rafah official, Jerusalem, November 2008.

ments. In particular, the stationing of the mission in Israel meant the authorities there not only could block the mission from undertaking monitoring functions, but also stop it from reaching the RCP for capacity-building purposes. As a result, various observers from civil society have asserted that Israeli authorities have unduly influenced the activities of EUBAM Rafah. The Gaza-based Palestinian Centre for Human Rights, for example, has argued that EU acceptance of Israeli restrictions has actively encouraged Israel's systematic closure of RCP, and 'continuing closure and siege of the entire Gaza Strip'.[13]

It is also unclear whether the Israeli authorities consider the mission impartial, reliable and capable. Among other factors, the mission has been made possible by a shift in Israeli attitudes towards greater willingness to concede a European role in matters with direct bearing on Israeli security. One explanation for this change is that Israeli officials felt Europeans had shifted from 'megaphone diplomacy' to a better understanding of the threats Israel faces.[14] Another explanation posits fresh Israeli willingness to partially outsource their security needs and control of the OPT to their neighbours and other third parties. Israeli government frustration at the reluctance of the mission to take on a more executive and interventionist role in response to its requests, as well as concerns over international monitoring in Lebanon, may have checked this trend.[15] An apparent unwillingness to share information with the mission regarding opening and closing of the RCP during the period of limited opening, and on a number of matters affecting the operations and personnel of the mission indeed suggest a low level of trust. Other areas may have also been affected. Lengthy authorisation processes with the Israeli authorities complicated the procurement of basic equipment for the mission, with an alleged one-year wait for the acquisition of weapons for staff. Later, while the mission was on standby, efforts to transfer armoured vehicles to EUPOL COPPS met with considerable delays as well.[16]

With a view to the second challenge, while there are regular calls for the reopening of the RCP under EU monitoring from a variety of international actors, the deterioration of the situation at the RCP since June 2007 has led some non-governmental

---

13. PCHR Situation Assessment, 'Palestinians continue to be stranded at Rafah International Crossing Point and in Al-Arish', 7 December 2007, Palestinian Center for Human Rights.

14. According to this view, after 9/11, European threat perceptions shifted closer to that of Israelis on questions of terrorism. Interview, Israeli Ministry of Foreign Affairs, Jerusalem, November 2008.

15. Phone interview, *Haaretz* journalist, March 2009. For an example of Israeli demands see 'Israel, EU, PA to extend EU's Monitoring Mission', *Haaretz*, 24 May 2007.

16. Interviews with EUBAM Rafah and other EU officials, Jerusalem, November 2008; interviews with EU officials, Brussels, January 2009 and March 2009.

organisations to call for the EU's complete withdrawal from the AMA arrangements if they remain suspended, in keeping with their obligations under international law and international humanitarian law. The Israeli organisations GISHA and Physicians for Human Rights have argued, for example, that the EU must do everything it can to prevent violations of the Fourth Geneva Convention involved in the closure of RCP. They argue that if unable to change the situation, 'the EU must renounce its involvement in the AMA so that its actions do not constitute recognition, tacit approval or complicity in an act of collective punishment, in violation of the Geneva Convention.'[17] Overall, notwithstanding the EU's repeated expressions of readiness to redeploy at Rafah in the event of an agreement among Palestinians, Israelis and Egyptians, the EU has been perceived by a number of observers as implicated in an increasingly harsh closure regime that inflicts collective punishment and hardship on the population of the Gaza Strip, and has consolidated the economic and demographic fragmentation of the OPT. While the precise legal implications remain to be defined, this would appear to weaken the EU's image as a credible third party and suggest a possible disconnect between the mission's activities and overall EU objectives of a two-state solution.

Achievements and lessons learned

A number of partial achievements have been drawn from the mission's implementation; for each there appears to be a closely related cautionary lesson. This section will examine four. First, the rapid deployment of the mission, in response to an external joint request from conflicting parties, is cited as an achievement, especially when viewed in terms of developing the EU's civilian crisis response capacity. The rapid deployment was impressive in operational terms, but a longer interim period in which the specifics of the AMA and the details of the mission were more fully explored with the parties before the EU agreed to deploy, as well as the drafting of a Status of Forces Agreement, might have strengthened the mission in its interaction with the parties. Given political developments, it is questionable whether changes to the 2005 AMA would have altered the overall fate to date of the RCP and EUBAM Rafah's monitoring role. Yet it is worth noting, especially for subsequent ESDP border assistance missions, or if the terms of the AMA are revisited, that the agreement could have been more specific, formally comprised all concerned parties, and established more robust mechanisms for addressing non-compliance and other issues of implementation. EUBAM Rafah might have been empowered in its appeals to the sides to comply with the terms of the AMA.

---

17. 'Rafah Crossing: Who Holds the Keys?', op. cit. in note 7, p. 172.

Second, the mission made a difference on the ground, carrying out its monitoring and advisory mandate almost daily for the seven months the crossing point was fully operational. Furthermore, the mission's presence and the efforts of the Head of Mission may have increased the number of crossings during the subsequent period in which regular openings were suspended. In total, 443,975 passengers crossed through the RCP in the 18 months during which the monitors were present.[18] The fact that the Rafah border crossing arrangements for passengers were the only part of the AMA implemented suggests that the mission's presence has had some bearing on their (albeit short-lived) implementation.[19]

However, the gulf between operational effect and overall political impact invites pause for thought. A British parliamentary report has suggested that the two ESDP missions' 'symbolic and political significance has outstripped their operational impact.'[20] EUBAM Rafah's standby status, in particular, has become symbolic of the difficult situation in which the EU finds itself in relation to the conflict. Recent calls for the mission to withdraw completely if the RCP remains closed seem to reflect in part this thinking.

Third, the mission has been considered by some policymakers as good value, in terms of the relatively high visibility achieved with relatively low financial and administrative costs. To this may be added the relatively high level of acceptance from EU Member States that the mission has enjoyed from its inception to its hibernation, creating relatively little controversy or tension internally. However, the level of political and diplomatic back-up provided by EU institutions and Member States has not always been sufficient for upholding the credibility and integrity of the mission. It is thus too early to establish the overall political costs and benefits of the mission.

Fourth, the mission is frequently described by policymakers and observers as having established a major precedent. However, given its fate so far, it is unclear what precise precedent the mission has set. Clearly an initial precedent was set in terms of a monitoring role on a sensitive issue for the EU, welcomed by many Palestinians and deemed a noteworthy political breakthrough in terms of Israeli acceptance. It clearly demonstrated the willingness of the EU to undertake such a role. On the flipside, both Palestinians and Israelis have also witnessed how political and security

---

18. EUBAM Rafah Fact Sheet, EU Council Secretariat, January 2009.

19. The agreement's provisions on other crossing points, the link between Gaza and the West Bank, movement within the West Bank, the Gaza seaport and airport were not implemented. See 'The Agreement on Movement & Access: One Year on', OCHA, November 2006.

20. House of Lords European Union Committee Report, 'The EU and the Middle East Peace Process', July 2007, p. 45.

dynamics quickly rendered the mission inoperable.

The mission thus constitutes a cautionary precedent in the face of suggestions for other third-party monitoring or executive roles for the EU in the region. Most specifically, given the experience at Rafah, the EU should be cautious about proposals for an extension of the EUBAM Rafah model to crossing points between the Gaza Strip and Israel, which constitute a very different, arguably more difficult, arena for impartial and independent EU monitoring. More generally, each proposal should be examined not only in terms of its operational viability, but also to determine whether it contributes to wider EU objectives towards the conflict and region. In its eagerness to assist, the EU should not underplay its ability to help define arrangements and maximise chances of implementation and should build leverage over potential spoilers to arrangements in which it invests its resources and soft power. Overall, albeit in a very difficult political context, EUBAM Rafah exemplifies the difficulty of effectively linking the EU's political and economic power, interests and objectives, and its ESDP missions on the ground.

BIBLIOGRAPHY

Asseburg, Muriel. 'European Conflict Management in the Middle East: Toward a More Effective Approach', *SWP Research Paper* 2009/RP 04, February 2009.

Centro Internacional de Toledo Para la Paz. 'EU Civil Missions in the Palestinian Territories: Frustrated Reform and Suspended Security', *Middle East Special Report* no. 1, Summer 2006.

House of Lords European Union Committee Report. 'The EU and the Middle East Peace Process', July 2007.

Nasrallah, Rami and Santoro, Simona. *The External Image of the European Union: Report on Palestine* (West Bank and Gaza), Jointly Executed Research Project 5.2.1, GARNET-Forum Per l Problemi Della Pace e Della Guerra, Florence, undated.

Pirozzi, Nicoletta. 'Building Security in the Palestinian Territories,' *European Security Review* no. 28, February 2006.

'Rafah Crossing: Who Holds the Keys?', GISHA-Legal Center for Freedom of Movement and Physicians for Human Rights-Israel report, March 2009.

Scobbie, Iain. 'Is Gaza still occupied territory?', *Forced Migration Review*, no. 26, August 2006.

Tocci, Nathalie. 'Active but Acquiescent: The EU's Response to the Israeli Military Offensive in the Gaza Strip', Euro-Mediterranean Human Rights Network Report, May 2009.

UNOCHA. 'The Gaza Strip: Access Report April 2006', UN Office for the Coordination of Humanitarian Affairs, 30 April 2006.

18. EUFOR RD Congo

The military operation EUFOR RD Congo 2006

Claudia Major

Legal basis: Council Joint Action 2006/319/CFSP of 27 April 2006.

Highlights of the mission's mandate:

■ Support the UN mission in place (MONUC) in its stabilising role during the election process.

■ Deterrence, protection of civilians, airport protection, evacuation.

Duration: 30 July 2006-30 November 2006.

Budget: €23 million 'common costs' administered by ATHENA. Germany contributed about €26 million, France about €27 million.

Mission strength: 2,400.

Contributing states: 21 Member States (Austria, Belgium, Cyprus, Czech Republic, Finland, France, Germany, Greece, Hungary, Ireland, Italy, Lithuania, Luxembourg, Netherlands, Poland, Portugal, Slovakia, Slovenia, Spain, Sweden, United Kingdom) and 2 third states (Turkey and Switzerland).

Background and context

Since the early 1990s, the African Great Lakes region has been troubled by interlocking civil wars, inter-state conflict and flawed democratic transitions. Concerted efforts of the international community and local players eventually led to peace agreements which, at the end of the 1990s, engaged the region in a transition process. To support this process in DRC, the UN Security Council (UNSC) established the mission MONUC in 1999.[1] With a yearly budget exceeding one billion dollars and about 18,000 personnel, MONUC is currently the largest and most expensive UN mission.[2] The international support for political aspects of the transition process has been led by the "International Committee to Assist the Transition" (CIAT).[3] The goal was to reach a sustainable conflict solution as a precondition for a transition towards peace, stability and development. An important step herein was the scheduling of democratic elections for 2006. In fact, the DRC has become a showcase of the capacity of the international community to manage the process of reconstruction and nation building from start to finish.

The EU, who is a member of the CIAT, considerably supported the transition process in DRC. SG/HR Javier Solana, Development Commissioner Louis Michel and EU Special Representative for the Great Lakes region, Aldo Ajello, played an important role in moving the transition process forward at critical junctures. Besides, since 2002, some €750 million have been provided by the European Commission for institution building, macro-economic support and the fight against poverty under the Cotonou Agreement. Overall, the EU is the largest donor of official humanitarian aid.[4] Moreover, in addition to the military operation *Artemis* (2003), three civilian ESDP missions have been deployed to DRC. EUPOL Kinshasa (2005-2007), EUPOL RD Congo (since 2007) and EUSEC RD Congo (since 2005) offer(ed) support and advice on various aspects of security sector reform.[5]

---

1. MONUC = Mission de l'Organisation des Nations unies en République démocratique du Congo. UN Mission in DR Congo Security Council resolution 1279 (1999) on the Establishment of MONUC, S/RES/1279, 30 November 1999.

2. Figures as on 31 Mars 2009: 18,431 personnel, out of which 16,601 soldiers, 737 military observers, 1,093 police, 965 international civilian personnel, 2,251 local civilian personnel, 578 UN volunteers. See: http://www.un.org/french/peace/peace/cu_mission/monuc/monucF.htm.

3. CIAT: Comité International d'Accompagnement de la Transition. It was set up following the signature of the peace agreement in Pretoria in December 2002 to support the democratic transition process in DRC. It is composed of the five permanent Member States of the UNSC (China, the United States, France, United Kingdom, Russia), South Africa, Angola, Belgium, Canada, Gabon, Zambia, the African Union, the EU and MONUC.

4. Cornelis Wittebrod, 'Protecting the humanitarian space in Africa', in *The EU's Africa Strategy: What are the lessons of the Congo Mission?* SDA Discussion Paper, Brussels, 2007, pp. 24-26, p. 24.

5. See the chapter on EUPOL Kinshasa and EUPOL RD Congo and the chapter on EUSEC RD Congo both in this book.

The operation's main features

In December 2005, the UN invited the EU to consider the possibility of deploying a military force to assist MONUC during the election process in DRC, planned for summer 2006. In March 2006, the EU Council approved of an option paper to express EU support to MONUC and decided to launch the military-strategic planning process. Once the EU had decided about the command structures and the contributing states, the UN authorised the EU's military engagement in the DRC by adopting UNSC resolution 1671 on 25 April 2006.[6] It authorised the EU to deploy forces to support MONUC. Placed under Chapter VII, EUFOR was charged to:

- support MONUC to stabilise a situation, in case MONUC faces serious difficulties in fulfilling its mandate within its existing capabilities

- contribute to the protection of civilians under imminent threat of physical violence in the areas of its deployment

- contribute to airport protection in Kinshasa

- ensure the security and freedom of movement of the personnel as well as the protection of the installations of EUFOR Congo[7]

- execute operations of limited character in order to extract individuals in danger.

Subsequently, on 27 April 2006, the EU Council adopted the Joint Action (JA) 2006/319/CFSP, which refers to the tasks outlined in UNSC Res 1671. Lieutenant General Karlheinz Viereck (Germany) was appointed EU Operation Commander (OpCdr), Major General Christian Damay (France) was appointed EU Force Commander (FCdr). EUFOR was to be conducted in 'full agreement with the authorities of the DRC and in close coordination with them and MONUC.' The precise cooperation arrangements between the EU and the UN, including a technical agreement for logistics and intelligence, were finalised separately in July 2006.

In terms of forces, EUFOR DR Congo was composed of three pillars, namely an advance element deployed in Kinshasa, an on-call force stationed in Libreville/Gabon, and a strategic reserve in Europe. The major part of EUFOR would be stationed

---

6. UN Resolution 1671 (2006), S/RES/1671, 25 April 2006.

7. In this particular case, it is to be noted that the force had to ensure its own protection and did not rely on other actors to do so.

outside the theatre. Thereby, EUFOR intended to simultaneously ensure a deterrent capacity while avoiding unnecessary heavy military presence in Kinshasa.

Pillars one and two involved 2,400 troops drawn from 21 EU Member States. Third countries were also invited to contribute, which led to the participation of Turkey and Switzerland. The biggest contributors were France (1,090 troops), Germany (780), Spain (130) and Poland (130).[8] Together with the strategic reserve in Europe, EUFOR had at its disposal about 4,000 troops, stationed in DRC, Gabon, France and Germany, and Chad-based air support. The rapid reaction capability was mainly composed of the Spanish Legion's *Grupo Táctico Valenzuela*. Special forces provided by France (two companies), Sweden (one company) and Portugal (25 troops) strengthened EUFOR's deterrent, reaction and intervention capabilities.

The chain of command (CoC) comprised three levels. The Political and Security Committee (PSC) maintained the overall political guidance and strategic control. At the military strategic level, the German-led OHQ in Potsdam under OpCdr Viereck assured the military planning and command of the operation. The French-led FHQ under FCdr Damay, acting at the operational level, was located in Kinshasa at the N'Dolo airfield. EUFOR was supported by respectively two legal and political advisors in the OHQ and FHQ, a cultural advisor in the FHQ and, for the first time ever, a gender advisor based in the OHQ.

According to the technical agreement between the EU and the UN, MONUC was responsible for providing logistics for EUFOR. With regard to airlift between Europe, Gabon and Kinshasa, the EU drew upon the SALIS (Strategic Airlift Interim Solution) system.[9] Flights between Europe and Africa were coordinated by the Strategic Airlift Coordination Centre in Eindhoven, Netherlands, in liaison with the OHQ. Logistical support and the transport of troops from Gabon to the DRC and within the country were provided 'on the spot' by tactical airlift capabilities based in Libreville and Kinshasa.

EUFOR had electronic observation and intelligence-gathering capabilities, including four B-Hunter Drones (UAV), at its disposal. Customised analysis of satellite imagery provided by the EU Satellite Centre offered additional support.

---

8. The numbers vary depending upon the source. These have been communicated by the French Ministry of Defence, 'Opération EUFOR RD Congo – BENGA'. See www.defense.gouv.fr/ema/layout/set/popup/layout/set/popup/layout/set/popup/content/view/full/24657.

9. SALIS was set up in June 2004 by 15 European NATO member states. It has been operational since March 2006. Resources have been pooled to charter special aircrafts to gain the capability to quickly transport heavy equipment by air. Russian and Ukrainian Antonov aircraft are used as an interim solution to meet shortfalls in European strategic airlift capabilities, pending deliveries of Airbus A400M. See: www.nato.int/issues/strategic-lift-air/index.html.

In terms of geographical scope, EUFOR focused on Kinshasa, but on request it was allowed to intervene in the whole DRC. Particular national provisions restricted however the geographical scope of deployment for the different units within EU-FOR. The German and the Spanish units were for example restricted to Kinshasa.

EUFOR was deployed for 4 months, from 30 July – 30 November 2006, starting with the first round of the elections. Overall, including pre-deployment and withdrawal phases, EUFOR has been present about 6 months in DRC. The question of extending EUFOR's timeframe was raised several times. France and Belgium in particular wished to extend the operation as a precaution against the danger of riots after the withdrawal of EUFOR. However, although the European authorities in the field agreed that the timing of the withdrawal was unfortunate, Germany, and parts of the military personnel, insisted on the departure in time. The operation was not extended.

The overall cost of EUFOR was about €100 million. ATHENA administered the financing of the common costs of ca. €23 million.[10] Germany contributed about €26 million, France about €27 million.[11] The remaining expenditure dealt with by the participating member states has not yet been made entirely accessible.

Internal challenges

Delays in the early stages of the planning process and a tedious force generation process complicated the run-up to EUFOR RD Congo. Once set up, the terms of the mandate, national caveats and material shortcomings affected its execution.

While the political agreement on EUFOR's deployment was reached rather smoothly, the force generation process turned out to be very cumbersome due to the reluctant commitment of the Member States. Pressured by its peers, Germany eventually accepted to take a leading role in terms of both providing troops and command structures. It contributed one third of the troops and the OHQ, while France provided the FHQ and another third of the troops.

The parliamentary approval, which is required in Germany for each military deployment, imposed several limitations on the German units. First, they were only

---

10. EU Council Secretariat Fact Sheet, 'Financing of ESDP operations', Brussels, June 2007. Available at: http://www.consilium.europa.eu/uedocs/cmsUpload/ATHENA_june_2007.pdf. According to the Joint Action, art 13.1, the financial reference amount for the common costs for EUFOR for a four-month period would be €16,700,000. Common costs refer mainly to headquarters and C3I systems (command, control, communications and information).

11. Interviews in the German and French Ministries of Defence, January 2009.

allowed to operate in Kinshasa, whereas most of the other units were allowed to operate throughout DRC. Second, Germany insisted on a four-month timeframe. Third, German combat troops were stationed in Gabon, which limited the probability of their deployment.

Once in the theatre, the interoperability within EUFOR proved to be challenging. EUFOR was undoubtedly a good quality force, but the integration of different national contributions with their particular doctrines, practices and instructions, was difficult. It led to frictions among the countries involved, with some feeling that they were more exposed and having to bear greater responsibilities than others.

Besides, the European CoC proved to be very complex. At the political-strategic level, the PSC, the SG/HR Solana, the chairman of the European Union Military Committee (EUMC) and DG E VIII were involved. Both the OHQ and the FHQ comprised comparatively large numbers of staff when compared to the number of troops deployed in the theatre. The OHQ was gradually built up. From initially about 20 personnel at the moment of activation, the staffing reached 146 personnel when it was completed in June 2006. 19 Member States contributed, with Germany (86) and France (16) providing the largest numbers. The FHQ comprised 122 personnel, 77 of which were French and 16 German. Eventually, the FHQ which commanded about 2,400 troops had more staff than the MONUC FHQ which commanded about 18,000 troops.

Moreover, the OpCdr, also due to political pressure, sought to exert close military control over the operation down the CoC, which some observers critically called 'micromanagement'.[12] This resulted in some tension in the interaction within the CoC.

EUFOR also faced constraints in the realm of airlift, where it was two aircraft short of the capabilities requested during the planning phase. Hence, only one deployment at a time beyond Kinshasa would have been possible. The different terms of use of the tactical air transport and the distance between Gabon and Kinshasa were also constrictive. The time needed to deploy the over-horizon-force from Gabon to Kinshasa (a 2 hour flight) restricted EUFOR's capacity to act. An estimated 72 hours was required to engage at full capacity if the point of application was not Kinshasa. Fortunately, EUFOR eventually did not face a situation where it needed to deploy its over-the-horizon force rapidly, and beyond Kinshasa.

---

12. Interviews with French and German personnel involved in EUFOR, December 2007, February and April 2008.

Challenges on the ground

The main challenges on the ground were the adaptation to the particular environment and the interaction with MONUC. Initially, the local population doubted EUFOR's neutrality and its military capability. Considering EUFOR a small force with a limited mandate, it quickly mocked it by nicknaming it 'EU-Faible' – faible meaning 'weak' in French. Besides, the local population suspected EUFOR of partiality and support for the outgoing President Kabila. EUFOR thus engaged in a focused media campaign to explain its presence, to clarify its role compared to MONUC, to build up a deterrent image, and to develop a specific identity. This was flanked by civil-military actions to improve EUFOR's image and win over hearts and minds, such as supporting local hospitals, and the publication of a journal, La Paillotte.

Cooperation with MONUC proved to be a major challenge. It suffered from inadequate cooperation mechanisms, coordination problems and a lack of mutual understanding.[13] First, the different assignment of responsibilities within the respective CoCs impeded, particularly at the early stage, both communication and coordinated decision-making between EUFOR and MONUC. The MONUC FCdr enjoyed comparatively more strategic and operational room for manoeuvre than the EU FCdr who, within the complex EU CoC, often had to revert to the OHQ.

Second, the complex procedures for committing EUFOR in support of MONUC amplified the cooperation problems rooted in the CoC. EUFOR's intervention could only be envisaged in response to exceptional circumstances beyond MONUC's capacities. With the exception of emergency cases, EUFOR's commitment was to be obtained through a formal request by the UNSG to the EU SG/HR. It required a lengthy and complex authorisation process which made a quick intervention difficult to assure.[14]

Additionally, cooperation between the two operations was affected by the lack of a formal agreement on the exchange of secure information. The technical agreement of July 2006 invited EUFOR and MONUC to share situation assessment, mainly to be able to anticipate a possible request to EUFOR. They eventually exchanged op-

13. Claudia Major, 'EU-UN cooperation in military crisis management: the experience of EUFOR RD Congo 2006', Occasional Paper no. 72, European Union Institute for Security Studies, Paris, September 2008.

14. The command post exercise MUZURRI of July 2006 revealed the lengthy and complex nature of this process. It was set up to test procedures between MONUC FHQ, UNDPKO, EU OHQ, EU FHQ and the EU PSC for requesting the engagement of EUFOR. The result was disastrous. The EU's answer arrived at MONUC FHQ 24h after the request. The call had to go up the UN line of command and then down the EU line of command. German Federal Ministry of Defence, contributions to the conference: 'Military aspects of UN-EU cooperation in crisis management operations in the light of EUFOR RD Congo', Berlin, 19-21 March 2007.

erational documents, such as daily and weekly situation reports. However, analysis was shared to a lesser extent given the sensitivity of such issues and the lack of an agreement on the exchange of classified information. Consequently, the two forces partly generated independent threat assessments, which led to diverging views over when deterrent action was necessary.[15]

Equally problematic was cooperation in the area of logistics, which MONUC was partly responsible for providing to EUFOR. Logistics and support are key for the success of an operation. This entails tasks as various as assuring living and working accommodation, medical support, surface transport; water and food; fuel; office equipment and furniture; general services; janitorial work; waste disposal etc. The significant differences between the logistical practices and systems quickly led to coordination problems and possible competition for scarce resources. Thanks to its presence in the whole DRC, MONUC was able to facilitate EUFOR deployments outside Kinshasa. This included providing petroleum during force projection exercises to the point of application, depots and transit camps and support to reconnaissance missions. Overall however, pointing out delays and the quality of the services provided, EUFOR questioned MONUC's capacity to take in charge EUFOR's logistical support.

The mission's implementation and performance

EUFOR was deployed to assure the smooth running of the presidential and parliamentary elections in DRC. The best placed candidates for the presidential elections were outgoing President Joseph Kabila and Vice-President Jean Pierre Bemba. After the first round of the presidential elections on 30 July 2006 did not yield a winner, a second round took place on 29 October 2006. As a result, the Congolese Supreme Court of Justice declared Joseph Kabila president of DRC with 58.05% of the votes.

With some exceptions, EUFOR's activities were concentrated in Kinshasa. In close cooperation with MONUC and EUPOL, they aimed to ensure EUFOR's visibility and credibility in order to dissuade potential attacks on the electoral process and to reassure the population. Both EUFOR and MONUC patrolled the streets of the capital during the electoral period, in parallel to the local police and the mixed patrols composed of the security forces of both election candidates. In addition, two temporary deployments of Mirage F1 assured deterrence for EUFOR (25-30 July; 7-15 August).

---

15. Richard Gowan, 'EUFOR RD Congo, UNIFIL and future European support to the UN', in *The EU's Africa Strategy: What are the lessons of the Congo Mission?*, SDA Discussion Paper, Brussels, 2007, pp: 29-31, p. 30; Interviews in the French Ministry of Defence, April 2008.

Overall, EUFOR did not face serious military challenges. It engaged however in stabilising tasks on three occasions: in August, after the announcement of the elections results; in September, when Bemba's TV station was attacked, and in November when the final results were announced.

The incidents with the greatest potential for destabilisation occurred 20-22 August 2006. At MONUC's request, EUFOR intervened together with MONUC when violent confrontations followed the announcement of the results of the first round of the presidential elections. The main intervention took place when Vice-President and presidential candidate Jean Pierre Bemba's HQ came under attack. At that moment, Bemba was receiving the members of CIAT. The concerted intervention of MONUC and EUFOR made it possible to separate the conflict parties and brought the CIAT representatives to safety. In parallel, additional forces were brought in from Gabon.

Generally, EUFOR profited from an overall favourable environment. Once it had dispelled doubts about its strength and impartiality, EUFOR operated in a mostly friendly environment. The Congolese population showed enormous interest in the elections and strongly supported them. EUFOR also benefited from an overall positive evolution of the security situation. Eventually, the security challenges were concentrated in Kinshasa, which considerably simplified EUFOR's action. EUFOR clearly fulfilled its mandate as outlined in the JA: it successfully supported MONUC in securing the election process in DRC. Except for the August events, it was not involved in violent clashes. EUFOR did not suffer casualties.

The EU and most observers considered EUFOR's deployment a success.[16] During the August incidents, EUFOR was able to transform into a deterrent force and demonstrated the capacity to react rapidly. Overall, and despite the procedural disconnects described above, EUFOR was, in cooperation with MONUC, decisive in limiting the number of incidents and in containing the potential spread of violence at sensitive moments in the election process.

However, other international observers were more cautious. The International Crisis Group claimed that 'neither the MONUC nor EU troops in Kinshasa acted quickly

---

16. UN Security Council, Presentation by Javier Solana, EU HR for CFSP, on the Democratic Republic of Congo/ EUFOR, New York, 9 January 2007, S005/07; Summary of remarks by Javier Solana, Informal Meeting of the EU defence ministers. Levi, Finland, 3 October 2006, S273/06; Hans-Georg Erhardt, 'Nichts wie weg? Zum Ende des EU Militäreinsatzes im Kongo', in *Hamburger Informationen zur Friedensforschung und Sicherheitspolitik* (Hamburg: IFSH, 41/ Dezember 2006); Security and Defence Agenda, *The EU's Africa Strategy: What are the lessons of the Congo Mission?*, SDA Discussion Paper, Brussels, 2007.

enough to prevent the August violence from escalating.'[17] Moreover, while recognising that EUFOR fulfilled its mandate in terms of assuring the elections, they argue that EUFOR would not have been able to confront bigger military challenges. They also made the criticism that the limited timeframe affected the dissuasive character of the mission.

These comments echo the criticism voiced prior to the operation where EUFOR was mocked as an inappropriate 'cosmetic operation', which had more to do with European form than African substance, and more with rhetoric than with relevant action.[18] According to this view, EUFOR fitted more what the EU had to offer than what the DRC and MONUC needed. The geographical restriction to Kinshasa, the timeframe, the troops number and the mandate were also cited to demonstrate EUFOR's 'cosmetic character'.[19] Besides, the arguments goes, the Union welcomed the operation mainly for internal purposes in that it afforded an opportunity to show the EU flag and to demonstrate the Union's military capabilities and autonomy.

These allegations are certainly valid in that to substantially support the transition process, a larger deployment, with a longer timeframe and a different mandate would have been necessary. In fact, while EUFOR certainly fulfilled its mission and allowed the EU to gain greater visibility and international recognition, it was less decisive in influencing the long-term political situation in DRC. Once EUFOR had left the country, the conflict between the new Congolese president and the opposition erupted again. In March 2007, Kabila's Republican Guard attacked the personnel charged with protecting unsuccessful candidate and opposition leader Bemba's residence. The confrontations reached a much higher intensity than those of August 2006. Bemba escaped and MONUC escorted him later on to the airport from which he departed into exile.

Nevertheless, this criticism seems to miss the point. The EU is very active in DRC, in political, economic, technical, diplomatic and also military terms. These different dimensions should certainly be brought under a more effective single strategy. But one mission, EUFOR, can neither make up for this lack nor can it be criticised for not doing so. EUFOR was neither supposed to replace MONUC nor to assure in a

---

17. International Crisis Group, 'Securing Congo's Elections: Lessons from the Kinshasa Showdown', *Africa Briefing* no. 42, Nairobi/Brussels, 2 October 2006, p. 4; see also Georges Nzongola-Ntalaja, 'Lessons learned from the *Artemis* and EUFOR operations in the Democratic Republic of the Congo', in *The EU's Africa Strategy: What are the lessons of the Congo Mission?*, SDA Discussion Paper, Brussels, 2007, pp: 32-33; Societecivile.cd, 'Espoir pour tous : La bataille de Kinshasa : MONUC et EUFOR impuissants ?', 23 August 2006, see: http://www.societecivile.cd/node/3032.

18. Jean Yves Haine and Bastian Giegerich, 'In Congo, a cosmetic EU operation', *International Herald Tribune*, 12 June 2006.

19. International Crisis Group, op. cit. in note 17.

long-term perspective the overall transition process in DRC. On UN request, it was set up to support MONUC in a particular and limited moment of time, with MONUC remaining in charge of the overall situation. Certainly, from an EU perspective, EUFOR has been politically and symbolically relevant in that it showed the EU capacity to intervene for the benefit of international security with military means in a distant theatre. However, this does not alter the fact that EUFOR indeed fulfilled its mandate as outlined in the UNSC Resolution and the following joint action.

Achievements and shortcomings

Although EUFOR can be considered a success, several shortcomings have to be recognised.[20] On the one hand, the differences between EU Member States and their impact on EUFOR affected the operation's capacity to act. While certainly a good quality force, EUFOR suffered from national caveats and a high degree of diversity. The cumbersome European decision-making and force generation processes, and the reluctance of EU Member States to support EUFOR in both financial and material terms put the deployment at risk, while also undermining the declarative and normative commitment of the EU to Africa, UN support and crisis management as expressed for example in the European Security Strategy or the EU-UN Joint declarations of 2003 and 2007.

These intra-European problems were, on the other hand, amplified by the cooperation settings with the UN. The lack of an agreement on information exchange, the complex procedures for committing EUFOR in support of MONUC, the failures in the areas of logistics and lack of communication seriously affected the cooperation. If these shortcomings eventually did not compromise EUFOR's effectiveness and the overall successful outcome, they affected the smooth running of the mission and could have damaged its overall result at sensitive moments, such as the August incidents.

On the whole, due to its particular settings, EUFOR provides only a limited test case for the effectiveness of EU military operations. EUFOR's deployment was not an example of rapid deployment or rapid response intervention, given that the Member States had enough time (roughly 8 months since December 1995/January 2006, when the UN had formulated its request) to set up the force. It was not a blueprint for a stand alone operation either, since EUFOR cooperated with MONUC which

20. A 'lessons learned review' for EUFOR has been published in March 2007 by the Council. It has however only been partly de-classified. Council of the European Union/DG E VIII/ EUMS, 'Analysis of Lessons from Operation EUFOR RD Congo', 22 March 2007, 7633/07.

was already present in the theatre, and relied on MONUC to a great extent for logistical help. Finally, although the August intervention demonstrated EUFOR's military effectiveness, the operation cannot be considered an example of dealing alone with serious military challenges as MONUC carried out most of these interventions.

BIBLIOGRAPHY

Damay, Christian. 'La contribution de l'UE à la sécurité du processus électoral en république démocratique du Congo', in *Les cahiers de Mars*, no. 191, 2007, pp. 89-92.

Gowan, Richard. 'EUFOR RD Congo, UNFIL and future European support to the UN', in *The EU's Africa Strategy: What are the lessons of the Congo Mission?*, SDA Discussion Paper, Brussels, 2007, pp. 29-31

Gutiérrez, Ignació Cosido. Report submitted on behalf of the Defence Committee, Assembly of the Western European Union, Doc A/1954, Paris, 29 December 2006.

Haine, Jean-Yves Haine and Giegerich, Bastian. 'In Congo, a cosmetic EU operation', *International Herald Tribune*, 12 June 2006.

International Crisis Group. 'Securing Congo's Elections: Lessons from the Kinshasa Showdown', *Africa Briefing* no.42, Nairobi/Brussels, 2 October 2006.

Major, Claudia. 'EU-UN cooperation in military crisis management: the experience of EUFOR RD Congo 2006', *Occasional Paper* no. 72, European Union Institute for Security Studies, Paris, September 2008.

Nzongola-Ntalaja, Georges. 'Lessons learned from the Artemis and EUFOR operations in the Democratic Republic of the Congo', in *The EU's Africa Strategy: What are the lessons of the Congo Mission?*, SDA Discussion Paper, Brussels, 2007, pp. 32-33.

Schmidt, Peter. 'Freiwillige vor! Bundeswehreinsatz im Kongo – Zur Dialektik einer Führungsrolle wider Willen', in *Internationale Politik*, Deutsche Gesellschaft für Auswärtige Politik, Berlin, November 2006, pp. 68-77.

Tull, Denis M. 'Die Führung und Beteiligung der Bundeswehr an EUFOR RD Congo', in Stefan Meir, (ed.), *Auslandseinsätze der Bundeswehr. Leitfragen, Entscheidungsspielräume und Lehren*, SWP Studie, S 27, Stiftung Wissenschaft und Politik, Berlin, September 2007, pp. 68-77.

Viereck, Karlheinz. 'EUFOR RD Congo. Europe can do it', in *Truppendienst* 3/2007, pp. 253-58.

Wittebrod, Cornelis. 'Protecting the humanitarian space in Africa', in *The EU's Africa Strategy: What are the lessons of the Congo Mission?*, SDA Discussion Paper, Brussels, 2007, pp. 24-6, p. 24.

19. EUPOL Afghanistan

The EU Police Mission in Afghanistan (EUPOL Afghanistan)

Luis Peral*

Legal basis: Council Joint Action 2007/369/CFSP of 30 May 2007.

Highlights of the mission's mandate:

■ To contribute significantly to the establishment under Afghan ownership of sustainable and effective policing arrangements, which will ensure appropriate interaction with the wider criminal justice system.

■ To support the reform process towards a trusted and efficient police service, which works in accordance with international standards, within the framework of the rule of law and respects human rights.

Duration: 15 June 2007 to date.

Budget: €43.6 million until 30 November 2008; €64 million, financial reference for the period 1 December 2008 to 30 November 2009.

Mission strength: 400 authorised. 225 by mid-March 2009.

Contributing states: 16 EU Member States (Czech Republic, Denmark, Estonia, Finland, France, Germany, Hungary, Italy, Latvia, Lithuania, the Netherlands, Poland, Romania, Spain, Sweden, United Kingdom) and 4 third states.

---

* The author is grateful to Eva Gross for her comments on an earlier version of this chapter.

Background and context

Following the terrorist attacks of 11 September 2001 in New York and Washington, the UN Security Council adopted Resolution 1373, which paved the way for the American-led military operation in Afghanistan in autumn 2001, known as Operation Enduring Freedom (OEF). OEF concentrated on overthrowing the Taliban regime, and eliminating al-Qaeda and other terrorist groups operating in the country. Almost simultaneously, in December 2001, the UN-led process for rebuilding Afghanistan began at the Bonn conference. In March 2002, the UN Security Council created the UN Assistance Mission to Afghanistan (UNAMA), under Resolution 1401, as an 'integrated mission' of some 17 specialised UN humanitarian and developmental agencies, with a common mandate to contribute to reconstruction and national reconciliation. The International Security Assistance Force (ISAF), a peacekeeping force set up under the framework of UNSC Resolution 1378, was to aid the interim government in developing national security structures, to assist the country's reconstruction, and to assist in developing and training future Afghan security forces.

The reconstruction of Afghanistan has proved an extremely difficult task in the midst of US and NATO-led military operations. After a first phase in which countries such as the United Kingdom and Australia joined OEF, the US obtained material and manpower support from nearly 30 countries, which began to act through smaller structures spread over the entire country. These Provincial Reconstruction Teams (PRTs) were created by leading nations to develop civilian projects, even if their staff are predominantly military. In October 2006, all the existing PRTs in Afghanistan were formally placed under the ISAF umbrella, which has been under NATO command since August 2003. However, the PRTs have been operating by and large autonomously from one another, with strong links to respective national capitals and little coordination on the ground. The US-led operation OEF includes an important component tasked with training and mentoring the Afghan security forces (army and police): the Combined Security Transition Command – Afghanistan (CSTC-A). In the wake of a further increase of US troops, and also for the sake of improved coordination, since spring 2009 both CSTC-A and ISAF are under the command of the US General Stanley McChrystal.

The involvement of the international community in the reconstruction of Afghanistan is broad and varied. In 2002, on the occasion of a conference on Security Sector

Reform (SSR) hosted by the UN in Geneva, the G8 launched a lead-nation approach to key areas for state building. Germany took the lead on police, creating the German Police Project Office (GPPO); the US assumed responsibility for army reform; Japan provided financial assistance to Disarmament, Demobilisation and Reintegration (DDR) programmes addressing militia forces that had fought the Taliban; the UK took the lead on counter-narcotics and Italy on the reform of the judicial system.

In the midst of a number of fragmented and overlapping civilian and military mandates, the international community agreed on a broad common strategy aligning all international actors and the Afghan government at the London Conference of February 2006.[1] According to the main outcome of the Conference, the so-called Afghan Compact, stability can only be achieved by combining security measures with good governance and economic and social development. In practice, this has proved extremely difficult to implement due to the poor coordination among different international actors and the pre-eminence of the military response to security concerns. In this complex context, the EU identified police reform as a key dimension of the stabilisation effort in Afghanistan. However, by the time consensus in Brussels for exploring the launch of an ESDP operation was achieved in 2006, the insurgency against US and NATO-led forces had not only revived but also consolidated. Establishing an effective, coherent and coordinated work programme among a multitude of actors engaged in Afghanistan's reconstruction, including police reform, and in a deteriorating security environment has posed a significant challenge for EUPOL Afghanistan.

The mandate

The Council Secretariat first sent an exploratory mission to Afghanistan in July 2006, followed by a Joint Council/Commission EU Assessment Mission (JEUAM) in September, to assess the situation of the Afghan police forces and judiciary. The Political and Security Committee (PSC) sent another mission between 27 November and 14 December to consider the feasibility of an ESDP mission. Following on from its conclusions, on 12 February 2007 the Council approved the Crisis Management Concept (CMC). The Council subsequently approved the Concept of Operations (CONOPS) in April 2007 and finally adopted the Joint Action establishing EUPOL

---

1. See 'The Afghanistan Compact', adopted at the London Conference on Afghanistan, 31 January-1 February 2006.

Afghanistan as a non-executive mission on 30 May 2007 with a mandate to help develop the Afghan police force.[2]

It was especially difficult to reach consensus on whether and how the EU should contribute to the improvement of the rule of law in Afghanistan. The Nordic countries supported the German request to the EU for help in its endeavour as leading nation for the police reform. The United Kingdom was willing to lead the eventual EU mission even if it could not make substantial contributions to it. Other Member States were reluctant to commit resources not channelled through the respective PRTs. In the end, the bulk of the GPPO was integrated in EUPOL Afghanistan, and the mission was headed by a German national. Brigadier-General Friedrich Eichele was appointed as head of the EU police mission in Afghanistan in June 2007, and replaced by General Jürgen Scholz, also German, only two months later. In October 2008 Police Commissioner Kai Vittrup, Danish, was designated head of EUPOL Afghanistan.

In Brussels, the director of the Civilian Planning and Conduct Capability (CPCC) exercises the command of the mission at the strategic operational level. EUPOL Afghanistan works under the overall authority of the High Representative for CFSP and receives strategic direction from the PSC as well as 'local political guidance' from the European Union Special Representative (EUSR) in Kabul. This position was held by Ambassador Francesc Vendrell until September 2008, and is currently held by Ambassador Ettore Sequi, whose remit has recently been extended to Pakistan.

Initially planned to comprise 240 international personnel, the PSC agreed in May 2008 to significantly increase the size of the mission with the aim to reach 400 international personnel, of which 269 should be police officers. By October 2009, the mission strength was 268 internationals, 170 of whom were police officers, 20 rule-of-law experts and the rest 78 civilian experts, plus 166 local staff. The majority of the police officers come from Germany (45), since the EU mission built upon German efforts.[3] Countries such as Italy (31), Finland (24), the United Kingdom (21), Sweden (19), Denmark (19), the Netherlands (16), France (12), Canada (12) also provide significant contributions. The mission has been recently reorganised along

---

2. Council Joint Action 2007/369/CFSP of 30 May 2007 on establishment of the European Union Police Mission in Afghanistan (EUPOL AFGANISTAN).

3. By the time EUPOL was established, Germany had spent over 70 million on police training in Afghanistan and trained some 17,000 Afghans in policing with 4,200 participating in one- or three-year training courses. On the German and US approaches to police training see Eva Gross, 'Security Sector Reform in Afghanistan: the EU's contribution', *Occasional Paper* no. 78, European Union Institute for Security Studies, Paris, April 2009.

three basic working lines: police, rule of law and mission support. EUPOL is now deployed to central, northern, western, southern and eastern regions, covering 15 Afghan provinces.

The remit of EUPOL as a non-executive mission is focused on institution-building. The mission implements its mandate through advising, mentoring, monitoring and training (including direct training and the 'train-the-trainers' scheme). The mission operates at different levels: at the strategic level (interior ministry reform, institutional development, support to the Afghan government in developing strategies and legislative frameworks), and at the operational and tactical levels (police chain of command, regional and provincial ANP headquarters, city police projects). From this standpoint, a constructive working relationship with the Afghan government – and its endorsement of EUPOL – is indispensable. A letter from the current Afghan Minister of the Interior, Mohammad Hanif Atmar, to the Head of EUPOL in October 2008, shortly after both the Minister and the new Head of Mission took office, offered a clearer framework for the implementation of the mission mandate. The letter allowed EUPOL to adapt and narrow down its mandate within the broad priorities established by the EU Council, which in turn helped build a constructive relationship with the US CSTC-A, whose mandate included the reform of all Afghan Security Forces, and had in fact led and financed the bulk of the effort on police reform.

Specifically, the priorities indicated by Minister Atmar for EUPOL Afghanistan included the following: accelerating and expanding the US Focused District Development (FDD) training programme and other similar existing programmes; implementing a comprehensive anti-corruption strategy; reinforcing intelligence and investigative capacity to curb organised crime, reducing civilian and police casualties, and supporting counter-terrorism and counter-insurgency campaigns; completing and expanding the police *tashkeel* (recruiting system), especially to medium- and high-risk districts; improving security in principal cities and along highways; and ensuring security for free, fair and transparent elections in August 2009.

Most of these priorities (anti-corruption, intelligence-led policing, criminal investigations, *tashkeel* increases and related training, support to ANP training for elections, security plans for principal cities) already fell under EUPOL's remit or capabilities. Atmar's letter demonstrated the Afghan commitment to police reform, with EUPOL's active input. This constitutes a crucial element for effective and sustainable institutional reforms and, as a result, EUPOL has been able to better target its activities in line with Afghan priorities. For some of these priorities, EUPOL has been requested to take the lead by Minister Atmar (such as anti-corruption, intelligence-led policing, Cities Police Projects, ANP elections training and criminal investigations).

As part of its mandate, EUPOL also seeks to support the coordination of international efforts in the field of police reform. The International Police Coordination Board (IPCB), which was created in 2007, was supposed to play an important role in this respect as it brings together all international actors involved in police reform under Afghan chairmanship. Coordination with other EU actors on the ground has also been reinforced (EUSR office, EC delegation). EUPOL has also been able to establish close working relationships both with UNAMA and the US (CSTC-A, Bureau of International Narcotics and Law Enforcement Affairs – INL). Since January 2009, the revised IPCB has contributed to reinvigorating the coordination of the international community.

Implementation

In the midst of other initiatives targeting police reform, illustrated below, EUPOL aims to contribute expertise on civilian policing through advising, monitoring mentoring and training, at the central, regional and provincial levels. In so doing, the ESDP mission seeks to strengthen the governance structures of the Afghan police and to form police officers operating in accordance with international standards and under the rule of law. The European Commission finances more than 50 percent of the Law and Order Trust Fund for Afghanistan (LOTFA), which pays the salaries of the Afghan National Police (ANP). EUPOL's tasks include: mentoring at the Ministry of the Interior and ANP headquarters; supporting the ANP Policing Plan; working on *tashkeel*; helping police and prosecutors work more closely together; and supporting the ANP on developing a training strategy (including curricula development).

Moreover, EUPOL has been tasked to take the lead in writing and implementing an anti-corruption strategy, which is being done in coordination with UNDP, the United Nations Office on Drugs and Crime (UNODC), and CSTC-A. Implementation has already started, focusing on: (i) establishing an adequate legislative and regulatory framework for the Afghan police and the Ministry of the Interior; (ii) prevention through specialised training and public awareness campaigns; (iii) enforcement through the conduct of internal investigations of alleged corruption cases with the interior ministry through the Inspector General. EUPOL is also providing mentoring and advice to the newly established anti-corruption unit within the Attorney General's Office. The mission is currently rolling out its main areas of activities to the provinces.

On the particular task of helping to improve security in certain cities, EUPOL is developing the so-called Kabul City Project, which is being applied in other major Afghan cities (Herat, Mazar, Kandahar, Lashkar Gah, Tarin Kowt etc) at the request of Minister Atmar. The project involves conducting a district-by-district SWOT (strengths, weaknesses, opportunities, threats) assessment, enhancing the command and control function for a self-sustained police force, and establishing a District Support Unit for each of the city districts, including an intelligence system. EUPOL has also supported improving control of the road entrances to Kabul city by enforcing checkpoints and introducing mobile teams, together with streamlining the work of traffic police.

Among the most successful specific projects, EUPOL has advised on establishing a hotline (number 100) for denouncing police misbehaviour in Helmand – where EUPOL opened its provincial headquarters thanks to a US government $9 million grant. This initiative has led to the conviction of nearly 30 police officers as a result of investigation upon evidence provided by as many as 60-80 daily phone calls (although only a fraction haved proved trustworthy).

In the area of training, the mission has run courses for 400 ANP officials to train ANP staff through the *Train the Trainers* programme, the final goal being to produce a permanent Afghan-owned training capacity. EUPOL is also devising a follow-up programme to ensure the sustainability of these efforts, and is planning to engage in civic education and public awareness campaigns to enhance confidence in the police service.

Challenges

EUPOL Afghanistan has experienced many of the problems that have affected other ESDP civilian missions. The start-up phase of the mission proved particularly challenging, due to both political uncertainty in Brussels and logistical difficulties in a very difficult theatre.[4] The planning and deployment phases were protracted because of difficulties recruiting personnel. The slowness of the recruiting process has affected the capacity of EUPOL to be present outside Kabul. The reluctance of EU

4. Scott Chilton, Schiewek Eckart, and Tim Bremmers, 'Evaluation of the appropriate size of the Afghan National Police Force Manning List (Tashkil)', Final Report, European Commission Contrat no. 2009/207401 – Version 1; Kabul, 15 July 2009, p. 42.

Member States to contribute the necessary personnel was one of the main factors that delayed the implementation of the mission. Over and above these difficulties, however, the mission has been confronted with broader political challenges related to the state of the Afghan security sector and, above all, to the arduous coordination of different police reform efforts.

The poor state of the ANP leaves limited margin for progress in the medium term.[5] Among other problems, the fact that the salary paid to ANP officers through the LOTFA remains low only aggravates the problem of corruption. Insurgents can offer double or triple that amount and corrupt institutional structures impede the establishment of an accountable police force. Besides, the Afghan government took time to clarify its needs, which made the definition of a precise and workable mandate all the more difficult. The deteriorating situation on the ground further lessened the potential and actual impact of EUPOL. Carrying out state-building operations in a war-like situation poses a particularly serious challenge. Thus EUPOL faces both the risk of being too 'sophisticated' for an institution that is still in its infancy and the difficulty of finding a complementary role that suited its capacities within the complex international network already in place, given in particular the overwhelming role of the US. In principle, there is scope for synergy between different contributions to police reform. In practice, so far, achieving synergy has proven very difficult. In perspective, EUPOL's distinctive approach focusing on the civilian model of policing should take more prominence as the ANP develops and best practices are introduced beyond basic police training.

Once deployed, EUPOL has had to adjust its ambitions to the complex situation on the ground. The IPCB did not function effectively as the intended coordination mechanism, despite EUPOL's efforts to help it in this role. The performance of this body has however improved in 2009 following reforms introduced by EUPOL to strengthen the Board.

Up until very recently, the prevailing US-led military strategy has not only been unable to create a secure environment for civilian operations in Afghanistan; it has also implied a 'militarisation' of some aspects of civilian efforts, particularly police

5. See Andrew Wilder, 'Cops or Robbers? The Struggle to Reform the Afghan National Police', AREU, *Issues* Paper Series, July 2007; see also Report on the Implementation of the Afghanistan Compact, Joint Coordination and Monitoring Board, International Conference in Support of Afghanistan, Paris, June 2008. A recent report sets a framework of 20 to 30 years to establish a police that is able to uphold the rule of law in Afghanistan: see Chilton, Schiewek and Bremmers, op. cit. in note 4.

reform.[6] Against this background, the US approach to police reform has evolved over time, with the launch of a new approach to police training, the so-called Focused District Development (FDD) programme. Since 2007, OEF military and private contractors offer intensive training of two months and subsequent mentoring to Afghan police units, with a view to improving the security of the local population and not just to tracking down insurgents or terrorists. However, the revised programme of November 2008 removed training on domestic violence, community policing, democratic policing and human rights, which were replaced with advanced shooting and further survival skills.[7] In spite of this renewed counterinsurgency orientation of the training, FDD intends to build up a functioning police force from the district level, and the programme is eventually meant to reach all provinces in Afghanistan by 2014.[8]

A certain discrepancy remains between the civilian model of police reform advocated by EUPOL and the more 'militarised' counterinsurgency model, in which the police complements the role of the army, pursued by the US. In short, the US has been focusing on increasing the quantity of police resources available on the ground, and conducted training mainly at the district level, whereas EUPOL has prioritised more qualitative aspects of training and mostly targeted mid- to senior-levels of management, as well as adopting a train-the-trainers approach with a view to building some sustainability of training knowledge in the ANP. Both US programmes and the EUPOL mandate include mentoring and advising at police headquarters in Kabul and in the provinces. It is important that this underlying difference between the US and the European approaches to police reform does not become a serious obstacle to integrated police reform. Efforts have been made to define joint approaches and strategies, and to coordinate EU and US mentors' activities and their deployments in the interior ministry and the ANP headquarters.

The absence of a comprehensive EU-NATO agreement on the provision of security for EUPOL staff through ISAF, and their inability to formally exchange classified information, due to the different membership of the two organisations, has hindered closer cooperation between the EU and NATO in the critical Afghan theatre. As a result, EUPOL had to conclude individual agreements with PRT lead nations,

---

6. 'With just 10 days of training and equipped with a minimum of firepower, [the Police] are used as a military force ... or tripwire to flush out the Taliban': Andrew Wilder, op. cit. in note 5, p. 94. Moreover, development projects are being further streamlined as a counterinsurgency tool according to high-level advisers of ISAF (interviews conducted by the author in July 2009).

7. Chilton, Schiewek and Bremmers, op. cit. in note 4, p. 60.

8. Frederik Rosén, 'Third Generation Civil-Military Relations and the "New Revolution in Military Affairs"', *DIIS Working Paper*, March 2009, pp. 12-20.

and the PRTs have sometimes acted as informal 'go-betweens' to share some information on an *ad hoc* basis between NATO and EUPOL personnel. The PRTs are predominantly military structures directly involved in development and state-building projects, often undertaking efforts for which other civilian actors, such as UNAMA and specialised NGOs, have long-standing expertise.

Concluding agreements with individual PRTs has not proved an easy process, whether leading nations are EU Member States or not. The capacity of the PRTs to host international personnel is especially limited in terms of accommodation and office space. Besides, security agreements between EUPOL and individual PRTs only provide *in extremis* coverage, offering EUPOL staff protection 'within means and capabilities'. As a result, EUPOL has been obliged to hire a private company to guarantee its security and adopt an extremely tight security policy in contrast with other international actors' regulations – for example, not allowing civilian staff in Kabul to leave EUPOL premises at certain times, since they do not carry weapons. The difficulty of ensuring adequate security for the mission staff not only slowed down but also limited EUPOL's geographic deployment. Even though the original deployment plan foresaw working with Turkish and US-led PRTs, Turkey and the US, for different reasons, did not conclude bilateral technical agreements with EUPOL.

The deployment of the NATO Training Mission-Afghanistan (NTM-A), as agreed at the Strasbourg-Kehl NATO Summit in April 2009, is imminent. Mandated to enhance the capacity of the Afghan army and police, and including a large contingent of *gendarmerie* forces from EU Member States in the framework of the European Gendarmerie Force, the new mission will represent another major actor in the fragmented panorama of police reform efforts.[9]

In addition, EUPOL has not been able to channel or better coordinate EU Member State efforts on police reform. Among the main bilateral police training projects, which are rather short-term and generally connected to their respective PRT activities, are the French surveillance training and German forensic training programme. The Italian *Carabinieri* have developed a programme for training the Afghanistan National Civil Order Police (ANCOP), considered to be the best corps within the

---

9. On July 20, 2006 the European Gendarmerie Force (EGF) was declared fully operational at a meeting of the high-level inter-ministerial committee (CIMIN) held in Madrid. On 19 March 2009, the six EU countries that are part of the EGF - France, Italy, the Netherlands, Portugal, Romania and Spain - decided to mobilise their joint forces to help bolster Afghanistan's police force in response to a proposal by France. See Federiga Bindi, 'Europe's Problematic Contribution to Police Training in Afghanistan', Brookings Institution, 4 May 2009.

ANP.[10] Spain is currently considering the secondment of specialists of the *Guardia Civil* on crime prevention and prosecution to the Afghan Minister of the Interior and Germany is about to expand its SSR personnel in the country. While these pro-grammes offer a significant contribution to police reform, it is important to achieve better coordination of these initiatives with EUPOL's efforts in the planning and implementation phases.

As to EU inter-institutional relations, some observers have considered the links be-tween the EUSR office and EUPOL as 'tenuous', and the European Commission programmes formulated and implemented 'separate' from EUPOL efforts. While all three institutions sit on the IPCB, 'there is little sense of who directs policy.'[11] At the same time, EU personnel from different institutions acknowledge that mutual relations are steadily improving.[12] In addition, there has been a discrepancy between the significant funds the Commission administers and the inability of EUPOL to finance even minor renovation work in the field in which it is deployed. In fact, one of the main challenges of the mission is to meaningfully mentor and advise ANP commanders while it gets daily requests to contribute to solve basic problems such as fixing the roof of a police station. Although officials from EUPOL and the Commission Delegation as well as the EUSR are well aware of the problem, not much progress has been achieved so far to better match the Commission financial resources and EUPOL's expertise and political profile in security sector reform.[13]

Conclusion

The EU has struggled to find common ground in Afghanistan. Political differenc-es between EU Member States have resulted in a piecemeal approach to the coun-try – the last contribution being the recently launched EU Electoral Observation Mission, under the direction of General Morillon.[14] EUPOL has suffered from a lack of consensus in Brussels, delayed deployment and recruitment shortages, and a challenging mandate that has not proven fully in tune with actual circumstances

10. For example, Italy's contribution in the police sector totals approximately 70 people, mainly *Carabinieri* and *Guardia di Finanza*: 34 *Carabinieri* in Adraskan (Western Afghanistan) train the Afghan National Civil Order Police (ANCOP) in cooperation with CSTC-A; 13 *Guardia di Finanza* officers in Herat train the Afghan Border Police (ABP) and custom officers in cooperation with CSTC-A; and the rest are integrated in EUPOL Afghanistan.

11. International Crisis Group, 'Policing in Afghanistan: Still Searching for a Strategy', *Asia Briefing* no. 85, Kabul/Brussels, 18 December 2008, p.10.

12. Interviews with EU officials from EUPOL, the EUSR office, the Council Secretariat and the Commission, July and September 2009.

13. It should be noted, however, that EUPOL's ability to finance some projects has improved since it can now con-duct some small-scale initiatives (e.g. delivery of equipment).

14. For an assessment of the EU contribution and proposals for enhancing it, see Daniel Korski, 'Shaping Europe's Afghan Surge', *Policy Brief*, European Council on Foreign Relations, March 2009.

on the ground. The operation has not managed to channel or better coordinate existing EU Member States' activities in Afghanistan, and the deployment of national resources outside EUPOL has been progressing. 150 French *Gendarmes*, 240 *Carabinieri* and smaller contingents from other European countries in the framework of the European Gendarmerie Force are expected to be deployed in the autumn within the new NTM-A mission. Nor has EUPOL managed to escape the traditional tensions between the different representatives of the Brussels institutions in the field. Proposals currently under discussion in Brussels to double-hat the EUSR as head of the European Commission delegation would help improve coordination.

However, since it was entrusted with a set of important tasks by the new Afghan Minister of the Interior in 2008, the mission has demonstrated flexibility in adapting to the complex and not always welcoming framework of international actors on the ground. EUPOL furthermore constitutes a unique example of a multinational civilian-led approach to state building in Afghanistan. In this context, a degree of integration with UNAMA should be considered in order to support effective multilateralism while progressively implementing a civilian police model that is rooted in a broader rule-of-law strategy for Afghanistan. As Javier Solana has recently confirmed in Kabul, EUPOL will continue to focus on civilian police.[15] However, not least with a view to the growing engagement of the US and NATO, its footprint may prove too light to make a clear difference on the ground in the absence of renewed efforts by EU Member States to contribute relevant personnel and to further coordinate their initiatives, and of a stronger political drive to make different police reform programmes more complementary.

BIBLIOGRAPHY

Bindi, Federiga. 'Europe's Problematic Contribution to Police Training in Afghanistan', Brookings Institution, 4 May 2009.

Chilton, Scott, Schiewek, Eckart and Bremmers, Tim. 'Evaluation of the appropriate size of the Afghan National Police Force Manning List (Tashkil)', Final Report, European Commission Contrat no. 2009/207401 – Version 1, Kabul, 15 July 2009.

---

15. Notes taken by the author at the press conference by Javier Solana, EU High Representative for CFSP, Kabul, 21 July 2009.

Gross, Eva. 'Security Sector Reform in Afghanistan: the EU's contribution', *Occasional Paper* no. 78, EU Institute for Security Studies, Paris, April 2009.

International Crisis Group, 'Policing in Afghanistan: Still Searching for a Strategy', *Asia Briefing* no. 85, Kabul/Brussels, 18 December 2008.

Korski, Daniel. 'Shaping Europe's Afghan Surge', *Policy Brief*, European Council on Foreign Relations, March 2009.

Rosen, Frederik. 'Third Generation Civil-Military Relations and the "New Revolution in Military Affairs"', *DIIS Working Paper*, March 2009.

Wilder, Andrew. 'Cops or Robbers? The Struggle to Reform the Afghan National Police', AREU, *Issues* Paper Series, July 2007.

20. EUFOR Tchad/RCA

The EU military operation in the Republic of Chad and in the Central African Republic (Operation EUFOR Tchad/RCA)

Damien Helly

Legal basis: Council Joint Action 2007/677/CFSP of 15 October 2007.

Highlights of the mission's mandate:

■ To contribute to protecting civilians in danger, particularly refugees and displaced persons.

■ To facilitate the delivery of humanitarian aid and the free movement of humanitarian personnel by helping to improve security in the area of operations.

■ To contribute to protecting United Nations personnel, facilities, installations and equipment and to ensuring the security and freedom of movement of its own staff and United Nations and associated personnel.

Duration: 15 March 2008-15 March 2009.

Budget: Around €120 million for common costs and nearly €1 billion (estimate) in total.

Mission strength: 3,700.

Contributiong states: 23 contributing Member States (all but Denmark, Estonia, Latvia and Malta) and 3 third states (Russia, Albania, Croatia).

Background

Chad has been at war since 1964. Instability on the Chad-Sudan-CAR borders is linked to the presence of groups living across them while being involved (directly or not) in various types of violence. The first massive flows of refugees from Darfur started to cross the border with Chad in 2003-2004. As of 2006, conflicts linked to the Chadian internal political crisis and local grievances between ethnic groups worsened the humanitarian situation.[1] Attacks from Sudanese (sometimes via the Central African Republic) and Chadian armed groups and Janjaweed militias against specific ethnic communities, the use of certain camps in Chad for recruitment of combatants and child soldiers, combined with banditism and impunity, led international organisations and NGOs to call for an international intervention to restore security in the area.

France had been trying since 2006 to find a way to address the consequences of the Darfur humanitarian crisis. Since it would have been difficult and counterproductive to intervene directly in Darfur at the time when the UN was about to reach an agreement with the government of Sudan on the deployment of an UN-AU operation, one alternative was to act on the margin of Darfur, i.e. in the neighbouring region of Chad where around 400,000 refugees and displaced people had fled.[2]

Initial proposals to engage the EU in Chad were made on 21 May 2007 by the French foreign affairs ministry and led to a joint Commission-Council Secretariat options paper on 13 July 2007. Following the 23 July GAERC meeting, a Crisis Management Concept (CMC) was prepared by the Council Secretariat and a Joint Planning Group relying mostly on the French planning capacity (*Centre de planification et de conduite des opérations* - CPCO) was set up.[3] The CMC was adopted on 12 September by the

---

1. For more details on historical facts, see International Crisis Group, 'Chad: A New Conflict Resolution Framework', *Africa Report* no. 144, Brussels, 24 September 2008, pp. 25-8.

2. UNHCR figures are about 235,000 refugees as of 31 December 2007 in Eastern Chad. This figure does not include IDPs. See: http://www.reliefweb.int.

3. On the initial planning phase, see Alexander Mattelaer, 'The Strategic Planning of EU Military. Operations - The Case of EUFOR TCHAD / RCA', *IES Working Paper* no. 5, 2008.

Council. The French diplomatic machinery was then mobilised to convince European partners as well as reluctant Chadian authorities to engage in and contribute to a new ESDP operation. The acceptance of EUFOR was based on a degree of political ambiguity: on the one hand, President Déby, a controversial leader propped up by France,[4] believed EUFOR would protect him against Sudan-backed rebel attacks, and on the other Paris convinced European partners that the force would remain 'neutral and impartial.' In the meantime, a UN resolution was being drafted and a force generation process had started painstakingly, with very few Member States (France, Ireland, Poland) willing to contribute significant (in absolute or relative terms) troops and resources.

Mandate and deployment

The joint action referred to UN Security Council Resolution 1778 of 25 September 2007 and was adopted on 15 October. It established the OHQ in Mont Valérien (France) and appointed Lieutenant General Patrick Nash (Ireland) as Operation Commander and Brigadier General Jean-Philippe Ganascia (France) as Force Commander based in Abéché. The mandate, given in Resolution 1778, was complementary to the UN Mission to Central African Republic and Chad (MINURCAT) and was threefold: (i) to contribute to protecting civilians in danger, particularly refugees and internally-displaced-persons (IDPs); (ii) to facilitate the delivery of humanitarian aid and the free movement of humanitarian personnel by helping to improve security in the area of operations; (iii) to contribute to protecting United Nations personnel, facilities, installations and equipment and to ensuring the security and freedom of movement of its staff and United Nations and associated personnel (estimated at around a couple of hundred).[5]

The Concept of Operation (CONOPS) adopted on 12 November 2007 by the Council, was followed by five force generation conferences during which it proved most difficult to get the required sufficient number of troops and critical enablers. France, at the fifth meeting, and despite its preference to limit its contribution, had to increase it by providing half of the troops, tactical air transportation and logistics assets. Italy provided a field hospital.

The Initiating Military Directive (IMD) and the CONOPS mandated the force to create a Safe and Secure Environment (SASE) and to remain impartial and neutral. The IMD and the statement of requirement identified the need for ten companies

---

4. Chad: 'A New Conflict Resolution Framework', op. cit. in note 1.
5. Broad estimates, based on interview with Council staff member, 16 July 2009.

(over three battalions), tactical transport capability and reconnaissance assets.[6] Nine companies were provided and deployed progressively.[7] Special operations forces (Belgium, Sweden, Austria, Ireland and France), a protection force (Finland) and a field hospital (Italy) were to be based in Abéché. Most of the Force Headquarters officers (Force Commander, Chief of Staff, JOC staff, Logistics Officer, political advisor) were French but with key positions occupied by other countries. Some national contingents had national caveats. Capabilities consisted of combat and transport helicopters, tactical transport aircrafts, armoured amphibian vehicles, refuelling and water supply trucks, reconnaissance assets and military containers.[8]

The Operation Plan (OPLAN) was approved and the operation launched by the Council on 28 January 2008. Three Status of Force Agreements (SOFAs) legalising and regulating the action of EU troops were signed with Chad, Central African Republic and Cameroon.

Some observers have cited 'serious disagreements over the reference amount for the common costs':[9] from €420 million initially presented to the RELEX group as a first ballpark figure by the Council General Secretariat, negotiations led to a reduction down to €99.2 million and a subsequent increase up to €120 million in January 2008. As of November 2008, overall costs, including bilateral contributions, were estimated at around €1 billion but there is no centralised accounting system to calculate the cost of such an operation.[10]

To date, EUFOR Tchad/RCA is the logistically most complex operation that the ESDP has had to deploy in a landlocked and underdeveloped area located 4,500 km from Brussels, where the average freight delay for a container is 35 to 45 days through a very limited number of bottlenecked land routes via Cameroon or Libya. Water scarcity and the natural fragility of the local environment have also entailed specific efforts for self-sustainability. The main contributing countries (France, Ireland and Poland) flew in and/or shipped their troops and equipment themselves. Troops had to build their own camps on bare land and most of the raw materials for the construction of camps and landing strips had to be imported.[11] Food supply was organised by each battalion,

---

6. For more details on these aspects of the planning, see Alexander Mattelaer, op. cit. in note 3, p. 23.

7. A French logistical battalion in Abéché, an Irish battalion in the South based in Goz Beida with a Dutch section, one French battalion in Forchana (East of Abéché and closer to the border with Sudan) and a detachment in Birao (CAR) and a Polish battalion in Iriba (North), later joined by Croation troops.

8. 13 helicopters were available at the end of 2008 (4 French Pumas and 2 Gazelles, 3 Polish Mi17 and 4 Russian Mi8) and a few large transport aircrafts (1 French A C-160 and 2 Transal, 1 Spanish 235s and 1 Greek C-130).

9. Alexander Mattelaer, op. cit. in note 3, p. 16.

10. Interview with an EU official, Brussels, November 2008.

11. For more figures, see interviews with Lt Gen Nash, 23 June 2008, Radio France International.

except for catering in Abéché 'stars camp' subcontracted by the French logistical body *Economat des Armées* (EDA) to a private company from the Gulf. In Abéché, national contingents had their own facilities and built or brought specific infrastructure depending on national cultural factors and practices.

The European Commission tried to ensure some coherence between the ESDP intervention and its aid package. €30 million were spent annually for humanitarian aid to Sudanese refugees and Chadian IDPs; €10 million from the Instrument for Stability financed the training of a special Chadian police (*Détachement Intégré de Sécurité* – DIS – a joint police and *gendarmerie* force set up to provide security for refugee and IDP camps and humanitarian workers) to intervene in camps in the East; €10 million was committed in January 2008 for a short-term rehabilitation/reconstruction programme (*Programme d'Accompagnement à la Stabilisation* – PAS) to accompany the ESDP operation. Under the 10th European Development Fund (EDF), governance programme funds were pledged for the reform of internal security forces (€25 million) and penitentiary and justice reform (€28 million) yet questions about the country's absorption capacity and political readiness remained.[12]

Implementation and performance

The operation got off to a perilous start when its deployment was called into question following a rebel attack against N'Djamena on 3 February.[13] After the rebels were defeated by Déby thanks to intelligence and medical support from the long-established French *Epervier* operation in Chad,[14] deployment could restart in mid-February. Troops had to prove the value-added of ESDP by deploying as quickly as possible, setting up defence infrastructure, paving the ground for a smooth handover to a UN follow-on force, and successfully protecting civilians, including IDPs.

However, UN work with the DIS to ensure Law and Order, which was supposed to complement EUFOR, was dramatically delayed due to slow cooperation, if not downright obstruction, from the Chadian authorities. This left EUFOR with no

12. France and Germany's water programmes were also instrumental in supporting communities in the East and prevent conflicts. Interviews with EC staff, Brussels, April 2008, and European and Chadian representatives, N'Djamena, 9-13 November 2008.

13. Some rebels feared EUFOR would be an ally of Déby against them. EU Presidency Statement on the Republic of Chad, 3 February 2008 and 'Le déploiement de l'EUFOR reprend', EUFOR Tchad/RCA press communiqué, 12 February 2008.

14. See: http://www.defense.gouv.fr. Epervier is an operation deployed in the framework of the 1976 bilateral defence agreement between France and Chad. French support to Chad was legitimised by the 4 February UN Security Council Statement S/PRST/2008/3 calling upon 'Members States to provide support, in conformity with the United Nations Charter, as requested by the Government of Chad.' See also 'Obscénité franco-tchadienne', *Le Monde*, 13 February 2009.

choice but to use military deterrence against two main threats: possible Janjaweed attacks as well as banditry and crime, the latter often originating from regular Chadian security forces or volatile Zaghawa armed groups benefiting from ethnically based impunity.[15]

As of May, there was a growing awareness of the need to develop closer cooperation with the diverse and numerous humanitarian community[16] through weekly meetings, the organisation of joint convoys and strong information-sharing channels through enhanced civil-military cooperation (CIMIC). The troops and the humanitarian community had to learn mutual recognition by respecting each other's space and methods.[17]

After initial statements about its non-interference in internal politics,[18] June 2008 was a key occasion for the operation to clearly demonstrate in Goz Beida that it would not interfere in clashes between rebel groups and the Chadian National Army (ANT). However, since tensions also impacted on the security of humanitarian workers (equipment and vehicles were robbed or destroyed), Irish and Dutch troops had to evacuate around 300 staff under threat.

EU-UN cooperation, which intensified with the mid-term review process (which, among its other objectives, aimed at planning the hand-over), reflected the strategic ambiguities mentioned above. From the start, some in the UN Department of Peacekeeping Operations (UN DPKO) had expressed resistance to the very idea of a peacekeeping operation in Eastern Chad on the grounds that conditions identified by the Brahimi Report (a peace to keep, firm commitments of troops, clarity of mandate and instructions) were not met.[19] The Chadian authorities, who probably feared that an increased international presence would limit their margin of manoeuvre, were also hard to convince.[20]

---

15. As an illustration, see France 24 report and interview with the Force Commander, 28 September 2008, available at: http://www.france24.com/fr/20080928-limites-mandat-eufor-tchad-soudan-darfour. For more details on the Zaghawa, the group of President Déby, Jérôme Tubiana, 'The Chad–Sudan Proxy War and the "Darfurization" of Chad: Myths and Reality', *Small Arms Survey*, HSBA Working Paper no. 12, 16 April 2008.

16. The death of one aid worker from Save the Children on 1 May 2008 could not be prevented. Around 50 humanitarian organisations and agencies were active. Phone interview with UN OCHA staff, 22 July 2008.

17. 'Document de référence. Structures et mécanismes de coordination civilo-militaire lors du mandat d'EUFOR Tchad/RCA', 16 March 2008, signed by Brig. General Ganascia and OCHA coordinator Kingsley Amaning.

18. Summary of Remarks by Lt General Patrick Nash, Operation Commander EUFOR Tchad/RCA, Press Conference, Brussels, 29 January 2008. See: www.consilium.europa.eu.

19. Report of the Panel on United Nations Peace Operations, 2000. See: http://www.un.org/peace/reports/peace_operations/

20. For more details on the EU-UN-Chadian negotiations on the UN follow-on force, Winrich Kuehne, 'How the EU Organizes and Conducts Peace Operations in Africa: EUFOR/MINURCAT', *ZIF Report* 0309, Berlin, 13 March 2009.

UN DPKO and the UN Police (UNPOL) were struggling to obtain Chadian support on the training of the DIS while the force generation process to enlarge MINUR-CAT also proved hesitant.[21] It soon appeared that a smooth hand-over to MINUR-CAT would not happen without a significant 're-hatting' of EUFOR troops, which eventually took place on 15 March 2009. Significant Polish, Irish and French presence was maintained temporarily on the ground together with smaller contingents (Finland, Austria, Croatia). Brigadier General Gerald Aherne from Ireland was appointed as Deputy Force Commander of MINURCAT under the command of Major General Elhadji Mahamadou Kandji from Senegal, and a large part of the UN FHQ, including his Swedish Chief of Staff, was composed of European officers. Other troops (Togo, Ghana, Norway) have slowly taken over in the course of 2009.[22]

At the end of the mandate, there seemed to be a consensus that the operation had proceeded without major difficulties or incidents and contributed, where its soldiers patrolled and were present, to a safer environment and a certain 'sense of security' among both the population and the humanitarian community. This was partly acknowledged by NGOs like OXFAM and International Crisis Group, who initially called for the operation to be launched but remained critical of a weak foreign policy regarding human rights and democratisation.[23] Overall and with few exceptions, humanitarian organisations and UN agencies expressed their satisfaction with EUFOR's security performance and showed concerns that its departure would create a security vacuum.[24] In total, over 2,500 short-range patrols in the immediate environment and 260 long-range patrols were carried out during the period of full operational capability.[25] The operation has also provided an important 'contribution in kind' with the construction of six military camps handed over to the UN with the consent of the Chadian authorities to whom infrastructures would eventually be returned after MINURCAT's departure.[26]

---

21. Part of DIS training, deployment, procurement and activity (community policing) was financed by the European Commission. Around 900 guns were provided by France but it was unclear how these arms would be stored, and their usage managed and controlled. Cars were provided by the UN although DIS Command and UN Police considered that they were inadequate for the task. Interviews, Abéché and N'Djamena, 9-13 November 2008.

22. See: http://www.un.org/Depts/dpko/missions/minurcat/facts.html.

23. International Crisis Group, op. cit. in note 1; Oxfam, 'Mission incomplete: why civilians remain at risk in eastern Chad', Briefing Paper, September 2008. Amnesty International has denounced Chad's human rights violations during and after the February 2008 crisis: Amnesty International Report, 'Double malheur, aggravation de la crise des droits humains au Tchad', December 2008.

24. Interviews with humanitarian aid representatives from OCHA, Oxfam, MSF France, Abéché and N'Djamena, 9-13 November 2008. One ICRC (International Committee of the Red Cross) staff member was saved by EUFOR hospital. In November 2008, NGO personnel was evacuated by helicopter from Ouandja in the Central African Republic.

25. EUFOR OHQ Tchad RCA, Operation Eufor Tchad/RCA, Booklet, 'Patrols' (undated).

26. The UN, as a result of its negotiations with the Chadian government, took over four out of six EUFOR sites with their infrastructure and was to build extra airport parking space for its own use. Report of the Secretary-General on the United Nations Mission in the Central African Republic and Chad, S/2009/199, 14 April 2009.

Challenges

The operation generated several political and operational debates. Some ambiguities lingered regarding the objectives of the operation and several positions could be identified, beyond an overall consensus on the need to deploy ESDP in Africa at an unprecedented level. Some contributing countries (like the UK or Germany), who probably would have preferred not to act at all, gave their green light for a short bridging mission without being fully convinced of the foreign policy rationale. France's intentions were unclear to many European partners who feared Paris would use the European flag to mask a policy aimed at supporting an authoritarian regime.[27] In France itself, the soundness of the operation was contested internally.[28] Paris's justification for the mission was based on a mix of hopes that the operation would maintain the *status quo* in Chad between the government and the rebels backed by Sudan (which eventually happened in May 2009 when Déby defeated the rebels) while effectively protecting populations in the East and thereby indirectly addressing the Darfur crisis. Many (Austria, Finland, Sweden, Ireland), who had a genuine interest in acting on the margin of Darfur and in promoting ESDP but feared being dragged into a mere regime protection measure, insisted on the neutrality and the impartiality of the force. This debate proved to be essential when in June 2008 the mandate and the rules of engagement had to be interpreted in the light of rebels' offensives in Goz Beida.

On the ground several debates sprung up regarding the return of IDPs and civil-military activities. Strong French diplomatic pressure was aimed at obtaining substantial IDP returns to prove the success of the operation.[29] This objective led to a debate on the appropriateness of encouraging the return of IDPs to areas that were not yet secured, and on the difficulty of using and verifying statistics in such a volatile and complex context. Such a policy was opposed by the humanitarian community and forced the military to engage in a deep and ultimately fruitful dialogue with non-military actors on the ground. As a result, EUFOR FHQ and the humanitarian actors agreed to limit the number and scope of return-related CIMIC projects implemented.

---

27. Charlemagne, 'Colonial baggage', *The Economist*, 7 February 2008.

28. 'Au Tchad, l'Eufor est désormais associée à un processus de liquidation de l'opposition démocrate', 'Interactive web interview with Jean-François Bayart on www.lemonde.fr', 14 February 2009; Jean-François Bayart, 'Le Baiser de la mort', *La Croix*, 19 March 2008 ; 'Au Tchad, la Force européenne reste neutre', *Le Monde*, 19 June 2008; Interview, Ministry of Defence official, Paris, 6 June 2008.

29. 'Chad: A New Conflict Resolution Framework', op. cit. in note 1, p. 34.

Despite efforts by Brussels staff in the planning phase, the cooperation between ESDP and the European Commission has been disappointingly sub-optimal because of a combination of unfortunate factors. The delegation of the Commission partly shared some of the humanitarian community's concerns regarding the role of EUFOR and, while in charge of supporting internal political dialogue, viewed the military operation with some mistrust. The strained relationship between the Force Commander and the EC Head of Delegation, who only started to cooperate at the very end of EUFOR's mandate, did not favour coherence either. Expected synergies between the PAS and EUFOR have thus developed slowly but the programme started to be implemented late 2008 and went on after the re-hatting of EUFOR.[30]

Lessons learned

The mandate of EUFOR Tchad/RCA was the result of a compromise between Member States pushing a variety of agendas. The rather strong mandate focused on civilian and aid workers protection, with clearly defined rules of engagement, but did not provide the mission with enough guidance and strength to manage initial political ambiguities. From a broader CFSP perspective, to say the least, the EU has not obtained any progress in the internal Chadian political dialogue and on democratisation. Relations between Chad and Sudan have not particularly improved either. More generally, this raises questions about the political profile of ESDP operations and how can EU policy considerations be more strongly linked to ESDP planning and operations. In the case of EUFOR Tchad/RCA, synergies and coherence between the ESDP operation, French diplomatic representation and the EU Special Representatives could have been optimised, through a more permanent and appropriate EU political presence in Chad.[31]

Another lesson to be learned is that the clearer the policy objectives are, the easier they can be communicated to the media and the public. With approximately 400 media personnel visiting the area of operation, EUFOR Tchad/RCA confirmed the absolute necessity for the EU to have at its disposal strong external communication and media teams able to coordinate with all EU players with a view to communicating externally in a consistent and effective manner.[32]

---

30. Interviews, EC and EUFOR staff, N'Djamena and Brussels, 11 November 2008 and 13 May 2009.

31. Ambassador Torben Brylle, from Denmark, has been EUSR for Sudan and his mandate was broadened to Eastern Chad on 12 February 2008. Ambassador Georg Lennkh, from Austria, was the EU Presidency Special Representative in charge of Chadian internal political dialogue. In practice the EU rotating presidency has mostly been represented locally by France.

32. General Nash's press conference, Brussels, 18 March 2009. See: www.consilium.europa.eu.

The operation's added value, however, is probably to have clarified, for European chancelleries and European public opinion, the nature of challenges inside Chad (state violence and rebellion, impunity, local ethnic and land-related conflicts) and in the region (the proxy war between Khartoum and N'Djamena and the violence in Darfur). This in turn should hopefully strengthen European foreign policy in the region.

As for coordination with other international organisations, new modes of coordination were set up at all levels between the EU (mainly DGE VIII, OHQ and FHQ, European Commission) and the UN (DPKO, Support office, UNPOL, office of the Special Representative of the Secretary General - SRSG). Contradictions between the EU and the UN emerged frequently during the coordination process and affected the mid-term review and the handover process, but they did not hamper joint work during which, at times, both organisations had to agree to disagree. Beyond certain disagreements, EU-UN coordination has deepened and reached unprecedented levels, and put new procedures in place that will be available for future joint operations.

The whole concept of intervention, as negotiated with Chad, was a hybrid set-up combining EU and UN interventions based on the idea of a bridging operation. It proved difficult to implement efficiently. The EU was expected to provide a military umbrella in the East to civilians, the humanitarian community, UN staff and police as well as UN-trained Chadian DIS. On paper, the components of this hybrid set-up were supposed to start their work simultaneously, but this did not happen due to the serious delays mentioned above. This experience raises questions about the mechanisms required for efficient future hybrid EU-UN formulas so as to avoid planning and deployment disconnects. Early definitive commitment of the follow-on force seems key in that respect. As for the bridging function, it would not have worked in this particular case without the significant (although temporary) re-hatting of EU contingents until the arrival of UN follow-on troops. In April 2009, there were still 817 French, 405 Irish, 316 Polish, 112 Austrians, 65 Finnish and several other European personnel deployed in Eastern Chad under the UN banner.

EUFOR Tchad/RCA was an important experience and highly instructive for ESDP. It has demonstrated once again that the EU could successfully project several thousand troops away from Europe without NATO, to carry out Petersberg tasks, including combat if need be, in coordination with the United Nations where necessary.

In theatre, their participation in the operation encouraged contributing countries to support each other on behalf of collective European objectives. Once the operation was launched, the initial reservations and ambiguities were not revealed in public and there was a convergence of efforts to optimise the conduct of the operation. This happened for instance with the use of national caveats. On several occasions some contingents referred to last-minute national caveats which prevented them from implementing certain missions ordered by the Force Commander. These tensions, rather usual in multinational operations, were not made public. They could have been avoided if more clarity had existed earlier on among contributing states about their respective caveats. In the future, it would be useful to anticipate and clarify issues around national caveats at the planning stage to avoid delays and internal tensions.

The framework nation concept proved effective with French troops being the backbone of the operation. The presence of other armies created a genuine inter-cultural environment where joint work between Europeans (especially among officers) resulted in inter-individual and multi-cultural learning processes which will eventually contribute to create an embryonic European military culture.[33]

While strategic airlift capabilities were ensured through internal cooperation between contributors, tactical air assets proved more problematic. It took months to obtain a limited number of additional transport helicopters – thanks to, among others, a contribution from Russia[34] – to complement a small and overstretched fleet constantly exposed to harsh climate conditions.

There is room for improvement in intelligence sharing and centralisation. Perhaps more coordination could have been achieved between national intelligence channels operating in theatre but the use of French assets from the *Epervier* operation remained sensitive because of the European force's neutral status. More unmanned equipment as well as more numerous special forces able to gather intelligence in sensitive areas would, like in any operation, have been welcome, in addition to available satellite imagery provided by SatCen. This being said, the data gathered by EUFOR and handed over to MINURCAT is rather substantial.

Lessons learned should also focus on the use of local resources by the operation and the way EU forces should communicate about it. Water scarcity and management,

---

33. Interviews with various members of EUFOR contingents, Stars Camp, Abéché, 10-13 November 2008.

34. The Russian contribution, delivered after its war against Georgia, was slightly controversial in Brussels but cooperation in theatre proved excellent. Interviews, EUFOR and Council staff, Brussels, 3 June and 20 July 2009.

for instance, are certainly challenges to be addressed by using adequate technologies while remaining aware of the impact on the perceptions of the local population.[35]

The Eastern Chad experience also required some flexibility and context-sensitive approaches in Civilian-Military Cooperation (CIMIC). More dialogue engagement with the humanitarian community as early as during the planning phase and early deployment is crucial in order to establish smooth working relations from day one.

In a context of economic downturn and lack of enthusiasm from other Member States, France had to agree to be the main financial (shouldering probably 80% of the total costs) and troop contributor. This predominant French role raises a fundamental question: are ESDP military operations, in Africa and elsewhere, possible without France acting as the main initiator and framework nation?

Given its size, the diversity of troops contributors, the complexity of the challenges, and the degree of cooperation with the UN, EUFOR Tchad/RCA is going to remain a milestone in the development of ESDP. It remains to be seen how and when its experience will inspire future missions in Africa and beyond.

BIBLIOGRAPHY

Amnesty International. 'Double malheur, aggravation de la crise des droits humains au Tchad', December 2008.

Brahimi, Lakhdar et al. Report of the Panel on United Nations Peace Operations, A/55/502, United Nations, New York, August 2000.

International Crisis Group. 'Chad: A New Conflict Resolution Framework', Crisis Group *Africa Report* no. 144, 24 September 2008.

Kuehne, Winrich. 'How the EU Organizes and Conducts Peace Operations in Africa: EUFOR / MINURCAT', *ZIF (Zentrum für Internationale Friedenseinsätze) Report*, Berlin, March 2009.

---

35. In Abéché Stars Camp, the Austrian contingent used a water recycling system and allegedly consumed 4 times less than other troops. The sometimes excessive use of water by troops was also witnessed by Chadian staff, well aware of water scarcity difficulties. Water recycling systems were also used by the Irish in Goz Beida.

Mattelaer, Alexander. 'The Strategic Planning of EU Military. Operations – The Case of EUFOR TCHAD/RCA', *IES Working Paper* no. 5, 2008.

Oxfam. 'Mission incomplete: why civilians remain at risk in eastern Chad', *Briefing Paper*, September 2008.

Seibert, Bjoern H. 'African Adventure? Assessing the European Union's Military Intervention in Chad and Central African Republic', MIT Security Studies Program Working Paper, November 2007.

Tubiana, Jérôme. 'The Chad–Sudan Proxy War and the "Darfurization" of Chad: Myths and Reality', Small Arms Survey HSBA *Working Paper* no. 12, 16 April 2008.

21. EULEX Kosovo

The EU rule-of-law mission in Kosovo (EULEX Kosovo)

Giovanni Grevi

Legal basis: Council Joint Action 2008/124/CFSP of 4 February 2008.

Highlights of the mission's mandate:

■ Assist the Kosovo institutions, judicial authorities and law enforcement agencies in their progress towards sustainability and accountability and in further developing an independent multi-ethnic justice system and multi-ethnic police and customs service, free from political interference and adhering to international standards and European best practices. EULEX shall carry out monitoring, mentoring and advising while retaining certain executive responsibilities.

■ Ensure the maintenance and promotion of the rule of law, public order and security.

■ Ensure that cases of war crimes, terrorism, organised and serious crime are properly investigated, adjudicated and enforced.

■ Contribute to the fight against corruption, fraud and financial crime.

Duration: 9 December 2008 to date (operational phase).

Budget: €265 million from February 2008 to June 2010.

Mission strength: In September 2009, 1,642 international staff and 1,000 local staff. Envisaged full mission strength: 1,900 international staff and 1,100 local staff.

Contributing states: 26 Member States (all but Cyprus) and 6 third countries (Canada, Croatia, Norway, Switzerland, Turkey and the United States).

Background and context

EULEX Kosovo was deployed and entered its operational phase under very difficult political conditions. A brief overview of the events that culminated in Kosovo's declaration of independence on 17 February 2008 seems in order to grasp the complexity of the political context of this mission. The Milosevic regime abolished the autonomous status of the Kosovo province within Serbia in 1989 and implemented discriminatory policies against the Albanian majority in Kosovo. With no political solution in sight, simmering tensions broke out into civil war between the Kosovo Liberation Army and the (then) Yugoslav army in 1998. In spring 1999 a NATO bombing campaign drove Serbian troops, responsible for large-scale abuses against the Albanian population, out of Kosovo. The UN Security Council (UNSC) Resolution 1244 of 10 June 1999 established that an international civilian and security presence would be deployed in this territory under UN auspices. NATO took over the military security dimension and deployed the 60,000-strong KFOR operation, which remains on the ground today albeit scaled back to around 15,000 personnel. The UN Interim Administration Mission in Kosovo (UNMIK), under the authority of a Special Representative of the UN Secretary General (SRSG), was mandated to take charge of the interim civilian administration of Kosovo.[1]

UNMIK's mandate was unprecedented in scope and depth, as it extended not only to promoting substantial autonomy and self-government in Kosovo, to performing basic civilian administrative functions and to maintaining law and order, but also to facilitating the political process designed to determine the future status of Kosovo.[2] Over the years, UNMIK has set up provisional institutions of self-government and progressively transferred competences to them. The so-called 'standards-before-status' approach driving these reform efforts since 2002 allowed some progress but could not substitute for the need for a political perspective on the future of Kosovo.

---

1. United Nations Security Council, Resolution 1244, 10 June 1999.

2. In short, the mandate was at the same time broad, executive, highly political and somewhat ambiguous. While the mission was given the greatest authority on the ground, from a legal standpoint the sovereignty and the territorial integrity of the (then) Federal Republic of Yugoslavia were not put into question. For broader considerations on the nature of UNMIK's mandate and on the first years of its implementation, see Alexandros Yannis, 'The UN as Government in Kosovo', *Global Governance* no. 10, 2004.

The absence of the latter precluded real local ownership of reforms and hampered sustainable progress towards self-government.[3]

With a view to unblocking the political stalemate, in November 2005 the UN Secretary General tasked former Finnish President Martti Ahtisaari with exploring the options to settle the future status of Kosovo and report on the matter. This mandate opened a process of two years of intensive negotiations, under the overall guidance of the Contact Group including France, Germany, Italy, Russia, the UK and the US.[4] In parallel to the start of this process, within the EU, the Council of Ministers welcomed in December 2005 a joint report by the High Representative Solana and Commissioner Rehn on 'The future EU role and contribution in Kosovo' that envisaged, among many other measures, the need to prepare for a possible integrated ESDP mission in Kosovo in the field of rule of law. An EU Planning Team meant to pave the way for this mission was set up in Pristina in April 2006.[5]

The Ahtisaari package was unveiled in March 2007. The Report recommended 'supervised independence' as the only viable option for Kosovo and included in annex a 'Comprehensive proposal for the Kosovo status settlement' outlining the key principles underpinning independence and the structures supervising it.[6] Crucially, under this plan, an International Civilian Representative (ICR) double-hatted as EU Special Representative (EUSR) was to supervise the implementation of the settlement agreement and to be endowed with 'strong corrective powers' to that end, along the lines of those attributed to the Office of the High Representative in Bosnia. It was also envisaged that an ESDP mission would 'mentor, monitor and advise on all areas related to the rule of law in Kosovo' and be invested with limited executive authority in the fields of justice, police and borders.

Serbia strenuously opposed this set of recommendations and Russia threatened to veto any attempt by the UNSC to endorse it. Consequently, the UNSC dispatched a US-EU-Russia diplomatic troika led by German Ambassador Wolfgang Ischinger in

---

3. Oisín Tansey, 'Kosovo: independence and tutelage', *Journal of Democracy*, vol. 20, no. 2, April 2009. See also Andreas Heinemann-Grüder and Igor Grebenschikov, 'Security governance by internationals: The case of Kosovo', *International Peacekeeping*, vol. 13, no. 1, March 2006.

4. For an exhaustive analysis of this process, see Marc Weller, 'Negotiating the final status of Kosovo', *Chaillot Paper* no. 114, EU Institute for Security Studies, Paris, December 2008.

5. Joint Report by Javier Solana, EU High Representative for CFSP, and Olli Rehn, EU Commissioner for enlargement, 'The future EU role and contribution in Kosovo', 6 December 2005. Council Joint Action 2006/304/CFSP of 10 April 2006 on the establishment of an EU Planning Team (EUPT Kosovo) regarding a possible EU crisis management operation in the field of rule of law and possible other areas in Kosovo, *Official Journal* L 112/18, 26 April 2004.

6. Letter of the UN Secretary General to the President of the Security Council, UN doc. S/2007/168, 26 March 2007. The letter accompanied the Report of the Special Envoy of the Secretary General on Kosovo's Future Status' and the 'Comprehensive Proposal for the Kosovo Status Settlement', UN doc. S/2007/168/Add.1.

an attempt to bring the parties to an agreement by the end of 2007. Following the failure of the troika to identify a consensual solution, the road was open to the unilateral declaration of independence by Pristina on 17 February 2008. On 4 February, the EU Council had adopted the joint action establishing EULEX Kosovo and had appointed the senior Dutch diplomat Pieter Feith as EUSR in Kosovo.[7] On the day after the declaration of independence, the Council noted that EU Member States 'will decide in accordance with national practice and international law, on their relations with Kosovo'.[8] In short, while consensus could be achieved within the Union to launch an ESDP operation mandated to reform and support Kosovo's rule-of-law institutions, Member States diverged on the recognition of Kosovo as an independent state. To date, 62 countries have recognised Kosovo, 22 of which from within the EU. However five EU Member States, namely Cyprus, Greece, Romania, Slovakia and Spain, have not.

Planning and mandate: the assumptions-reality gap

In January 2006, the EU dispatched a joint Council-Commission Fact Finding Mission (FFM) to Kosovo to explore the scope for an ESDP mission in the field of rule of law. The FFM recommended that the EU set up a planning team to prepare a possible integrated rule-of-law mission, potentially encompassing the justice, police and customs dimensions. When the European Union Planning Team (EUPT) for Kosovo was set up in April 2006, the EU and its Member States based their approach on a set of assumptions. They expected that the negotiations on the future status of Kosovo would end by late 2006/early 2007, that under the new terms of a consensual agreement UNMIK would withdraw and that the UNSC would request the EU to replace the UN mission in the field of rule of law.

The EUPT grew to include a staff of 80 international and 55 local staff and was divided into a justice team, a police team and an administration team. It was mandated to initiate planning to ensure a smooth transition between selected tasks of UNMIK and a possible ESDP operation.[9] EUPT worked alongside the separate EU

---

7. Council Joint Action 2008/124/CFSP of 4 February 2008 on the European Union Rule of Law Mission in Kosovo, EULEX Kosovo, *Official Journal* L 42/92, 16 February 2008 and Council Joint Action 2008/123/CFSP of 4 February 2008 appointing a European Union Special Representative in Kosovo, *Official Journal* L 42/88, 16 February 2008.

8. External Relations Council meeting, Brussels, 18 February 2008, 6496/08 (Presse 41).

9. That included the progressive definition of the mandate, objectives and tasks of the ESDP mission to come and of related requirements in terms of personnel, procurement, logistics and mission security. See Council Joint Action 2006/304/CFSP, op. cit. in note 6, Articles 1 and 2.

team charged with preparing the setting up of the ICO/EUSR office.[10] In its September 2006 report, the EUPT presented Member States with three options regarding the future mission's strength – light, medium (800/900 international officials) and robust – as a basis for discussion. The work of the EUPT was based on yet another assumption, namely that the future mission would very much focus on tasks of monitoring, mentoring and advising through extensive co-location of international officials in local structures, and would limit executive powers to the minimum. The purpose was to transfer responsibility and ownership as swiftly as possible to local authorities, put them in the 'driver's seat' and build stronger local capacity.

The mandate of EULEX, eventually adopted in February 2008, is vast. The central aim of EULEX is to assist and support Kosovo's institutions, judicial authorities and law enforcement agencies in becoming more sustainable and accountable, developing into inter-ethnic services and acting independently from political interference and according to best international and European standards.[11] In this perspective, the mission was to monitor, mentor and advise relevant authorities, ensure public order, fight against corruption, fraud and financial crime and ensure that all serious crime cases would be properly investigated and prosecuted. In performing these tasks, the mission was attributed some circumscribed executive powers in the police and judicial fields. These included carrying out sensitive investigations, conducting prosecution and running trials, as well as overruling where necessary the decisions of local authorities. Of course, the ability of the mission to implement this ambitious mandate largely depended on the political circumstances surrounding its deployment, and those were not favourable.

The postponement of the final phase of the negotiations concerning the status of Kosovo by around one year and its drastic conclusion with the unilateral declaration of independence of Pristina in February 2008 turned many of the original planning assumptions upside down. The declaration of independence stressed its 'full accordance' with the Ahtisaari plan and committed to its implementation. Such a plan, however, had not been endorsed by the UNSC, the independence of Kosovo was firmly opposed by Serbia and Russia (among others) and the Serbian minority in Kosovo (about 6 percent of the population of two million) rejected the declaration of independence. Kosovo Serbs disengaged from participation in public

10. Council Joint Action 2006/623/CFSP of 15 September 2006 on the establishment of a EU-team to contribute to the preparations of the establishment of a possible international civilian mission in Kosovo, including a European Union Special Representative component (ICM/EUSR Preparation Team), *Official Journal* L 253/29, 16 September 2006.

11. See Council Joint Action 2008/124/CFSP, op. cit. in note 8, Articles 2 and 3.

services and began to establish parallel structures of self-government, in particular in the area north of the Ibar river where half of them live.[12] The new state of play had five main, closely inter-related implications for EULEX.

First, the assumption that EULEX would take charge of security sector reform and institution building in the area of rule of law in the wider context of the implementation of the Ahtisaari plan was undermined.[13] Second, the expectation that EULEX would deploy all over Kosovo could not, at first, be fulfilled. North of the Ibar, Kosovo Serbs attacked and destroyed two border points (gates 1 and 31) and in March occupied the court building in Northern Mitrovica, making both customs collection and the exercise of jurisdiction in the North temporarily impossible. Furthermore, Serb-majority municipalities participated in Serbian elections in May and elected new councils outside the Kosovo state jurisdiction. Third, considerable confusion as to the applicable law in police, judicial and customs activities (among other public services) followed political fragmentation. Kosovo Serb authorities insisted on applying the so-called UNMIK law (the legislation adopted under the rule of the SRSG between 1999 and 2007) or earlier Yugoslav codes and regulations, while the new Kosovar authorities enacted fresh legislation in a growing number of fields which was meant to apply country-wide.

Fourth, the expected transition of authority *and* equipment, vehicles, buildings and information from UNMIK to EULEX did not happen. The two missions co-existed uncomfortably side-by-side in the course of 2008 with UNMIK unable to scale down as fast as envisaged and EULEX unable to deploy according to the planned schedule, which led to inevitable frictions. Fifth, the political impasse squeezed the new position of the double-hatted ICR/EUSR and complicated its relations with EULEX. On 28 February, the EUSR Pieter Feith was appointed International Civilian Representative, heading the International Civilian Office (ICO), by a group of 25 like-minded countries (the International Steering Group). The ICR is supposed to assist the Kosovo government with the implementation of Ahtisaari's comprehensive proposal.[14] However, the legality and legitimacy of the ICO are questioned

---

12. For an insightful report of the developments following the declaration of independence by the Kosovo Assembly up to summer 2008, see International Crisis Group, 'Kosovo's Fragile Transition', *Europe Report* no. 196, 25 September 2008.

13. The comprehensive proposal envisaged a transition period of 120 days for the Kosovo Assembly to adopt the new Constitution and relevant legislation in compliance with the proposal. The new Constitution came into force on 15 June and various other laws were adopted. However, the comprehensive proposal itself remained a subject of dispute at the international level and Kosovo Serb municipalities rejected the new legislation.

14. In particular, the ICR has final authority to interpret the civilian aspects of this proposal and to take corrective measures to remedy action taken by Kosovo authorities if need be.

by Serbia and Russia and the UNSG still makes no reference to this office in his reports on the situation in Kosovo. As EUSR, on the other hand, Feith can continue to hold and develop contacts with the parties that do not recognise the ICR authority. Doing so, however, can upset the Pristina authorities and necessitates a difficult, permanent balancing act.

Facing the dilemma of whether to deploy only in parts of Kosovo (Albanian majority areas), with the risk of paving the way towards the eventual split of the country along ethnic divides, or to wait for an improvement of the political context to deploy Kosovo-wide, EULEX entered a period of operational hibernation until December 2008, when initial operational capability was finally declared. The path to this turning point was politically bumpy and paved with considerable ambiguity. In his June report on UNMIK, the UNSG acknowledged the need for a 'recalibrated international presence' to confront the 'new reality in Kosovo'. However, due to the stalemate in the UNSC on the Kosovo status question, he went no further than recognising that the EU would perform an enhanced operational role in the field of rule of law 'under the framework of resolution 1244 (1999) and the overall authority of the UN'.[15] The 'reconfiguration' – or scaling down – of UNMIK was cautiously launched on 26 June but it was only in his November report on UNMIK that the UNSG could note that all parties had accepted the reconfiguration of the international presence in Kosovo and the consequent operational role of EULEX throughout Kosovo. However, it was once again specified that EULEX would respect resolution 1244 and would 'operate under the overall authority and within the status neutral framework of the United Nations'.[16]

In short, resolution 1244 formally remained the legal framework of a mission originally envisaged to help implement the comprehensive proposal that would succeed 1244 itself.[17] This was the somewhat paradoxical political condition that enabled the launch of the mission. The distinctive features of EULEX, the further challenges that confronted the mission and its accomplishments during the first six months of operational activity are illustrated in what follows.

---

15. UN Security Council, Report of the Secretary General on the United Nations Interim Administration Mission in Kosovo, S/2998/354, 12 June 2008.

16. UN Security Council, Report of the Secretary General on the United Nations Interim Administration Mission in Kosovo, S/2008/692, 24 November 2008. Para 21-29 and 48-51.

17. On the legal debate surrounding the legality of EULEX mandate, see Erika de Wet, 'The Governance of Kosovo: Security Council Resolution 1244 and the Establishment and Functioning of EULEX', American Journal of International Law, vol. 103, no. 1, January 2009.

Unique mission: distinctive challenges

EULEX Kosovo is unique in many respects and marks a change of gear in the level of ambition of civilian ESDP. Four distinctive features can be highlighted that single this mission out from all others. First, its sheer size. The work of the EUPT has permitted a realistic estimation of the mission strength required to fulfil the broad mandate of EULEX. Of the three options concerning the scope and size of the mission outlined in September 2006, Member States somewhat reluctantly came to endorse the most demanding one. It is foreseen that, at full strength, EULEX should include 1,900 international and 1,100 local staff. As of September 2009, the mission staff amounted to 1,642 internationals (around 250 of whom contracted) and 1,000 local.[18] Looking at the composition of the mission staff, EULEX is also unique as it is the first ESDP civilian mission including US personnel among other contributions by third countries. 77 American civilian police have been put under EU command in the context of the mission.

Second, as stressed above, the mandate of EULEX is very large and in many ways unprecedented in the context of civilian ESDP. For one, previous operational experience demonstrated that a clear-cut distinction between police and judicial affairs was untenable. EULEX is the first fully integrated rule-of-law mission spanning across the fields of (civil and criminal) justice, police and customs. For another, EULEX is the first civilian mission mandated not only with the traditional tasks of monitoring, mentoring and advising but also with delicate executive tasks, as noted above. Besides, EULEX is the first ESDP mission including a customs component. This is a key dimension of EULEX's work, as about two thirds of Kosovo's revenues still flow from the collection of customs duties.

Third, not least given its size and the consequent management requirements in the field, EULEX has centralised a whole range of important horizontal tasks at its headquarters in Pristina. These include programming, procurement, personnel, training and best practices, human rights and gender policies, the anti-corruption unit and the bodies responsible for communication and outreach to civil society and NGOs. The units in charge of personnel and training have been playing a crucial role in processing the selection and reception to the mission of hundreds of officials at a time.[19]

18. In September 2009, the largest contributors (including seconded and contracted personnel) were France, Italy and Romania with around 190 nationals each, followed by Poland (134), Germany (107), Sweden (87), Finland (72), and the UK (66).

19. With a view to ensuring a better linkage between Brussels and the field, some EULEX personnel have also been placed at the Civilian Planning and Conduct Capability in the Council Secretariat.

Fourth, EULEX is distinctive because of the thorough programmatic approach that has been devised by the EUPT on the basis of the stated aims and objectives of the mission.[20] In a nutshell, this approach consists of a detailed set of programme activities accompanied by performance indicators designed for the police, justice and customs sectors (and their subfields). EULEX officials, in conjunction with the relevant counterparts, are tasked to assess the performance of Kosovo's institutions based on these indicators over successive six-month cycles. That would enable EULEX and Kosovo's institutions to flexibly adjust their activities on the basis of the reports concluding each cycle. Under such an approach, the first six months of the operation were dedicated to a major stocktaking exercise to identify specific priorities for future action.

If EULEX is a unique mission, the challenges that it has met in deploying and going operational look nonetheless quite familiar to civilian ESDP. However, these challenges have played out on a whole different scale given the size, ambition and distinctive political context of EULEX. The planning process fell short of anticipating all the mission needs and indicating some of its operational priorities. Progress was surely achieved with regard to earlier planning experience, as the very launch of such a large and complex mission testifies. However, the political conundrum surrounding the mission's deployment overstretched the process and altered some of the planning assumptions. It followed that contingencies such as the need to take over executive functions in the turbulent area north of the Ibar were not anticipated. More generally, earlier focus on the monitoring, mentoring and advising dimension needed to be rebalanced at a late stage into the process by more attention to the requirements of executive tasks, such as the fight against organised crime.[21] Besides, reportedly, the integrated nature of EULEX was not always reflected in its planning stages, with different teams in EUPT and in the early stages of EULEX largely working side-by-side with little dialogue and weak coordination.[22] By the end of 2008, planning documents such as the CONOPS and the OPLAN, adopted respectively in autumn 2007 and February 2008, were partially outdated. The shift in the political environment of EULEX had serious repercussions on procurement activities as well.

As has been the case for other ESDP missions, cumbersome procedures hampered the procurement process, which was coordinated in Pristina. However, three addi-

---

20. See EULEX Programme Strategy, available at http://www.eulex-kosovo.eu/?id=27.

21. EULEX staff lamented the absence of EU concept and planning documents concerning executive policing activities, except from the deployment and tasks of integrated police units and formed police units. Faced with upcoming contingencies on the ground, the mission staff had to devise relevant procedures on the spot. Interview with EULEX officials, March 2009.

22. Interview with EULEX officials, Pristina, March 2009.

tional factors intervened to complicate procurement in the case of EULEX. First and foremost, the original assumption that EULEX would take over premises and vehicles from UNMIK did not materialise for many months, as noted above. UNMIK remained on the ground for much longer than expected and sent mixed messages to EULEX on whether and when specific compounds or equipments could be taken over. Second, the existing framework contract to procure armoured vehicles did not work properly and serious delay was accumulated, leaving EULEX short of cars. Third, uncertainty on the evolution of the political context entailed that Member States were reluctant to speed up major tenders when it was not clear at which point and under what circumstances the mission would go operational. More broadly, specific needs related to executive tasks, such as investigations requiring adequate technological equipment, had not been anticipated and necessary means were not available well into the operational phase of the mission.

Given the size of EULEX, the recruitment of personnel posed a distinct challenge and exposed the limitations of the system under civilian ESDP. Seven calls for contributions followed one another between October 2007 and spring 2009. Yet, by May, just over 80% of the envisaged positions were filled and successive calls were met by decreasing contributions of Member States, while the quality and level of training of seconded personnel proved very uneven.[23] Much of the training needed to be carried out 'in mission', with the training unit organising 11,000 training days between late 2007 and March 2009. Many of the outstanding vacancies concern highly specialised functions, for example in the judicial sector.[24] As with the procurement process, the fact that the operational priorities of the mission shifted after the first call for contribution entailed delays in identifying all the relevant profiles for recruitment. Besides, the fact that the recruitment process of EULEX largely overlapped with that for the expansion of EUPOL Afghanistan and for EUMM Georgia further strained already scarce national resources.

Implementation and performance

EULEX entered the operational phase on 9 December 2008 and assumed full operational capacity on 6 April 2009. The mission has regularly undertaken its functions of monitoring, mentoring and advising Kosovo authorities at the central level, and progressively expanded its activities at the regional and local level. In particular, according to a recent report, the mission has been advising the Kosovo Judicial

23. In particular, the candidates put forward by Member States covered only 50% of the vacancies announced under the last call for contribution. Interviews with EULEX officials, March 2009.

24. Interviews with EULEX officials, March 2009.

Council and Supreme Court and supported the drafting of (yet to be implemented) national strategies on organised crime, counter-terrorism, narcotics and integrated border-management.[25] Anti-money laundering and anti-corruption have been other key fields of (often difficult) cooperation with Kosovo authorities, while EULEX has been closely monitoring the restructuring of the police service and the selection of senior officials.

In implementing the programmatic approach outlined above, EULEX officials concluded in June 2009 a precise mapping of relevant Kosovo's structures and institutions and the assessment of their needs, with a view to better targeting the mission's activities.[26] The resulting picture indicates considerable institutional weaknesses across the police, justice and customs sectors. In relative terms, the Kosovo police is a functioning, multi-ethnic service with adequate staff and equipment. Priorities for future development reveal, however, key shortcomings. Objectives include the development of intelligence-led policing, the strengthening of the directorates for organised crime and crime analysis, the establishment of a viable interface between police and prosecutors and better collection of criminal statistics. The justice sector is in a very precarious state, with as yet non-functioning leading bodies and very serious concerns related to the independence of the judiciary from political influence, to the personal security of the judges and prosecutors and to the ability to ensure witness protection. The customs service is in place and new legislation in line with European standards has been adopted in 2008. On the other hand, the service lacks infrastructure and equipment and is not prepared to deal with the serious challenge of organised crime. The implementation of the Integrated Border Management Strategy, which entails close cooperation between police and customs, is expected to enable stronger border controls to counter trans-national crime.

In addition to supporting Kosovo institutions in implementing these and other priorities, EULEX has been performing a range of executive tasks in partnership with Kosovo authorities. Concerning customs, EULEX took a prudent, incremental approach to reactivating Gates 1 and 31 in the north, which had been damaged in violent riots following the declaration of independence and abandoned by Kosovo Serb personnel. Since December 2008, the EULEX presence at both gates has been established including customs officials, border police and a formed police unit, backed

25. Report of the Secretary General and High Representative for the Common Foreign and Security Policy of the European Union to the Secretary General of the United Nations on the activities of the European Union Rule of Law Mission in Kosovo. The report can be found in Annex One to UN Security Council, Report of the Secretary General on the United Nations Interim Administration Mission in Kosovo, S/2009/300, 10 June 2009.

26. See EULEX Programme Report, July 2009, available at http://www.eulex-kosovo.eu/?id=8&n=123. EULEX officials stress that this is the most comprehensive report ever produced on Kosovo's rule-of-law institutions, resulting from over 2,500 assessments delivered by 400 EULEX monitors and advisers over six months.

by KFOR troops. In cooperation with Kosovo Serb customs officials, EULEX began 24/7 data collection for commercial traffic on 1 February and, on 20 May, it began to copy and stamp relevant documents of commercial vehicles and goods, sharing information with both Kosovo and Serb customs authorities. If a degree of control has therefore been re-established at these gates, the question of how to re-start collecting customs revenues, including issues of applicable law and division of the revenue between local (Kosovo-Serb dominated) and central authorities in Kosovo, remains to be addressed.

In the police field, EULEX managed to establish a reasonable working relationship with the Kosovo police in the North, which reports to EULEX and not directly to Kosovo police structures. EULEX has also contributed to setting up an ethnically mixed Kosovo police unit including Kosovo Serb, Bosniak and Albanian officers in Northern Mitrovica and monitors its performance. EULEX police have had to intervene on two main occasions to restore public order, namely in April, when Kosovo Serbs and Kosovo Albanians clashed on the question of the reconstruction of some houses for Kosovo Albanians in Serbian-populated areas, and in May, to manage the demonstrations staged by Kosovo Serbs to protest against protracted electricity cuts by KEK – the Kosovo power provider.

In the beginning, the exercise of jurisdiction by EULEX judges and prosecutors was hampered by a lack of support staff, such as court translators, the very slow transfer of over 400 case files from UNMIK (completed only in March 2009), and legal uncertainty on the applicable law, notably north of the Ibar where Kosovo Serbs reject the legislation adopted by institutions in Pristina. That said, between January and April 2009 over 100 hearings were held involving EULEX judges in mixed panels with Kosovo colleagues and, by the end of May, 16 verdicts had been passed in criminal cases, including two at the Kosovo Supreme Court. During the first nine months of operations, EULEX prosecutors have been involved in 467 prosecutions.[27] Mechanisms for the timely interaction between Kosovo police and EULEX prosecutors (in cooperation with local prosecutors) have been established. The reopening of the courthouse in Northern Mitrovica, which was stormed by Kosovo Serbs in March 2008 and was subsequently closed for eight months, is regarded as a notable success for EULEX (although only international officials have been serving there so far). EULEX officials have also begun to handle civil cases, including sensitive ones concerning inter-ethnic property disputes and the controversial privatisation process of state-owned enterprises.

---

27. EULEX Press Release, 'EULEX Justice Component – A successful beginning', 6 September 2009, available at http://www.eulex-kosovo.eu/?id=8&n=136.

The record of the first six months of operational activity of EULEX is reasonably good.[28] The mission has notably been able to deploy north of the Ibar and to achieve tangible progress in carrying out customs, police and judicial activities there. This has been done with the increasing cooperation of local services while fully briefing authorities in Pristina and keeping them closely associated to developments. That said, these achievements as well as further progress in strengthening the overall rule-of-law sector in Kosovo will only prove sustainable if more fundamental challenges are successfully addressed. Three of them top the agenda, namely improving inter-ethnic relations, still very tense, fighting pervasive organised crime and dealing with widespread corruption, including in political circles and public administration.[29] Managing the delicate process of de-centralisation (devolving competences to Kosovo-Serb majority municipalities), and re-starting the stagnating economy are the basic pre-conditions for effectively tackling these challenges.[30] In both respects, EULEX can provide much help but is not the core player.

Hence the importance of close cooperation and coordination with the other EU actors in the field, namely the EUSR and the European Commission Liaison Office (ECLO). Following the closing of the European Agency for Reconstruction in 2008, the latter is today responsible for the management and allocation of the substantial assistance package to Kosovo under the Stability and Association Process. Between 1999 and 2007, the EU and its Member States have earmarked €2.7 billion for Kosovo's recovery and reform (€1.9 billion of which through Community assistance).[31] Arguably, ten years after the Kosovo war and aside from humanitarian relief, the EU cannot claim much return for its big investment in this tiny country. Overall allocations through the Instrument for Pre-Accession Assistance for the 2008-2010 period amount to almost €260 million and are primarily targeted to political reform, socio-economic development and supporting Kosovo's regional integration. So far, EULEX and ECLO have developed rather good cooperation in identifying priorities for assistance in the rule-of-law sector and in monitoring the implementation of EC-funded programmes.

---

28. For another assessment in this direction, see European Parliament, Directorate General for External Policies, Policy department, 'EULEX Kosovo: lessons learned and future challenges', Brussels, September 2009. According to this report, over the first eight months of its operational phase, 'EULEX has made substantial progress in developing its role and providing technical support to Kosovo authorities' under the police, justice and customs component. At the same time, the report notes that serious political and legal complexities face the future implementation of the mission's mandate.

29. Elizabeth Pond, 'The EU's Test in Kosovo', *The Washington Quarterly*, Autumn 2008.

30. On the politically delicate process of decentralisation, see International Crisis Group, 'Serb integration in Kosovo: taking the plunge', *Europe Report* no. 200, 12 May 2009.

31. Instrument for Pre-Accession Assistance (IPA), Multi-Annual Indicative Planning Document (MIPD) 2008-2010 for Kosovo, pp. 3-9.

Conclusion

The very fact that EULEX is operating in Kosovo attests the coming of age of civilian ESDP. Besides, the relatively smooth deployment of the mission throughout Kosovo since December 2008 and the reasonably positive record of its first semester of operational activity go to the credit of the overall professionalism and commitment of the mission staff. The launch of such a large and ambitious mission in a turbulent political context invites, however, three questions.

The first concerns the discrepancy between foreign policy and ESDP. Unable to devise a common position of the question of the status of Kosovo, EU Member States have nevertheless agreed to deploy an ESDP mission that had been originally conceived to underpin the 'supervised' independence of Kosovo itself. It is understood that all EU Member States support the building of accountable and effective rule-of-law institutions in Kosovo and that, more broadly, all agree that the future of Kosovo and other Western Balkan countries lies in EU membership. However, launching EULEX as a quick technical fix of an unresolved political problem could only create tensions at both the political and operational level and, potentially, undermine the mission for good. A very substantial degree of political ambiguity and diplomatic skill within the EU and the UN has, in this case, averted this danger and enabled EULEX to enter its operational phase. In future, more thinking will have to be devoted by EU Member States to the intersection between foreign policy and ESDP, if the two are to be mutually reinforcing.

The second question regards EULEX itself and its ability to move on from initial achievements to structurally tackling the reform of rule-of-law institutions as well as the root causes of their fragility, namely corruption and organised crime. This challenge is closely linked to another issue facing the mission, namely striking the right balance between the direct exercise of executive functions and the transfer of ownership and responsibility to Kosovo authorities – the stated aim of the mission. So far, individual Kosovo officials may show great determination but most of the political class remains more committed in words than in deeds, while the lines between political, economic and criminal networks are sometimes blurred. Short of much stronger local commitment and capacity to address crime and corruption and uphold the rule of law, the impact of EULEX will not be decisive. From this standpoint, the specific efforts of EULEX to engage and support local civil society organisations are very important and should be pursued further.[32]

The third question relates to civilian ESDP as such, and to the potentially growing gap between the supply and the demand of resources. This is relevant both for EULEX, which has not yet reached full strength and perhaps never will, and for future ESDP missions. As noted above, mounting and running an operation like EULEX marks a change of gear in ESDP. It is legitimate to wonder whether such change of gear will prove sustainable, whether in terms of procurement and mission support, personnel requirements or planning and conduct structures. In other words, the question is whether the EULEX experience will help trigger the structural consolidation of civilian ESDP capabilities, or whether this mission will remain the only one of its kind for the foreseeable future.

BIBLIOGRAPHY

European Parliament, Directorate General for External Policies, Policy department. 'EULEX Kosovo: lessons learned and future challenges', Brussels, September 2009.

Heinemann-Grüder, Andreas and Grebenschikov, Igor. 'Security governance by internationals: The case of Kosovo', *International Peacekeeping*, vol. 13, no. 1, March 2006.

International Crisis Group. 'Kosovo's Fragile Transition', *Europe Report* no. 196, 25 September 2008.

International Crisis Group. 'Serb integration in Kosovo: taking the plunge', *Europe Report* no. 200, 12 May 2009.

Pond, Elizabeth. 'The EU's Test in Kosovo', *The Washington Quarterly*, Autumn 2008

Tansey, Oisín. 'Kosovo: independence and tutelage', *Journal of Democracy*, vol. 20, no. 2, April 2009.

Weller, Marc. 'Negotiating the final status of Kosovo', *Chaillot Paper* no. 114, EU Institute for Security Studies, Paris, December 2008.

---

32. Protests were staged in August against EULEX involving movements and organisations from civil society, following concerns expressed by Kosovo government representatives over a police protocol agreed by EULEX and Serbia. This indicates that much work remains to be done to engage relevant stakeholders and build confidence with a view to strengthening independent organisations and enhancing the accountability of public institutions.

de Wet, Erika. 'The Governance of Kosovo: Security Council Resolution 1244 and the Establishment and Functioning of EULEX', *American Journal of International Law,* vol. 103, no. 1, January 2009.

Yannis, Alexandros. 'The UN as Government in Kosovo', *Global Governance* no. 10, 2004.

22. EU SSR Guinea-Bissau

The EU mission in support of Security Sector Reform in Guinea-Bissau (EU SSR Guinea-Bissau)

Damien Helly

Legal basis: Council Joint Action 2008/112/CFSP of 12 February 2008.

Highlights of the mission's mandate:

■ Advice and assistance to local authorities in the implementation of the National SSR strategy comprising plans for downsizing/restructuring the army and the police .

■ Support to the adoption of SSR legal frameworks; and the preparation for further engagement by donors in capacity building and DDR.

■ Assess the perspectives for continued ESDP engagement.

Duration: June 2008 to date.

Budget: €5.6 million.

Mission strength: 14 seconded staff (out of 21 positions) and 13 local staff.

Contributing states: 6 Member States (France, Germany, Italy, Portugal, Spain, Sweden).

Background

Guinea-Bissau is a small country with a population of 1.3 million. It is considered to be a fragile state which has experienced very little economic development since its creation. It gained its independence in 1974 after a bloody war of liberation from Portugal and was then ruled with an iron fist by Nino Vieira, a war veteran, for two decades. It was then plunged into a civil war in 1998-1999. The country's history was thus marked by the predominance of the armed forces whose legitimacy as winners of the war has given them unchallenged power and prestige. With the army being controlled by and mainly composed of the Balanta ethnic group, political cleavages in Guinea Bissau have often – but not always – followed ethnic divisions. Guinea Bissau's security governance has also been affected by external destabilising factors such as links with the rebellion against Senegal in neighbouring Casamance and, more recently, drug trafficking from Latin America. Underdevelopment, recurring political violence and instability, the stranglehold of a small elite over the political process and widespread impunity have left state structures resembling an almost empty shell.[1]

The re-election of the former authoritarian ruler Nino Vieira in 2005, although the result of a trade-off with the army, opened a window of opportunity for international engagement in Security Sector Reform (SSR). The UK supported the drafting of a national Security Sector Reform national strategy which was adopted in October 2006 and presented at a donor round table in Geneva in November.[2] A year later, the country was on the agenda of the UN Peacebuilding Commission.[3] The EU, already engaged in the country through its development programmes, sent two joint Commission/Council Secretariat fact finding missions in May and October 2007 to develop an overall EU approach to support the national SSR process.[4] The idea of an ESDP civilian mission in the country was backed in particular by Portugal (given its links with its former colony), Spain (mainly for internal security reasons linked to migration), France and the UK (both having an interest – and interests – in Western

---

1. International Crisis Group, 'Guinea-Bissau: In Need of a State', *Africa Report* no. 142, 2 July 2007; Jean-Claude Marut, 'Guinée-Bissau, Casamance et Gambie: une zone à risques', *EUISS Opinion*, December 2008. See: http://www.iss.europa.eu. About 80% of the armed forces are from the Balanta group; International Crisis Group, 'Guinea-Bissau: Building a Real Stability Pact', *Africa Briefing* no. 57, 29 January 2009, p. 5. The Fulas are now considered the primary ethnic group in the country.

2. Republic of Guinea-Bissau, Interministerial Committee for the Restructuring and Modernisation of the Defence and Security Sector, Technical Committee, 'Restructuring and Modernisation of the Defence and Security Sector', Strategy Document, October 2006.

3. UN Peacebuilding Commission, 'Background Paper on Security Sector Reform in Guinea-Bissau', Peacebuilding Commission Country-Specific Configuration on Guinea-Bissau – Thematic Discussion on Security Sector Reform and the Rule of Law, 18 June 2008, p. 2.

4. Each mission lasted around two weeks and consisted of a group of about 15 people. Interview with an international official in Bissau, 16 June 2008.

Africa) who have all pursued bilateral cooperation agreements in the security sector. A written request from the Bissau-Guinean authorities on 10 January 2008 invited the EU to deploy an EU SSR mission and on 12 February the Council adopted the Joint Action launching the mission. EU SSR Guinea-Bissau, has shown the potential and the limits of ESDP civilian missions in a small-scale but politically challenging and increasingly competitive environment.

Mission and mandate

EU SSR Guinea-Bissau is one of the smallest ESDP operations with only 21 advisors to be deployed and a limited budget of less than €6 million. The mission's mandate was divided into three categories: assisting the authorities in developing implementation plans on the basis of their national SSR strategy; paving the ground for more engagement from donors on capacity building, training and equipment of the security sector; and assessing the relevance of a continued ESDP engagement. The 2006 national strategy established an SSR Steering Committee, a Technical Coordination Committee and a secretariat. The mission participated accordingly at various levels in the SSR coordination meetings.

The Head of Mission, Brigadier General Verastegui from Spain, supported by a Deputy and a political adviser/public information officer, managed a group including a number of Portuguese and Spanish officers seconded from armed forces, police and the *gendarmerie*/national guard. One adviser was in charge of the coordination with the secretariat of the Committee for Technical Coordination. Staff in charge of the justice sector worked under the authority of the police adviser. The mission renovated and equipped the former French chancery in the centre of Bissau where all the staff were located.

SSR advisors also work with their counterparts from various Bissau-Guinean institutions belonging to the security sector in order to assist them in the drafting of bills and internal administrative guidelines. Four staff members were supposed to work with the armed forces, four with security forces and two with the judiciary (prosecutor's office).

Recruitment of advisors proved difficult. The EU was already overstretched with ongoing or upcoming civilian missions, language requirements (Portuguese and French) were hard to meet and the country was not seen as of strategic importance by most Member States.[5] As a result, not all positions of the mission were filled,

5. Interview with a European official, Bissau, 17 June 2009.

some tasks had to be merged in order to be carried out, and gender-mainstreaming objectives in staffing could not be met.[6] Although the mission was supposed to benefit from new, swifter framework contracts for procurement, the mission had to rent vehicles for several months before receiving its own ones. Similarly, the mission building took several months to be renovated and the team had to work from a hotel in Bissau throughout most of its first year. Thanks to the experience of the procurement staff, drawn from previous ESDP missions, personnel were required to bring their own laptops to Bissau in anticipation of delays in the delivery of IT equipment.

The mission's work was quickly hampered by instability and political violence first when President Vieira's house was attacked in November 2008 in an alleged attempted *coup*,[7] then in March 2009 when he was assassinated hours after the Army's chief of staff Tagmé Na Wai. Political tensions (sometimes linked to ethnic factors) continued and a few killings took place in June during the following presidential campaign. In a climate of instability and heightened tensions around electoral campaigns, it became hard for the mission to engage deeply with its interlocutors.

Implementation, achievements and challenges

Implementation and achievements

Even though the mission's mandate, including an extension of six months, has not yet been fulfilled, there have been some achievements. The mission's headquarters have hosted work meetings with Bissau Guinean counterparts and a certain dynamic and confidence began to be built up with those interlocutors who had survived the political turmoil. In the police sector, progress was made on the drafting of organic laws for the Ministry of the Interior and of legislation dealing with various branches of the police (public order police, judicial police), yet these were not discussed by the parliament.

In the Army, cooperation and dialogue with former chief of staff Tagmé Na Wai proved more difficult than expected until he showed some interest in setting up a pension fund for veterans (designed by the European Commission), only a few weeks before he was killed in a bombing. Steady confidence-building efforts were being made at various levels of the armed forces, yet little progress could be achieved

---

6. Only one advisor was a woman, in charge of justice and under the authority of the police team leader.

7. David Zounmenou, 'Guinea-Bissau's legislative elections: what implications for stability?', *EUISS Opinion*, November 2008. See: http://www.iss.europa.eu.

because of the summer 2009 election campaign during which the mission prepared itself to help implement possible further progress on army reform.[8]

Divergences within the mission about the future of the Bissau-Guinean navy and air force – and the scope for their possible integration into a *Gendarmerie*/national guard on the Portuguese model of the *Guarda Nacional Republicana* (GNR) – have undermined its unity and its credibility.[9] In the justice sector, some progress in advising the general prosecutor's office was made with the adoption of internal guidelines and basic instructions on prosecution procedures and relations with the judicial police, as well as with the organisation of a training and information sharing seminar.

Needs assessments in capacity building (training, costs of assessment for the construction of new building and infrastructure) have also recently begun to be carried out in certain sectors (police and justice particularly). This being said, after 15 months, the mission's achievements appeared limited in the eyes of the staff, the international community present in Bissau and local public opinion, with the local populations still wondering about the purpose and the exact nature of its activities.[10]

Envisaged synergies with complementary EC-funded programmes under the European Development Fund and the Instrument for Stability[11] are still to take off: the censuses of the police and veterans have taken time, as well as the setting up of pension funds and other support measures for veterans.[12] Coordination with the European Commission went through various phases. First, a learning and negotiation phase took place focused on the definition of the mission's mandate and chain of command. It was decided that the operation would be under the civilian command of the Civilian Planning and Conduct Capability (CPCC) and that its justice reform component would be limited to the prosecutor's office.[13] Second, the deployment and implementation phase was carried out thanks to the crucial political

8. Interview with a mission staff member, Bissau, 16 June 2009.

9. Interviews in Bissau with members of the mission and international officials, 14 and 16 June 2009.

10. Interviews in Bissau with Bissau Guinean scholars, journalists and young people, 14-20 June 2009.

11. PARSS (Programme d'appui à la réforme du secteur sécuritaire) and PDRRI (Programme de réhabilitation et de réinsertion des anciens combattants).

12. The army census was carried out by the UNDP in 2008.

13. The main bulk of support to justice reform was supposed to be provided by the EC PAOSED programme, but this was poorly ranked in the evaluation report commissioned by the EC – Paolo Scalia and Roberto Lora, 'Avaliação do PAOSED e Preparação do Programa Sucessor, Atelier de restituição', 26 February 2009. A Justice programme matrix was designed by the ESDP justice adviser but coordination with PAOSED proved challenging. Interview with EUSSR mission staff, Bissau, 15 June 2009.

and logistical support from the EC and in particular its delegation in Bissau. Third, the EU SSR Head of Mission was involved in regular ambassadorial EU coordination meetings, although technical coordination between the mission's advisers and Member States has remained rather loose.[14]

The coordination bodies created by the national SSR strategy have not proved effective.[15] The leadership of the Minister of Defence as *primus inter pares* did not go down well with other members of the government concerned with the reform (notably in the ministries of the Interior and Justice). The weight and the inertia of the military staff and veterans significantly hampered any comprehensive progress. Coordination mechanisms were hindered by various factors, beyond instability in the government. Local ownership was limited by the fact that the Bissau-Guinean permanent staff of the national SSR secretariat did not receive income. Sometimes poor intercultural communication between EU SSR staff and their counterparts in the secretariat had negative effects. Despite an internal decision made at Prime Minister level, the Technical Committee met less regularly than initially foreseen, before seeing its very existence questioned by a new minister after the November 2007 elections.

In this quite chaotic environment, the three experts deployed by the EC under its Instrument for Stability had to struggle to find their space, role, and interlocutors to advise relevant authorities (Ministry of Defence) on SSR, coordinate flanking socio-economic measures, facilitate the coordination of SSR efforts (an SSR programmes matrix was finalised and terms of reference for the national SSR secretariat were developed) and prepare for the launch of EDF programmes in SSR/PARSS. While they were ready to complement the ESDP mission, the political vacuum and uncertainty left them with a reduced agenda.

Setbacks and challenges

The SSR mission in Guinea-Bissau, at first sight, looked like a relatively straightforward operation. All the ingredients were there to create an environment more conducive to tangible and sustainable achievements than previous experiences that had taken place in much larger countries such as EUSEC and EUPOL in DRC. Enabling conditions included a small country with clearly identified challenges, reformers

---

14. Group interview with experts involved in the SSR process, Bissau, 15 June.
15. Interviews with international and Bissau Guinean officials, Bissau, 16 June 2009.

and spoilers, and an internationally backed-up local leadership, with a comprehensive and long-term EU engagement based on an innovative policy mix. However, the mission suffered from the conjunction of a set of adverse circumstances.

First and foremost, the operation's initial planning assumptions were dramatically undermined by instability and political violence. With key SSR figures disappearing overnight because of the resumption of political tensions and violence linked to the electoral campaign, the window of opportunity disappeared for several months and European advisors found themselves operating in a political vacuum where very little could be done. Nonetheless, political violence did not lead to general insecurity in the country and the mission was able to continue to operate without seeing its members' safety threatened. New interlocutors were appointed and the SSR process was not officially put on hold. However, structural difficulties linked to the fragility of the state had to be faced. For instance it proved extremely challenging for the mission to find appropriate interlocutors in the armed forces either because very few officers were educated enough, or those who were had been sidelined for political or ethnic reasons.[16] Some advisers suggested that the initial planning missions had been too short to grasp the specificity of Guinea-Bissau's state fragility and the complexity of local ownership.[17]

Second, and notwithstanding the destructive impact of instability, the international community sadly failed to marshal a strong national and international consensus able to give some impetus to SSR. The EU SSR mission could probably have done more at the political level to communicate and share more widely and transparently its objectives, methods, timeframes and challenges without threatening its success. A lack of external communication coupled with poor coordination from other international organisations (namely UN agencies and key bilateral donors) confirmed the long-awaited risks of a 'war of experts'.[18]

Third, despite the best will, experience and flexibility from its leadership, internal weaknesses undermined the mission's potential and cohesion. It proved impossible to motivate Member States to provide adequate personnel for almost a fifth of key positions (including those of security officer, reporting officer and justice adviser). The mission therefore was under-staffed and overstretched, and this hampered its ability to shape the course of events or actually take the lead on key issues from the beginning.

---

16. Interview with a European security expert, Bissau, 16 June 2008.
17. Interviews, Bissau, 16 and 18 June 2009.
18. Observatoire de l'Afrique, 'Security Sector Reform (SSR) in Guinea-Bissau', *Africa Briefing Report*, Egmont Palace, Brussels, 28 January 2008, p.6.

More particularly, there was a debate about the co-location of ESDP advisers within Bissau-Guinean institutions, actually reflecting different understandings of the implementation of local ownership in a fragile state. Mission officials argued that co-location (a common practice for EC-funded technical assistance) was not appropriate. Without clear criteria to determine where advisers should be placed, it was felt that it would have created tensions among Bissau-Guinean institutions. Another reason given was that appropriate infrastructures were not in place in local institutions to allow advisors to work properly. Finally, remaining physically distant from Bissau Guinean interlocutors (which did not exclude occasional visits) was also seen as a way to respect local ownership and the (slow) pace of reform. Outside observers tended to consider that the mission's choice actually isolated ESDP advisers from the security sector, limited their proactiveness and their cultural sensitivity and undermined their image.[19] For them, centralising action in a brightly renovated HQ was a missed opportunity to create trust and an *esprit de corps* with key players in Bissau.

Lessons learned

In the case of EU SSR Guinea-Bissau, a strict interpretation of the extent to which benchmarks targets were fulfilled shows that, even if all planning assumptions had been confirmed – which was obviously not the case – they would have been hard to meet in one year. This however does not mean that the planners were wrong. The choice of adopting an ambitious mandate had the advantage of making clear that the EU had the political aspiration to lead on SSR. From the start it was anticipated that the EU would adopt a comprehensive SSR approach linking with regional[20] and international donors and partners (UN agencies, Interpol) as well as with other EU instruments. In the future, where possible, even more time should be dedicated to in-country analysis and planning of the political conditions on the ground as well as to coordination opportunities and challenges. More time for planning would also have allowed planners to work more deeply on an analysis and evaluation of previous SSR and DDR experiences, including the international coordination thereof.[21]

A second lesson is that it is absolutely vital for ESDP SSR advisers to develop close working relationships with their local counterparts while building a genuine ESDP

---

19. Interviews with international staff working on SSR, Bissau, 20 June 2009.

20. e.g. The Economic Community of West African States (ECOWAS), the Community of Portuguese Language Countries (CPLP).

21. André Monteiro and Michel Morgado, 'Last Chance for Security Sector Reform in Guinea Bissau', *IPRIS Viewpoints*, April 2009. Available at www. ipris.org.

team spirit. Several models exist, like co-locating experts within institutions (EU-JUST Themis) or prioritising team-building processes (EUSEC DRC in its first phase). Beyond co-location though, more work should be done to operationalise the concept of local ownership and to train ESDP practitioners more deeply about culturally-sensitive implementation in fragile states. Similarly, while respecting the principle of separation of powers and smooth relations with local counterparts, justice sector reform advisers should enjoy full autonomy in the framework of future SSR missions, while coordinating with their colleagues dealing with other sectors.

Third, matching ambitions with capabilities and adequate human resources – let alone meeting gender mainstreaming requirements – is a fundamental prerequisite as well as a constant challenge. EU SSR Guinea-Bissau is the latest confirmation of the need to boost Member States' efforts to increase the amount of human resources available for EU civilian crisis management.

Ultimately, the availability of adequate staff will always be linked to the strategic interests of Member States which should be more clearly identified in this region and in Africa as a whole. This would eventually lead to a more clearly defined EU foreign policy towards West Africa and the rest of the continent able to guide, frame and support ESDP deployment in coordination with other EU instruments and other partners.

BIBLIOGRAPHY

International Crisis Group. 'Guinea-Bissau: In Need of a State', *Africa Report* no. 142, 2 July 2007.

International Crisis Group. 'Guinea-Bissau: Building a Real Stability Pact', *Africa Briefing* no. 57, 29 January 2009.

International Crisis Group. 'Guinea-Bissau: Beyond Rule of the Gun', *Africa Briefing* no. 61, 25 June 2009.

Marut, Jean-Claude. 'Guinée-Bissau, Casamance et Gambie: une zone à risques', *EUISS Opinion*, December 2008.

Monteiro, André and Morgado, Michel. 'Last Chance for Security Sector Reform in Guinea Bissau', *IPRIS Viewpoints*, April 2009. Available at www. ipris.org.

Observatoire de l'Afrique. 'Security Sector Reform (SSR) in Guinea-Bissau', *Africa Briefing Report*, Egmont Palace, Brussels, 28 January 2008.

Republic of Guinea-Bissau, Interministerial Committee for the Restructuring and Modernisation of the Defence and Security Sector, Technical Committee. 'Restructuring and Modernisation of the Defence and Security Sector', Strategy Document, October 2006.

République de Guinée Bissau – Commission européenne. 'Document de stratégie pays et programme indicatif national pour la période 2008-2013', 9 December 2007.

UN Peacebuilding Commission. 'Background Paper on Security Sector Reform in Guinea-Bissau', Peacebuilding Commission Country-Specific Configuration on Guinea-Bissau, Thematic Discussion on Security Sector Reform and the Rule of Law, 18 June 2008.

Zounmenou, David. 'Guinea-Bissau's legislative elections: what implications for stability?', *EUISS Opinion*, November 2008.

23. EUMM Georgia

The European Union Monitoring Mission in Georgia (EUMM)

Sabine Fischer

Legal basis: Council Joint Action 2008/736/CFSP of 15 September 2008.

Highlights of the mission's mandate:

■ Provide civilian monitoring of the conflict parties' behaviour, including full compliance with the six-point Agreement of 12 August 2008.

■ Close cooperation with partners, namely the UN and the OSCE.

■ Main objectives: long-term stability throughout Georgia after the war.

■ Tasks: stabilisation, normalisation, confidence building, reporting.

Duration: 15 September 2008 to date.

Budget: €49.6 million (2008 to 2010).

Mission strength: 340 staff.

Contributing states: 24 Member States (Austria, Bulgaria, Czech Republic, Denmark, Estonia, Finland, France, Germany, Greece, Hungary, Ireland, Italy, Latvia, Lithuania, Luxembourg, Malta, Netherlands, Poland, Romania, Spain, Sweden, United Kingdom)

The European Union Monitoring Mission in Georgia (EUMM), operational since 1 October 2008, is one of the most significant and at the same time one of the most politically difficult ESDP missions. Its deployment helped to end the armed conflict between Georgia and Russia in August 2008 and to considerably stabilise the situation along the administrative borders between undisputed Georgian territory on the one hand and the breakaway regions of South Ossetia and Abkhazia, on the other.[1] At the same time, however, the mission operates under conditions which do not allow for the fulfilment of parts of its mandate. Moreover, the war in Georgia and the Union's direct involvement in post-conflict stabilisation directly impact on EU-Russia relations – one of the most difficult facets of EU foreign relations today.

The EU's role in ending the Russian-Georgian war

The outbreak of hostilities between Georgia, South Ossetia and Russia on 7 August 2008 paralysed the international actors hitherto involved in conflict resolution in Georgia. In this situation, the EU under the French Presidency quickly moved to close the gap. On 10 August the Presidency, in cooperation with the OSCE, launched a negotiation mission which ended with the signing by Russia and Georgia of the so-called six point Agreement on 12 August. The parties to the conflict committed themselves not to resort to force, to end hostilities, and to provide free access to humanitarian aid. Georgia agreed to withdraw its military forces to their bases, and Russia accepted the obligation to bring its troops back behind the lines held prior to the outbreak of hostilities (7 August). The agreement envisaged the deployment of an international mechanism to monitor the ceasefire. Moreover, it announced that international talks on the security and stability arrangements in Abkhazia and South Ossetia were to be rapidly initiated. Already at this point the EU Council committed itself to 'contribute actively to the effective implementation of these principles' and to 'including on the ground, [...] support every effort, including those of the UN and the OSCE, with a view to the peaceful and lasting solution to the conflict in Georgia'.[2]

Between 12 August and 1 September several EU structures set out to explore the situation on the ground and the conditions for an ESDP action. On 1 September

---

1. The term 'undisputed Georgian territory' is drawn from a Human Rights Watch Report where it circumscribes 'any part of Georgia, except South Ossetia and Abkhazia, both areas which are subject to dispute over their sovereignty and have made bids for independence'. Human Rights Watch, 'Up in Flames. Humanitarian Law Violations and Civilian Victims in the Conflict over South Ossetia', New York, January 2009, p. 2, fn1.

2. General Affairs and External Relations Council meeting on the situation in Georgia, Council Conclusion 12453/08, Brussels, 13 August 2008.

the French Presidency convened an extraordinary Council meeting on the crisis in Georgia. The Council Conclusions outlined a first, tentative schedule for the deployment of an ESDP mission to Georgia: 'The European Union has [...] decided on the immediate dispatch of a fact-finding mission with the task to gather information and defining the modalities for an increased European Union commitment on the ground, under the European Security and Defence Policy.' The Council asked the relevant EU bodies to take the necessary steps so as to make it possible to decide on an observer mission by 15 September.[3]

On 8 September 2008, Russia and the EU concluded an additional agreement on the implementation of the six-point plan. Russia committed itself to withdraw its troops from undisputed Georgian territory by 15 September and from the buffer zones adjoining South Ossetia and Abkhazia 'within 10 days from the deployment of international mechanisms in these zones, including at least 200 observers from the European Union', and no later than 1 October 2008.[4]

Already in August the Council Secretariat had set up a Crisis Management Co-ordination Team (CMCT) and had sent two small exploratory teams to Georgia. Their task was to explore the situation on the ground and to reinforce the Tbilisi-based team of the EUSR for the South Caucasus. The Commission, for its part, dispatched a crisis assessment team, and the European Commission's Humanitarian Aid Office (ECHO) sent a team to assess the humanitarian situation in Georgia. The extraordinary Council meeting on 1 September was followed by the deployment of another Council/Commission exploratory team in order to prepare the concept of operations (CONOPS). Ultimately, the Council Secretariat dispatched an advance team after the conclusion of the implementation agreement on 8 September to prepare the ground for the deployment of the actual mission. The Commission Delegation in Tbilisi and the Tbilisi-based team of the EUSR for the South Caucasus facilitated and coordinated the deployment and programme of the various teams.

The different exploratory and preparatory teams, together with the Council services, and the Commission all collaborated in the drafting of the CONOPS and Joint Action (JA) defining the mandate and main features of the mission. The JA had to be adapted to ongoing developments several times throughout September 2008. The number of monitors was a case in point. DG VIII and the Civilian Conduct and

---

3. Extraordinary European Council, Brussels, 1 September 2008. Presidency Conclusions, 12594/08, p. 3. Available at: http://register.consilium.europa.eu/pdf/en/08/st12/st12594.en08.pdf.

4. 'Russia steps back: Medvedev-Sarkozy agreement', 8 September 2008. Available at: www.moscowcorrespondent. wordpress.com (downloaded June 2009).

Planning Capability (CPCC) had initially planned to staff the mission with no more than 140 observers.[5] After the conclusion of the implementation agreement in Moscow on 8 September this number had to be considerably increased.

The mission mandate, implementation and performance

The mission's objectives as outlined in the JA are first 'to contribute to long-term stability throughout Georgia and the surrounding region', and secondly 'in the short term, to the stabilisation of the situation with a reduced risk of a resumption of hostilities, in full compliance with the six-point Agreement and the subsequent implementation measures'.[6] In order to achieve these aims, the JA focuses the EUMM's activities on four main tasks.

Stabilisation: The mission is supposed to monitor, analyse and report on the situation pertaining to the stabilisation process, the implementation of the six-point Agreement and violations of human rights and international humanitarian law. *Normalisation:* Moreover, the mission should monitor, analyse and report on the normalisation of civil governance in the conflict region, thereby focusing on rule of law, effective law enforcement structures and adequate public order. *Confidence building:* The mission's task is to contribute to the reduction of tensions through liaison, facilitation of contacts between parties and other measures. *Information:* Last but not least, the mission is tasked to support decision-making processes in Brussels and Member States by providing information on the situation on the ground.

The mission mandate by definition covers the whole of Georgia, hence including South Ossetia and Abkhazia.[7] The initial mandate of one year has been extended until 14 September 2010.[8] Within two weeks after the adoption of the JA the Union was able to establish the mission Headquarters in Tbilisi and four regional offices (Tbilisi, Gori, Kashuri and Zugdidi), and to deploy more than 200 monitors as well as technical and support staff. Member States demonstrated great willing-

---

5. Interview with EU official, Brussels, March 2009.

6. Council Joint Action 2008/736/CFSP of 15 September 2008 on the European Union Monitoring Mission in Georgia, EUMM, Georgia, *Official Journal of the European Union*, 17 September 2008, L 248/27.

7. See for example: 'EUMM's Mandate is Georgia-wide', EUMM Press Release 06/08, 5 November 2008. Available at: www.eumm.eu.

8. Council Joint Action 2009/572/CFSP, 27 July 2009. *Official Journal of the European Union*, 29 July 2009, L 197/110.

ness to contribute to the mission and make its quick implementation possible.[9] The EUMM's performance evolves around the four tasks outlined in the mandate (stabilisation, normalisation, confidence building, and information).

First of all, the EUMM monitors the Georgian side of the administrative borders. By doing so it focuses on movements of military and police forces as well as equipment and vehicles. The mission's most prominent and urgent task was to monitor and to report the withdrawal of Russian troops by 10 October. On 10 October Russian compliance with the deadline for its withdrawal was confirmed, despite the fact that there were still Russian troops in the village of Perevi on undisputed Georgian territory. Brussels, the Member States and the EUMM have repeatedly called upon the Russian and South Ossetian sides to withdraw military forces and militia from Perevi and to reduce the number of troops deployed in Abkhazia and South Ossetia according to the provisions of the ceasefire.[10] Moscow, for its part, argues that point 5 of the six-point agreement has become obsolete with the recognition of South Ossetia and Abkhazia by the Russian Federation.

At the same time the EUMM is monitoring Georgian movements in the areas adjacent to the administrative borders. On 26 December 2008 the mission called upon the Georgian government not to deploy armoured vehicles in those areas and cautioned against the potentially detrimental impact such a move could have on the upcoming round of the Geneva talks.[11] The Georgian side followed the EUMM's recommendations and postponed the deployment. On another occasion the EUMM denied Russian allegations that Georgia was increasing the number of its troops in the adjacent areas.[12]

The EUMM's monitoring activity is not limited to security developments in the narrow sense of the word. As outlined above the mission mandate encompasses 'soft areas' such as monitoring and reporting on the normalisation of civil governance with a focus on the rule of law, human rights and the humanitarian situation of the local population. For instance, the monitors have established close contacts with local administrations, schools and universities to build up a network and distribute

---

9. Member States contributed the following number of monitors: France 36, Italy 35, Poland 26, Sweden 25, Germany 25, Romania 20, United Kingdom 19, Denmark 10, Finland 10, Spain 10, Netherlands 8, Greece 8, Czech Republic 5, Lithuania 5, Ireland 4, Bulgaria 4, Austria 4, Latvia 3, Hungary 3, Malta 2, Luxembourg 2, Estonia 2.

10. 'The EUMM calls on the Russian Government to withdraw its units from the Perevi checkpoint without delay', 13 December 2008. See: www.eumm.eu.

11. 'EUMM expresses concern about deployment of new Georgian police vehicles', 26 December 2008. See: www.eumm.eu.

12. 'EU Monitors Deny Georgia Troops Build-Up', February 2009. See: www.civil.ge.

information about the mission and its activities. Facilitating the smooth return of internally displaced persons and improving their living conditions has been another focus of its monitoring activities during the mission's early phase.

The second area of the EUMM's activity is direct interaction with the Georgian government, aiming at stabilisation and normalisation of the situation in the conflict zones. The mission's main interlocutors to achieve these goals are the Ministry of the Interior and the Ministry of Defence.

An agreement on the exchange of liaison officers with the Ministry of the Interior guarantees the EUMM direct contact and a constant flow of information on developments and incidents in the conflict zones.[13] Moreover, the mission concluded a Memorandum of Understanding with the Ministry on 10 October 2008 according to which the Georgian side commits itself to give advance notification if it plans to deploy police forces in the adjacent zones. The MoU also foresees the establishment of a cooperation mechanism between law enforcement agencies on both sides of the administrative borders. This idea was later taken up in the Geneva talks, which ultimately led to the agreement on an Incident Prevention and Response Mechanism (IPRM) in February 2009. The latter provides the framework for regular meetings of the parties to the conflicts as well as the international actors involved to discuss the security situation in the conflict zones.[14]

Similar arrangements have been made with the Ministry of Defence. A Memorandum of Understanding was signed by the EUMM and the MoD on 26 January 2009. Under the MoU the MoD commits itself to refrain from significant movement or re-deployment of large troop numbers or heavy equipment in the zones adjacent to the administrative borders with South Ossetia and Abkhazia, and to provide in advance notification if movements are considered necessary for tactical purposes. The MoU concedes the right to the EUMM to conduct inspections of facilities and sites of the Georgian armed forces.

EUMM members assess their cooperation with the Ministry of the Interior and the MoD as generally good. Nevertheless, there have been some concerns regarding the Georgian government's efficiency in implementing the provisions of the agreements. One EUMM representative described the attitude of the Georgian government

---

13. Interview with EUMM staff, Tbilisi, January 2009.

14. 'Proposals for joint incident prevention and response mechanisms', 18 February 2009. See: www.civil.ge.

institutions regarding informational exchange as 'not proactive'.[15] The ability of the EU monitors to distinguish Georgian military and police forces in the conflict zones during the first months after the war was a matter of concern due to the fact that police often wore military uniforms and used vehicles which were not visibly flagged out as belonging to the police. With the gradual stabilisation of the situation along the borders, however, this issue has become less urgent.

The third area of the EUMM's activity is information. The mission's reporting has important functions at three levels. Firstly, it provides the EU institutions in Brussels and the capitals of the Member States with detailed weekly reports on the situation in Georgia. Secondly, EUMM reporting and analysis feeds into the preparation of the Geneva talks between the parties to the conflicts. The EUMM is also represented at the talks and provides perspectives and ideas from the ground. As noted above, it helped to initiate the development of the IPRM and also facilitates its implementation.[16] Thirdly, EUMM reporting discourages non-compliance with the six-point Agreement on the Georgian side.

One year after the deployment of the mission it is too early for a conclusive assessment on the EUMM's performance. The mission was heavily front-loaded in the sense that it had to fulfil its first and most prominent task, the monitoring of the withdrawal of Russian troops from undisputed Georgian territory, within the first 10 days of its existence.[17] Regardless of the fact that the Russian withdrawal was not complete, all sides agreed that the EUMM has delivered on the stabilisation process after the war in August 2008. With the liquidation of the OSCE Mission to Georgia and of the United Nations Observer Mission in Georgia (UNOMIG), the EUMM's presence becomes even more important for preserving stability along the boundaries between South Ossetia, Abkhazia and Georgia.

In the months after the war the EUMM monitored the normalisation of the situation of the civil population and the return of IDPs to the extent possible. Close interaction with local and national government structures has helped to restore civil governance. However, the EUMM's ability to fully implement the tasks of normalisation and stabilisation is hampered by the fact that the mission's activities are limited to the Georgian side of the conflict zones. This structural problem poses an even greater challenge regarding the third task,

---

15. Interview with EUMM staff, June 2009.
16. Interview with EUMM staff, June 2009.
17. Interview with EU official, Brussels, January 2009.

confidence building, which is being undermined by the Abkhaz, South Ossetian and Russian reluctance to provide the EUMM access to Abkhazia and South Ossetia. Although the EUMM rightly points out that stabilisation and confidence-building are linked,[18] it will remain difficult to make a direct contribution to confidence-building, beyond the IPRM framework, without functioning relations with all parties to the conflicts.

The EU and the EUMM find themselves in a difficult dilemma here. Abkhazia and South Ossetia deny the EUMM normal cooperation as long as the mission insists on access to their territories, invoking Georgian territorial integrity. On the other hand, the policy of non-recognition is crucial in the EUMM's relations with the Georgian government and helps to convince Tbilisi to make unilateral security commitments.[19]

Challenges

The EUMM is certainly one of the most politically difficult ESDP civilian missions. It has been established in a dangerous situation in which two important partner countries of the EU, Russia and Georgia, were engaged in a war against each other. It operates in a very crowded theatre and in a tense local context. Last but not least, it is interlinked with EU-Russia relations. As such, the mission faces a range of challenges stemming both from within the EU and from the situation on the ground.

In reviewing these challenges, it should be stressed that the deployment of a sizeable mission in a conflict area within less than a month represents in itself a remarkable achievement. That said, the implementation process was characterised by a number of technical, logistical and political problems.[20] These notably included a proliferation of teams on the ground, challenges with staffing and procurement and the difficult political context of the planning phase.

First, the deployment of numerous exploratory, preparatory and advance teams dispatched with different tasks by different EU institutions proved difficult to coordinate and generated confusion inside the EU as well as in the eyes of local and other international actors on the ground.

Second, because of the urgency of the situation the recruitment of the mission staff

18. Interview with EUMM staff, June 2009.

19. Interviews with EUMM staff, January and June 2009.

20. The following points are based on interviews with EUMM staff and EU officials conducted in Tbilisi and Brussels in January and March 2009.

did not follow the usual selection procedures. Instead, Member States were request-ed to contribute contingents of monitors and translators already endowed with technical equipment and vehicles. This led to the nationally biased composition of many teams on the ground, which later required their reorganisation. Furthermore, not all Member States did entirely live up to their initial commitments. In the start-ing phase, for instance, a number of teams lacked translators, which made commu-nication with the local population difficult.

Third, complex procurement procedures complicated the establishment and equip-ment of both the Headquarters in Tbilisi and the field offices. When the mission was first launched, technical and other equipment (such as cell phones, computers, desks, uniforms etc) was lacking and procurement went ahead only slowly. Mission members point out that this has been the biggest problem in the implementation phase and has had an impact on the further development of the mission.

Fourth, in the highly politicised and tense atmosphere during the planning phase, political decisions did not always coincide with technical realities and requirements. As outlined above, the final decision to staff the mission with more than 200 moni-tors was taken at the political level and on the basis of political rather than technical considerations. This had implications both for the planning process and the imple-mentation of the mission.

From a different standpoint, the mission needs to strike a difficult balance in its rela-tion with the parties to the conflict. As outlined above, the EUMM cooperates closely with Georgian authorities. Already well before the war the Saakashvili government had actively wooed deeper EU engagement in the unresolved conflicts in Georgia. From Tbilisi's perspective, Russia's dominant role in the peacekeeping mechanisms addressing the conflicts in both entities and Moscow's strong impact on OSCE and UN-led conflict resolution processes were clearly against Georgian interests. Closer co-operation with the EU and the Union's deeper involvement in conflict resolution were seen in Tbilisi as a tool to reduce Russian influence and gain more control via Mem-ber States with whom Georgia holds close relations. When the Union finally started to discuss the deployment of an ESDP engagement on the ground the Georgian side hoped for a military mission with a more robust mandate. The Georgian government had to accept that the EU was willing to commit itself only to a civilian mission but nevertheless shifted its political focus to cooperation with the EUMM, while other international actors were being regularly criticised for their inefficiency.[21] As a conse-

21. See for instance 'Saakashvili: UN Mission not effective', 24 January 2009. Available at: www.civil.ge.

quence, the EUMM came to be perceived as being very close to the Georgian side.

The EUMM's relations with Abkhazia and South Ossetia remain tense. The same can be said of the missions's relations with the Russian forces based in the two entities. Official Russian statements have mostly been dismissive of the EUMM's activities, with a slight improvement very recently. In Abkhazia, attitudes towards the EU and its policy in the region have changed radically since the war.[22] Before August 2008, the Abkhaz leadership repeatedly expressed interest in closer relations with the European Union. Many saw this as a tool to counterbalance increasing Russian influence and protect Abkhazian autonomy. Western public statements and actions in the run-up to, during and after the war, however, evoked harsh criticism in Abkhazia. In the context of this crisis of confidence, the EUMM came to be perceived as the materialisation of the West's pro-Georgian policy.[23] On the other hand, it is exactly the negative attitude of Sukhumi and Tskhinvali, backed by Moscow, which deprives the mission of any possibility to prove the opposite. It remains to be seen if the Geneva Talks and the IPRM, which after a bumpy start have come to be accepted by all parties to the conflicts as the main negotiation formats, will improve the atmosphere and pave the way for a more substantial dialogue in the future.

Overlap with the other international players in Georgia posed yet another challenge for the EUMM, before the OSCE mission and UNOMIG were withdrawn. When the EU decided to launch the mission, the UN and the OSCE had already been on the ground for about 15 years. Regardless of repeated public statements by all sides that the three missions did not overlap but complement each other, tensions could not be avoided altogether. The missions were also being ascribed different political affinities in relation to the parties to the conflicts. As outlined above, EUMM is perceived as being close to the Georgian side. UNOMIG, which had a field office in Sukhumi for nearly 15 years, on the other hand, was seen as relatively close to the Abkhaz side. This complicated the interaction on the ground and made it difficult for all sides to join forces.

Another challenge arises from the fact that Georgia is a very 'crowded' theatre for the EU. Since the August war, two new actors appeared on the Tbilisi scene – the EUMM

---

22. It is difficult to draw a picture of the situation in South Ossetia, where the political elite and civil society are much weaker, and politics is even more dependent on Moscow than in Abkhazia.

23. Interviews with representatives of the Abkhaz *de facto* authorities and civil society in Sukhumi, January 2009.

and the EUSR for the Crisis in Georgia, thus boosting the already significant EU presence in the country (EC Delegation and Office of the EUSR for the Southern Caucasus, including the Border Support Team, plus 15 Member States' embassies). While the mandates of EU actors in Georgia are different, they also overlap to a certain extent, particularly in the field of confidence building.[24] This situation requires a great effort by EU actors to develop a common strategy.

Last but not least, divisions within the European Union complicate the mission's situation on the ground. The main problem here is disagreement among Member States regarding an appropriate strategy and policy towards Russia. The difficulty to achieve a common position towards Russia and the Eastern neighbourhood often paralyses the Union's policy towards the region. After the Russian-Georgian war, the EU was not able to maintain the resolve which had driven its policy from the French Presidency's mediation mission at the beginning of August to the Extraordinary Council meeting on 1 September. The tough stance which had characterised the Council Conclusions soon gave way to the desire to normalise relations with Russia. The evolution of the broader context of EU-Russia relations in the so-called shared neighbourhood deprived the EUMM of important leverage (for instance with respect to the withdrawal of Russian troops from Perevi), and complicated its position on the ground.

Conclusion

The decision to deploy an ESDP mission in Georgia was a rare show of unity by the European Union. The record speed of its implementation proved the Union's capability to react quickly in a situation of serious crisis, provided that sufficient political will and strong leadership exist. Through the creation of the EUMM, the EUSR for the Crisis in Georgia, and the Geneva talks, the EU has considerably increased its profile in conflict resolution in Georgia. The mission has quickly delivered on its first and most prominent task, the stabilisation of the situation after the war. Despite some technical problems in the implementation process, the initial stage of the EUMM therefore represents a success for the ESDP.

---

24. Interviews with EU officials and EUMM staff in Brussels and Tbilisi, January and March 2009.

When looking at developments after the withdrawal of the Russian forces from undisputed Georgian territory as well as at the other tasks of the EUMM, the picture becomes more mixed. The complex political situation on the ground and the internal EU differences on the Eastern neighbourhood complicate the mission's work. Nevertheless the EUMM continues to make an important contribution to the stabilisation of this conflict-ridden region, particularly after the departure of the OSCE mission and UNOMIG. Its persistence on the ground remains, therefore, of utmost importance for peace and stability.

BIBLIOGRAPHY

Human Rights Watch. 'Up in Flames. Humanitarian Law Violations and Civilian Victims in the Conflict over South Ossetia', New York, January 2009.

International Crisis Group. 'Russia versus Georgia: The Fallout', *Europe Report* no. 195, Tbilisi/Brussels, 22 August 2008.

International Crisis Group. 'Georgia: The Risk of Winter', *Europe Briefing* no. 51, Tbilisi/Brussels, 26 November 2008.

International Crisis Group. 'Georgia and Russia: Still Insecure and Dangerous', *Europe Briefing* no. 53, ICG Tbilisi/Brussels, 22 June 2009.

24. EU NAVFOR Somalia

The EU military Operation *Atalanta*

Damien Helly

Legal basis: Council Joint Action 2008/851/CFSP of 10 November 2008.

Highlights of the mission's mandate:

- To provide protection to vessels chartered by the World Food Programme for Somalia.

- To provide protection, based on a case-by-case evaluation of needs, to merchant vessels cruising in the areas where it is deployed.

- To keep watch over areas off the Somali coast, including Somalia's territorial waters.

- To take the necessary measures, including the use of force, to deter, prevent and intervene in order to bring to an end acts of piracy and armed robbery.

- In view of prosecutions potentially being brought by states respecting EU human rights standards, to arrest, detain and transfer suspected pirates.

- To liaise with other actors working to combat acts of piracy and armed robbery off the Somali coast.

Duration: 8 December 2008 to date.

Budget: €8.4 million (common costs) for the first 12 months.
Total annual contributions estimated at around €400 million.

> **Mission strength:** Around 2,000.
>
> **Contributing states:** 19 Member States (all apart from Austria, Czech Republic, Denmark, Estonia, Latvia, Lithuania, Portugal and Slovakia) and 2 third states (Croatia and Norway) have contributed.

Introduction

On 10 November 2008, the first ESDP naval operation was officially launched by the Council to deter and combat piracy off the coast of Somalia and in the Gulf of Aden. Piracy off the coast of Somalia is a symptom of ongoing insecurity, political instability, clan-based violence and international geopolitical rivalries on the mainland. As a result, populations have been suffering from resource scarcity and displacement, as well as being subject to fear and intimidation. The local fishing industry has become increasingly threatened in the last decade by the illegal presence of foreign vessels in the country's territorial waters. While Somali piracy may originally have been motivated by local frustrations against these ships, it has now become highly profitable organised crime disconnected from socio-economic factors.

Background and context of the mission

In the last five years, the pirates' resources have dramatically increased thanks to the payment of large ransoms by governments, shipping companies or insurance groups. This income is believed to be shared between pirate leaders, local fishermen and gunmen, elements of the Somali Diaspora, and corrupt officials in the northeastern Somali province of Puntland and in the Federal Government, thereby exacerbating the situation in Somalia. Some of this money is reinvested to fund future piracy operations. There are probably around a thousand people actively involved in piracy in Somalia,[1] however it is hard to give a precise estimate of the population participating indirectly in piracy and related illicit activities.

Most pirates in the region are Somali, sometimes based on Yemen's coasts. Their leaders are rarely experienced sailors and employ local fishermen to navigate and take care of vessels. These groups use modern technologies and light speed boats, sometimes carrying several of the latter in 'mother ships' from which they can be

---

1. 'Le chaos somalien favorise le commerce des otages', *La Croix*, 12 November 2008.

launched onto the high seas. All groups rely on land support from local facilities and communities who have benefited from the income generated by profits made out of piracy (corruption, ransoms and cash inflows).

Piracy operations follow standard patterns divided into a number of action phases. The first phase consists of surveillance and targeting potential victims, i.e. vessels navigating at slow speed, far away from any maritime or air surveillance and protection. Most of the attacks take place in the Gulf of Aden where vessels frequently have to travel at slower speeds and where the distance from the coasts is less, which allows pirates to attack simultaneously from a variety of directions.[2] Sometimes, small arms (rocket-propelled grenades have been used) have been fired at the vessels to intimidate the crew, who are then threatened with fire arms. It rarely takes more than 30 minutes for an attack to take place, after which it is extremely difficult to intervene.

Piracy and European interests: a new challenge

Piracy is one of the consequences of Somalia's instability. Experts have recognised that the root causes of piracy lie in Somalia's protracted internal crisis and that any purely maritime operation will not directly address these issues.[3] African regional organisations and the UN have not managed to stabilise Somalia yet, despite a renewed debate since 2008 about the need to send peacekeeping troops or strengthen the Transitional Federal Government (TFG).

Pirates, by targeting daily food aid delivered from the sea by the World Food Programme, have posed a direct threat to Somalia itself. A moral and humanitarian imperative to assist more than three million Somalis depending on this aid (a priority for Nordic countries and the Netherlands) led several countries to provide escorts for World Food Programme (WFP) convoys. France, Denmark, the Netherlands and Canada did so in 2007 and 2008.

Moreover, strong economic and commercial interests have mobilised top European decision-makers. More than 15 per cent of global trade passes through the

---

2. There are other factors that increase the vessels' vulnerability: small crews working long shifts, limiting even more the number of personnel able to warn about an attack, lack of visibility to the rear of vessels, and the difficulty in distinguishing pirates from fishing boats in very crowded waters.

3. Pirates off the coasts of Somalia have been under the scrutiny of the UN and the International Maritime Organisation, international experts and military fleets patrolling in the region for some time. A UN Group of experts issued a report on piracy off the coasts of Somalia in 2008, providing recommendations to the international community for further action in this realm. A Contact Group on Piracy off the Coast of Somalia (CGPCS) was established and held its inaugural meeting on 14 January 2009. See also Roger Middleton, 'Piracy in Somalia: Threatening global trade, feeding local wars', *Briefing Paper*, Chatham House, October 2008.

Suez Canal and the Gulf of Aden annually.[4] A significant part of European energy and commodity supplies and exports thus depends on transit through the Gulf of Aden.[5] Maritime freight in this area is therefore a highly sensitive security matter not only for the EU and Europe in a broad sense, but for all major markets including India, China and the US. In a time of financial crisis and fluctuating oil prices, it has become clear that insecurity in the area could have a high commercial cost and some maritime operators have called for support from the navies.[6] War risk insurance premiums have suddenly peaked, alternative routes via the Cape of Good Hope imply extra costs (e.g. more expenditure on fuel, due to longer transport distances) or losses for littoral economies (like, in particular, Egypt, whose income from the Suez Canal has significantly dropped). For countries like France, Italy and Spain, where the fishing trade (including in the Indian Ocean) plays an important economic role, piracy has become a threat to national economic interests.

Furthermore, the seizure in early 2009 of the *Faina*, an Ukrainian cargo ship transporting heavy weaponry, unveiled the existence of clandestine arms trade deals in the region that some states might have wanted to keep secret. It also showed that a worst-case scenario was possible: large quantities of weapons, in addition to huge ransoms, could fall into the hands of uncontrollable groups with potential links to terrorist networks and/or arms traffickers. The capture of the *Sirius Star*, a Saudi oil tanker transporting cargo worth $100 million, on 15 November 2008 not only convinced major freight forwarders to avoid the Gulf of Aden but also triggered fears of environmental catastrophe, in addition to concerns about existing toxic waste off the Somali coast. Merchant ships are often staffed by international crews and insecurity in the area motivated numerous states to set about improving the protection of their nationals.[7]

The combination of all the above, added to high-profile media coverage, led to an increased commitment from governments to deploy naval assets in the framework of the EU. A first step was taken with the creation of a coordination cell, NAVCO, in September 2008, aimed at supporting the deployment of military assets with a

---

4. In 2007, the Suez Canal handled about 20,000 ships. Jean-Paul Rodrigue, 'The Strategic Space of International Transportation', in Jean-Paul Rodrigue, Claude Comtois and Brian Slack (eds.), *The Geography of Transport Systems* (New York: Routledge, 2009). Available at: http://people.hofstra.edu/geotrans/eng/ch5en/conc5en/ch5c1en.html.

5. 95% of EU Member States' trade (by volume) transported by sea passes through the Gulf of Aden. EU NAVFOR Operation *Atalanta*, Information brochure, Public information office, August 2009.

6. Concerns were expressed by shipping companies, freight forwarders, insurance companies and the International Maritime Organisation.

7. In November 2008, around 300 hostages were reported to be detained by pirates. 'Hostages fight Somali pirates as EU mulls daunting task', *Agence France Presse*, 9 December 2008.

view to assisting commercial and humanitarian vessels and ensuring their security.[8] NAVCO represented a first attempt to intensify coordination between navies, the shipping industry and the WFP and its activities were included in the mandate of the *Atalanta* operation launched in November the same year.

The first EU naval operation

Atalanta is a multidimensional maritime operation which, by virtue of its naval character, differs from other previous EU crisis management or peacekeeping missions. It implements several UN Security Council resolutions stipulating that all states cooperating with the TFG could use all necessary means in the fight against piracy off the coasts of Somalia.[9] The Council Joint Action[10] set two main objectives: the first one is to protect in priority the vessels of the World Food Programme delivering food aid to displaced persons in Somalia; the other, less specific, is to protect vulnerable vessels in the area and ensure 'deterrence, prevention and repression' of piracy and armed robbery at sea.

The area of operation (AOO) of 1.4 million square nautical miles is composed of several zones: the south of the Red Sea, the Gulf of Aden and Southern coasts of Somalia up to 500 miles and the area surrounding the Seychelles islands.[11] Fulfilling the mandate implied not only intelligence gathering and monitoring of the area of operation but also measures to secure maritime trade in these areas. Its law enforcement dimension, which consists of arrest, detention and transfer of suspects, goes beyond solely military action and requires that states contribute personnel with judicial expertise. Rules of engagement allow troops to board ships and use force against pirates where necessary.

The Operational Headquarters (OHQ) based in Northwood near London, is headed by Operation Commanders on a rotating basis. First OpCdrs were UK Rear-Admirals Philip Jones and Peter Hudson with Rear-Admirals Jean-Pierre Labonne from France and Thorsten Kähler from Germany as deputies. The Force Command

---

8. Council Joint Action 2008/749/CFSP, on the European Union military coordination action in support of UN Security Council resolution 1816 (2008) (EU NAVCO), 19 September 2008.

9. UN Security Council Resolutions 1814 of 15 May, 1816 of 2 June, 1838 of 7 October, 1846 of 2 December 2008. Resolutions 1814, 1838, 1853 urged states to coordinate anti-piracy activities, to protect WFP vessels and to enhance judicial and anti-crime cooperation.

10. Council Joint Action 2008/851/CFSP of 10 November 2008 on a European Union military operation to contribute to the deterrence, prevention and repression of acts of piracy and armed robbery off the Somali coast, 12 November 2008, *Official Journal* L301/33, pp. 33-37.

11. The AOO was extended in May 2009 after new attacks threatening the EU's interests took place outside the sphere of the initial AOO.

(around 20) works aboard ships in the area.[12] The OHQ also hosts the Maritime Security Centre – Horn of Africa (MSCHOA), which is one of the operation's innovations. It provides a secure web-portal with a range of services to merchant vessels including alerts of pirate activity/attacks, risk assessment based on military intelligence, regional and world navigation news and self-protection advisory measures. It is managed jointly by naval officers and private sector liaison staff all based in the OHQ operation centre in Northwood.[13] A rear logistics base for Maritime Patrol Reconnaissance Aircraft and the Force Headquarters (FHQ) support is located in Djibouti, in a French military base.

Atalanta's entire manpower, including the OHQ, FHQ, Support Area and military assets, amounts to approximately 2,000 personnel from 19 EU contributing countries. Third countries currently participating are Croatia and Norway. Other countries are expected to join.[14]

EUNAVOR capability started with 4-5 frigate-type vessels and less than 2 full-time surveillance aircrafts. This increased to a dozen ships assisted by 3 full-time Maritime Patrol and Reconnaissance Aircraft (MPRAs) provided by France, Spain and Germany and 8 helicopters.[15] Its annual cost is estimated at approximately €400 million.[16]

Implementation and performance

Atalanta's mandate reflects the multiplicity of tasks carried out by the operation. These range from escorting vessels to the coordination of information exchange with merchant vessels as well as liaison with other international fleets. The mandate also includes international judicial cooperation to ensure the prosecution of suspected pirates. The first 12 months were divided into three phases of four months

12. It has been headed by three successive commanders from, respectively, Greece (Commodore Papaioannou), Spain (Captain Garat Caramé) and the Netherlands (Commodore Bindt).

13. There are senior merchant navy personnel working in the OHQ from, among others, the following companies: BP, Intertanko, Maersk, Total, NYK (Japan).

14. 'Political and Security Committee decision on the setting-up of the Committee of Contributors for *Atalanta*', 2009/446/CFSP of 10 June 2009, *Official Journal*, L 148/52, 11 June 2009; Montenegro and Switzerland are mentioned informally by experts. Interviews, Brussels, 11 August 2009.

15. In August 2009 vessels included: ESPS *Numancia* (SP), ITS *Maestrale* (IT), ITS *Comandante Borsini* (IT), FGS *Rheinland-Pfalz* (DE), FGS *Brandenburg* (DE), FS *La Fayette* (FR), HS *Niciforos Fokas* (GR), HswMS *Stockholm* (SWE), HSwMS *Malmö* (SWE). Support units play also a key role: SPS *Marques de la Ensanada* (SP), HSwMS *Trossö* (SWE). Luxembourg also plans to charter a plane to assist with surveillance in the Indian Ocean. In the first six months, the force included: HMS *Northumberland* (UK), *Floréal* (FR), *Karlsruhe* (GER), *Victoria* (SP), *Psara* (GR). A French AWACs surveillance plan started operating end of August 2009.

16. Interviews with Council General Secretariat staff and OHQ-based staff, Brussels and Northwood, 12 May and 13 August 2009. This is based on estimates of costs for six frigate-type vessels, one tanker and three MPRAs.

each (December-March, April-July, August-November). On 15 June 2009, the Council decided to extend the operation for one more year. The Initial Operational Capacity was reached on 13 December 2008. As planned, Phase 1 was implemented by the UK, France and Greece who had the force command. Phase 2 saw the additional participation of Spain, Germany and Italy and Phase 3 foresaw the Netherlands and Belgium joining the operation.

MPRAs are used to monitor the area of operation and to deter pirates, especially in the Southern area and along Somali coasts. The setting up and management of an Internationally Recommended Transit Corridor (IRTC), in coordination with other fleets, to be used daily by merchant vessels in the Gulf of Aden, thanks to the MSCHOA, has enabled a more effective prevention of the attacks. Companies are encouraged to register on the centre's website to communicate their transit routes and to join groups of ships seeking to avail of naval protection along the corridor.[17] The MSCHOA has informed the adoption of a set of common best management practices for vessels' self protection and has been recognised by the International Maritime Organisation (IMO) as a key tool.[18] Escorting WFP vessels, the number one priority, represents on average less than 10 percent of Operation *Atalanta*'s tasks, the rest being equally shared between action in the Gulf of Aden and in the Seychelles area.[19]

It is worth mentioning that contributing ships can switch from EU to national operational command, a very usual practice in multilateral naval operations. This also allows them to use force in a differentiated manner, depending on the legal framework inside which they operate. For the sake of EU coherence however, reverting to national command is more the exception than the rule.[20]

Although it is almost impossible to define universally agreed criteria of success for crisis management operations, some data can be used to assess *Atalanta*'s effectiveness in combating piracy. As of mid-August 2009, 68 pirates had been transferred to

---

17. The registration rate of vessels transiting the area, monitored by the Operation, has significantly increased in less than 12 months and reached 70% in August 2009. Statement made by a European official during a workshop on maritime security in the framework of the conference 'Make the difference', 4 June 2009, Brussels and interview with Operation staff members, London, 13 August 2009.

18. International Maritime Organisation, 'Piracy and armed robbery against ships in waters off the coast of Somalia' (including an annex of best management practices to deter piracy in the Gulf of Aden and off the coasts of Somalia), MSC.1/Circ.1332, 16 June 2009.

19. In shipping days. Estimates given by Operation staff in Northwood and Brussels, 11 and 13 August 2009.

20. In the absence of precise international legal mechanisms, it has not been clear from the outset how EU troops could arrest and detain suspected pirates. This has given rise to various situations in which force was used differently by Member States, sometimes creating controversies or disapproval. Interview with an EU diplomat, Brussels, March 2009.

the Kenyan judicial authorities.[21] This proved to be a real added value. Several AMISOM vessels carrying sensitive cargo were also secured and 70 per cent of the vessels passing through the Gulf of Aden are registered on the MSCHOA system.

Although the intensity of attacks and hijackings vary throughout the year they have generally increased in 2009.[22] It was felt nonetheless that *Atalanta*'s joint presence with other international navies has had some deterrent impact. Improvements in prevention, self-protection measures and risk-awareness have also had an effect, with an increasing number of attacks being resisted.[23]

One of the results of the anti-piracy operations may also be an increased awareness in Europe of the need to contribute to the long-term stabilisation of Somalia. The EU has already been engaged in the country through its support to the Djibouti process and other diplomatic efforts, support to the African Union mission AMISOM, and Commission's programmes in humanitarian aid, support to civil society and police training.[24] The deterioration of the crisis in spring and summer 2009 however did not facilitate further international intervention to support stability in the country. The EU has committed to more resources during an AU-UN-EU pledging conference in June 2009 and is envisaging to upgrade its support to the country. Through its Instrument for Stability, the European Commission can support the Kenyan and Seychellois judicial systems. This form of support has allowed the EU to secure a transfer arrangement with Kenya and negotiations are underway with the Seychellois.

International coordination

With over 20 nations and two dozen international vessels patrolling in the area (China, India, Iran, Japan, Malaysia, Singapore, South Korea, Turkey and Russia all

---

21. On 11 March, suspected pirates were handed over to the Kenyan authorities for the first time. On 3 May, the NIVÔSE frigate intercepted eleven pirates, a mother ship and two skiffs after it was spotted by a Spanish MPRA. On 26 May, seven suspects were detained in the Gulf of Aden. In May, attacks against the MSC *Melody* were successfully deterred thanks to coordination between *Atalanta* and other fleets. *Atalanta*'s achievements are presented in press releases available at: http://consilium.europa.eu and www.mschoa.eu.

22. While the Gulf of Aden is not really affected by the monsoon, the rest of the AOO is, making it more difficult for pirates to operate. For various estimates on pirates attacks and captures, see a compilation made by Nicolas Gros-Verheyde in his Brussels2 blog on ESDP, 'Bilan anti-piraterie', August 2009. Available at: http://bruxelles2. over-blog.com.

23. Interview with EUMS and OHQ staff, Brussels and Northwood, 11 and 13 August 2009.

24. See chapters on AMISOM and EU-AU relations in this volume.

have ships in the area, in addition to the Combined Maritime Forces - CMF,[25] NATO and EU coalition vessels) the region has become a laboratory for international military naval coordination. On the other hand, the heavy presence of military vessels in this particularly sensitive area also reflects growing geostrategic competition between powers around Eurasia.[26] At the operational and tactical levels of command, coordination is pursued through a series of cooperative framework agreements allowing *Atalanta* to consult directly with other fleets, with the approval of the Political and Security Committee (PSC).[27] In the region, monthly coordination meetings conveyed under the SHADE (Shared Awareness and De-confliction) mechanism are organised in Bahrain by CMF and gather representatives of almost all the fleets navigating in the area. The meetings are currently co-chaired by *Atalanta* and CMF. Meetings at sea between force commanders and visits to the Northwood OHQ are organised regularly. *Atalanta* has also established an internet-based secured communication platform, *Mercury*, for real and private chat to facilitate information exchange between all the fleets and, importantly, a basic Common Operating Picture displaying merchant shipping transiting the Gulf of Aden.[28] Thanks to these innovations in coordination, *Atalanta* has been instrumental in developing dialogue with global actors like Russia or China.

In practice, the degree of synergy between *Atalanta* and other fleets varies from mere exchange of information regarding itineraries to intelligence sharing and coordinated action. Naval methods and tactics also differ from one country to another: for instance the Chinese, Russian and Indian fleets have mandates to escort their national merchant vessels.[29] In the Gulf of Aden, these national escorts take place along the IRTC where EU, NATO and the CMF coalition warships operate. China is present in the Indian Ocean for the first time in four centuries. Its navy has been keen to be seen as proactive in pursuing anti-piracy objectives, in shaping the course of events in the Gulf of Aden and in engaging in international coordination. The assertive presence of India reflects that country's ambitions as a regional power able

---

25. CMF is a US-led maritime coalition of the willing comprising three Combined Task Forces (CTF 150, 151 and 152) the first of which was established in 2002. CMF gathers around two dozens of nations operating in the Gulf of Aden, Gulf of Oman, the Arabian Sea, Red Sea and the Indian Ocean. Its task forces individually focus on counter-terrorist missions and maritime security around the Middle East and Iraq. Anti-piracy is a more recent focus of CTF 151. More information can be found at http://www.cusnc.navy.mil/cmf/152/index.html.

26. James Rogers, 'From Suez to Shanghai: The European Union and Eurasian maritime security', *Occasional Paper* no. 77, EUISS, Paris, March 2009. The author mentions the Chinese strategy of 'concirclement', p.17.

27. Interview with EUMS and OHQ staff, Brussels and Northwood, 11 and 13 August 2009

28. *Mercury* is a secure 'real time' chat system for military navies gathering 120 accounts from almost all the countries having warships in the area. It is for instance a key tool for the EU to communicate with the Chinese and the Russian fleets.

29. Anti-piracy legislation is evolving rapidly and new laws were passed in India, Japan and Russia in 2009.

to deploy and intervene around the Indian Ocean.[30] Russia has proved a cooperative partner for *Atalanta*.[31]

Arab countries are in principle opposed to the presence of international fleets in the Red Sea.[32] Some of the littoral Arab states are also investigating the possibility of developing their own counter-piracy force.[33] In Suez, *Atalanta* cooperates with Egypt on the dissemination of information to private operators.

Coordination with other Western fleets has been unprecedented and largely facilitated by contacts between European officers from states (the UK in particular) simultaneously involved in NATO (Operations *Active Endeavour*, *Allied Protector* and *Ocean Shield*),[34] CMF operations (CTF 150 and CTF 151)[35] and *Atalanta*. At the operational level, the coordination has significantly improved and after several months, it was recognised by the International Maritime Organisation that the EU MSCHOA plays a leading role in the international coordination of counter-piracy.[36]

Main challenges confronting the mission

Atalanta has faced at least four main challenges. First, the operation as such is not designed to put an end to piracy in the region on its own. It can tackle symptoms, but not the root cause of the issue. Its mandate does not comprise an end goal expressing a clear foreign policy strategy towards Somalia and the Indian Ocean as a whole.[37] It is recognised that a comprehensive EU approach towards Somalia and to maritime security more generally, in which *Atalanta* could play its role, is necessary in the long term.[38]

---

30. Indian interventions against pirates have taken place with the minimum level of coordination with other fleets. Some attacks against Somali skiffs have stirred controversy after the death of 15 Somali fishermen in November 2008. See Blog Brussels2, available at: http://bruxelles2.over-blog.com.

31. Interview with EUMS staff, Brussels, 11 August 2009.

32. Yemen Foreign Minister Abou Bakr Korbi expressed worries about an old Israel-led plan of internationalisation of the Red Sea that was rejected by Arab states. See 'Le chaos somalien favorise le commerce des otages', *La Croix*, 12 November 2008.

33. 'Arab countries agree to set up own anti-piracy force', *RIA Novosti*, 30 June 2009. Available at: http://en.rian.ru/world/20090630/155391292.html (accessed August 2009).

34. In 2008 NATO briefly took over for a period of 6 weeks the task of escorting WFP food aid vessels but until 2008 was not formally engaged in anti-piracy operations. To some extent the NATO maritime shipping centre and the EU MSCHOA websites overlap as far as the safety of merchant vessels is concerned.

35. Combined Task Force (CTF) 150 was mostly a counter-terrorism instrument with minor counter-piracy components. An anti-piracy task force, CTF 151 was set in motion from October until mid-December 2008 and reactivated in 2009. It comprises three ships from the US, the UK and Singapore.

36. Interviews with EUMS staff, 11 August 2009; IMO, op. cit. in note 18.

37. Interview with a maritime security expert, Paris, 5 June 2009.

38. Valentina Pop, 'MEPs say EU anti-pirate mission is "military nonsense"', *EUObserver*, 15 October 2008; Javier Solana, 'Il faut aider la Somalie à se stabiliser', *Le Figaro*, 12 août 2009 ; James Rogers, op. cit. in note 26.

Despite the US and UK initiatives in December 2008, there has been no consensus about what measures to adopt to combat Somali piracy on land and to address linkages between piracy and the local political elite, in Somaliland, Puntland and south central Somalia and at the national level. The operation has engaged Somali authorities who have made anti-piracy statements, but this is not enough. Assisting fragile Somali authorities to improve coastal security may prove a double-edged sword since in the past expertise and equipment passed to coast guards has reportedly subsequently been used to upgrade piracy techniques.[39]

Second, the operation had to carry out its tasks with insufficient assets in comparison to what it had requested. The extension of the AOO up to 1.4 million square nautical miles (about 10 times the size of Spain) made things even more difficult.[40] This challenge was addressed by increasing the capacities of the operation through more vessels and above all more MPRAs, which eventually happened, and by developing strong international coordination to maximise existing naval forces in the area.[41] Third, despite success in coordinating with the shipping industry and via the MSCHOA, reaching out to most vulnerable vessels will remain a challenge as those are usually registered in fragile flag states, run as family businesses and operated on the margins of international coordination. Fourth, the prosecution of suspected pirates by third states will continue to be a challenge if more arrests take place, as the capacities of regional partners like Kenya are already becoming overstretched.[42] Finding alternative options, through judicial agreements with Djibouti, Kenya and the Seychelles to prosecute, arrest, detain and, transfer suspects, is therefore a challenge for the future.

Lessons learned

Atalanta, by being the first EU naval operation, broke new ground in many respects. It developed links with NATO in a context of *rapprochement* between France and the

---

39. This has been the case with people trained by private and security companies in Somalia. Interviews with EU military staff, Northwood, 13 August 2009.

40. *BBC Monitoring Europe*, 3 February 2009.

41. This being said, the operation, as of August 2009, still requires a proper hospital at sea. Without it, staff are at risk if incidents take place far away from Mombasa or Djibouti. Interview with OHQ staff, Northwood, 13 August 2009.

42. Legal issues around piracy cannot be elaborated on here. EU Member States, although they are legally entitled to prosecute suspected pirates, have all been reluctant to do so. This has been motivated by strict immigration policies, the fear of encouraging asylum seeking by Somalis in the long run, and a growing sense that, according to the spirit of the EU-Africa partnership, African problems need to be solved by Africans. Hence the need for the EU to sign judicial transfer agreements with regional states. Interviews with EU diplomats and *Atalanta* staff, Brussels, London, March, July and August 2009; Bruno Waterfield, 'Somali pirates embrace capture as route to Europe', *Telegraph*, 19 May 2009.

organisation and this experience could help inform the future of ESDP and NATO relations.

Beyond piracy, the sudden increased presence of naval forces in the Indian Ocean and the Gulf of Aden shows that new maritime power games are developing. *Atalanta* has proved to be an essential tool for the EU to dialogue with global and regional maritime players like China and Russia, in addition to the links it established with the US-led coalition in the area.

Thanks to its comprehensive approach involving rule-of-law and Community instruments to support judicial systems in the region, the EU is able to ensure that suspected pirates are prosecuted according to international human rights standards. However, the judicial cooperation started by *Atalanta* will require long-term engagement from the EU with still rather fragile partner states such as Kenya or possibly the Seychelles.

Needs have been identified with a view to enhancing judicial harmonisation and cooperation in the field of piracy in Europe and more generally increase the profile and capacities of the EU's representation abroad when, for instance, it comes to negotiate international judicial agreements or Status of Force Agreements (SOFAs). The operation has also highlighted the complexity of operations in a law enforcement environment. At the tactical level, one key issue is the need for standardised secure EU military communications. Finally, one of the innovations of *Atalanta* lies in the cooperation between the military and the private sector (*inter alia* through the setting up of the MSCHOA) and this experience will hopefully inform further research on the business and security nexus.

BIBLIOGRAPHY

Middleton, Roger. 'Piracy in Somalia: Threatening global trade, feeding local wars', *Briefing Paper*, Chatham House, London, October 2008.

Rodrigue, Jean-Paul. 'The Strategic Space of International Transportation', in Jean-Paul Rodrigue, Claude Comtois and Brian Slack (eds.), *The Geography of Transport Systems* (New York: Routledge, 2009).

Rogers, James. 'From Suez to Shanghai: the European Union and Eurasian maritime security', *Occasional Paper* no. 77, EU Institute for Security Studies, Paris, March 2009.

Conclusion:
the next steps for ESDP

Giovanni Grevi, Damien Helly and Daniel Keohane

Ten years after its formal launch in June 1999, ESDP has established itself as a key component of the EU's external projection and international profile. It has provided tangible added value through many of the 20-plus military and civilian operations deployed in the last six years. It has channelled and fostered cooperation between EU Member States in the sensitive domains of security and defence. It has helped generate an original, comprehensive strategic approach to crisis management, and it has set in place some of the tools to implement it. ESDP is a success story, not least when one considers that it was born and developed in turbulent times, and at a time of profound change for the EU itself.

The Union expanded to include 12 new countries between 2004 and 2007, but failed for years to introduce the institutional reforms necessary to improve decision-making for internal and external policies. At the same time, the political cohesion of the Union has been put to serious test by external factors that could not be foreseen back in 1999. The 9/11 attacks dramatically changed the threat perception and security priorities of the US and of European countries. Two wars followed, in Afghanistan and Iraq, which involved many EU Member States, exposed divisions within the Union, and still represent (at least in the case of Afghanistan) formidable challenges for stabilisation and peace-building.

In large parts of Africa and elsewhere, state fragility and state failure pose serious security risks. These have required innovative, but inevitably complicated and sometimes messy, solutions to reform or re-build frameworks of governance while deterring violence. From the Middle East to the eastern neighbourhood of the EU, geopolitical tensions have been growing more acute, often leading to a deterioration of the political context where crisis management takes place. No quick fix is in sight.

In such an environment, it was not a given that EU Member States would succeed in sustaining and expanding their cooperation in security and defence matters at EU level, on top of all their other bilateral and multinational commitments and domestic pressures. However, ten years on, ESDP exists. If demand for intervention through ESDP is a benchmark, among others, of success, then it is fair to say that this policy has been doing rather well.

And yet, as this book shows, this is surely no time for complacency. On the contrary, a closer look at the experience of ESDP shows that the challenges ahead are as large as those that have been overcome, if not more arduous. Besides, while not detracting from its considerable achievements, it has to be acknowledged that in some cases the gap between the discourse and practice of ESDP has been significant. The aim should be to fill this gap over the next ten years, and move even further than that. Drawing from the extensive assessment included in this book, a few conditions need to be met to build on past accomplishments and ensure the future 'sustainable development' of ESDP. The entry into force of the Lisbon Treaty, following the positive outcome of the Irish referendum in October 2009, would offer a major opportunity for progress.

EU foreign policy and ESDP

The first condition is, of course, the political backing of EU Member States. Political support for ESDP is required at two levels: vision and decision. On the one hand, Member States need to express a shared vision of the remit and purpose of the security and defence policy of the EU. The original Franco-British St. Malo agreement in 1998 reflected an important point of convergence of essentially different national perspectives on ESDP. These perspectives have largely shaped – and sometimes stifled – the debate on ESDP in the last ten years and are still present. Relatively recent developments such as France's *rapprochement* to NATO and the endorsement of ESDP by the previous and current US administrations have set the stage for better cooperation between the EU, the US and NATO in crisis management. However, the basic political question of the autonomy of the Union as an international security actor across the civil and military dimensions of crisis management – which lay at the core of the St. Malo Declaration – remains to be addressed by EU Member States.

On the other hand, action through ESDP is predicated on the consensus of EU Member States on the need for and objectives of intervention. The relationship between CFSP and ESDP is the critical one here, and the experience of the last ten years has proven that this is a two-way street. The stronger the political cohesion between EU Member States, the larger the potential for an ESDP mission to be effective in the field. The EU monitoring mission in Georgia shows that the political determination of EU Member States can translate into a mission that is deployed in a matter of weeks and makes a difference on the ground, when no other international actor could intervene. Effective crisis diplomacy in FYROM in 2001 has made possible the deployment of two ESDP missions in that country. Deploying an ESDP mission can also help focus the minds of Member States and provide an incentive to advance towards common positions. The launch of *Artemis* and the other ESDP missions and measures supporting peacekeeping in Africa has triggered a broader debate on EU policy towards this continent and its relationship with the African Union (AU).

In many cases, however, the link between CFSP and ESDP has been rather loose, which has entailed serious problems for relevant ESDP operations. This has been the case, for example, for EUPOL Afghanistan, for the two ESDP missions in the Palestinian Territories and, in some respects, for EULEX Kosovo. For very different reasons, these missions have been facing considerable obstacles in implementing their mandates. This has been partly due to the ambiguity of the EU's foreign policy stance on the controversial political issues surrounding the intervention. From a different standpoint, a degree of discrepancy between foreign policy priorities and operational engagement can emerge over time, when missions outlast the political attention span in most capitals.

Aside from specific circumstances, the bottom line is that ESDP missions cannot replace the political convergence of EU Member States on sensitive foreign policy matters. Such convergence has proven stronger, the more EU countries have felt that their collective interests and security were affected. This explains, to take another example, the decision to launch the naval operation *Atalanta* off the coasts of Somalia to fight piracy, protect trade routes and enable the delivery of humanitarian aid. The 'sustainable development' of ESDP will depend on the joint political assessment of the challenges and threats facing EU Member States, on the ability to identify their key common interests, and on the decision on whether ESDP is the most suitable tool, or not, to protect them. Examination of a range of these matters started with the landmark European Security Strategy adopted in December 2003 and has continued with the report on the implementation of the strategy of December 2008, but it is by no means accomplished. National debates will play an important role in strengthening a shared strategic outlook and enhancing the political support and legitimacy of ESDP.

Stronger institutions

The second condition to support the consolidation of ESDP is that a strong, integrated institutional system is in place. Institutions are a means to an end, in this case effective action, but not an end in themselves. However, it is equally clear that effective action requires first and foremost the 'capacity to decide' together. That is the capacity to formulate, adopt and implement decisions while enhancing the convergence of national positions and improving the coherence of EU foreign policy. In a Union of 27, and in a policy area where decisions are taken by unanimity, a suitable institutional framework is essential to shape a timely, comprehensive response to crises, or to anticipate them where possible. That demands permanent interaction between the Brussels-based crisis management committees, the structures of the Council Secretariat headed by the SG/HR and the European Commission.

Over its first ten years, ESDP has had to make do with a relatively fragile and fragmented institutional framework. The fact that a number of missions have been launched and conducted, and that the beginning of a common strategic culture has been generated, is to the credit of the responsible officials at both national and EU levels. As explained in this book, sometimes difficult negotiations have produced piecemeal innovation to equip the Union with a stronger planning capacity for military and civilian operations. For civilian ESDP, the setting up of the Civilian Planning and Conduct Capability represents a notable achievement. Initiatives have also been taken to improve cooperation and coordination between EU institutions in Brussels and in the field, as recent EU interventions in Kosovo and Chad show. While a positive trend can be observed and much can be said in favour of preserving some flexibility in decision-making, a more structured system for coordination and planning should be developed, based on the reforms in the Lisbon Treaty.

In particular, based on operational experience, it is essential that EU institutions have adequate capacity to deliver top-level strategic analysis and assessments to Member States in a timely fashion. This would help ensure that EU governments consider the full range of options for EU intervention in crisis theatres, and identify and quickly implement key lessons from past and ongoing missions. Planning documents should include at the earliest stage not only the strategic objectives of EU action, but also a shared perspective on the division of labour between EU actors – whether ESDP missions or Community instruments – and the definition of effective coordinating mechanisms between them. The planned creation of the Crisis Management Planning Department (already agreed in principle in December 2008), in the broader context of the far-reaching reforms contained in the Lisbon Treaty, will mark an important step in this direction.

That said, coherence at EU level, although obviously important, cannot replace coherence between Member State action and initiatives. Having invested a lot of political capital and resources in EU instruments, including ESDP operations, Member States should be committed to making sure that EU action delivers in difficult theatres such as Afghanistan, and that their own policies are fully consistent with this goal. Stronger coordination at the level of the Foreign Affairs Council and of the European Council will be required. The fact that, as established by the Lisbon Treaty, a new double-hatted High Representative and a President of the European Council would preside over these two bodies, replacing the rotating Presidency, could help achieve that.

More resources

The third pre-requisite for the development of ESDP is the expansion, or better use, of the resources available to it. These resources include money, personnel and equipment and belong to the Member States (although a lot of the costs of civilian ESDP missions are covered by the Community budget). In many respects, progress has been made over the last ten years to improve ESDP capabilities. On the military side, EU governments have cut their armed forces personnel and some of their inventories of outdated equipment. However, military reform in Europe remains a slow process and there are still a number of key military equipment weaknesses across the EU. On the civilian side, steps have been taken to identify relevant personnel for deployment in ESDP missions, to create a pool of readily available experts, to cover the costs of early preparatory actions to set up ESDP missions, and to speed up the procurement of some categories of equipment. Since 2008, the EU has deployed well over 2,000 personnel in eleven ongoing civilian operations, which is a considerable result. In particular, dispatching versatile *gendarmerie*-type police forces has provided a distinctive contribution of ESDP to crisis management operations.

But ESDP is approaching the limits of what can be done within the scope of the resources made available so far. At one level, it is a matter for Member States to choose how to employ scarce resources such as, among others, professional soldiers, specialised military equipment, skilled policemen and judges. The demands put on ESDP and the expectations raised by its operations should be proportional to the resources that Member States have decided to allocate.

The 2008 Declaration on strengthening capabilities says that the EU should be able to carry out two or three military operations simultaneously, along with several civil operations in separate places. The EU is already doing this – Member States are currently carrying out 13 ESDP operations, two of which are military. This is an impressive number of simultaneous operations, even if most ESDP missions so far have been limited in size and scope. However, ESDP operations are starting to become larger and more challenging, such as the 2008 deployments in Georgia (EUMM), Kosovo (EULEX) and Chad (EUFOR Tchad/RCA). One key question for the future, therefore, may be less the number of ESDP operations, but more their size, mandate and political ambition.

At another level, ways to make the best use of existing resources should continue to be explored. This should entail a degree of pooling or multinationalisation of some military assets, which is envisaged by the Declaration on strengthening capabilities of December 2008, and which could be further developed through the permanent structured cooperation mechanism in the Lisbon Treaty. On the civilian side, Member States will need to devise national strategies to expand the pool of available personnel and enhance training schemes. At the same time, ongoing work should continue to improve the procedures for rapid financing and procurement in support of civilian missions.

Effective partnerships

Whatever the resources made available, however, in most theatres ESDP can only succeed if it works in close partnership with other major crisis management actors. The fourth condition for ESDP to deliver is therefore that these partnerships are developed further, with a focus on relations with the UN, NATO, the OSCE and the African Union, as well as other African regional organisations. Almost all ESDP missions have been deployed alongside the often sizeable presence of these organisations, or to pave the way for or follow their engagement on the ground. All ESDP military operations, except *Concordia*, have taken place under a UN mandate. Aside from clear benefits at the political, operational and tactical level, good cooperation and coordination with these actors is also a key dimension of EU support to effective multilateralism.

The experience of the last ten years has been mixed. Considering the complexity of the political debates within each of these organisations and the challenges they are confronted with in the field, this is not surprising. Besides, constructive dialogue at the institutional level does not always feeds into effective cooperation on the ground, and *vice versa*.

In Africa, ESDP was used to support MONUC twice, in 2003 with *Artemis* and in 2006 with EUFOR RD Congo. EUFOR Tchad/RCA was designed as a bridging operation paving the ground for UN deployment. However, the EU has not yet clarified the nature and scope of its long-term involvement in UN peacekeeping, as indicated by the 2008 decision not to intervene in Eastern Congo, following a request of the UN. In other regions, from Georgia to Kosovo, EU-UN cooperation has been weakened by the political constraints affecting the room for manoeuvre of either institution.

The partnership between the EU and the AU (involving also other African regional mechanisms and the European Commission), with a strong focus on the development of the African Peace and Security Architecture, will be reviewed in 2010 when the African Standby Force should be in place. Cooperation between the EU and NATO has long been hampered by differences between Turkey and Cyprus, which has made the formal exchange of confidential documents impossible for most issues, and has also been weakened by broader political debates between NATO countries on pressing issues such as the intervention in Afghanistan. While the political will is largely there to overcome differences and work more closely and effectively together, from Afghanistan to Kosovo, how precisely to move to a higher gear of cooperation remains to be defined.

Over the next few years, the EU will need to reinforce its partnerships not only with the UN and other key multilateral bodies, but also with major powers involved in crisis management such as the US and, among others, India, China, Brazil and Russia. The bottom line is that all of these actors are confronted with an ever more demanding crisis management agenda, in terms of both quantitative requirements and qualitative approach. In the last ten years, security sector reform, disarmament, demobilisation and reintegration and the broader concept of peace-building have taken centre-stage in the debate on crisis management, from conflict prevention to post-conflict stabilisation and beyond.

Next steps for ESDP

Lessons drawn from the crisis management debate point to two fundamental factors of success. First, a comprehensive, possibly integrated approach across the different actors involved in the field. Second, given the scale of the challenge to stabilise conflict areas and build the conditions for lasting peace, the resilience of the political and material commitment of crisis management actors, possibly over many years. Both these factors pose important questions for the future of ESDP.

These questions are not new. The comprehensive approach has been at the core of the EU's strategic vision since the launch of ESDP and it has become clear that operations initially planned for periods of one or two years actually require much longer timeframes to deliver. The fifth and last condition of the 'sustainable development' of ESDP, therefore, is a consolidated effort to collect and implement the lessons of the first ten years of activity with a focus on the coherence of EU action, and on the sequencing over time of different tools for managing crises and building peace. On the latter point, the interesting experiences of the Aceh Monitoring Mission and of the transition from EUPOL *Proxima* to EUPAT to Community programmes in FYROM can be built upon.

These lessons have to be gathered on a more systemic basis than has been done so far, and need to be translated into tangible innovations at the operational level. The need for a stronger 'lessons' policy is largely acknowledged by EU institutions. Lessons from operational experiences should drive the development of military and civilian capabilities. Some mechanisms have been recently devised or revamped to both closely monitor the conduct of ESDP operations and identify lessons from their performance. The more integrated institutional framework established under the Lisbon Treaty will hopefully create the conditions for a more joined up effort across currently separate departments.

As a contribution to this process, this book ends by pointing at five main lessons on the practice of ESDP that deserve deeper analysis and research.

First, the distinction between military and civilian crisis management operations reflects established institutional patterns rather than the reality on the ground. As the Swedish Foreign Minister Carl Bildt stressed at a recent EUISS conference on 28 July 2009, most crises are first and foremost political ones and require a political response.[1] Such responses may require a different mix of military and civilian means at different times. When it comes to the EU, Member States need to arrive at a shared assessment of the nature of the crisis and the purpose of intervention to begin with, and need to put their combined political weight behind ESDP missions. In other

---

1. The speech is available on the EUISS website at: http://www.iss.europa.eu/fileadmin/fichiers/pdf/seminars/2009/ESDP_10-Bildt_speech.pdf

words, ESDP should be a key tool for a broader foreign policy strategy, which benefits from tailored and informed analysis.

Second, when outlining the mandates of ESDP operations, the relation between the conditions on the ground, available resources and attainable objectives needs to be the subject of more careful attention. From this standpoint, the existing practice of joint fact-finding missions should be developed further and be connected with more joined up planning structures in Brussels. Short of a good match between the mandate of the mission and the requirements on the ground, the risk may be to embark on 'declaratory' missions that cannot really make much difference.

Third, a comprehensive approach demands, at some point, 'comprehensive' responsibility. In other words, without necessarily envisaging rigid hierarchical frameworks, a clearer allocation of the responsibility to coordinate different EU actors – and, when differences arise, to arbitrate – would seem in order both in Brussels and in the field. Aside from a question of effectiveness, this is also a matter of accountability. The establishment of the European External Action Service could provide scope for important innovations drawing from the pioneering experiences of 'double hatting' some EU Special Representatives.

Fourth, while some progress has been made in this respect, more needs to be done to establish the capacity for the rapid deployment of ESDP assets and missions and, in the case of civilian ones, to guarantee adequate mission support including in dangerous theatres. In particular, revisiting the concepts and the actual degree of readiness of the Battlegroups and of the Civilian Response Teams, among other formats for rapid intervention, could suggest adjustments to improve the performance of ESDP when time is pressing and action is of the essence. Work along these lines should go hand-in-hand with improving the procedures for rapid financing, including exploring the options for the start-up fund envisaged by the Lisbon Treaty.

Fifth, aside from ensuring internal support for ESDP, the EU needs to be more aware of the perception of ESDP outside Europe. The effectiveness of ESDP operations is a function of good planning and adequate resources. On top of that, however, ESDP missions have to connect with local leaders and public opinion in the field, and do so in ways that are consistent with the engagement and messages of other EU actors. The 'narrative' associated with each mission is a critical dimension of its political profile and visibility in the eyes of local interlocutors, potential spoilers and other crisis management partners.

Writing in 2000, to describe what ESDP was about, Javier Solana, the EU's High Representative for the Common Foreign and Security Policy, explained: 'What the EU will offer, unlike any other international organisation, is the capacity to deliver the fullest possible range of crisis management measures within a single framework. This new capability will help the EU to advance its core objectives: the alleviation of poverty, the promotion of democracy and the rule of law, and the protection of human rights. It will allow us to make a greater contribution to the development of international stability and the preservation of peace and security.'[2] The EU's contribution to international security has substantially increased and improved because of the development of ESDP over the last ten years. In the words of Javier Solana, writing in 2009: 'We have come a long way in developing ESDP as a tool enabling Europe to project itself through action in response to crises. ESDP is no longer an aspiration; it is a reality.'[3]

---

2. Javier Solana, 'Why Europe needs the military option', *Financial Times*, 29 September 2000.

3. Javier Solana, 'Preface', in Álvaro de Vasconcelos (ed.), *What ambitions for European defence in 2020?* (Paris: European Union Institute for Security Studies, July 2009).

Annexes

- Member States' contributions to military ESDP operations

- Member States' contributions to ongoing civilian ESDP operations

- ESDP operations at a glance

Annex 1:

Member States' contributions to military ESDP operations*

Member States	Concordia	Artemis	Althea	EUFOR RD Congo	EUFOR Tchad / RCA	Total contributions
Austria	11	3	203	0	55	272
Belgium	26	82	60	86	50	304
Bulgaria	1	0	139	0	0	140
Cyprus	0	1	0	0	0	1
Czech Republic	2	0	90	0	0	92
Estonia	1	0	3	0	0	4
Finland	9	0	182	0	65	256
France	149	1,785	439	1,002	2,095	5,470
Germany	16	7	1,242	780	0	2,045
Greece	21	7	179	0	15	222
Hungary	1	1	143	0	0	145
Ireland	0	5	55	0	440	500
Italy	27	1	1,119	72	55	1,274
Latvia	2	0	3	0	0	5
Lithuania	1	0	1	0	0	2
Luxembourg	0	0	1	0	0	1
Malta	0	0	0	0	0	0
Netherlands	2	1	438	0	65	504
Poland	17	0	227	130	400	774
Portugal	6	2	234	56	15	313
Romania	3	0	110	0	120	233
Slovakia	1	0	40	0	0	41
Slovenia	0	0	124	0	15	139
Spain	17	1	469	131	90	708
Sweden	14	81	80	62	235	472
United Kingdom	3	111	691	0	0	805
TOTAL	**330**	**2,088**	**6,297**	**2,319**	**3,715**	**14,722**

*Source: Anne-Claire Marangoni. 'Le financement des opérations militaires de l'UE : des choix nationaux pour une politique européenne de sécurité et de défense ?', *EU Diplomacy Paper* no. 6, College of Europe, November 2008. (Estimates gathered on the basis of working documents from the French military staff).

Figures indicate the number of military personnel and do not take rotation of personnel into account. Total for *Concordia*, *Artemis* and all of the operations have been added by the editors on the basis of data available in the reference document. Figures for EUNAVFOR *Atalanta* are not included.

Annex 2:

Member States' contributions to ongoing civilian ESDP operations*

Member States	Seconded personnel/ Total per Member State	Contracted personnel / Total per Member State	Total
Austria	37	5	42
Belgium	45	10	55
Bulgaria	57	25	82
Cyprus	2	0	2
Czech Republic	43	3	46
Denmark	80	7	87
Estonia	10	6	16
Finland	99	25	124
France	247	28	275
Germany	236	23	259
Greece	42	9	51
Hungary	60	8	68
Ireland	19	15	34
Italy	242	40	282
Latvia	14	4	18
Lithuania	15	4	19
Luxembourg	4	0	4
Malta	3	1	4
Netherlands	57	5	62
Poland	141	17	158
Portugal	34	12	46
Romania	214	16	230
Slovakia	15	2	17
Slovenia	18	3	21
Spain	45	19	64
Sweden	131	12	143
United Kingdom	66	59	125
Total	**1,976**	**358**	**2,334**

* *Source*: Data based on statistics produced by the CPCC, April 2009.

The precise amount of contributions is constantly evolving. Figures do not take rotation of personnel into account.

Annex 3:

ESDP operations at a glance*

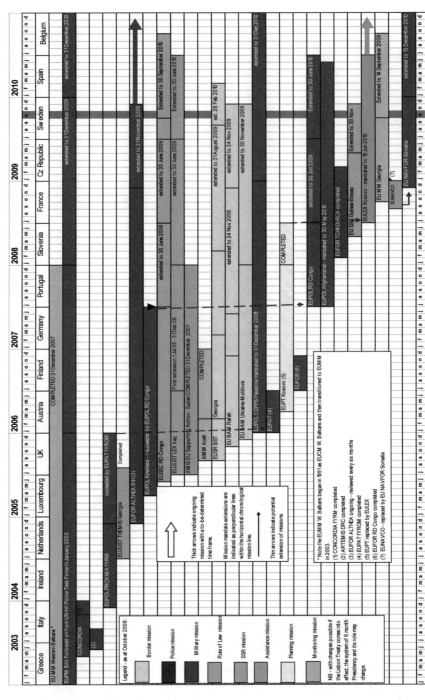

* Chart of ongoing and completed ESDP and EU missions, updated version October 2009, copyright Giji Gya, ESDP MAP (www.esdpmap.org). This table, more information and regular updates are available at the ISIS Europe website (www.isis-europe.org).

About the authors

Esra Bulut is Research Fellow at the EUISS where she deals with governance, reform, conflict and security in the Middle East and Mediterranean, Islamist politics and EU policy towards the Mediterranean and Middle East. Previously, she worked as research officer, research analyst and EU advocacy manager for the International Crisis Group (2005-2008), as a consultant for the United Nations Development Programme Bureau for Crisis Prevention and Recovery (2007), and in various research, editorial and teaching capacities at LSE (2000-2005).

Caty Clément is faculty member at the Geneva Centre for Security Policy where she is co-director for the New Issues in Security course. She holds a Ph.D in International Relations and Comparative Politics. She has worked extensively on conflict and mediation both as an academic and a practitioner with a strong Africa focus.

George Dura is a researcher at the Centre for European Policy Studies in Brussels and a Ph.D candidate in Political Science at the Catholic University of Louvain in Belgium. His research interests include EU CFSP/ESDP, the ENP, Romanian foreign policy and conflict resolution in Moldova.

Sabine Fischer is Senior Research Fellow at the EUISS where she deals with EU-Russia relations, domestic and foreign policy in Russia and the other countries of the former USSR and EU policy towards the former Soviet Union. Previously she was a Research Fellow at the German Institute for International and Security Affairs (2006-2007), the Freie Universitaet Berlin (2003-2006), the Mannheim Centre for European Social Research (2002-2003) and the Peace Research Institute Frankfurt (1998-2002).

Benedikt Franke is a Visiting Research Fellow at the University of Oxford. He holds a Ph.D from the University of Cambridge and an MA from the Johns Hopkins University Paul H. Nitze School of Advanced International Studies (SAIS). His book *Security Cooperation in Africa: A Reappraisal* has just been published by Lynne Rienner.

Richard Gowan is Associate Director for Multilateral Diplomacy at New York University's Center on International Cooperation. He is also the UN policy fellow at the European Council on Foreign Relations. From 2005 to 2007, he coordinated the first two editions of the Annual Review of Global Peace Operations, the most comprehensive source of data and analysis on peacekeeping in the public domain.

Giovanni Grevi is Senior Research Fellow at the EUISS where he deals with the development of the EU foreign and security policy, institutional questions and civilian crisis management. He previously worked at the European Policy Centre (EPC) in Brussels, where he was Associate Director of Studies from 2002 to 2005.

Eva Gross is Senior Research Fellow for European Foreign and Security Policy at the Institute for European Studies, Free University Brussels. Her research interests include the role of the EU as a global actor, the Europeanization of national foreign and security policy, transatlantic relations, and EU conflict prevention and crisis management policies.

Damien Helly is Research Fellow at the EUISS where he deals with conflict prevention and crisis management, and linkages between security, development and governance, mainly in sub-Saharian Africa. Before joining the EUISS, he worked as lecturer in Azerbaijan for the French Ministry of Foreign Affairs, for the International Crisis Group as Caucasus project director, Moldova consultant and Haiti Senior Analyst, and for Saferworld as European policy and advocacy coordinator.

Isabelle Ioannides is a Post-Doctoral Research Fellow at the Faculty of Social Sciences of the Free University of Amsterdam (ULB). She holds a Ph.D in International Relations and Security Studies from the Department of Peace Studies, University of Bradford, UK. She has published widely on EU crisis management, police missions and SSR, among other subjects.

Daniel Keohane is Senior Research Fellow at the EUISS where he deals with ESDP, counter-terrorism and defence industry issues. He was previously Senior Research Fellow at the Centre for European Reform (CER) in London, and a Research Associate at the Institute for National Strategic Studies, National Defense University, in Washington DC.

Daniel Korski is a Senior Policy Fellow at the European Council on Foreign Relations. He previously worked for the British government in Iraq, Afghanistan, and the US as well as in London. He also worked in Bosnia-Herzegovina for the Office of the High Representative.

Xymena Kurowska is an Assistant Professor in the Department of International Relations and European Studies at the Central European University and a grant holder within the European Foreign and Security Policies Programme. She has conducted research and published on different aspects of European security and EU's policies in the Eastern neighbourhood.

Dov Lynch has a doctorate from the University of Oxford and has published extensively on EU policy and security developments in the former Soviet Union. He was Senior Research Fellow at the EUISS from 2002 to 2006 and now works as Senior Advisor to the Secretary General of the OSCE.

Claudia Major is Research Fellow at the Center for Security Studies, ETH Zurich. Previously she worked as policy analyst and consultant in public affairs in Berlin, Paris and Brussels. Claudia graduated from the Free University Berlin and Sciences Po, Paris and holds a Ph.D from the University of Birmingham (UK). She will take up a research position at SWP Berlin in late 2009.

Michael Merlingen is an Associate Professor at Central European University in Budapest. His research focuses on CFSP/ESDP and on IR theory. Among other publications, he has published two books on the ESDP with his co-author Rasa Ostrauskaite and a number of articles on Foucauldian IR.

Luis Peral is Research Fellow at the EUISS where he deals with the EU contribution to multilateralism and in particular to the international security system, EU-Asia relations with a focus on India, and international responses to conflict situations such as that of Afghanistan. He was formerly Lecturer in International Law at the University Carlos III of Madrid (1992 to 2004), Ramon y Cajal researcher at the Ministry of the Presidency of the Spanish Government (2004 to 2008), Senior Fellow at FRIDE (2004-2006) and Director of the Conflict Prevention and Resolution Programme at the Toledo International Centre for Peace, CITpax (2006-2008).

Kirsten E. Schulze is Senior Lecturer in International History at the London School of Economics. Her main areas of research are the Aceh Conflict, the Maluku Conflict, the Indonesian military, and militant Islam in Indonesia. She is the author of *The Free Aceh Movement (GAM): Anatomy of a Separatist Organisation (2004)* and the co-author of *Tolerance on Trial: Democracy and Conflict in Indonesia (2010)*. She has published widely on the Aceh conflict.

Thierry Vircoulon is Associate Researcher at the Institut français des Relations internationales (IFRI) where his research focuses on Central Africa and the Great Lakes Region, South Africa and Zimbabwe, governance and post-conflict reconstruction, security sector reform and Sino-African relations. He is a graduate of the Ecole Nationale d'Administration (ENA) and holds a DEA in political science from the Sorbonne. He has formerly worked for the Quai d'Orsay and for the European Commission.

Bibliography

- Aalto, Erkki. 'Interpretations of Article 296', in Daniel Keohane (ed.), 'Towards a European Defence Market', *Chaillot Paper* no. 113, EU Institute for Security Studies, Paris, November 2008, pp. 13-49.

- Altana, Gabriele and Baldi, Stefano. 'Vademecum della PESD: Breve guida della Politica Europea di Sicurezza e Difesa', *Manuali diplomatici*, 2009.

- Amnesty International. 'Double malheur, aggravation de la crise des droits humains au Tchad', London, 18 December 2008.

- Andréani, Jacques. *Le Piège: Helsinki et la chute du communisme* (Paris: Odile Jacob, 2005).

- Appiah-Mensah, Seth. 'The African Mission in Sudan: Darfur Dilemmas', in *African Security Review*, vol. 15, no. 1, 2006, pp. 2-9.

- Arloth, Jana and Seidensticker, Frauke. *The ESDP Crisis Management Operations of the European Union and Human Rights* (Berlin: German Institute for Human Rights, April 2007).

- Aspinall, Edward. 'The Helsinki Agreement', *Policy Studies* no. 20, East West Center, Washington D.C., 2006.

- Aspinall, Edward and Crouch, Harold. 'The Aceh Peace Process: Why it Failed', *Policy Studies*, no. 1, East West Center, Washington D.C., November 2003.

- Assanvo, William and Pout, Christian. 'The European Union: African Peace and Security Environment's Champion?', Fondation pour la Recherche Stratégique, Paris, 2007.

- Asseburg, Muriel. 'European Conflict Management in the Middle East: Towards a More Effective Approach', *Carnegie Endowment/SWP Working Paper*, February 2009.

- Augustin, Col. Pierre. 'Lessons learned: Operation *Concordia/Altaïr* in Macedonia', *Doctrine* no. 6, March 2005

■ Avello, María. 'European efforts in Transitional Justice', *Working Paper* no. 58, Fundación para las Relaciones Internacionales y el Diálogo Exterior (FRIDE), Madrid, June 2008.

■ Avery, Graham, Missiroli, Antonio et al. 'The EU Foreign Service: how to build a more effective common policy', *EPC Working Paper* no. 28, Brussels, November 2007.

■ Bagayoko, Niagalé. 'L'Opération Artémis, un tournant pour la politique européenne de sécurité et de défense?', *Revue Afrique contemporaine*, no. 209, 2004, pp. 101-16.

■ Bagayoko, Niagalé. 'The EU and the member-states: African capabilities building programmes' in Christophe Cazelles (ed.), *Europe's activity in Africa in the field of security* (Paris: Centre d'analyse stratégique, 2007).

■ Bah, A. Sarjoh and Jones, Bruce D. 'Peace Operations Partnerships' in Center on International Cooperation, *Annual Review of Global Peace Operations 2008* (Boulder, CO: Lynne Rienner, 2008).

■ Ball, Nicole et al. 'Squaring the Circle: Security-Sector Reform and Transformation and Fiscal Stabilisation in Palestine', Report prepared for the UK Department for Industrial Development, 16 January 2006.

■ Bayart, Jean-François. 'Africa in the World, A History of Extraversion', *African Affairs*, vol. 99, no. 395, April 2000, pp. 217-67.

■ Bergeon, Sébastien. 'Le Partenariat stratégique « UE-Afrique » face aux « situations de fragilité »', *Studia Diplomatica*, vol. LXII, no. 2, 2009, pp. 53-64.

■ Bertin, Thomas. 'The EU Military Operation in Bosnia', in Michael Merlingen and Rasa Ostrauskaite (eds.), *European Security and Defence Policy: An Implementation Perspective* (Abingdon,Oxon/New York: Routledge 2008).

■ Bindi, Federiga. 'Europe's Problematic Contribution to Police Training in Afghanistan', Brookings Institution, 4 May 2009.

■ Binnendijk, Hans and Kugler, Richard. 'Transforming European Forces', *Survival*, vol. 44, no. 3, 2002, pp. 117-32.

■ Biscop, Sven. 'Permanent Structured Cooperation and the future of ESDP', *Egmont Paper* no. 20, The Royal Institute for International Relations, Brussels, April 2008.

■ Biscop, Sven and Andersson, Jan Joel (eds.) *The EU and the European Security Strategy: Forging a Global Europe* (New York: Routledge, 2008)

■ Bogland, Karin, Egnell, Robert and Lagerström, Maria. 'The African Union – A Study Focusing on Conflict Management', *Swedish Defence Research Agency Report* no. 2475, Swedish Defence Research Agency, Stockholm, 2008.

■ Brahimi, Lakhdar et al. 'Report of the Panel on United Nations Peace Operations', Doc. A/55/502, United Nations, New York, August 2000.

■ Braud, Pierre-Antoine. 'Implementing ESDP Operations in Africa', in Anne Deighton and Victor Mauer (eds.), *Securing Europe? Implementing the European Security Strategy* (Zurich: ETH Centre for Security Studies, 2006).

■ Braud, Pierre-Antoine and Grevi, Giovanni. 'The EU mission in Aceh: implementing peace', *Occasional Paper* no. 61, EU Institute for Security Studies, Paris, December 2005.

■ Burwell, Fran et al. 'Transatlantic Transformation: Building a NATO-EU Security Architecture', *Policy Paper*, Atlantic Council of the United States, March 2006.

■ Cameron, Fraser. 'The EU and International Organisations: Partners in Crisis Management', *EPC Issue Paper* no. 41, Brussels, 22 October 2005.

■ Cazelles, Christophe. 'The EU as an international organisation: the case of Darfur' (Paris: Centre d'analyse stratégique, 2007).

■ Centro Internacional de Toledo Para la Paz. 'EU Civil Missions in the Palestinian Territories: Frustrated Reform and Suspended Security', *Middle East Special Report* no. 1, Summer 2006.

■ Chandler, David. 'EU Statebuilding: Securing the Liberal Peace through EU Enlargement', in *Global Society: Journal of Interdisciplinary International Relations* (London: Routledge, 2007), pp. 593-607.

■ Chandran, Rahul, Sherman, Jake and Jones, Bruce D. 'Rapid Deployment of Civilians for Peace Operations: Status, Gaps and Options', Center on International Cooperation, New York University, April 2009.

■ Charillon, Frédéric (ed.) 'L'européanisation de la défense', *Les Champs de Mars*, no. 16, 2005.

■ Chilton, Scott, Schiewek, Eckart and Bremmers, Tim. 'Evaluation of the appropriate size of the Afghan National Police Force Manning List (Tashkil)', Final Report, European Commission Contrat no. 2009/207401 – Version 1; Kabul, 15 July 2009.

■ Cilliers, Jakkie. 'The African Standby Force: an update on progress', *ISS paper* no. 160, Pretoria, March 2008.

■ Collantes Celador, Gemma. 'The European Union Police Mission: The Beginning of a New Future for Bosnia and Herzegovina?', *IBEI Working Paper* no. 9, Institut Barcelona d'Estudis Internacionals, Barcelona, October 2007.

■ Collantes Celador, Gemma et al. 'Fostering an EU Strategy for Security Sector Reform in the Mediterranean: Learning from Turkish and Palestinian Police Reform Experiences', *EuroMeSCo Paper* no. 66, 2008.

■ Cornish, Paul. 'EU and NATO: Co-operation or competition?', Policy department of external policies, European Parliament, October 2006.

■ Damay, Christian. 'La contribution de l'UE à la sécurité du processus électoral en République démocratique du Congo', in *Les cahiers de Mars*, no. 191, 2007, pp. 89-92.

■ Darnis, Jean-Pierre, Gasparini, Giovanni, Grams, Christoph, Keohane, Daniel, Liberti, Fabio, Maulny, Jean-Pierre and Stumbaum, May-Britt. 'Lessons learned from European defence equipment programmes', *Occasional Paper* no. 69, EU Institute for Security Studies, Paris, October 2007.

■ Davis, Laura. 'Justice-Sensitive Security Reform in the Democratic Republic of Congo', International Center for Transitional Justice, New York, February 2009.

■ Davis, Laura. 'Small Steps, Large Hurdles: the EU's role in Promoting Justice in Peacemaking in the DRC', International Center for Transitional Justice, New York, May 2009.

■ Delcourt, Barbara, Martinelli, Marta and Klimis, Emmanuel (eds.) *L'Union européenne et la gestion de crises* (Brussels, Editions de l'université de Bruxelles, 2008).

■ de Montclos, Marc-Antoine Pérouse. 'Les Occidentaux peuvent-ils sauver l'Afrique?', *Politique étrangère*, mars 2006, pp. 547-56.

■ Derblom, Markus, Hagström Frisell, Eva and Schmidt, Jennifer. 'UN-EU-AU Coordination in Peace Operations in Africa', *Swedish Defence Research Agency Report* no. 2602, Swedish Defence Research Agency, Stockholm, 2008.

- Derks, Marie and More, Sylvie. 'The European Union and Internal Challenges for Effectively Supporting Security Sector Reform', The Clingendael Institute, June 2009.

- de Schoutheete, Philippe. 'La cohérence par la défense. Une autre lecture de la PESD', *Chaillot Paper* no. 71, EU Institute for Security Studies, Paris, October 2004.

- de Vasconcelos, Álvaro (ed.) 'The European Security Strategy 2003-2008: Building on common interests', *ISS Report* no. 5, EU Institute for Security Studies, February 2009.

- de Vasconcelos, Álvaro (ed.) *What ambitions for European defence in 2020?*, (Paris: EU Institute for Security Studies, 2009).

- de Waal, Alex (ed.) *War in Darfur and the Search for Peace* (Cambridge , MA : Harvard University Press, 2007).

- de Wet, Erika. 'The Governance of Kosovo: Security Council Resolution 1244 and the Establishment and Functioning of EULEX', *American Journal of International Law*, vol. 103, no. 1, January 2009, pp. 83-96.

- Dobbins, James et al. *Europe's Role in Nation-Building: from the Balkans to the Congo* (Santa Monica CA: RAND, 2008).

- Dodge, Toby, Luciani, Giacomo and Neugart, Felix. *The European Union and Iraq: Present Dilemmas and Recommendations for Future Action* (London/Florence/Munich: Bertelsmann Stiftung Foundation, Mediterranean Programme and Robert Schuman Centre for Advanced Studies, June 2004).

- Duke, Simon. 'The Linchpin COPS: Assessing the workings and institutional relations of the Political and Security Committee', *Working Paper* 2005/W/05, European Institute of Public Administration, Maastricht, 2005.

- Dumoulin, André, Mathieu, Raphaël and Sarlet, Gordon. *La politique européenne de sécurité et de défense (PESD). De l'opératoire à l'identitaire* (Brussels: Bruylant, 2003).

- Dura, George. 'EU border guards set to ensure Moldova's economic reintegration', *Eurojournal*, 8 April 2004.

- Durch, William J., Holt, Victoria K., Earle, Caroline R. and Shanahan, Moira K. *The Brahimi Report and the Future of UN Peace Operations*, Henry L. Stimson Center, Washington D.C.2003

■ Engelbrekt, Kjell and Hallenberg, Jan (eds.) *European Union and Strategy. An Emerging Actor* (London: Routledge, 2009).

■ European Commission, *From warning to action: Reportage on the EU's Instrument for Stability* (Luxembourg: Office for Official Publications of the European Communities, 2008).

■ European Defence Agency. 'An Initial Long-Term Vision for European Defence Capability and Capacity Needs', Brussels, 3 October 2006.

■ European Parliament, Directorate General for External Policies, Policy department, 'EULEX Kosovo: lessons learned and future challenges', Brussels, September 2009.

■ 'European security and defence: Core documents 2004, vol. V', *Chaillot Paper* no. 75, EU Institute for Security Studies, Paris, February 2005.

■ Everts, Steven, Freedman, Lawrence, Grant, Charles, Heisbourg, François, Keohane, Daniel, and O'Hanlon, Michael. *A European way of war* (London: Centre for European Reform, London, May 2004).

■ Flessekemper, Tobias. 'EUPOL *Proxima* in Macedonia, 2003-05', in Michael Merlingen and Rasa Ostrauskaite (eds.), *European Security and Defence Policy: An Implementation Perspective* (London: Routledge, 2008), pp. 78-97.

■ Franke, Benedikt. 'EU-AU cooperation in capacity building', in Joachim A. Koops (ed.), 'Military Crisis Management – The Challenge of Effective Inter-Organizationalism', *Studia Diplomatica*, vol. 62, no. 3, Egmont, Royal Institute for International Relations, forthcoming, 2009.

■ Franke, Benedikt. *Security Cooperation in Africa: A Reappraisal* (Boulder, CO: Lynne Rienner, 2009).

■ Freidrich, Roland and Luethold, Arnold (eds.) *Entry Points to Palestinian Security Sector Reform* (Geneva/Ramallah: DCAF, 2007).

■ Fritsch, Helmut. 'EUFOR RD CONGO: A Misunderstood Operation', Queen's Center for International Relations, *Martello Papers* no. 33, Kingston, Ontario, 2008.

■ Gégout, Catherine. 'Causes and Consequences of the EU's Military Intervention in the Democratic Republic of Congo: A Realist Explanation', *European Foreign Affairs Review*, vol. 10, no. 3, Autumn 2005, pp. 427-43.

- Giegerich, Bastian and Nicoll, Alexander. 'European Military Capabilities', *Strategic Dossier*, International Institute for Strategic Studies, London, June 2008.

- GISHA-Legal Center for Freedom of Movement. 'Rafah Crossing: Who Holds the Keys?', GISHA-Legal Center for Freedom of Movement and Physicians for Human Rights-Israel report, March 2009.

- Glière, Catherine (ed.) 'European security and defence: Core documents 2008, vol. IX', *Chaillot Paper* no. 117, EU Institute for Security Studies, Paris, July 2009.

- Gnesotto, Nicole (ed.) *EU Security and Defence Policy: the first five years* (1999-2004) (Paris: EU Institute for Security Studies, 2004).

- Gordon, Philip. 'Their own army?', *Foreign Affairs*, vol. 79, no. 4, July/August 2000, pp. 12-17.

- Gourlay, Catriona. 'Civil-Civil Coordination in EU crisis management' in Agnieszka Nowak (ed.), 'Civilian crisis management: the EU way', *Chaillot Paper* no. 90, EU Institute for Security Studies, Paris, June 2006, pp. 103-22.

- Gourlay, Catriona. 'Community instruments for civilian crisis management', in Agnieszka Nowak, 'Civilian crisis management: the EU way', *Chaillot Paper* no. 90, EU Institute for Security Studies, Paris, June 2006, pp. 49-67.

- Gourlay, Catriona. 'The emerging EU civilian crisis response capacity', in *Faster and more united? The debate about Europe's crisis reponse capacity* (Luxembourg: Office for the Official Publications of the European Communities, 2006).

- Gowan, Richard. 'EUFOR RD Congo, UNIFIL and future European support to the UN', in 'The EU's Africa Strategy: What are the lessons of the Congo Mission?', *SDA Discussion Paper*, Brussels, 2007, pp: 29-31, p. 30.

- Gowan, Richard. 'The European Security Strategy's Global Objective: Effective Multilateralism', in Sven Biscop and Jan Joel Andersson (eds.), *The EU and the European Security Strategy: Forging a Global Europe* (New York: Routledge, 2008).

- Gowan, Richard and Brantner, Franziska. *A Global Force for Human Rights? An Audit of European Power at the UN* (London: European Council on Foreign Relations, 2008).

- Grant, Charles. 'EU defence takes a step forward', Centre for European Reform *Briefing Note*, London, December 2003.

■ Grant, Charles. *Is Europe doomed to fail as a power?* (London: Centre for European Reform, July 2009).

■ Grevi, Giovanni. 'The Institutional Framework of External Action' and 'The Common Foreign, Security and Defence Policy', both chapters in Giuliano Amato, Hervé Bribosia, Bruno de Witte (eds.), *Genesis and Destiny of the European Constitution* (Brussels: Bruylant 2007).

■ Grevi, Giovanni. 'Pioneering foreign policy: the EU Special Representatives', *Chaillot Paper* no. 106, EU Institute for Security Studies, Paris, October 2007.

■ Grevi, Giovanni, Manca, Daniela and Quille, Gerrard. 'The EU Foreign Minister: Beyond Double-Hatting', *The International Spectator*, vol. XL, no. 1, 2005, pp. 59-75.

■ Grignon, François and Kroslak, Daniela. 'The Problem with Peacekeeping', *Current History*, vol. 107, no. 708, April 2008, pp.186-87.

■ Gross, Eva. *The Europeanization of national foreign policy: continuity and change in European crisis management* (Basingstoke: Palgrave Macmillan, 2009).

■ Gross, Eva. 'Security Sector Reform in Afghanistan: the EU's contribution', *Occasional Paper* no. 78, EU Institute for Security Studies, Paris, April 2009.

■ Gros-Verheyde, Nicolas. 'Mission Eubam Moldavie/Ukraine', *Europolitique*, Dossier Spécial, no. 3516, 23 April 2008, pp. 9-16.

■ Groupe Mixte de Réflexion et la Réorganisation de la Police Nationale Congolaise. *Travaux de réflexion sur la réforme de la police nationale congolaise* (Kinshasa: Ministère de l'Intérieur, 2005).

■ Gutiérrez, Ignació Cosido. 'European Union Operations in the Democratic Republic of Congo (DRC) – reply to the annual report of the Council', Report submitted on behalf of the Defence Committee, Assembly of the Western European Union, Doc A/1954, Paris, 29 December 2006.

■ Gya, Giji, Isaksson, Charlotte and Martinelli, Marta. 'Report on ESDP Missions in the Democratic Republic of the Congo. Background paper', UNIFEM, Brussels, October 2008.

■ Haine, Jean-Yves (ed.) 'From Laeken to Copenhagen. European defence: Core Documents, vol. III', *Chaillot Paper* no. 57, EU Institute for Security Studies, Paris, February 2003.

■ Haine, Jean-Yves Haine and Giegerich, Bastian. 'In Congo, a cosmetic EU operation', *International Herald Tribune*, 12 June 2006.

■ Hamilton, Daniel et al. 'Alliance reborn: An Atlantic compact for the 21st century', Washington NATO Project, February 2009.

■ Hamilton, Douglas. 'European Rapid Reaction Force Unlikely by 2003' *Reuters*, 29 March 2000.

■ Hartley, Keith. 'The future of European defence policy: an economic perspective', *Defence and Peace Economics*, vol. 14, no. 2, January 2003, pp.107-15.

■ Heinemann-Grüder, Andreas and Grebenschikov, Igor. 'Security governance by internationals: The case of Kosovo', *International Peacekeeping*, vol. 13, no. 1, March 2006, pp. 43-59.

■ Helly, Damien. 'EUJUST THEMIS in Georgia: an ambitious Bet on Rule of Law', in Agnieszka Nowak (ed.), 'Civilian crisis management: the EU way', *Chaillot Paper* no. 90, EU Institute for Security Studies, Paris, June 2006, pp. 89-102.

■ Hoebeke Hans, Carette, Stéphanie and Vlassenroot, Koen. 'EU Support to the Democratic Republic of the Congo', Centre d'analyse stratégique, République Française (Brussels: IRRI-KIIB, 2007).

■ Homan, Kees. 'Operation Artemis in the Democratic Republic of Congo', in European Commission (ed.), *Faster and more united ? The debate about Europe's crisis response capacity* (Luxembourg: OPOCE, May 2007), pages 151-55.

■ House of Lords European Union Committee Report. 'The EU and the Middle East Peace Process', July 2008.

■ Howorth, Jolyon. *Security and Defence Policy in the European Union* (Basingstoke, Hampshire: Palgrave Macmillan, 2007).

■ Howorth, Jolyon. 'A new institutional architecture for the transatlantic relationship?', Europe Visions no. 5, Institut français des relations internationales (IFRI), Paris, June 2009.

■ Howorth, Jolyon. 'The Political and Security Committee: a case study in supranational inter-governmentalism', in Renaud Dehousse (ed.), *The Community Method in Perspective: New Approaches* (New York: Palgrave, 2009).

■ Hull, Cecilia and Svensson, Emma. 'The African Union Mission in Somalia (AMISOM): Exemplifying African Union Peacekeeping Challenges', *Swedish Defence Research Agency Report* no. 2596, Swedish Defence Research Agency, Stockholm, 2008.

■ Human Rights Watch. 'Internal Fight: Palestinian abuses in Gaza and the West Bank', New York, July 2008.

■ Human Rights Watch. 'Up in Flames. Humanitarian Law Violations and Civilian Victims in the Conflict over South Ossetia', New York, January 2009.

■ Hunter, Robert E. *The European Security and Defense Policy: NATO's Companion or Competitor?* (Santa Monica, CA: RAND, 2002).

■ International Crisis Group. 'Securing Congo's Elections: Lessons from the Kinshasa Showdown', *Africa Briefing* no. 42, Nairobi/Brussels, 2 October 2006.

■ International Crisis Group. 'Guinea-Bissau: Building a Real Stability Pact', *Africa Briefing* no. 57, 29 January 2009.

■ International Crisis Group. 'Guinea-Bissau: Beyond Rule of the Gun', *Africa Briefing* no. 6 , 25 June 2009.

■ International Crisis Group. 'Security Sector Reform in the Congo', *Africa Report* no. 14, 13 February 2006.

■ International Crisis Group, 'Guinea-Bissau: In Need of a State', *Africa Report* no. 142, 2 July 2007.

■ International Crisis Group. 'Chad: A New Conflict Resolution Framework', *Africa Report* no. 144, 24 September 2008.

■ International Crisis Group. 'Congo: Five Priorities for a Peacebuilding Strategy', *Africa Report* no. 150, 11 May 2009, pp. 10-13.

■ International Crisis Group. 'Aceh's Local Elections: The Role of the Free Aceh Movement (GAM)', *Asia Briefing* no. 57, Jakarta/Brussels, 29 November 2006.

■ International Crisis Group, 'Policing in Afghanistan: Still Searching for a Strategy', *Asia Briefing* no. 85, Kabul/Brussels, 18 December 2008.

■ International Crisis Group. 'EUFOR: Changing Bosnia's security arrangements', *Europe*

Briefing no. 31, Sarajevo/Brussels, 29 June 2004.

■ International Crisis Group. 'Georgia: The Risk of Winter', *Europe Briefing* no. 51, ICG Tbilisi/Brussels, 26 November 2008.

■ International Crisis Group. 'Georgia and Russia: Still Insecure and Dangerous', *Europe Briefing* no. 53, ICG Tbilisi/Brussels, 22 June 2009.

■ International Crisis Group. 'Macedonia: No Room for Complacency', *Europe Report* no. 149, Skopje/Brussels, 23 October 2003.

■ International Crisis Group. 'Moldova: Regional Tensions Over Transdniestria', *Europe Report* no. 157, 17 June 2004.

■ International Crisis Group. 'Russia versus Georgia: The Fallout', *Europe Report* no. 195, Tbilisi/Brussels, 22 August 2008.

■ International Crisis Group. 'Kosovo's Fragile Transition', *Europe Report* no. 196, 25 September 2008.

■ International Crisis Group, 'Serb integration in Kosovo: taking the plunge', *Europe Report* no. 200, 12 May 2009.

■ International Crisis Group. 'Ruling Palestine II: The West Bank Model', *Middle East Report* no. 79, 17 July 2008.

■ *International Peacekeeping*, vol. 16, no. 2, 2009, pp. 215-286.

■ International Rescue Committee. 'Mortality in the Democratic Republic of Congo: an ongoing crisis', New York, January 2008.

■ Ioannides, Isabelle. 'EU Police Mission *Proxima*: testing the "European" Approach to Building Peace', in Agnieszka Nowak (ed.), 'Civilian Crisis Management: the EU Way', *Chaillot Paper* no. 90, EU Institute for Security Studies, Paris, June 2006, pp. 69-86.

■ Ioannides, Isabelle. 'Police Mission in Macedonia', in Michael Emerson and Eva Gross (eds.), *Evaluating the EU's Crisis Missions in the Balkans* (Brussels: Centre for European Policy Studies, 2007), pp. 81-125.

■ Jakobsen, Peter Vigo. 'The ESDP and Civilian Rapid Reaction: Adding Value is Harder than Expected', *European Security* vol. 15, no. 3, September 2006, pp. 299-321.

■ Jones, James L. et al. *Report of the Independent Commission on the Security Forces of Iraq*, September 2007.

■ Juncos, Ana E. 'Bosnia and Herzegovina: A Testing Ground for the ESDP?', *CFSP Forum*, vol. 4, no. 3, Fornet, May 2006.

■ Juncos, Ana E. 'Police Mission in Bosnia and Herzegovina', in Michael Emerson and Eva Gross (eds.), *Evaluating the EU's Crisis Missions in the Balkans*, Centre for European Policy Studies, Brussels, 2007, pp. 46-80.

■ Keohane, Daniel. 'The EU and armaments cooperation', *Working Paper*, Centre for European Reform, London, December 2002.

■ Keohane, Daniel. 'Europe's new defence agency', *Policy brief*, Centre for European Reform, London, June 2004.

■ Keohane, Daniel and Valasek, Tomas. 'Willing and able? EU defence in 2020', *EU2020 essay*, Centre for European Reform, London, June 2008.

■ Kerkkanen, Ari et al. 'Building Capacity for the Palestinian Civil Police: EUPOL COPPS and Communications Project', *Finland Civilian Crisis Management Centre Report*, 2008.

■ Khol, Radek. 'Civil-Military Coordination in EU crisis management', in Agnieszka Nowak (ed.), 'Civilian crisis management: the EU way', *Chaillot Paper* no. 90, EU Institute for Security Studies, Paris, June 2006, pp. 123-38.

■ Kim, Julie. 'Bosnia and the European Union Military Force (EUFOR): Post-NATO peacekeeping', CRS Report for Congress RS21774, Congressional Research Service, Washington D.C., 5 December 2006.

■ Koops, Joachim A. 'Military Crisis Management – The Challenge of Effective Inter-Organizationalism', *Studia Diplomatica*, vol. 62, no. 3, Egmont – Royal Institute for International Relations, forthcoming, 2009.

■ Kuehne, Winrich. 'How the EU Organizes and Conducts Peace Operations in Africa: EUFOR / MINURCAT', ZIF Report, Berlin, March 2009.

■ Kühnhardt, Ludger. 'African Regional Integration and the Role of the European Union', *ZEI Discussion Paper* C184, 2008.

■ Kurowska, Xymena. 'The Role of ESDP Operations' in Michael Merlingen and Rasa Ostrauskaite (eds.), *The European Security and Defence Policy: An Implementation Perspective* (Abingdon, Oxon/New York: Routledge, 2008).

■ Kurowska, Xymena. 'The transformative European Security and Defence Policy: between international refashioning and domestic rise of politics', in *Consent for Europe*, vol. 3, 2007.

■ Kurowska, Xymena. 'More than a Balkan Crisis Manager: The EUJUST Themis to Georgia' in Michael Merlingen and Rasa Ostrauskaite (eds.), *The European Security and Defence Policy: Implementation Perspective* (London and New York: Routledge, 2008), pp. 97–110.

■ Kurowska, Xymena. '"Solana Milieu": Framing Security Policy', *Perspectives on European Politics and Society*, vol. 10, no, 4, Taylor & Francis, forthcoming, December 2009.

■ Kurowska, Xymena and Tallis, Benjamin. 'EU Border Assistance Mission: Beyond Border Monitoring', *European Foreign Affairs Review*, vol. 14, no. 1, Kluwer Law International, London, 2009, pp. 47–64.

■ Le More, Anne. *International Assistance to the Palestinians after Oslo: Political Guilt, Wasted Money* (London: Taylor & Francis, 2008).

■ Leakey, David. 'ESDP and Civil/Military Cooperation: Bosnia and Herzegovina, 2005', in Anne Deighton and Victor Mauer (eds.), 'Securing Europe? Implementing the European Security Strategy', *Zürcher Beiträge zur Sicherheitspolitik*, no. 77, 2006.

■ Lia, Brynjar. *A Police Force Without a State: A History of the Palestinian Security Forces in the West Bank And Gaza* (London: Ithaca Press, 2006).

■ Lia, Brynjar. *Building Arafat's Police: The Politics of International Police Assistance in the Palestinian Territories after the Oslo Agreement* (London: Ithaca Press, 2007).

■ Lieb, Julia and Maurer, Andreas. 'Making EU Foreign Policy more effective, consistent and democratic. The options and variables for the European External Action Service', *Working Paper* FG 1, SWP (Stiftung Wissenschaft und Politik), Berlin, July 2007.

■ Lieb, Julia and Maurer, Andreas. 'Creating a European External Action Service. Preconditions for avoiding a rude awakening', *SWP Comments* 13, SWP (Stiftung Wissenschaft und Politik), Berlin, June 2008.

■ Lindstrom, Gustav. 'On the ground: ESDP operations', in Nicole Gnesotto (ed.), *EU Security and Defence Policy. The first five years (1999-2004)* (Paris: EU Institute for Security Studies, 2004), pp. 111-30.

■ Lindstrom, Gustav. 'Enter the EU Battlegroups', *Chaillot Paper* no. 97, EU Institute for Security Studies, Paris, February 2007.

■ Lynch, Dov. 'Russia faces Europe', *Chaillot Paper* no. 60, EU Institute for Security Studies, Paris, May 2003.

■ Lynch, Dov. 'Why Georgia Matters', *Chaillot Paper* no. 86, EU Institute for Security Studies, Paris, 2006.

■ Major, Claudia. 'EU-UN cooperation in military crisis management: the experience of EUFOR RD Congo 2006', *Occasional Paper* no. 72, EU Institute for Security Studies, Paris, September 2008.

■ Mandelbaum, Michael. *The Case for Goliath: How America Acts as the World's Government in the 21st Century* (New York: Public Affairs, 2005).

■ Marangoni, Anne-Claire. 'Le financement des opérations militaires de l'UE : des choix nationaux pour une politique européenne de sécurité et de défense ?', *EU Diplomacy Paper* no. 6, College of Europe, Bruges, November 2008.

■ Maresca, John J. *To Helsinki: the Conference on Security and Co-operation in Europe, 1973-1975* (Durham, NC: Duke University Press, 1985).

■ Marut, Jean-Claude. 'Guinée-Bissau, Casamance et Gambie: une zone à risques', EUISS *Opinion*, December 2008.

■ Matlary, Janne Haaland. *European Union Security Dynamics: In the New National Interest* (Basingstoke: Palgrave Macmillan, 2009).

■ Mattelaer, Alexander. 'The Strategic Planning of EU Military. Operations – The Case of EUFOR TCHAD/RCA', *IES Working Paper* no. 5, Institute for European Studies, Brussels, 2008.

■ Matveeva, Anna et al. *Macedonia: Guns, Policing and Ethnic Division* (London/Bonn: Saferworld and Bonn International Centre for Conversion, 2003).

■ Melmot, Sébastien. 'Candide au Congo. L'échec annoncé de la réforme du secteur de la sécurité – RSS', *Focus Stratégique* no. 9, Laboratoire de Recherche sur la Défense, Institut français des relations internationales (IFRI), Paris, Septembre 2008.

■ Menon, Anand. 'Empowering paradise? The ESDP at ten', *International Affairs*, vol. 85, no. 2, 2009, pp. 227-46.

■ Merchet, Jean-Dominique. *Défense européenne, la grande illusion* (Paris: Larousse, 2009).

■ Merlingen, Michael and Ostrauskaite, Rasa. 'ESDP Police Missions: Meaning, Context and Operational Challenges', *European Foreign Affairs Review*, vol. 10, no. 2, 2005, pp. 215-35.

■ Merlingen, Michael and Ostrauskaite, Rasa. 'Power/Knowledge in International Peace-building: The Case of the EU Police Mission in Bosnia', in *Alternatives: Global, Local, Political*, vol. 30, no. 3, 2005, pp. 297-323.

■ Merlingen, Michael with Ostrauskaite, Rasa. *European Union Peacebuilding and Policing: Governance and the European Security and Defence Policy* (London: Routledge, 2006).

■ Michel, Leo. 'NATO and the European Union: Improving Practical Cooperation', Institute for National Strategic Studies, National Defense University, Washington D.C., 2006.

■ Michel, Leo. 'NATO-EU cooperation in operations', NATO Defense College, *Research Paper* no. 31, February 2007.

■ Middleton, Roger. 'Piracy in Somalia: Threatening global trade, feeding local wars', *Briefing Paper*, Chatham House, London, October 2008.

■ Milton-Edwards, Beverley. 'Order Without Law? An Anatomy of Hamas Security: The Executive Force (Tanfithya)', *International Peacekeeping*, vol. 15, no. 5, 2008, pp.663-76.

■ Missiroli, Antonio (ed.) 'From Copenhagen to Brussels: European Defence: Core documents, vol. IV', *Chaillot Paper* no. 67, EU Institute for Security Studies, Paris, December 2003.

■ Missiroli, Antonio. 'The impact of the Lisbon Treaty on ESDP', *Briefing Paper*, Policy Department External Policies, European Parliament, January 2008.

■ Missiroli, Antonio and Pansa, Alessandro. *La difesa europea* (Genoa: Il Melangolo, 2007).

■ Monaco, Annalise. 'Operation Concordia and Berlin Plus: NATO and the EU take stock', *NATO notes*, vol. 5, no. 8, International Security Information Service (ISIS) Europe, Brussels, December 2003.

■ Monteiro, André and Morgado, Michel. 'Last Chance for Security Sector Reform in Guinea Bissau', IPRIS *Viewpoints*, April 2009.

■ Morfit, Michael. 'Staying on the Road to Helsinki: Why the Aceh Agreement was possible in August 2005', paper for the international conference on *Building a Permanent Peace in Aceh: One Year After the Helsinki Accord*, sponsored by the Indonesian Council for World Affairs, Jakarta, 14 August 2006.

■ Mühlmann, Thomas. 'Police Restructuring in Bosnia-Herzegovina: Problems of Internationally-led Security Sector Reform', in *Journal of Intervention and Statebuilding*, vol. 2, no. 1, March 2008, pp. 1-22.

■ Mühlmann, Thomas. 'The Police Mission EUPM in Bosnia, 2003-05', in Michael Merlingen and Rasa Ostrauskaite (eds.), *The European Security and Defence Policy: An Implementation Perspective* (London: Routledge, 2008), pp. 43-60.

■ Nasrallah, Rami and Santoro, Simona. *The External Image of the European Union: Report on Palestine (West Bank and Gaza)*, Jointly Executed Research Project 5.2.1, GARNET-Forum Per i Problemi Della Pace e Della Guerra, Florence, undated.

■ Nickel, Dietmar and Quille, Gerrard. 'In the Shadow of the Constitution: Adapting to a Changing External Environment', paper presented at EUSA Tenth Biennial International Conference, Montreal, 17-19 May 2007.

■ Novosseloff, Alexandra. 'EU-UN Partnership in Crisis Management: Development and Prospects', International Peace Academy, New York, June 2004.

■ Nowak, Agnieszka. 'Civilian crisis management within ESDP', in Agnieszka Nowak (ed.), 'Civilian crisis management: the EU way', *Chaillot Paper* no. 90, EU Institute for Security Studies, Paris, June 2006.

■ Nzongola-Ntalaja, Georges. 'Lessons learned from the Artemis and EUFOR operations in the Democratic Republic of the Congo', in *The EU's Africa Strategy: What are the lessons of the Congo Mission?*, SDA Discussion Paper, Brussels, 2007, pp: 32-33.

■ Observatoire de l'Afrique. 'Security Sector Reform (SSR) in Guinea-Bissau', *Africa Briefing Report*, Egmont Palace, Brussels, 28 January 2008.

■ Ojanen, Hanna (ed.) 'Peacekeeping-Peacebuilding: Preparing for the Future', Finnish Institute of International Affairs *Report* no. 14, September 2006.

■ Orsini, Dominique. 'Future of ESDP: Lessons from Bosnia', *European Security Review* no. 29, ISIS Europe, Brussels, June 2006, pp. 9-12.

■ Ortega, Martin (ed.) 'The European Union and the United Nations – Partners in effective multilateralism', *Chaillot Paper* no. 78, EU Institute for Security Studies, Paris, June 2005.

■ Overhaus, Marco. 'La Politique européenne de sécurité et de défense en Bosnie-Herzégovine : les limites de la gestion de crise à l'européenne', *Politique étrangère*, no. 3, 2009, pp. 625-36.

■ Oxfam. 'Mission incomplete: why civilians remain at risk in eastern Chad', *Briefing Paper*, September 2008.

■ Penska, Susan E. 'Policing Bosnia and Herzegovina 2003-05: Issues of Mandates and Management in ESDP Missions', CEPS *Working Document*, no. 255, Centre for European Policy Studies, Brussels, 2006.

■ Petroska-Beska, Violeta et al. *Early Warning Report FYR Macedonia* (Skopje: United Nations Development Programme, UNDP, June 2005).

■ Pirozzi, Nicoletta. 'Building Security in the Palestinian Territories,' *European Security Review* no. 28, February 2006.

■ Pirozzi, Nicoletta. 'EU support to African security architecture: funding and training components', *Occasional Paper* no. 76, EU Institute for Security Studies, Paris, February 2009.

■ Pond, Elizabeth. 'The EU's Test in Kosovo', *The Washington Quarterly*, Autumn 2008.

■ Quille, Gerrard. 'The Lisbon Treaty and its implications for CFSP/ESDP', *Briefing Paper*, Policy Department External Studies, European Parliament, February 2008.

■ Quille, Gerrard, Gasparini, Giovanni, Menotti, Roberto, Pirozzi, Nicoletta and Pullinger, Stephen. 'Developing EU Civil Military Coordination: The Role of the new Civilian Military Cell', Joint Report by ISIS Europe and CeMISS, Brussels, June 2006.

■ Rácz, András. 'EU border assistance mission to Ukraine and Moldova: a preliminary analysis', *Eurojournal*, October 2005.

■ Ramel, Frédéric (ed.), *La présidence française de l'Union européenne et la PESD. Contraintes, opportunités, tendances*, Cahier du CEREM, no. 7, January 2009.

■ Rathmell, Andrew. 'Reforming Iraq's Security Sector', *RUSI Journal*, February 2005, pp. 8-11.

■ Republic of Guinea-Bissau, Interministerial Committee for the Restructuring and Modernisation of the Defence and Security Sector, Technical Committee. 'Restructuring and Modernisation of the Defence and Security Sector', *Strategy Document*, October 2006.

■ République de Guinée Bissau – Commission européenne. 'Document de stratégie pays et programme indicatif national pour la période 2008-2013', 9 December 2007.

■ Rodrigue, Jean-Paul. 'The Strategic Space of International Transportation', in Jean-Paul Rodrigue, Claude Comtois and Brian Slack (eds.), *The Geography of Transport Systems* (New York: Routledge, 2009).

■ Roger-Lacan, Véronique. 'Traité de Lisbonne et défense européenne', *Défense nationale et sécurité collective*, vol. 64, no. 2, février 2008, pp. 55-62.

■ Rogers, James. 'From Suez to Shanghai: The European Union and Eurasian maritime security', *Occasional Paper* no. 77, EU Institute for Security Studies, Paris, March 2009.

■ Ronzitti, Natalino (ed.) *Le forze di pace dell'Unione Europea* (Soveria Mannelli: Rubettino Editore, 2005).

■ Rosen, Frederik. 'Third Generation Civil-Military Relations and the "New Revolution in Military Affairs"', DIIS Working Paper, Danish Institute for International Studies, March 2009.

■ Rutten, Maartje (ed.) 'From Saint Malo to Nice. European Defence: Core documents, vol. I', *Chaillot Paper* no. 47, EU Institute for Security Studies, Paris, May 2001.

■ Rutten, Maartje (ed.) 'From Nice to Laeken. European Defence: Core documents, vol. II', *Chaillot Paper* no. 51, EU Institute for Security Studies, Paris, April 2002.

■ Sayigh, Yezid. 'Inducing a Failed State in Palestine', *Survival*, vol. 49, no. 3, 2007, pp. 7-39.

■ Schake, Kori. 'Constructive duplication: Reducing EU reliance on US military assets', *Working Paper*, Centre for European Reform, London, January 2002.

■ Schmidt, Peter. 'Freiwillige vor! Bundeswehreinsatz im Kongo – Zur Dialektik einer Führungsrolle wider Willen', in *Internationale Politik*, Deutsche Gesellschaft für Auswärtige Politik, Berlin, November 2006, pp. 68-77.

■ Schroeder, Ursula C. 'Governance of EU crisis-management', in Michael Emerson and Eva Gross (eds.), *Evaluating the EU Crisis Missions in the Balkans* (Brussels: Centre for European Policy Studies, 2007).

■ Schulze, Kirsten E. 'The Free Aceh Movement (GAM): Anatomy of a Separatist Organization', *Policy Studies*, no. 2, East West Center, Washington D.C., September 2004.

■ Schulze, Kirsten E. 'From the battlefield to the negotiating table: GAM and the Indonesian government, 1999-2005', *Asian Security*, vol. 3, no. 2, Special Issue on Internal Conflicts in Southeast Asia: The Nature, Legitimacy, and (Changing) Role of the State, July 2007, pp.80-98.

■ Schulze, Kirsten E. 'Human Security, the AMM, and the Transition from Conflict to Peace in Aceh, 2005-2006' in Mary Martin and Mary Kaldor (eds.), *A European Way of Security: The European Union and Human Security* (London: Routledge, 2009).

■ Schwok, René and Mérand, Frédéric (eds.). *L'Union européenne et la sécurité internationale. Théories et pratiques* (Brussels/Geneva: Bruylant/Université de Genève, 2009).

■ Scobbie, Iain. 'Is Gaza still occupied territory?', *Forced Migration Review*, no. 26, August 2006.

■ Seibert, Bjoern H. 'African Adventure? Assessing the European Union's Military Intervention in Chad and Central African Republic', MIT Security Studies Program *Working Paper*, November 2007.

■ Smith, Karen E. *The Making of EU Foreign Policy: the Case of Eastern Europe* (Basingstoke: Palgrave Macmillan, 2004).

■ Solana, Javier. 'Why Europe needs the military option', *Financial Times*, 29 September 2000.

■ Solana, Javier, 'Preface' in Álvaro de Vasconcelos (ed.), *What ambitions for European defence in 2020?* (Paris: European Union Institute for Security Studies, July 2009).

■ Spence, David and Fluri, Philipp (eds.) *The European Union and Security Sector Reform*, Geneva Centre for the Democratic Control of Armed Forces (London: John Harper Publishing, 2008).

■ Spinoza, Jérôme. 'L'Afrique dans le regard allemand', *Revue Défense Nationale*, no. 1, January 2007.

■ Spruds, Andris et al. 'Analysis of the EU's Assistance to Moldova', European Parliament, Committee on Foreign Affairs, *Briefing Paper*, 25 November 2008.

■ Tansey, Oisín. 'Kosovo: independence and tutelage', *Journal of Democracy*, vol. 20, no. 2, April 2009, pp. 153-66.

■ Tardy, Thierry. 'Limits and Opportunities of UN-EU Relations in Peace Operations: Implications for DPKO', UN Peacekeeping Best Practices Unit, New York, September 2003.

■ Tardy, Thierry. 'The European Union, a regional security actor with global aspirations' in Thierry Tardy (ed.), *European security in a global context: Internal and external dynamics* (London: Routledge, 2009), pp. 17-36.

■ Tardy, Thierry. 'UN-EU Relations in Crisis Management. Taking Stock and Looking Ahead', Background paper presented at the International Forum for the Challenges of Peace Operations, October 2008.

■ Terpan, Fabien. 'The political dimension of ESDP', *Revue Défense Nationale*, no. 2, February 2006.

■ Thym, Daniel. 'Beyond Parliament's Reach? The Role of the European Parliament in the CFSP', *European Foreign Affairs Review*, vol. 11, no. 1, Spring 2006.

■ Tocci, Nathalie. *The EU and Conflict Resolution: Promoting Peace in the Backyard* (London: Routledge, 2008).

■ Tocci, Nathalie, 'Active but Acquiescent: The EU's Response to the Israeli Military Offensive in the Gaza Strip', Euro-Mediterranean Human Rights Network Report, May 2009.

■ Tubiana, Jérôme. 'The Chad–Sudan Proxy War and the "Darfurization" of Chad: Myths and Reality', Small Arms Survey, HSBA *Working Paper* no. 12, 16 April 2008.

- Tull, Denis M. 'Die Führung und Beteiligung der Bundeswehr an EUFOR RD Congo', in Stefan Meir (ed.), *Auslandseinsätze der Bundeswehr. Leitfragen, Entscheidungsspielräume und Lehren*, SWP Studie, S 27, Stiftung Wissenschaft und Politik, Berlin, September 2007, pp. 68-77.

- Tywuschik, Veronika and Sherriff, Andrew. 'Beyond Structures: Reflections on the implementation of the Joint Africa-EU strategy', ECDPM *Discussion Paper*, European Centre for Development Policy Management (ECDPM), 2009.

- Ulriksen, Ståle, Gourlay, Catriona and Mace, Catriona. 'Operation Artemis: The Shape of Things to Come?' in *International Peacekeeping*, vol. 11, no. 3, 2004, pp. 508-25.

- UN Office for the Coordination of Humanitarian Affairs, 'The Gaza Strip: Access Report April 2006', UNOCHA, 30 April 2006.

- UN Office for the Coordination of Humanitarian Affairs, 'The Agreement on Movement & Access: One Year on', UNOCHA, November 2006.

- UN Peacebuilding Commission. 'Background Paper on Security Sector Reform in Guinea-Bissau', Peacebuilding Commission Country-Specific Configuration on Guinea-Bissau, Thematic Discussion on Security Sector Reform and the Rule of Law, 18 June 2008.

- Valasek, Tomas. 'France, NATO and European defence', *Policy Brief*, Centre for European Reform, London, May 2008.

- Vervaeke, Koen. 'EU-AU Cooperation in Military Crisis Management and Capacity-Building: A View From Practice', in Joachim A. Koops (ed.), 'Military Crisis Management – The Challenge of Effective Inter-Organizationalism', *Studia Diplomatica*, vol. 62, no. 3, Egmont – Royal Institute for International Relations, forthcoming, 2009.

- Viereck, Karlheinz. 'EUFOR RD Congo. Europe can do it', in *Truppendienst*, no. 3, 2007, pp. 253-58.

- Vines, Alex and Middleton, Roger. 'Options for the EU to Support the African Peace and Security Architecture', Study for the European Parliament, February 2008.

- Vircoulon, Thierry. 'Reconstruire l'Etat de droit, le système de sécurité ou les forces de sécurité ? Dilemmes et paradoxes de la réforme du secteur de sécurité', in Jean-Marc Châtaigner et Hervé Magro (eds.), *Etats et sociétés fragiles* (Paris: Karthala, 2007).

■ Weiler, Quentin. 'The European Union and Security Sector Reform in Africa: a Leader in Theory, a Laggard in Reality?', United Nations University CRIS, *Bruges Regional Integration & Global Governance Papers*, January 2009.

■ Weller, Marc. 'Negotiating the final status of Kosovo', *Chaillot Paper* no. 114, EU Institute for Security Studies, Paris, December 2008.

■ White, Stephen. 'EUJUST LEX – The EU integrated rule of law mission for Iraq', in *Journal of Defense and Strategy*, vol. 8, no. 2, December 2008, pp. 97-103.

■ Wilder, Andrew. 'Cops or Robbers? The Struggle to Reform the Afghan National Police', *Issues* Paper Series, AREU (Afghanistan Research and Evaluation Unit), Kabul, July 2007.

■ Witney, Nick. 'Re-energising Europe's security and defence policy', *Policy Paper*, European Council on Foreign Relations, London, July 2008.

■ Witney, Nick. 'European Defence - now with added elan?', European Council on Foreign Relations, 19 December 2008.

■ Wittebrod, Cornelis. 'Protecting the humanitarian space in Africa', in *The EU's Africa Strategy: What are the lessons of the Congo Mission?* SDA Discussion Paper, Brussels, 2007, pp. 24-26.

■ Wright, Richard and Auvinen, Juha. 'What ambitions for the civilian ESDP?', in Alvaro de Vasconcelos (ed.), *What ambitions for European Defence in 2020?*, EU Institute for Security Studies, Paris, July 2009, pp. 111-22.

■ Yannis, Alexandros. 'The UN as Government in Kosovo', *Global Governance* no. 10, January-March 2004.

■ Yost, David S. 'NATO and International Organisations', *Forum Paper* 3, NATO Defense College, Rome, September 2007.

■ Youngs, Richard. 'Europe and Iraq: From Stand-off to Engagement?,' The Foreign Policy Centre, London, October 2004.

■ Youngs, Richard. 'The European Union and Palestine: A New Engagement', OpenDemocracy, 28 March 2007.

■ Zounmenou, David. 'Guinea-Bissau's legislative elections: what implications for stability?', EUISS *Opinion*, November 2008.

Abbreviations

ABP	Afghan Border Police
ACP	Africa, Caribbean and Pacific
AFET	Committee on Foreign Affairs of the European Parliament
AFSOUTH	Allied Forces Southern Europe
AMA	Agreement on Movement and Access
AMIS	African Union Mission in Sudan
AMISEC	African Union Mission for Support to the Elections in the Comoros
AMISOM	African Union Mission in Somalia
AMM	Aceh Monitoring Mission
ANCOP	Afghanistan National Civil Order Police
ANP	Afghan National Police
ANT	Chadian National Army (*Armée nationale du Tchad*)
AOO	Area of Operation
AP	Action Plan
APF	African Peace Facility
APSA	African Peace and Security Architecture
ASEAN	Association of South-East Asian Nations
ASF	African Standby Force
AU	African Union
AWACS	Airborne Warning and Control System
BiH	Bosnia and Herzegovina
BRA	Aceh Reintegration Board (*Badan Reintegrasi Damai Aceh*)
CAG	Community Advisory Group
CAR	Central African Republic
CARDS	Community Assistance for Reconstruction, Development and Stabilisation
CCMT	Civilian Capabilities Management Tool
CFE	Conventional Forces in Europe
CFSP	Common Foreign and Security Policy
CHG	Civilian Headline Goal
CIAT	International Committee to Assist the Transition (*Comité international d'Accompagnement de la Transition*)
CIMIC	Civil-Military Cooperation
CIS	Commonwealth of Independent States
CIVCOM	Committee for the Civilian Aspects of Crisis Management

CivOpCdr	Civilian Operations Commander
CMB	Crisis Management Board
CMC	Crisis Management Concept
CMCT	Crisis Management Coordination Team
CMF	Combined Maritime Forces
CMPD	Crisis Management Planning Department
CNDP	National Congress for the Defence of the People (*Congrès national pour la Défense du Peuple*)
CoC	Chain of Command
CONOPS	Concept of Operations
COREPER	Committee of Permanent Representatives
COREU	*Correspondance européenne* (Communication network between EU Member States and the European Commission for cooperation in foreign policy)
CPA	Coalition Provisional Authority
CPCC	Civilian Planning and Conduct Capability
CRCT	Crisis Reponse Coordination Team
CRT	Civilian Response Team
CSCE	Conference on Security and Cooperation in Europe
CSO	Civilian Strategic Option
CSP	Country Strategy Paper
CSTC-A	Combined Security Transition Command – Afghanistan
CTF	Combined Task Force
DAC	Development Assistance Committee
DCI	(i) Defence Capabilities Initiative (ii) Development and Cooperation Instrument
DDR	Disarmament, Demobilisation and Reintegration
DG E	Directorate General: External Economic Relations, CFSP
DfID	Department for International Development
DIS	*Détachement intégré de Sécurité* (Chadian joint police and gendarmerie force)
DITF	Darfur Integrated Task Force
DPKO	Department of Peacekeeping Operations
DRC	Democratic Republic of Congo
DSACEUR	Deputy Supreme Allied Commander Europe
EAR	European Agency for Reconstruction
EC	European Commission
ECAP	European Capabilities Action Plan
ECHO	European Commission Humanitarian Office
ECJ	European Court of Justice
EDA	European Defence Agency
EDF	European Development Force
EEAS	European External Action Service

EGF	European Gendarmerie Force
EIDHR	European Instrument for Democracy and Human Rights
ENP	European Neighbourhood Policy
ENPI	European Neighbourhood and Partnership Instrument
EP	European Parliament
EPC	European Political Cooperation
ESDP	European Security and Defence Policy
ESS	European Security Strategy
EUBAM	European Union Border Assistance Mission
EUFOR	European Union Military Force
EUJUST	European Union Rule of Law Mission
EUMC	European Union Military Committee
EUMM	European Union Monitoring Mission
EUMS	European Union Military Staff
EUPAT	European Union Police Advisory Team
EUPOL	European Union Police Mission
EUPM	EU Police Mission in Bosnia and Herzegovina
EUPT	European Union Planning Team (for Kosovo)
EUSR	European Union Special Representative
FCdr	Force Commander
FDD	Focused District Development
FFM	Fact-Finding Mission
FHQ	Force Headquarters
FPRI	*Front de résistance patriotique de l'Ituri*
FPU	Formed Police Unit
FYROM	Former Yugoslav Republic of Macedonia
GAERC	General Affairs and External Relations Council
GAM	Free Aceh Movement (*Gerakan Aceh Merdeka*)
GPPO	German Police Project Office
HoD	Head of Delegation
HoM	Head of Mission
HQ	Headquarters
HR	High Representative
HUMA	Humanitarian Aid
ICO	International Civilian Office
ICR	International Civilian Representative
IDP	Internally Displaced Person
IET	Iraq Expert Team
IFOR	Implementation Force
IfS	Instrument for Stability

IGAD	Intergovernmental Authority on Development
IIA	Inter-Institutional Agreement
IMD	Initiating Military Directive
IMO	International Maritime Organisation
IOM	International Organisation for Migration
IPA	Instrument for Pre-Accession Assistance
IPCB	International Police Coordination Board
IPTF	International Police Task Force
IPU	Integrated Police Unit
IRTC	Internationally Recommended Transit Corridor
ISAF	International Security Assistance Force
IT	Information Technology
JA	Joint Action
JHA	Justice and Home Affairs
JOC	Joint Operations Centre
JSF	Joint-Strike-Fighter
KFOR	Kosovo Force
LoGA	Law on the Governance of Aceh
LOTFA	Law and Order Trust Fund for Afghanistan
MAP	Military Assessment and Planning Unit
MDG	Millennium Development Goal
MFA	Ministry of Foreign Affairs
MIA	Ministry of Internal Affairs
MINURCAT	United Nations Mission in the Central African Republic and Chad
MoD	Ministry of Defence
MOI	Ministry of Interior
MONUC	United Nations Organisation Mission in DR Congo (*Mission de l'Organisation des Nations unies en République démocratique du Congo*)
MoU	Memorandum of Understanding
MPRA	Maritime Patrol and Reconnaissance Aircraft
MSCHOA	Maritime Security Centre-Horn of Africa
MSF	*Médecins Sans Frontières*
MSO	Military Strategic Option
NAC	North Atlantic Council
NATO	North Atlantic Treaty Organisation
NGO	Non-governmental Organisation
NRF	NATO Response Force
NTM-A	NATO Training Mission-Afghanistan
OCHA	Office for the Coordination of Humanitarian Affairs
ODA	Official Development Aid

OECD	Organisation for Economic Cooperation and Development
OEF	Operation Enduring Freedom
OHQ	Operational Headquarters
OMIK	OSCE Mission in Kosovo
OpCdr	Operation Commander
OPLAN	Operation Plan
OPT	Occupied Palestinian Territory
OSCE	Organisation for Security and Cooperation in Europe
OUA	Organisation for African Unity (*Organisation de l'Unité africaine*)
PA	Palestinian Authority
PARSS	*Programme d'appui à la réforme du secteur sécuritaire*
PAS	*Programme d'accompagnement à la stabilisation*
PCC	Prague Capabilities Commitment
PCP	Palestinian Civil Police
PCPDP	Palestinian Civil Police Development Programme
PfP	Partnership for Peace
PIR	*Police d'intervention rapide*
PMC	Political Military Committee
PMG	Political Military Group
pMS	Participating Member States
PNC	*Police nationale congolaise*
PRDP	Palestinian Reform and Development Plan
PRT	Provincial Reconstruction Team
PSC	Political and Security Committee
PU	Policy Unit
R2P	Responsibility to Protect
RCP	Rafah Crossing Point
RECs	Regional Economic Communities
RM	Regional Mechanisms
RRM	Rapid Reaction Mechanism
SAA	Stabilisation and Association Agreement
SACEUR	Supreme Allied Commander Europe
SALW	Small arms and light weapons
SAP	Stabilisation and Association Process
SEDE	Subcommittee on Security and Defence of the European Parliament
SG/HR	Secretary General/High Representative
SHAPE	Supreme Headquarters Allied Powers Europe
SIAC	Single Intelligence Analysis Capacity
SIPA	State Investigation and Protection Agency
SitCen	Joint Situation Centre

SOFA	Status of Forces Agreement
SPMU	Strategic Planning and Management Unit
SRSG	Special Representative of the Secretary General
SSR	Security Sector Reform
SSRT	Security Sector Reform and Transformation
TACIS	Technical Aid to the Commonwealth of Independent States
TEU	Treaty on European Union
TFG	Transitional Federal Government
TNI	Indonesian Military (*Tentara Nasional Indonesia*)
UAV	Unmanned Aerial Vehicle
UIC	Union of Islamic Courts
UN	United Nations
UNAMA	United Nations Assistance Mission to Afghanistan
UNAMID	United Nations African Mission in Darfur
UNDP	United Nations Development Programme
UN DPKO	United Nations Department of Peacekeeping Operations
UNMIK	United Nations Interim Administration Mission in Kosovo
UNOMIG	United Nations Observer Mission in Georgia
UNPOL	United Nations Police
UNSC	United Nations Security Council
UNSCR	United Nations Security Council Resolution
UNSG	United Nations Secretary General
UPC	*Union des patriotes congolais*
USD	United States Dollars
WEAG	Western European Armaments Group
WEU	Western European Union
WFP	World Food Programme
WKC	Watchkeeping Capability